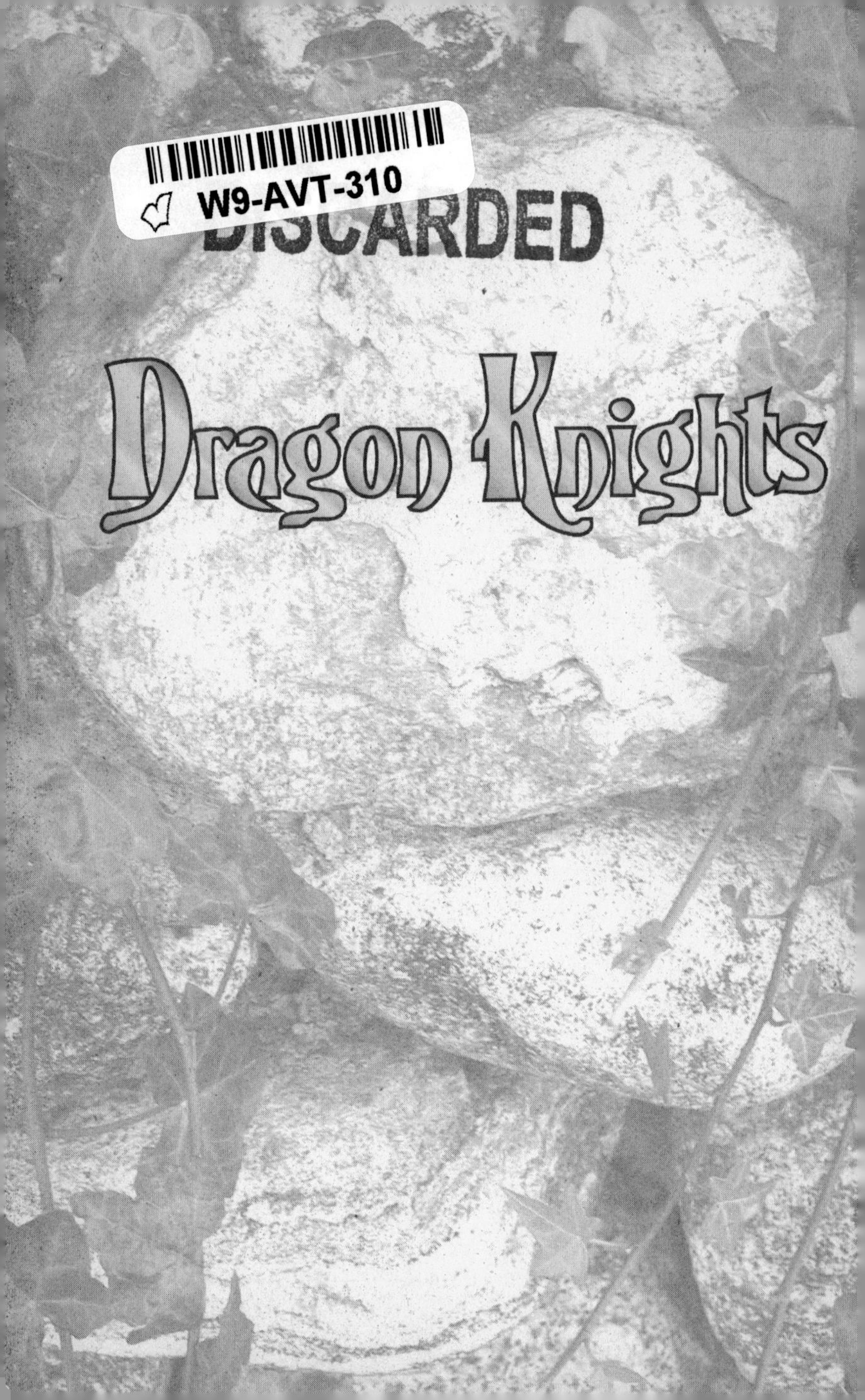

Dragon Knights

ALSO AVAILABLE FROM  TOKYOPOP®

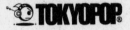

TOKYOPOP®

Presents

Dragon Knights

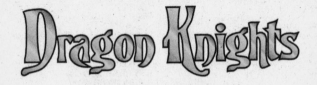

Written and Illustrated by
Mineko Ohkami

Volume 1

TOKYOPOP®

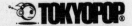

Los Angeles • Tokyo • London

Translator - Yuki Ichimura
English Adaptation - Mary DeMarle
Editor - Stephanie Donnelly
Associate Editor - Robert Coyner
Retouch and Lettering - Jinky De Leon
Cover Layout - Raseel El-Djoundi
Graphic Designer - Anna Kernbaum

Digital Imaging Manager - Chris Buford
Pre-Press Manager - Antonio DePietro
Production Managers - Jennifer Miller and Mutsumi Miyazaki
Art Director - Matt Alford
Managing Editor - Jill Freshney
VP of Production - Ron Klamert
President & C.O.O. - John Parker
Publisher & C.E.O. - Stuart Levy

E-mail: info@TOKYOPOP.com
Come visit us online at www.TOKYOPOP.com

A **TOKYOPOP** Manga

TOKYOPOP Inc.
5900 Wilshire Blvd. Suite 2000
Los Angeles, CA 90036

Dragon Knights Vol. 1

ISBN: 1-931514-40-2

First TOKYOPOP printing: March 2002

15 14 13 12 11 10 9 8 7 6
Printed in the USA

Dragon Knights

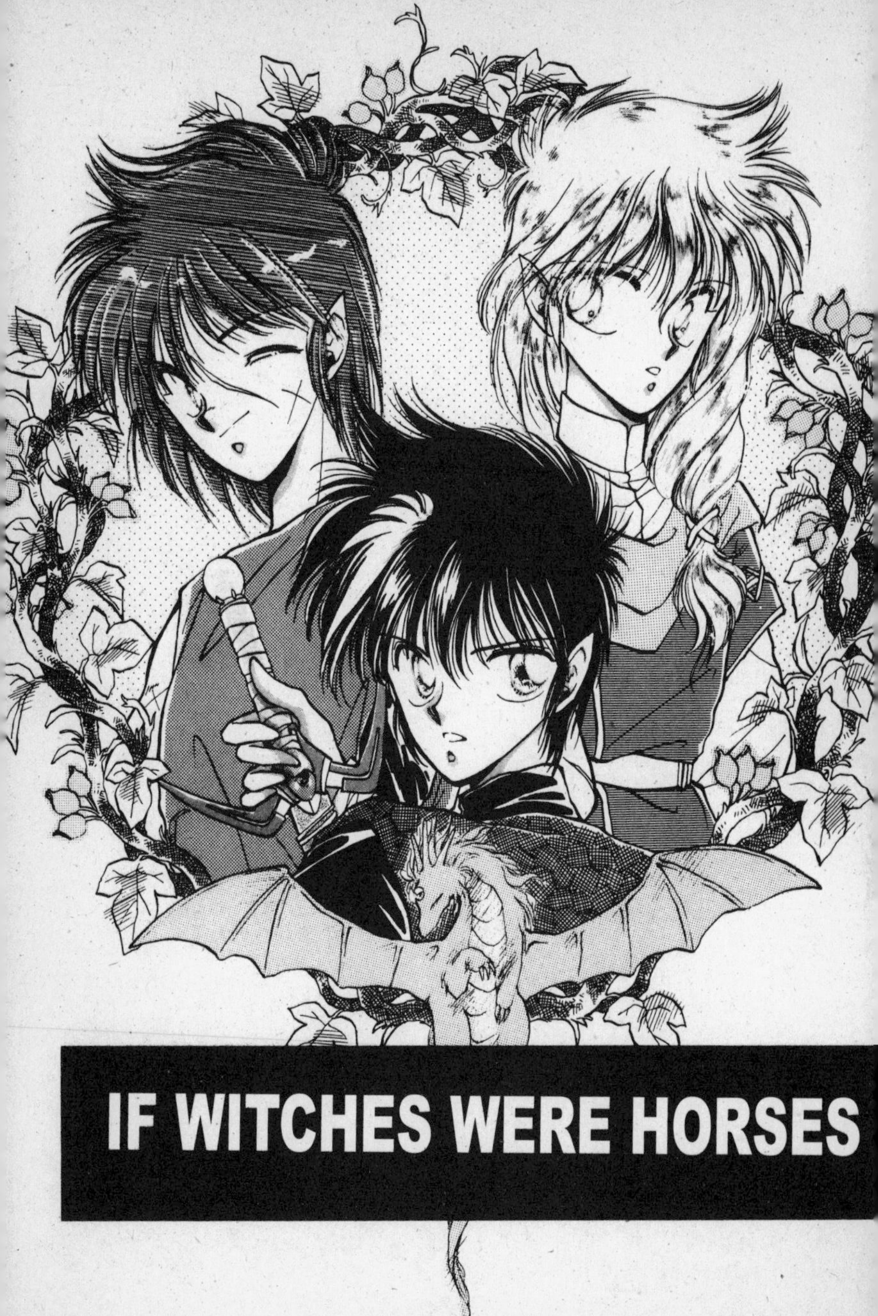

IF WITCHES WERE HORSES

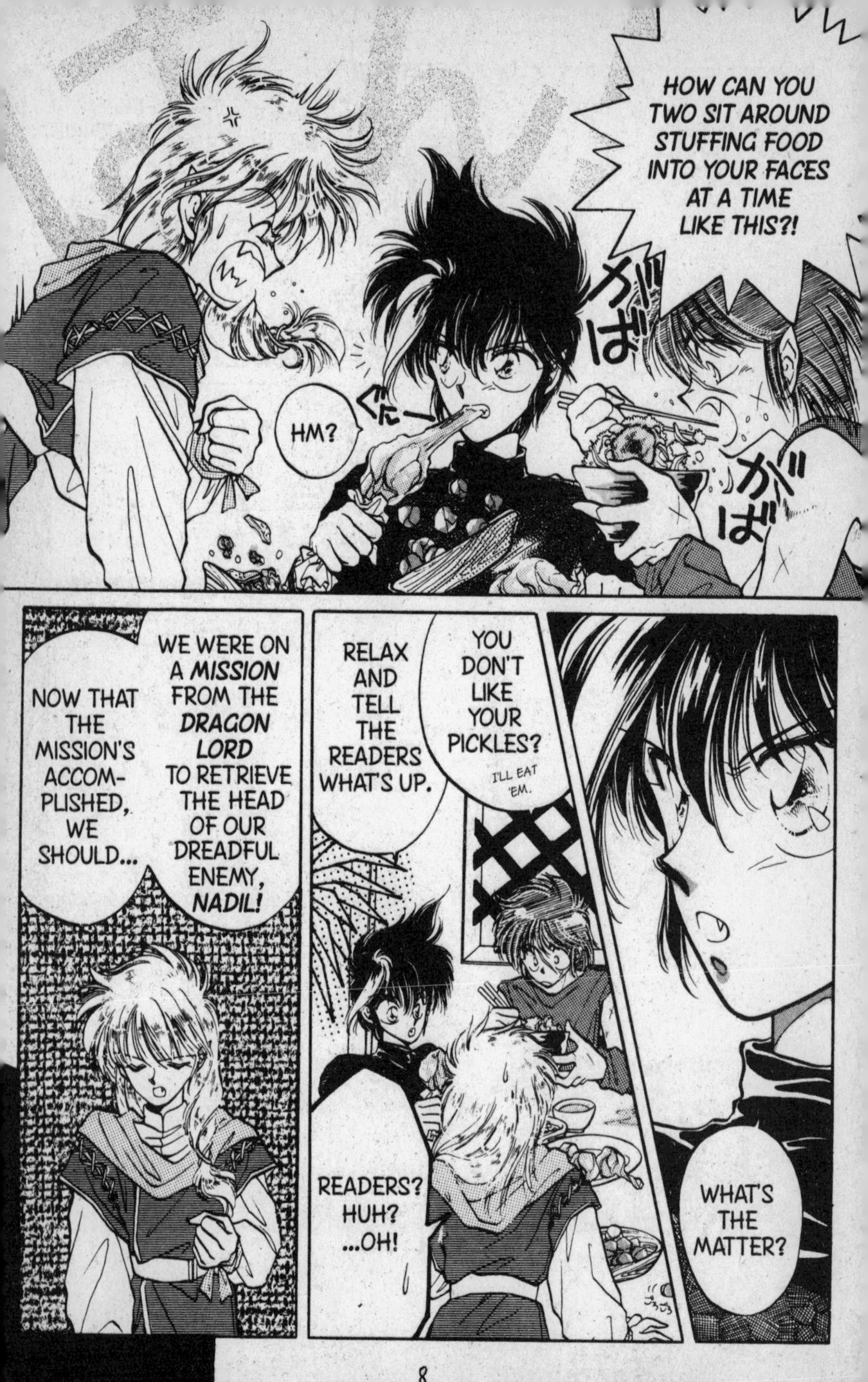
HOW CAN YOU TWO SIT AROUND STUFFING FOOD INTO YOUR FACES AT A TIME LIKE THIS?!
がば
がば
HM?
WHAT'S THE MATTER?
YOU DON'T LIKE YOUR PICKLES?
I'LL EAT 'EM.
RELAX AND TELL THE READERS WHAT'S UP.
READERS? HUH? ...OH!
WE WERE ON A *MISSION* FROM THE *DRAGON LORD* TO RETRIEVE THE HEAD OF OUR DREADFUL ENEMY, *NADIL!*
NOW THAT THE MISSION'S ACCOM-PLISHED, WE SHOULD...

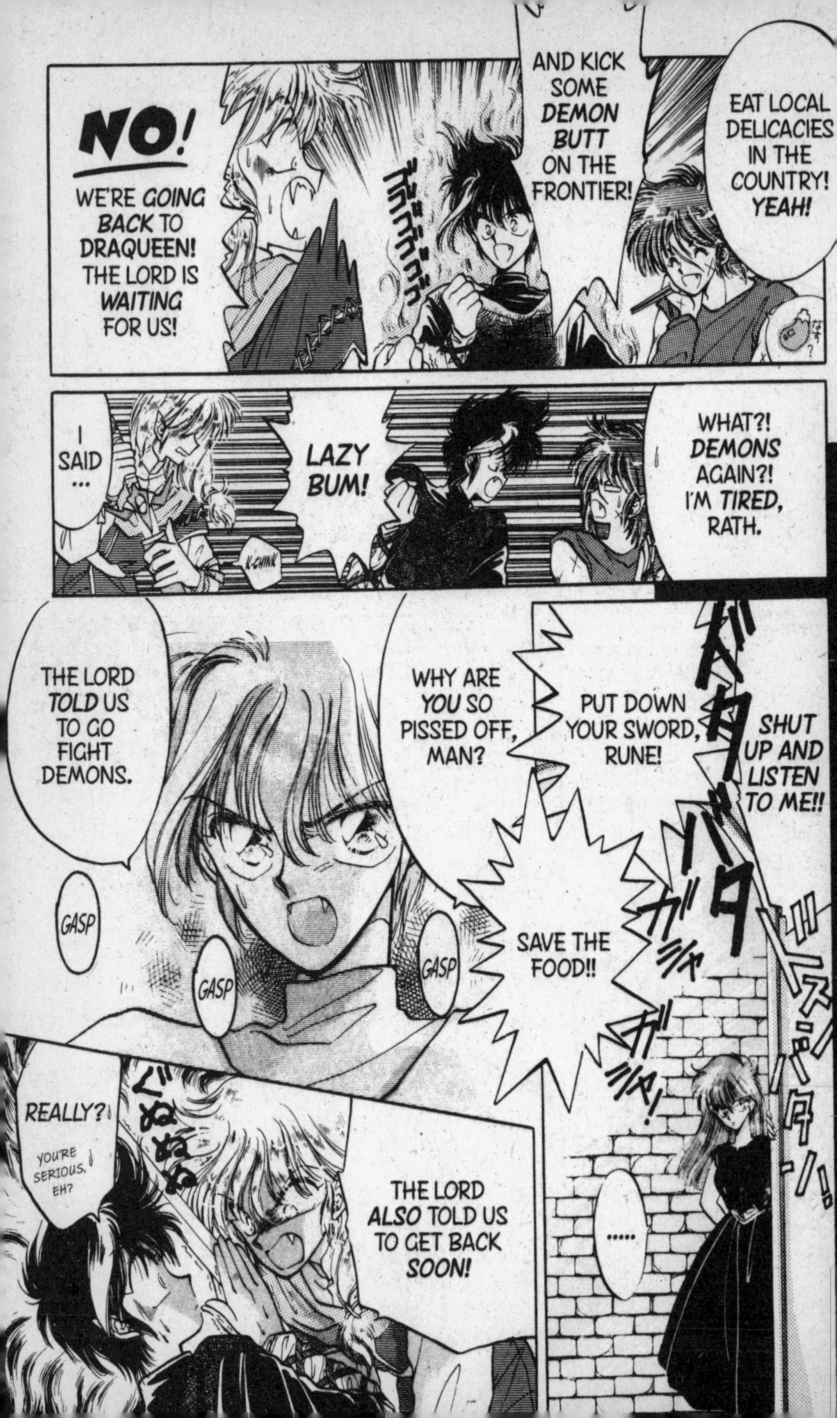
EAT LOCAL DELICACIES IN THE COUNTRY! YEAH!
AND KICK SOME DEMON BUTT ON THE FRONTIER!
NO! WE'RE GOING BACK TO DRAQUEEN! THE LORD IS WAITING FOR US!
WHAT?! DEMONS AGAIN?! I'M TIRED, RATH.
LAZY BUM!
K-CHINK
I SAID ...
SHUT UP AND LISTEN TO ME!!
PUT DOWN YOUR SWORD, RUNE!
SAVE THE FOOD!!
WHY ARE YOU SO PISSED OFF, MAN?
GASP
THE LORD TOLD US TO GO FIGHT DEMONS.
GASP
GASP
.....
THE LORD ALSO TOLD US TO GET BACK SOON!
REALLY?
YOU'RE SERIOUS, EH?

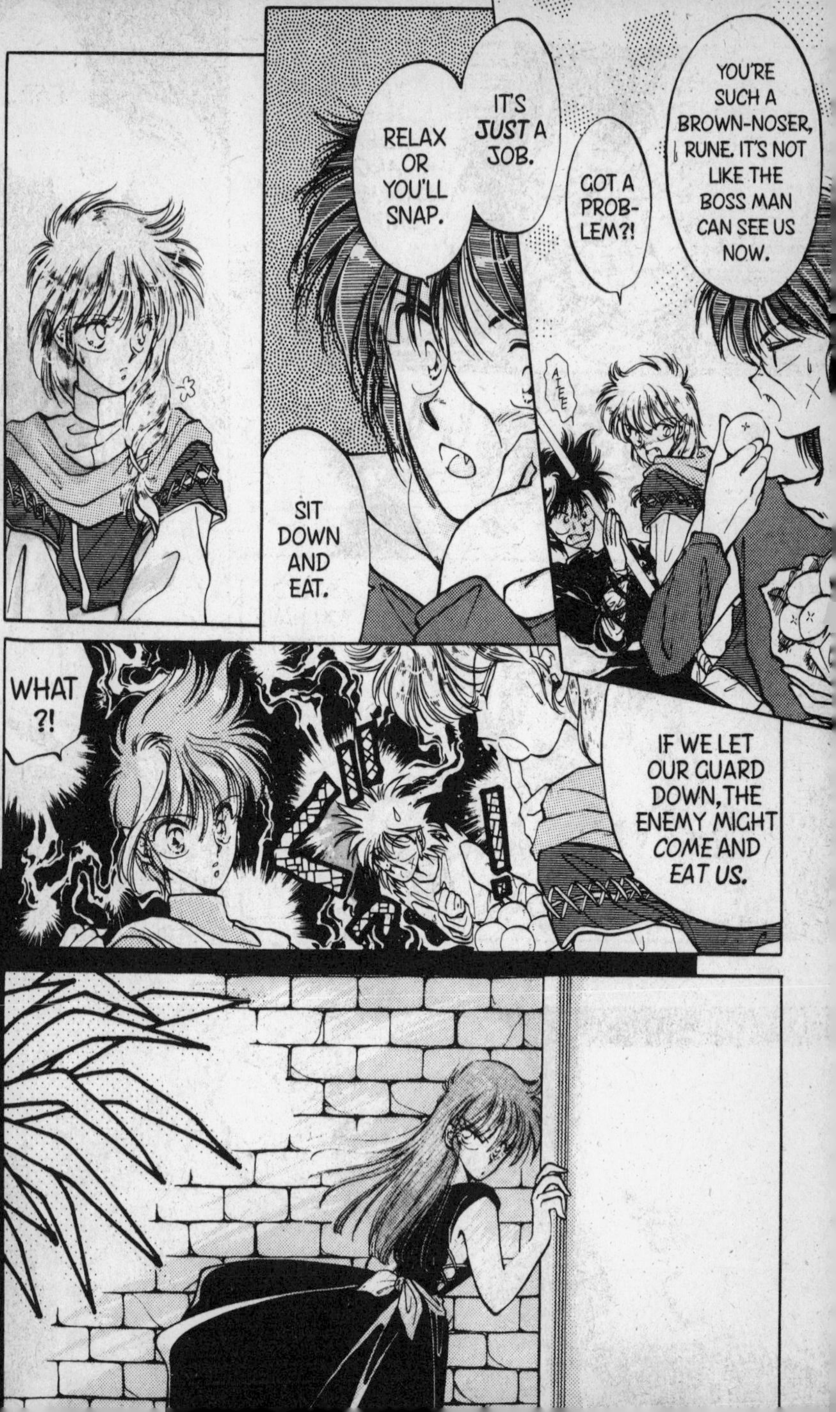

YOU'RE SUCH A BROWN-NOSER, RUNE. IT'S NOT LIKE THE BOSS MAN CAN SEE US NOW.
GOT A PROB-LEM?!
AIEE
IT'S *JUST* A JOB.
RELAX OR YOU'LL SNAP.
SIT DOWN AND EAT.
IF WE LET OUR GUARD DOWN, THE ENEMY MIGHT *COME* AND *EAT US.*
WHAT?!

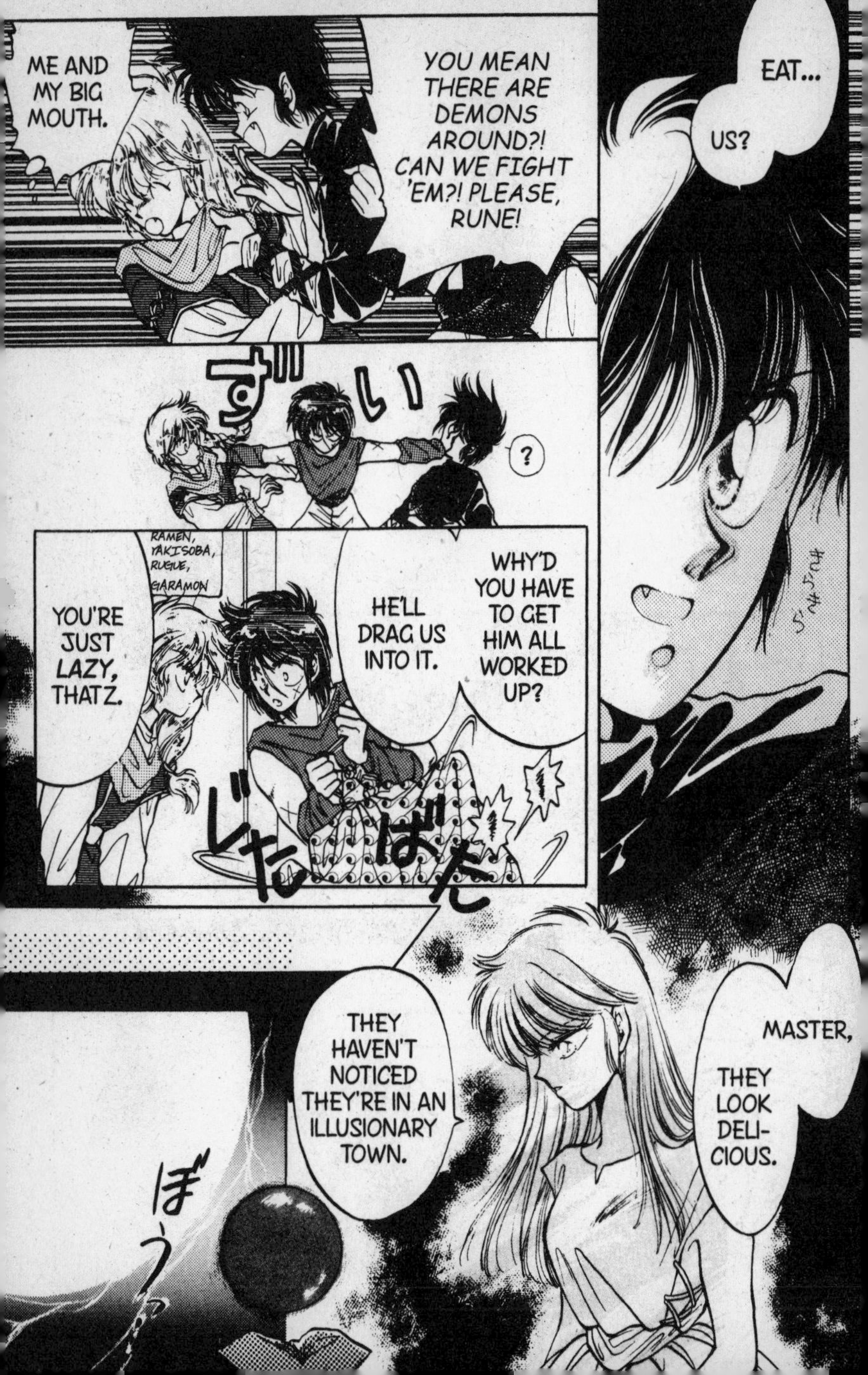
EAT...
US?
YOU MEAN THERE ARE DEMONS AROUND?! CAN WE FIGHT 'EM?! PLEASE, RUNE!
ME AND MY BIG MOUTH.
すい
?
WHY'D YOU HAVE TO GET HIM ALL WORKED UP?
HE'LL DRAG US INTO IT.
YOU'RE JUST LAZY, THATZ.
RAMEN, YAKISOBA, RUGUE, GARAMON
じたばた
MASTER,
THEY LOOK DELICIOUS.
THEY HAVEN'T NOTICED THEY'RE IN AN ILLUSIONARY TOWN.
ぼう

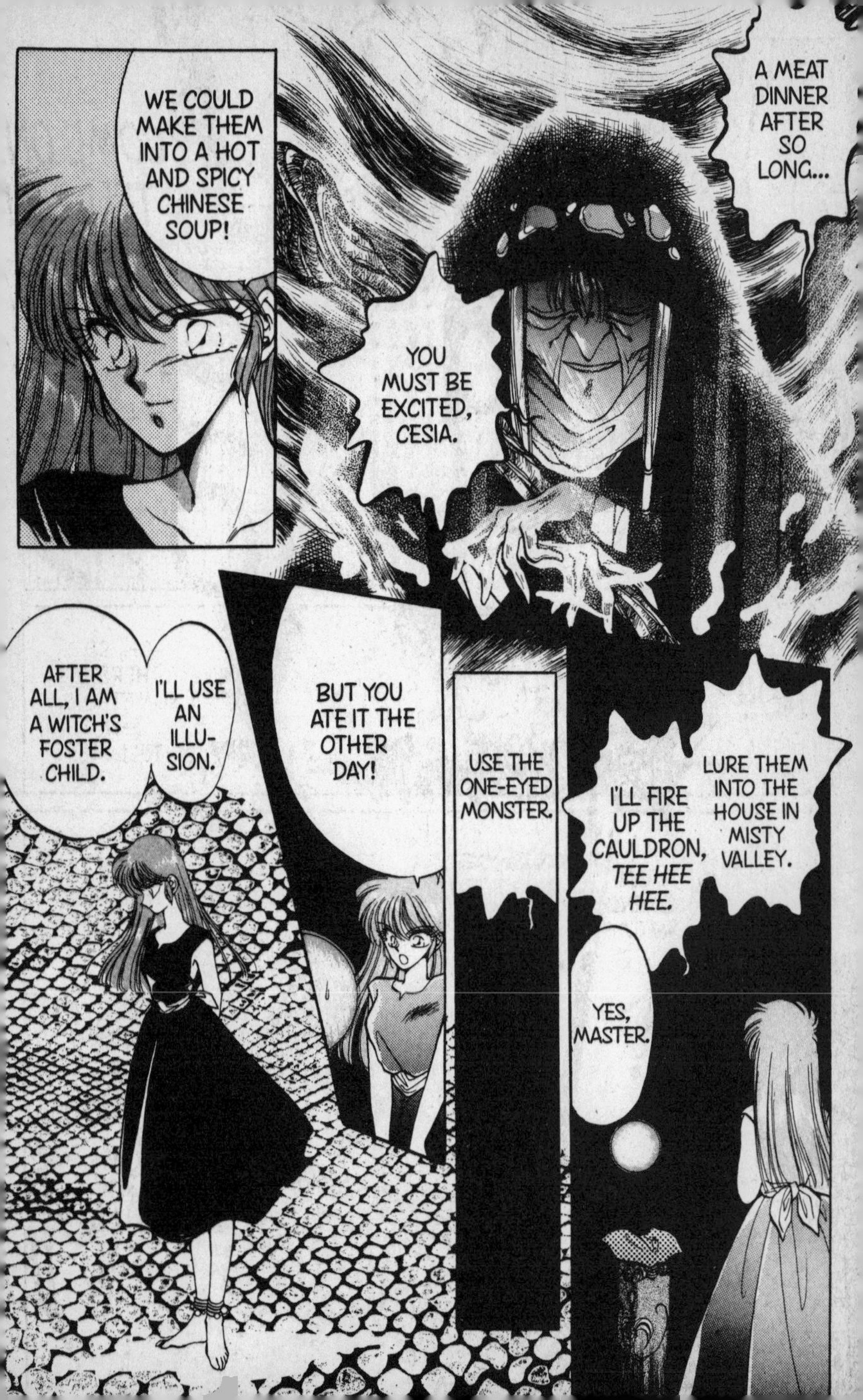
A MEAT DINNER AFTER SO LONG...
YOU MUST BE EXCITED, CESIA.
WE COULD MAKE THEM INTO A HOT AND SPICY CHINESE SOUP!
LURE THEM INTO THE HOUSE IN MISTY VALLEY.
I'LL FIRE UP THE CAULDRON, TEE HEE HEE.
YES, MASTER.
USE THE ONE-EYED MONSTER.
BUT YOU ATE IT THE OTHER DAY!
I'LL USE AN ILLU-SION.
AFTER ALL, I AM A WITCH'S FOSTER CHILD.

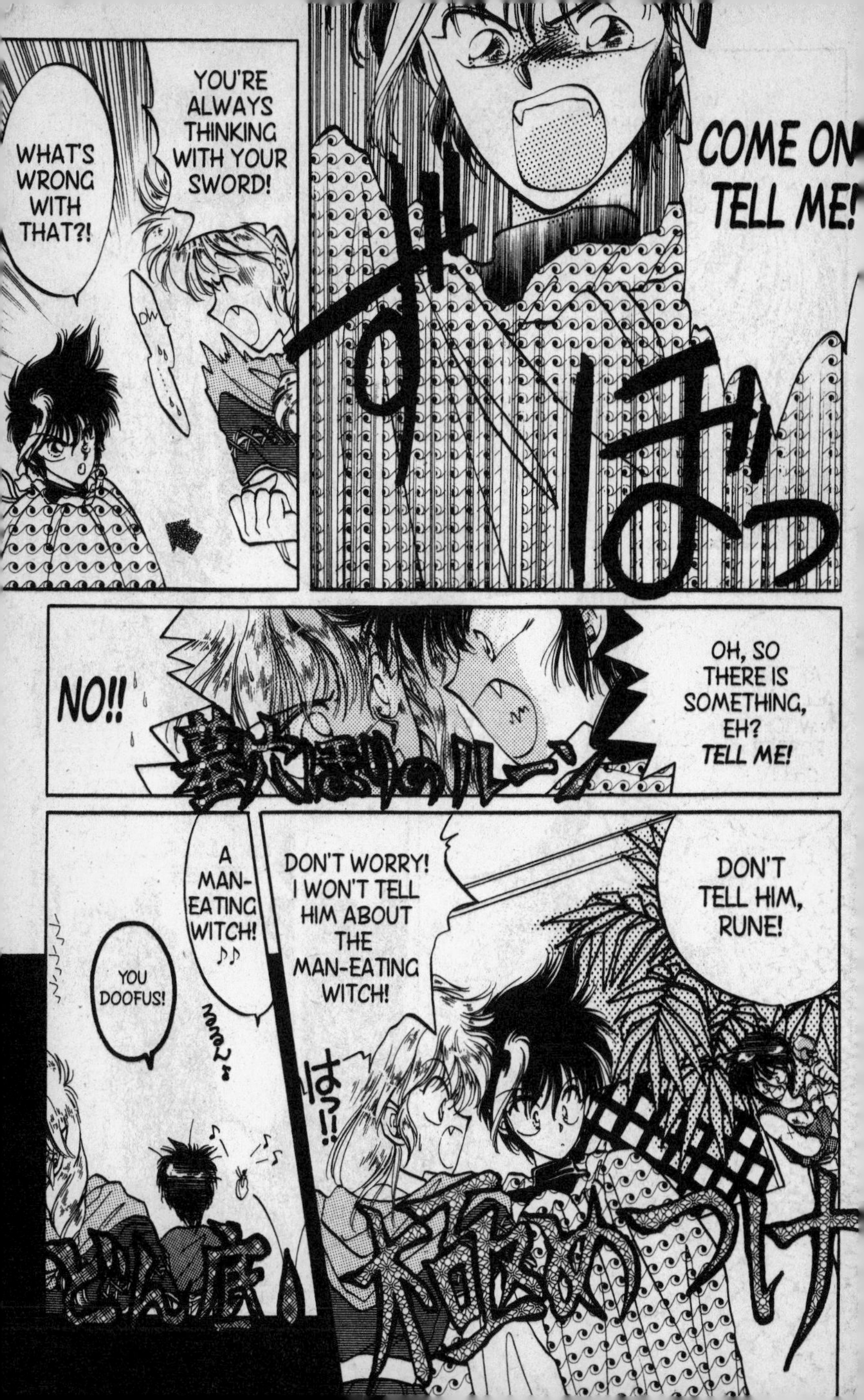
COME ON TELL ME!
YOU'RE ALWAYS THINKING WITH YOUR SWORD!
OW
WHAT'S WRONG WITH THAT?!
OH, SO THERE IS SOMETHING, EH? TELL ME!
NO!!
DON'T TELL HIM, RUNE!
DON'T WORRY! I WON'T TELL HIM ABOUT THE MAN-EATING WITCH!
はっ!!
A MAN-EATING WITCH! ♪♪
YOU DOOFUS!

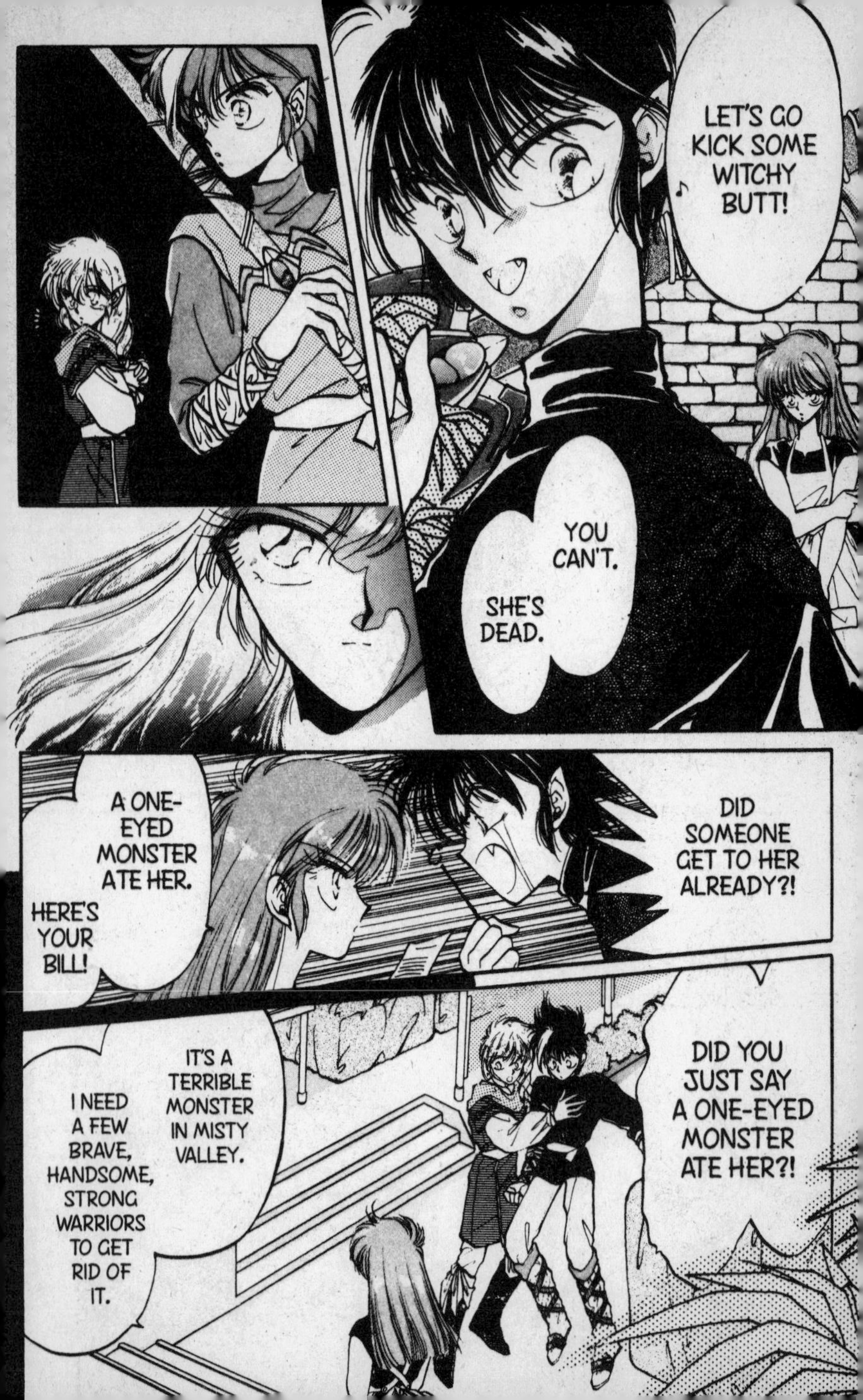
LET'S GO KICK SOME WITCHY BUTT! ♪
YOU CAN'T.
SHE'S DEAD.
DID SOMEONE GET TO HER ALREADY?!
A ONE-EYED MONSTER ATE HER.
HERE'S YOUR BILL!
DID YOU JUST SAY A ONE-EYED MONSTER ATE HER?!
IT'S A TERRIBLE MONSTER IN MISTY VALLEY.
I NEED A FEW BRAVE, HANDSOME, STRONG WARRIORS TO GET RID OF IT.

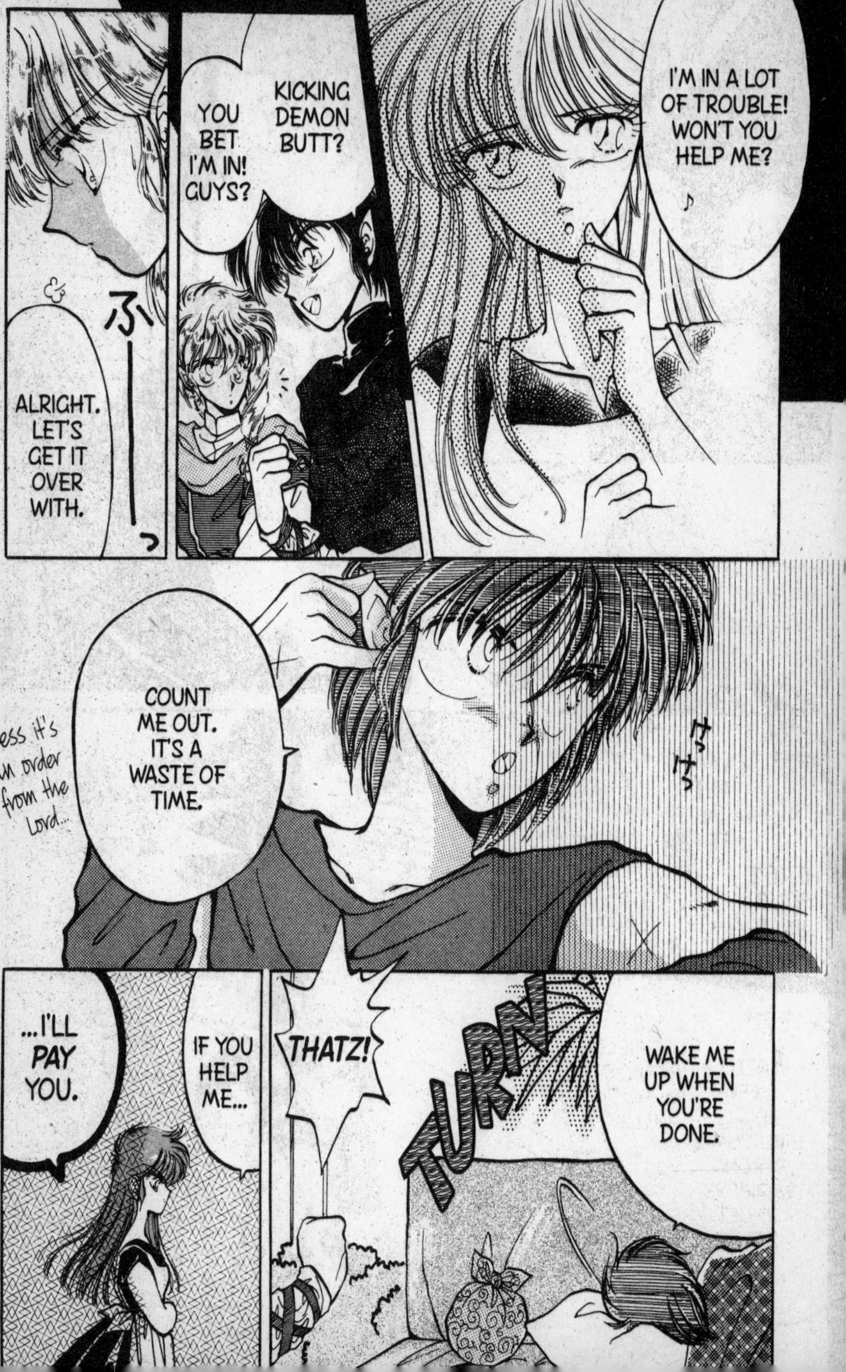
I'M IN A LOT OF TROUBLE! WON'T YOU HELP ME? ♪
KICKING DEMON BUTT?
YOU BET I'M IN! GUYS?
ふー
ALRIGHT. LET'S GET IT OVER WITH.
COUNT ME OUT. IT'S A WASTE OF TIME.
ess it's an order from the Lord...
WAKE ME UP WHEN YOU'RE DONE.
TURN
THATZ!
IF YOU HELP ME...
...I'LL PAY YOU.

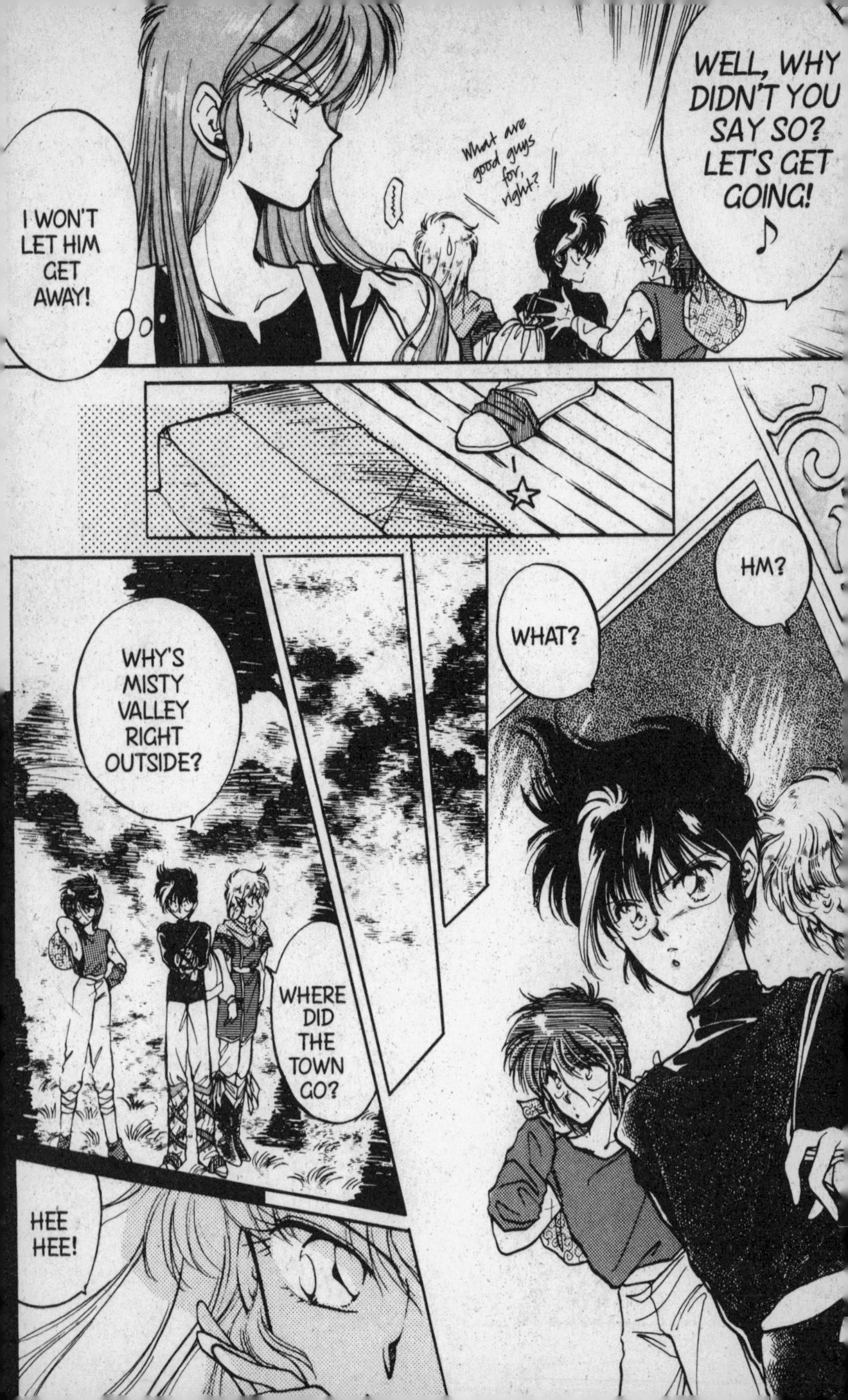
WELL, WHY DIDN'T YOU SAY SO? LET'S GET GOING! ♪
What are good guys for, right?
I WON'T LET HIM GET AWAY!
HM?
WHAT?
WHY'S MISTY VALLEY RIGHT OUTSIDE?
WHERE DID THE TOWN GO?
HEE HEE!

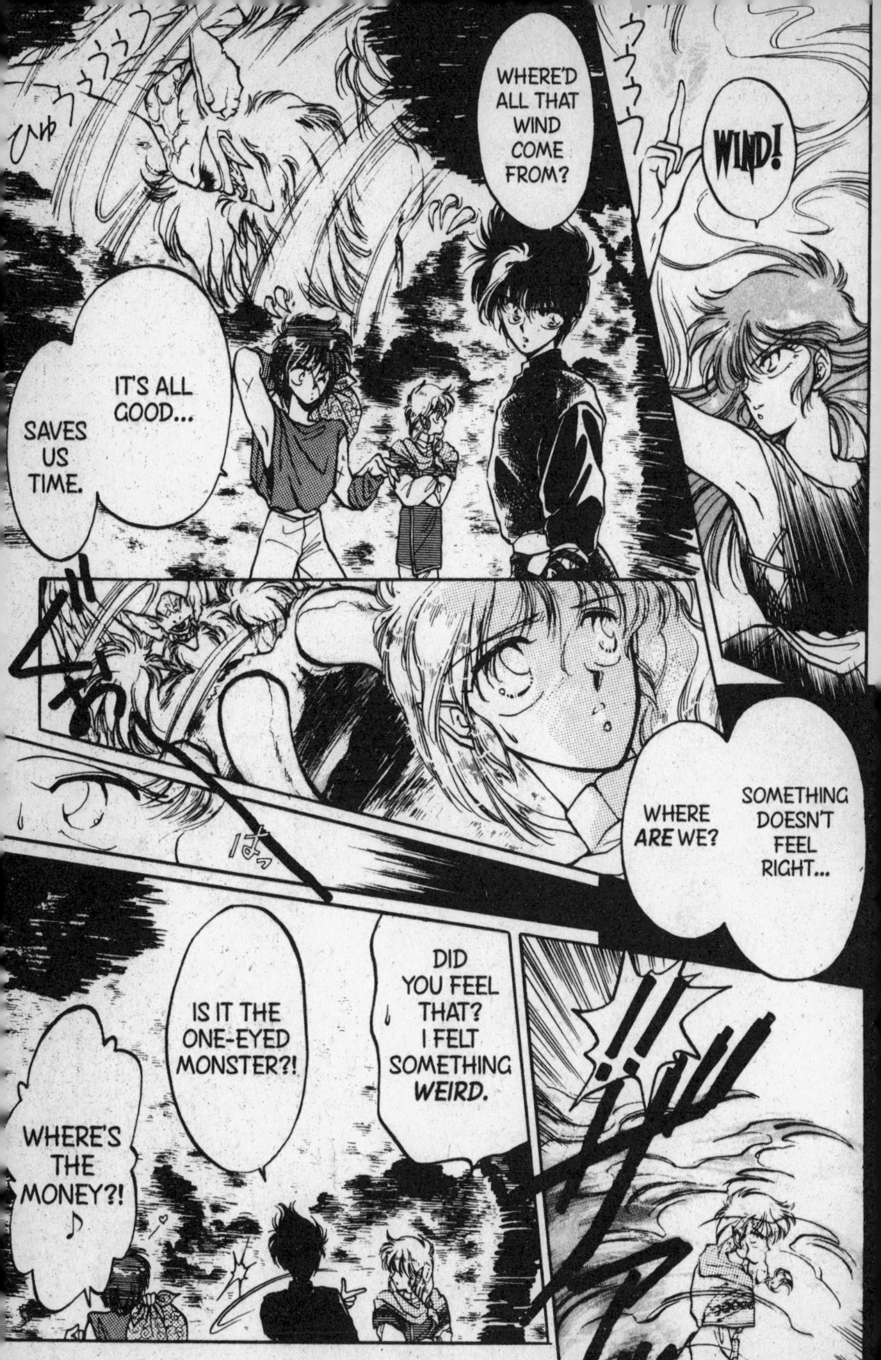
WIND!
WHERE'D ALL THAT WIND COME FROM?
IT'S ALL GOOD...
SAVES US TIME.
SOMETHING DOESN'T FEEL RIGHT...
WHERE *ARE* WE?
はっ
!!
DID YOU FEEL THAT? I FELT SOMETHING *WEIRD.*
IS IT THE ONE-EYED MONSTER?!
WHERE'S THE MONEY?! ♪

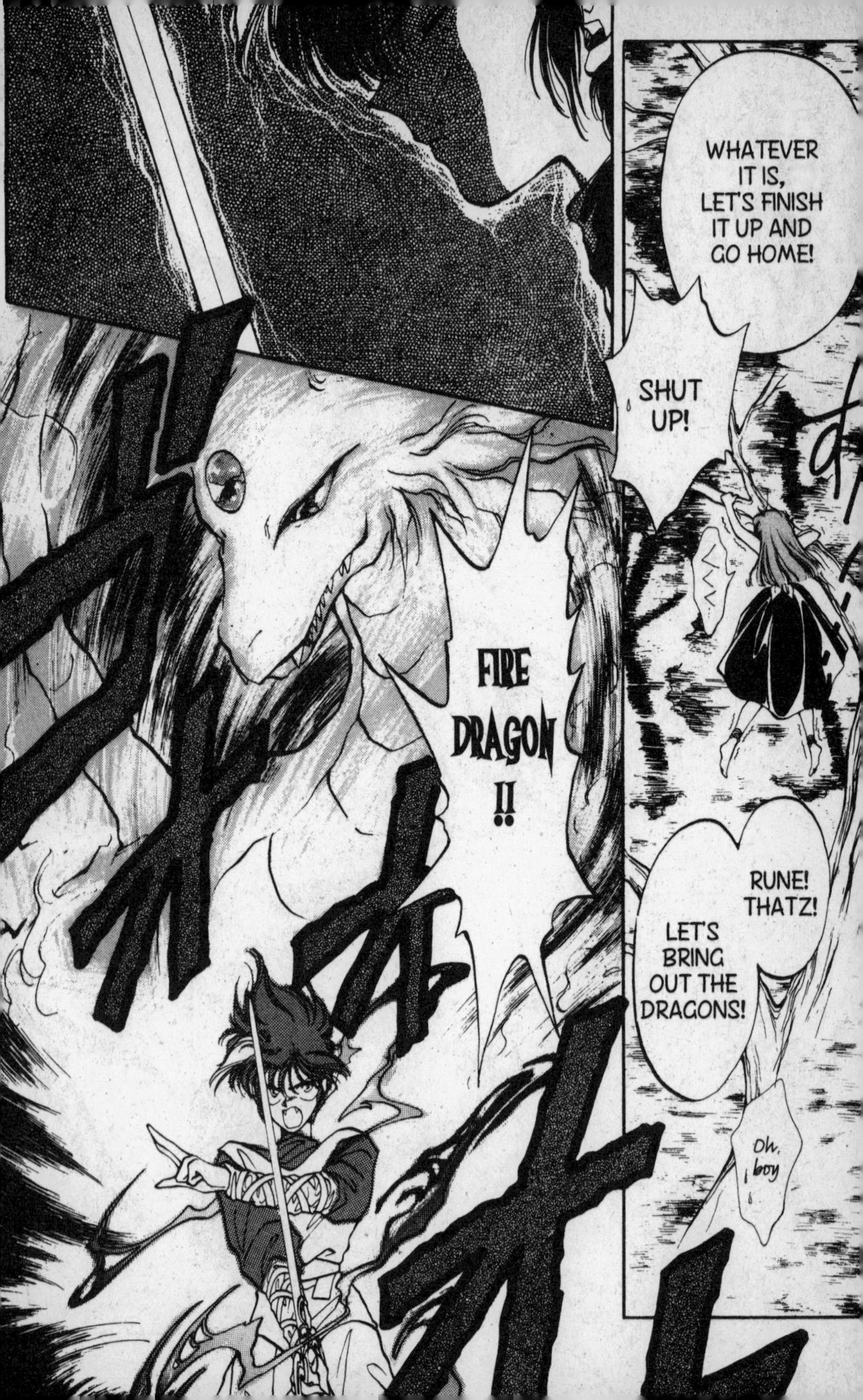
WHATEVER IT IS, LET'S FINISH IT UP AND GO HOME!
SHUT UP!
RUNE! THATZ!
LET'S BRING OUT THE DRAGONS!
Oh, boy
FIRE DRAGON!!

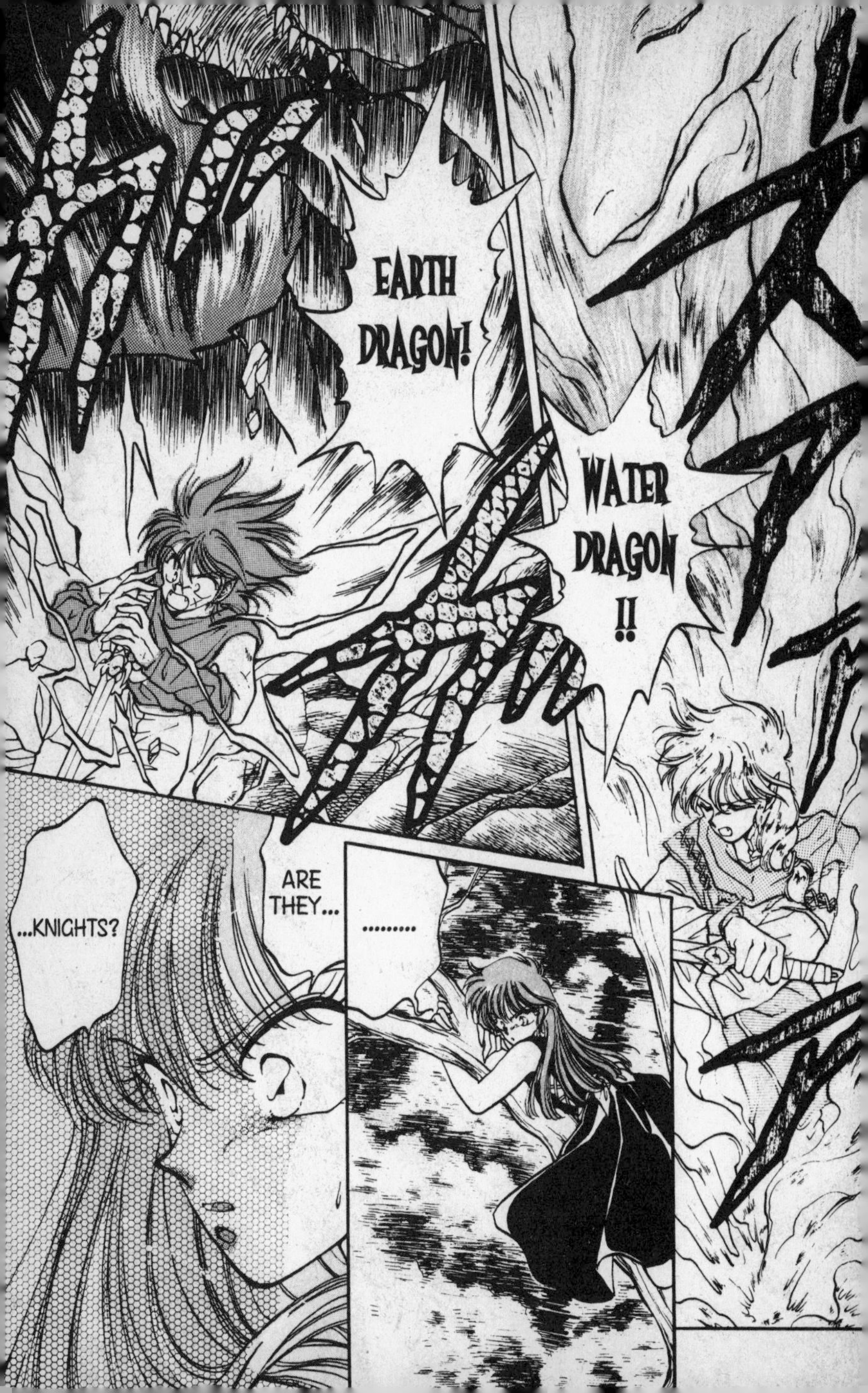
EARTH DRAGON!
WATER DRAGON !!
....
ARE THEY...
...KNIGHTS?

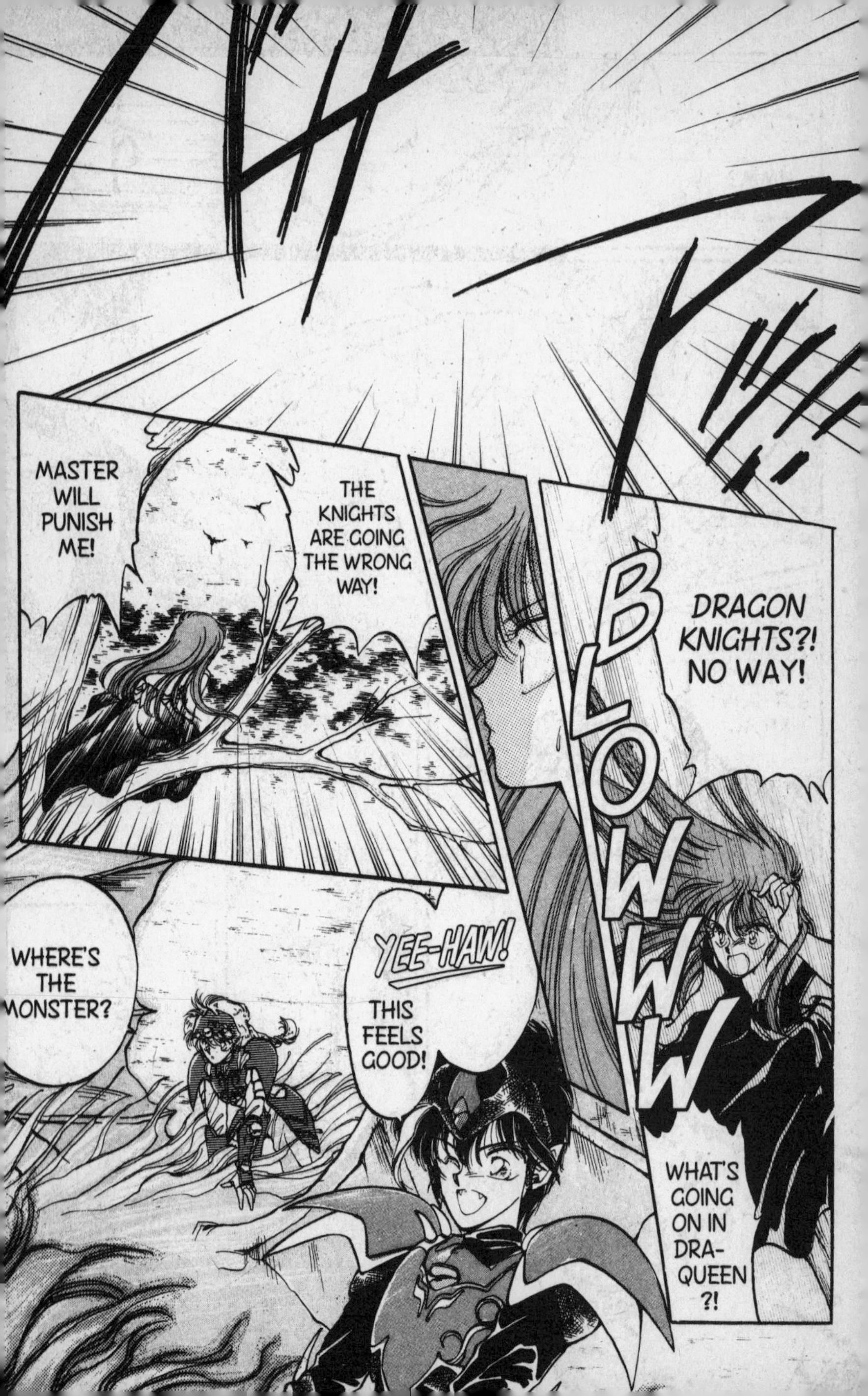

DRAGON KNIGHTS?! NO WAY!
BLOWWWW
WHAT'S GOING ON IN DRA-QUEEN?!
THE KNIGHTS ARE GOING THE WRONG WAY!
MASTER WILL PUNISH ME!
YEE-HAW!
THIS FEELS GOOD!
WHERE'S THE MONSTER?

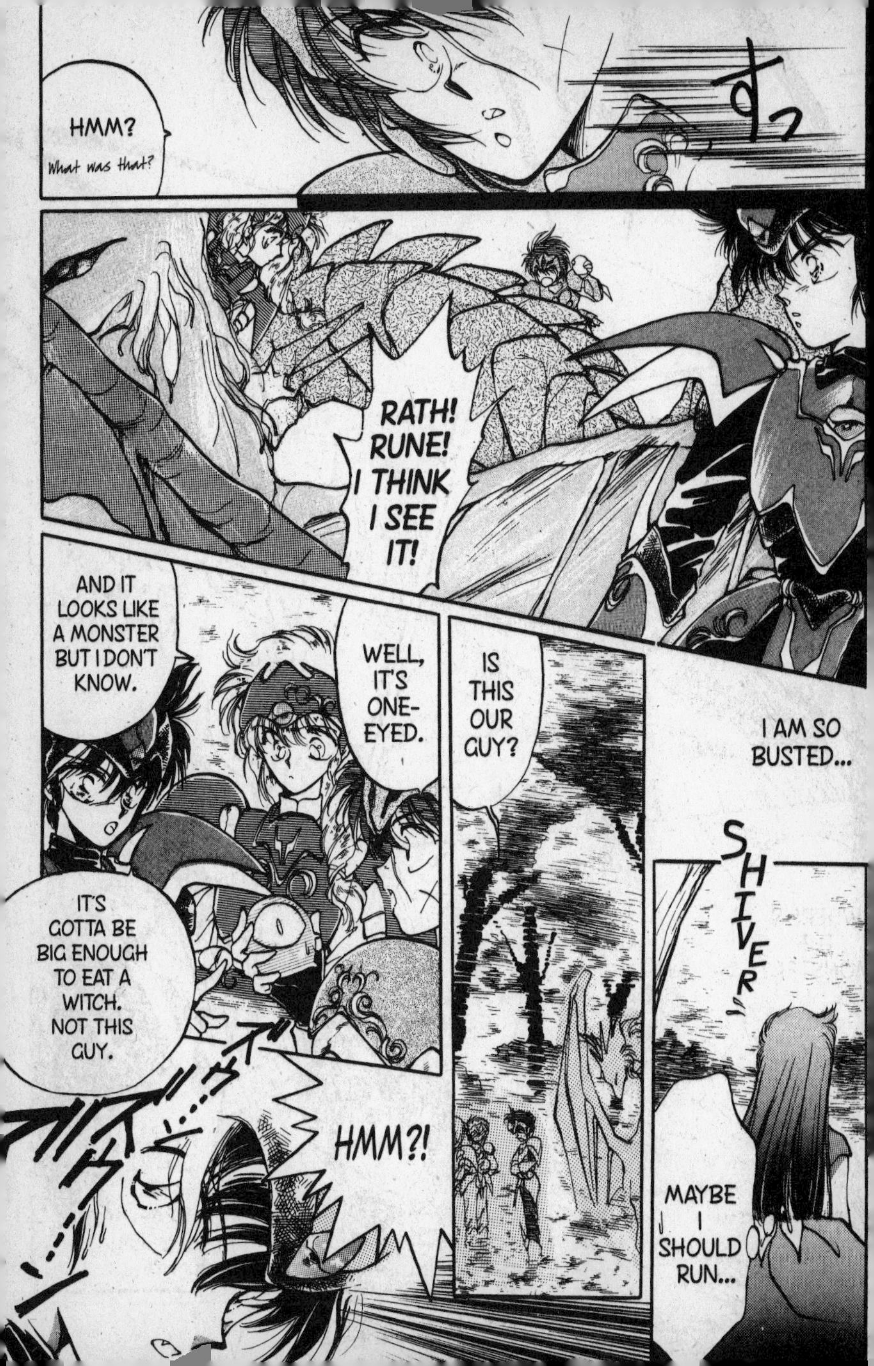

HMM?
What was that?
すっ
RATH! RUNE! I THINK I SEE IT!
I AM SO BUSTED...
SHIVER
MAYBE I SHOULD RUN...
IS THIS OUR GUY?
WELL, IT'S ONE-EYED.
AND IT LOOKS LIKE A MONSTER BUT I DON'T KNOW.
IT'S GOTTA BE BIG ENOUGH TO EAT A WITCH. NOT THIS GUY.
HMM?!

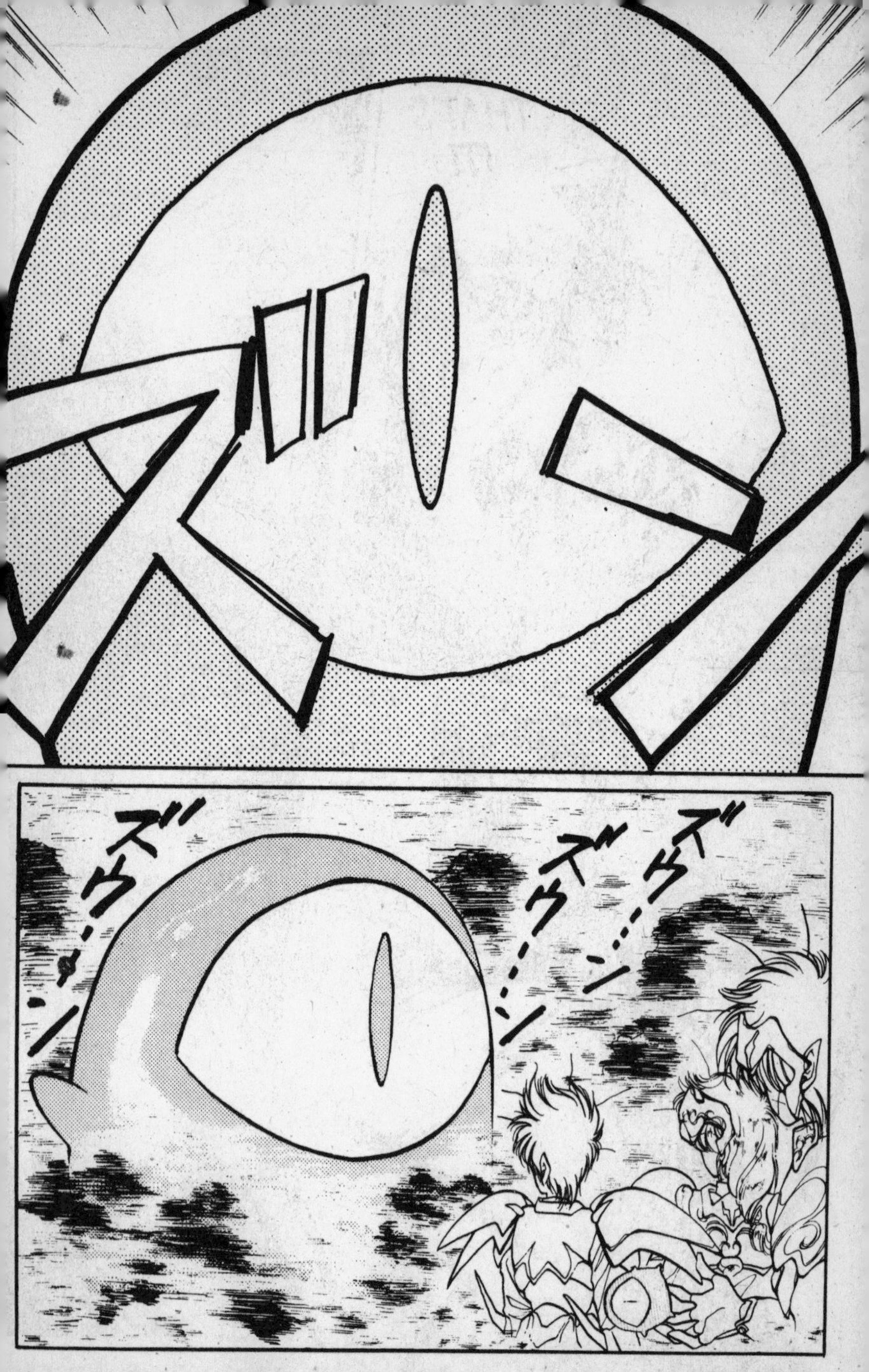
ズウ…ン
ズウ…ン
ズウ…ン

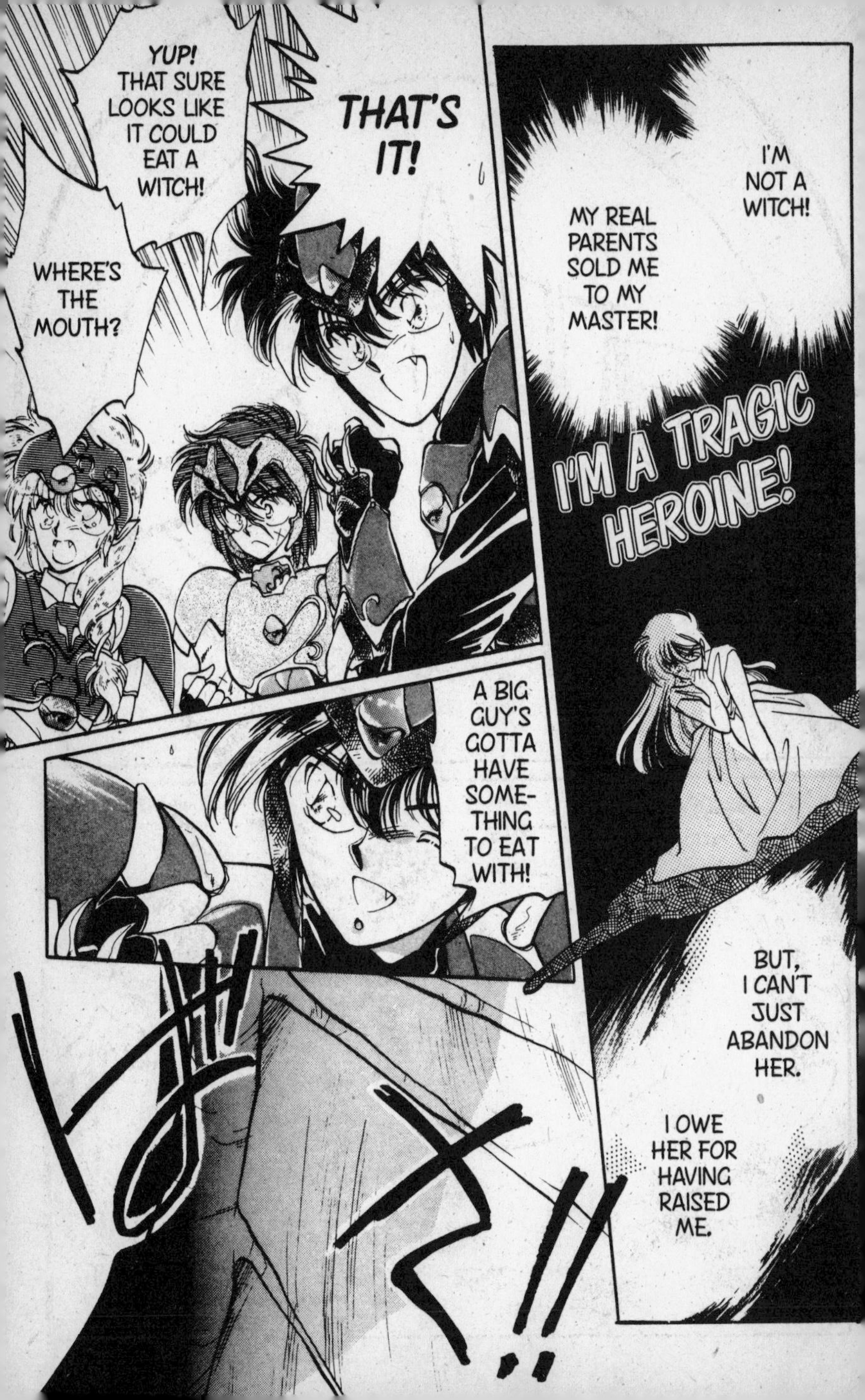
I'M NOT A WITCH!
MY REAL PARENTS SOLD ME TO MY MASTER!
I'M A TRAGIC HEROINE!
BUT, I CAN'T JUST ABANDON HER.
I OWE HER FOR HAVING RAISED ME.
THAT'S IT!
YUP! THAT SURE LOOKS LIKE IT COULD EAT A WITCH!
WHERE'S THE MOUTH?
A BIG GUY'S GOTTA HAVE SOME-THING TO EAT WITH!

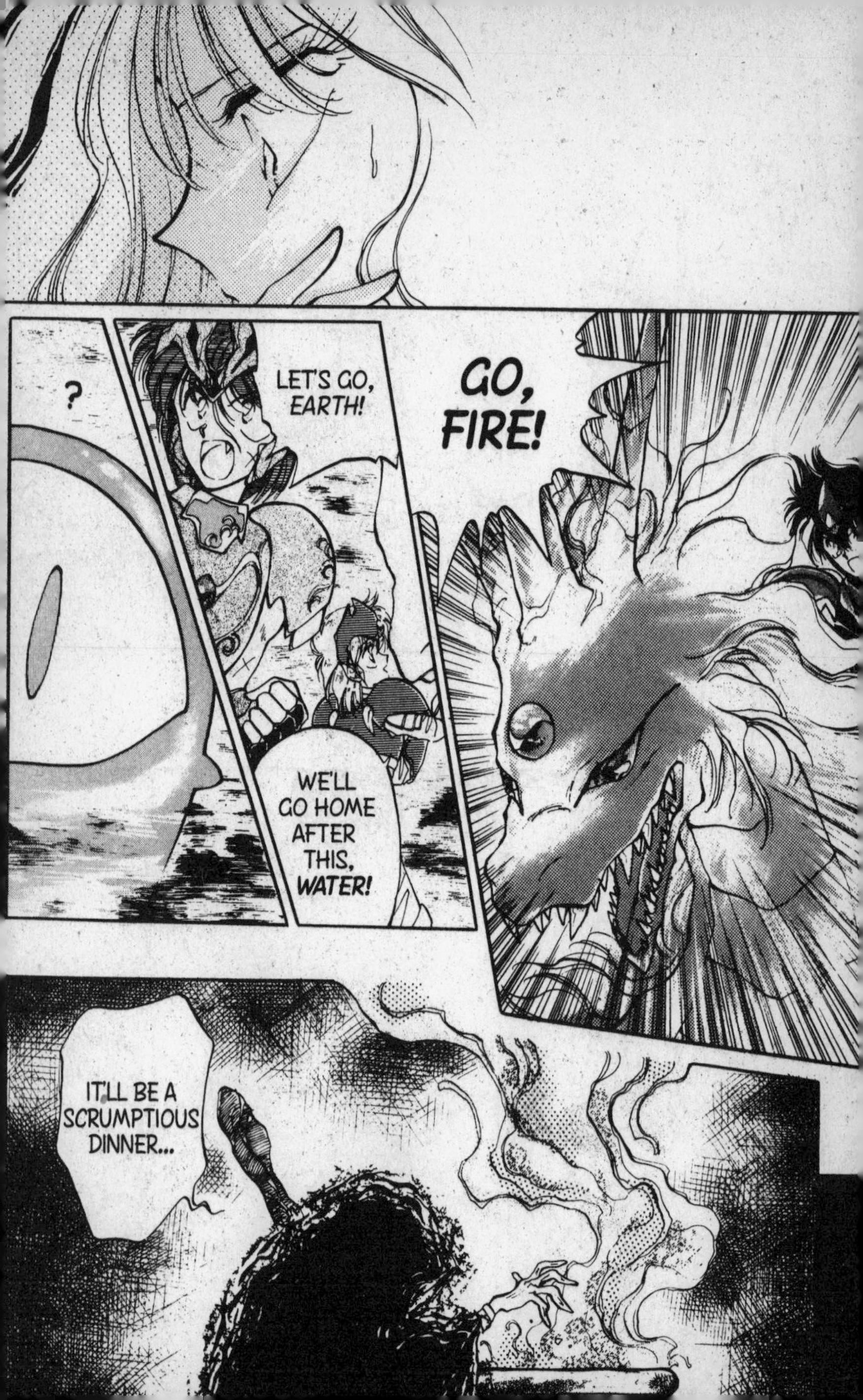
GO, FIRE!
LET'S GO, EARTH!
WE'LL GO HOME AFTER THIS, WATER!
?
IT'LL BE A SCRUMPTIOUS DINNER...

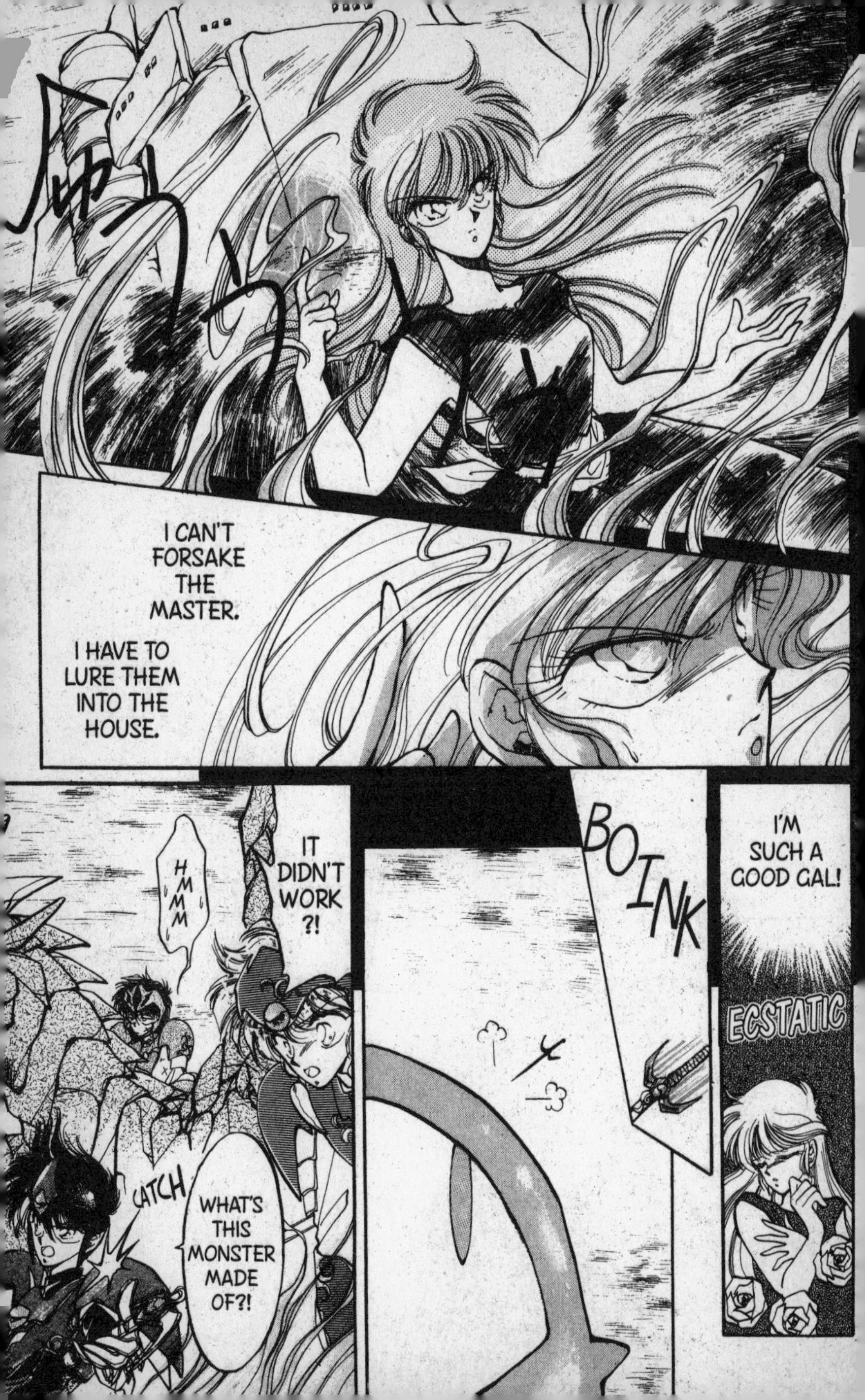
I CAN'T FORSAKE THE MASTER.
I HAVE TO LURE THEM INTO THE HOUSE.
I'M SUCH A GOOD GAL!
ECSTATIC
BOINK
IT DIDN'T WORK ?!
HMMM
WHAT'S THIS MONSTER MADE OF?!
CATCH

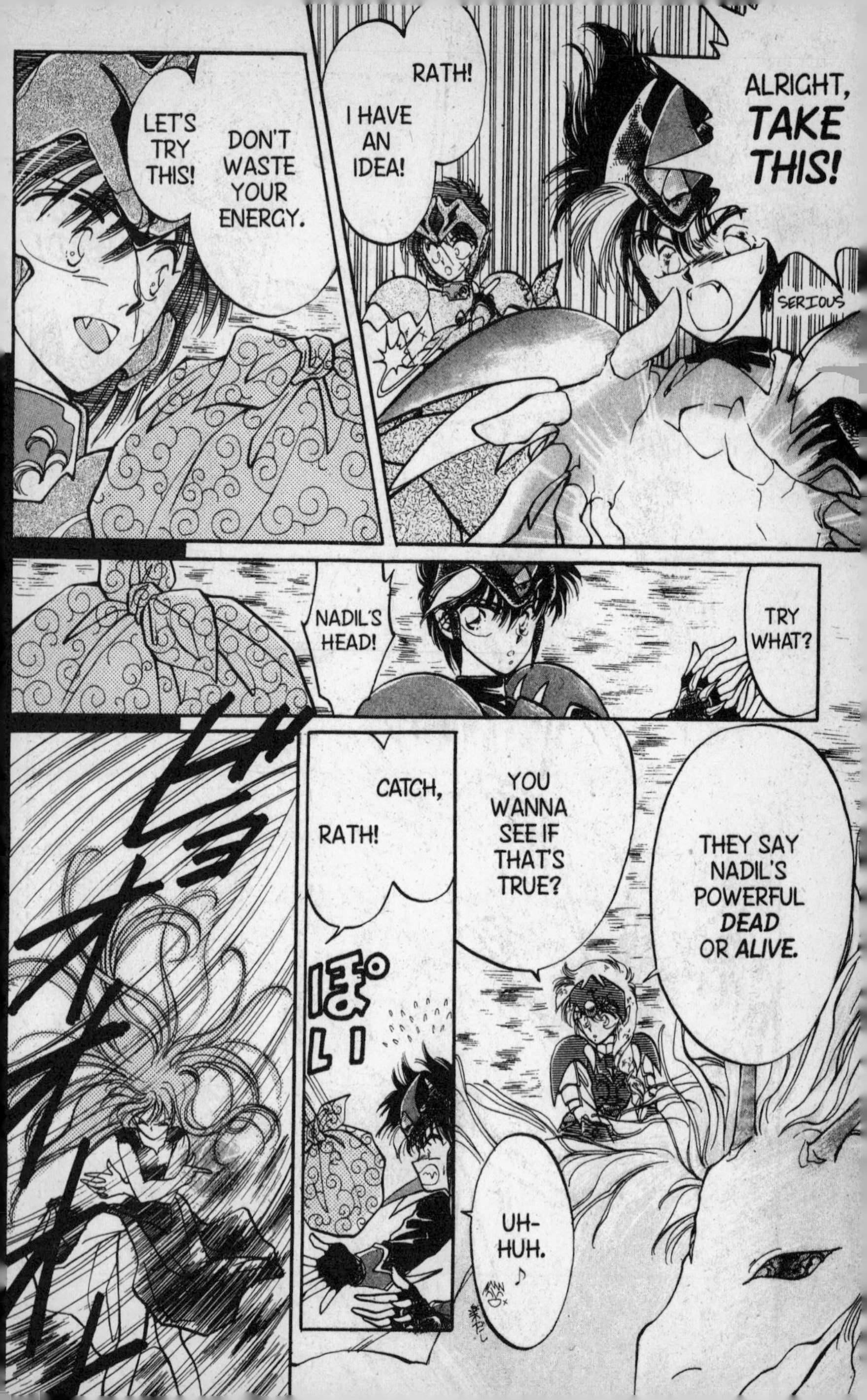
ALRIGHT, TAKE THIS!
SERIOUS
RATH!
I HAVE AN IDEA!
DON'T WASTE YOUR ENERGY.
LET'S TRY THIS!
TRY WHAT?
NADIL'S HEAD!
THEY SAY NADIL'S POWERFUL DEAD OR ALIVE.
YOU WANNA SEE IF THAT'S TRUE?
UH-HUH. ♪
CATCH,
RATH!
ぽい

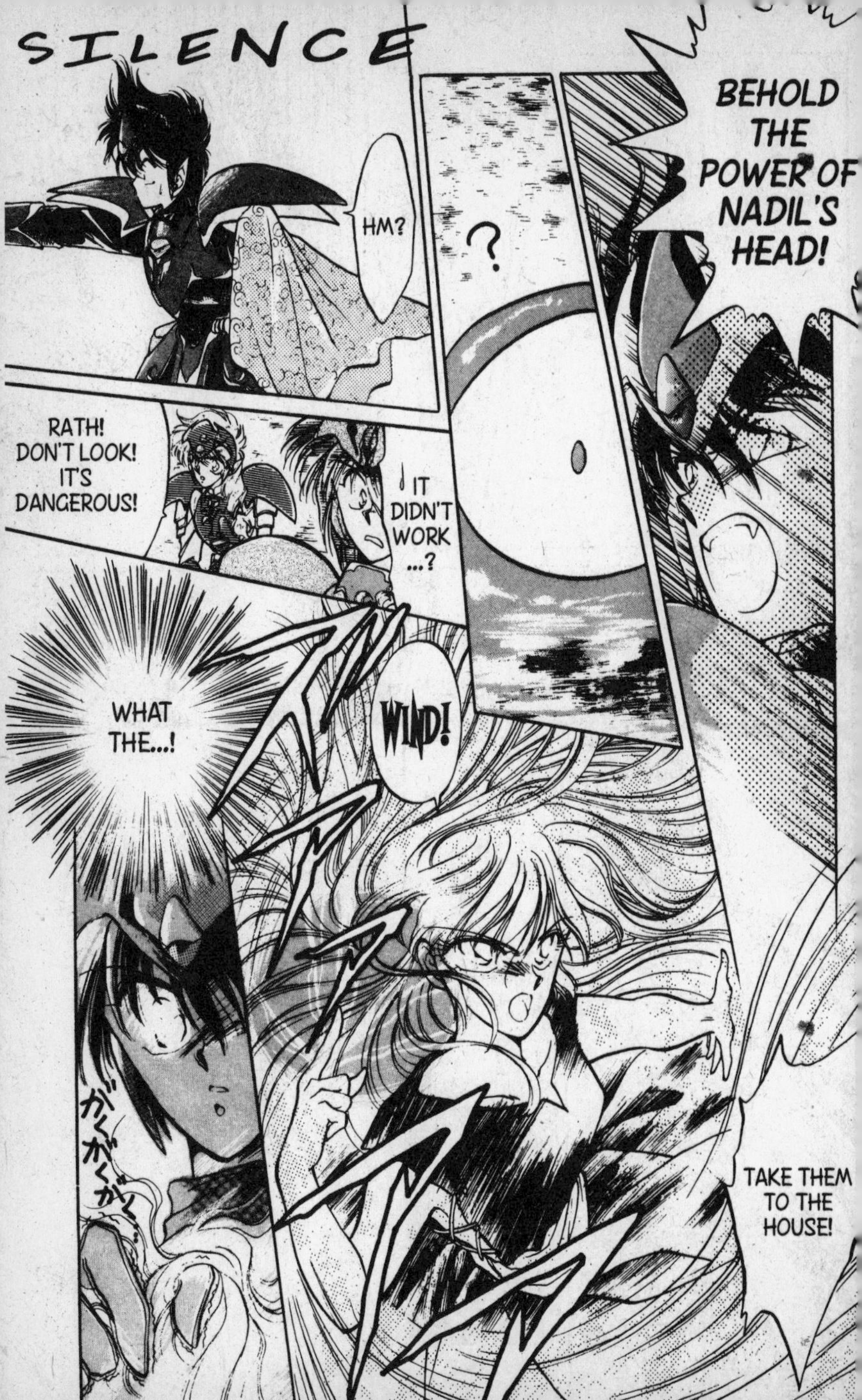
BEHOLD THE POWER OF NADIL'S HEAD!
?
HM?
SILENCE
IT DIDN'T WORK...?
RATH! DON'T LOOK! IT'S DANGEROUS!
WIND!
TAKE THEM TO THE HOUSE!
WHAT THE...!
がくがくがく…

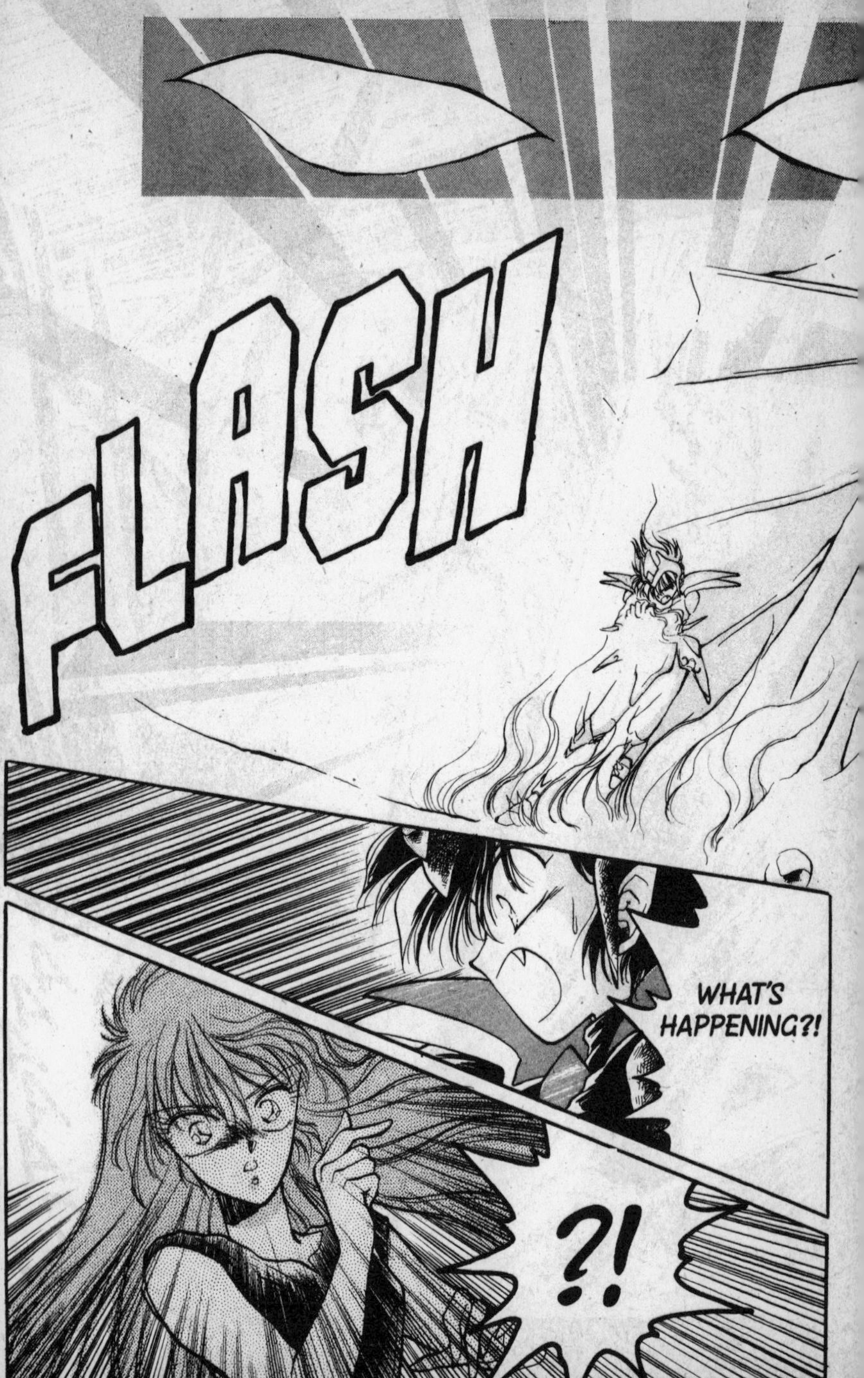
FLASH
WHAT'S HAPPENING?!
?!

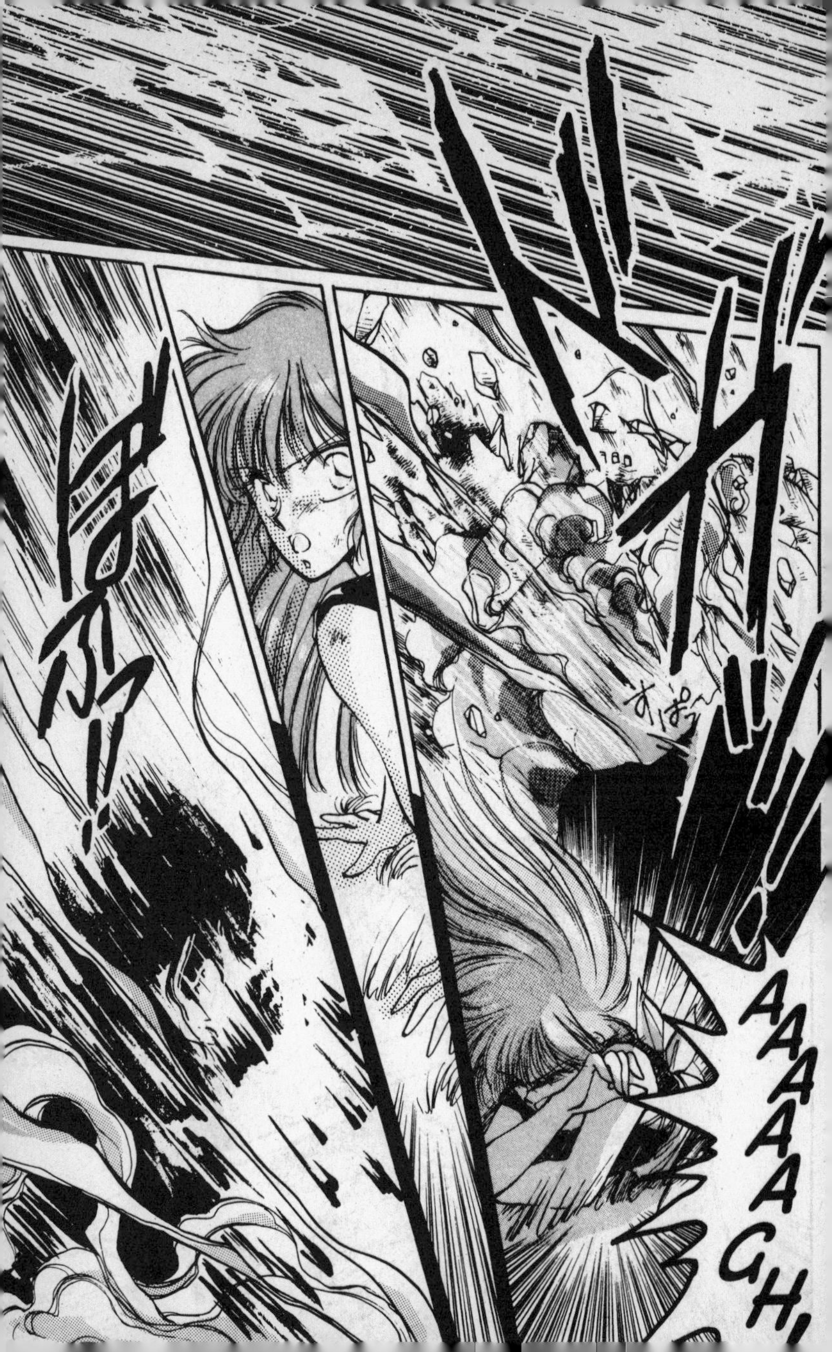

ぼふっ!!
すぽっ
AAAAAAGH!

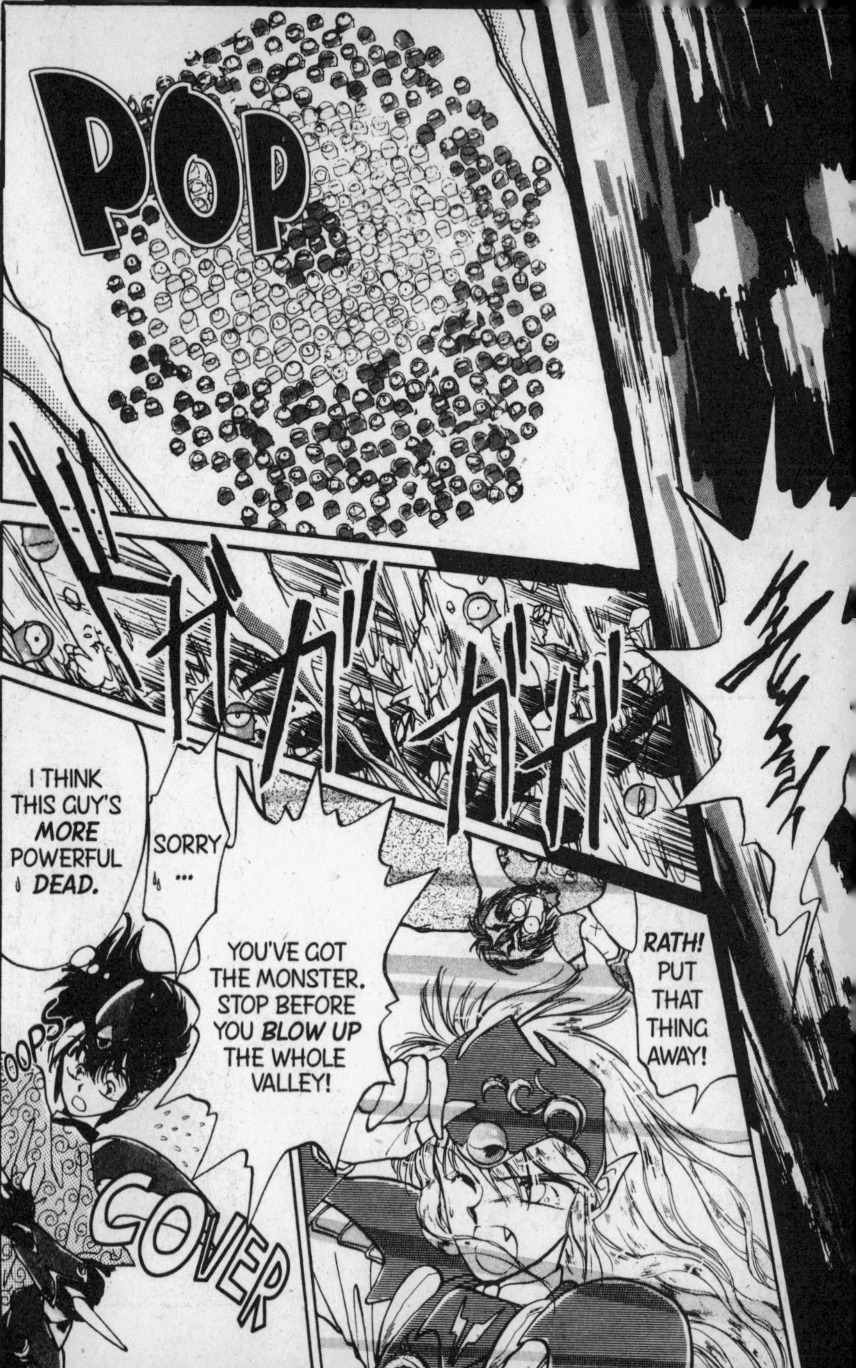
POP
RATH! PUT THAT THING AWAY!
YOU'VE GOT THE MONSTER. STOP BEFORE YOU BLOW UP THE WHOLE VALLEY!
SORRY...
I THINK THIS GUY'S MORE POWERFUL DEAD.
OOPS
COVER

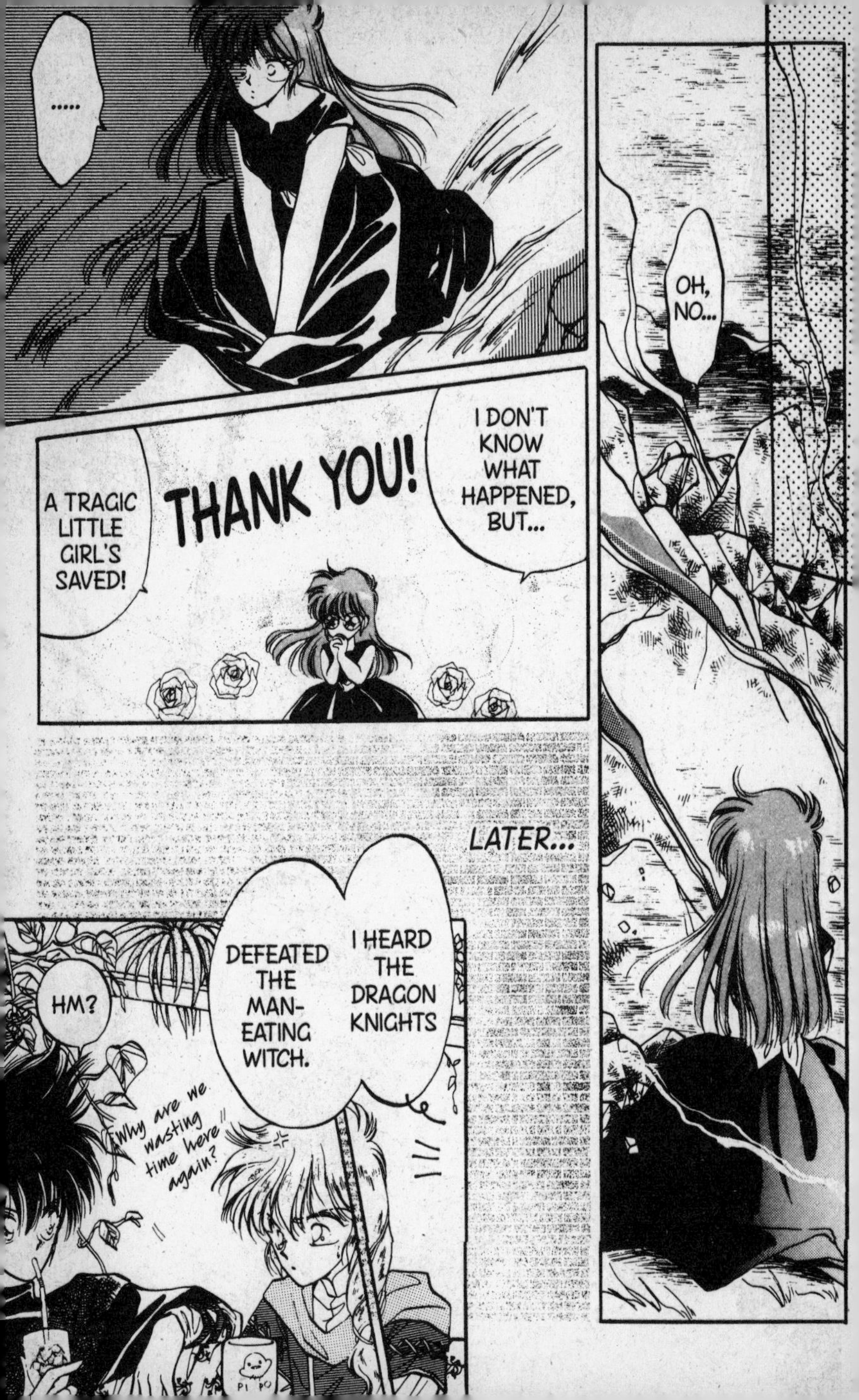
OH, NO...
.....
I DON'T KNOW WHAT HAPPENED, BUT...
THANK YOU!
A TRAGIC LITTLE GIRL'S SAVED!
LATER...
I HEARD THE DRAGON KNIGHTS
DEFEATED THE MAN-EATING WITCH.
HM?
Why are we wasting time here again?
PI PO

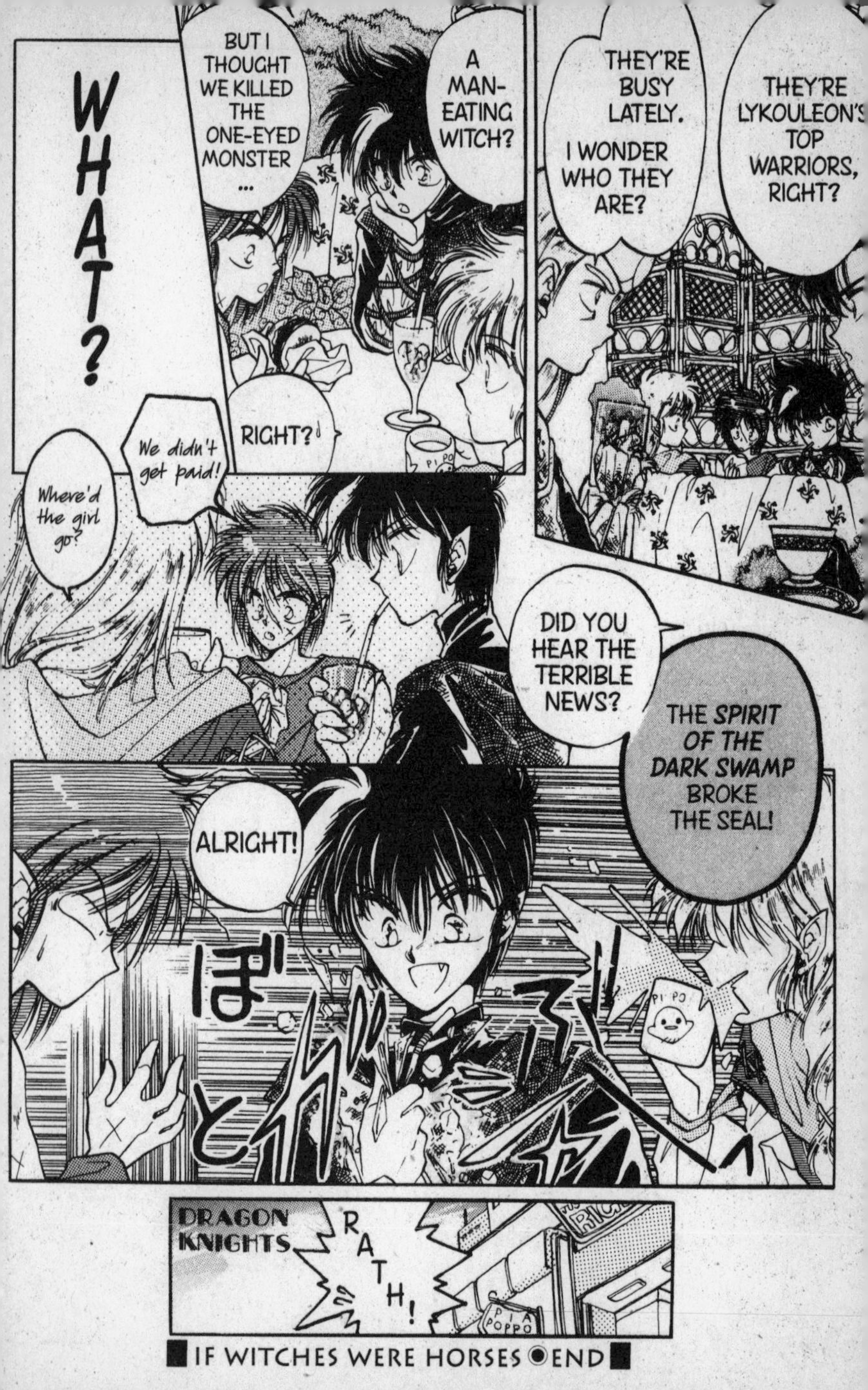
THEY'RE LYKOULEON'S TOP WARRIORS, RIGHT?
THEY'RE BUSY LATELY.
I WONDER WHO THEY ARE?
A MAN-EATING WITCH?
BUT I THOUGHT WE KILLED THE ONE-EYED MONSTER ...
RIGHT?
WHAT?
DID YOU HEAR THE TERRIBLE NEWS?
THE SPIRIT OF THE DARK SWAMP BROKE THE SEAL!
We didn't get paid!
Where'd the girl go?
ALRIGHT!
DRAGON KNIGHTS
RATH!
PI PO
PIA POPPO

■ IF WITCHES WERE HORSES ◉ END ■

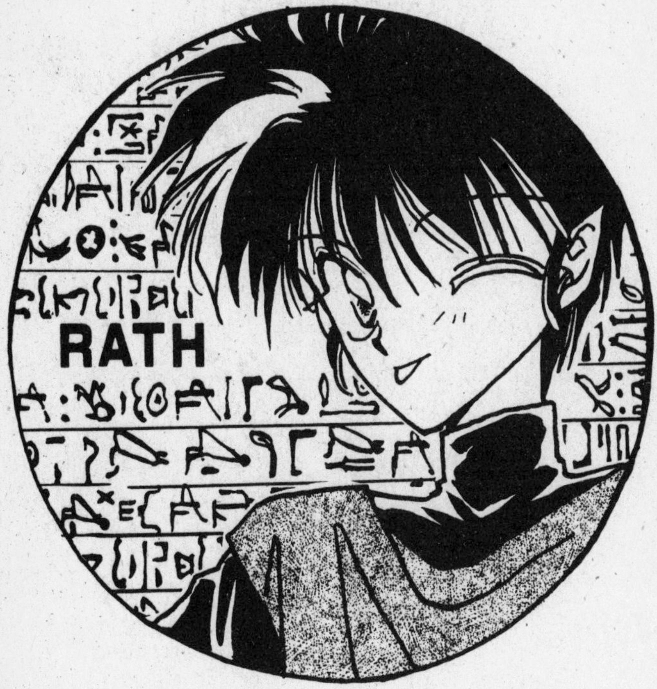
RATH

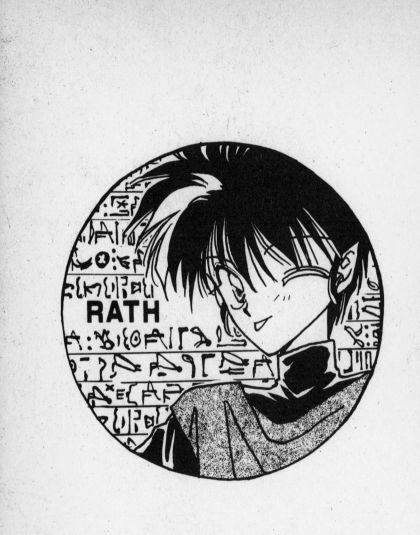

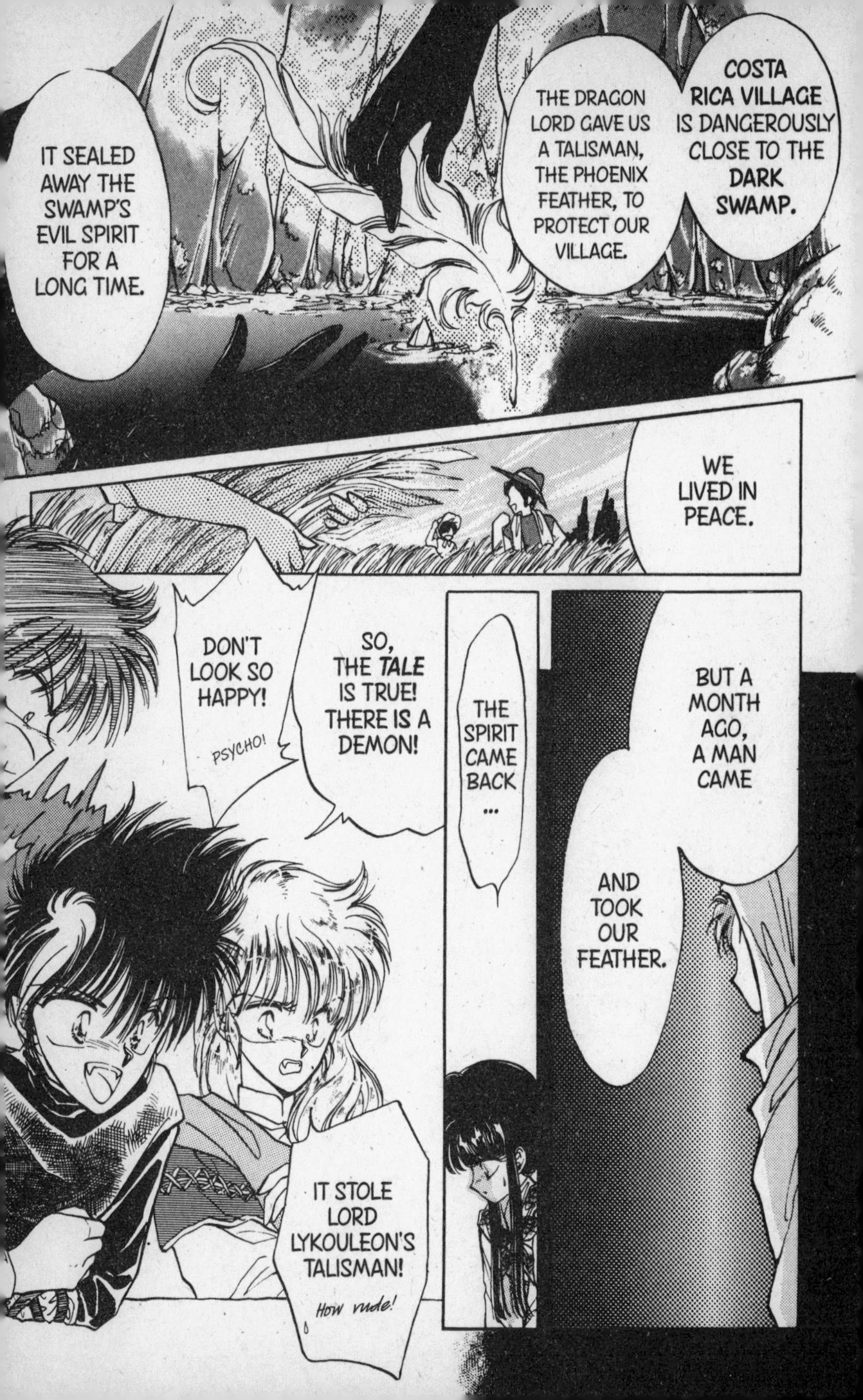

COSTA RICA VILLAGE IS DANGEROUSLY CLOSE TO THE DARK SWAMP.
THE DRAGON LORD GAVE US A TALISMAN, THE PHOENIX FEATHER, TO PROTECT OUR VILLAGE.
IT SEALED AWAY THE SWAMP'S EVIL SPIRIT FOR A LONG TIME.
WE LIVED IN PEACE.
BUT A MONTH AGO, A MAN CAME
AND TOOK OUR FEATHER.
THE SPIRIT CAME BACK ...
SO, THE TALE IS TRUE! THERE IS A DEMON!
DON'T LOOK SO HAPPY!
PSYCHO!
IT STOLE LORD LYKOULEON'S TALISMAN!
How rude!

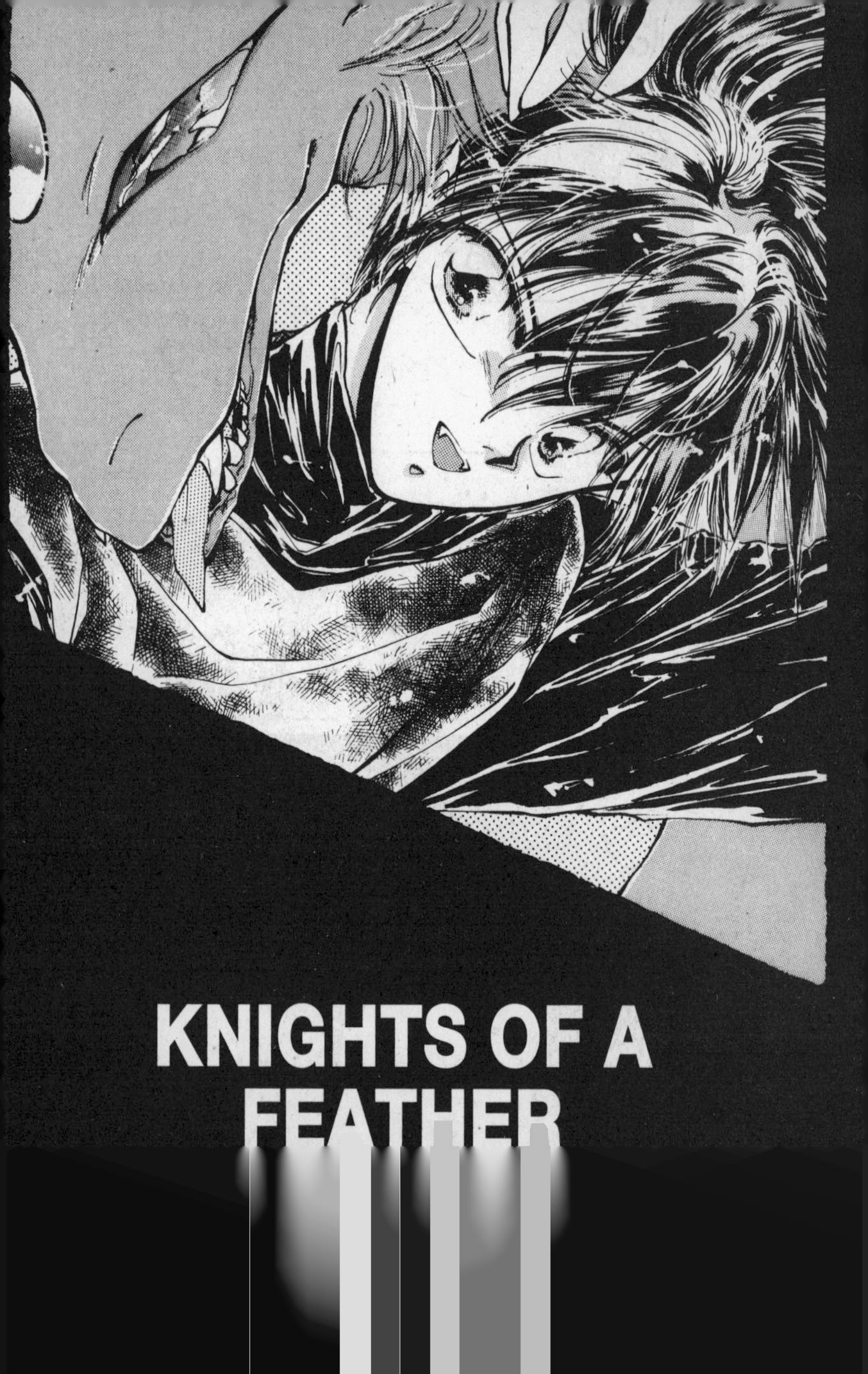

KNIGHTS OF A FEATHER

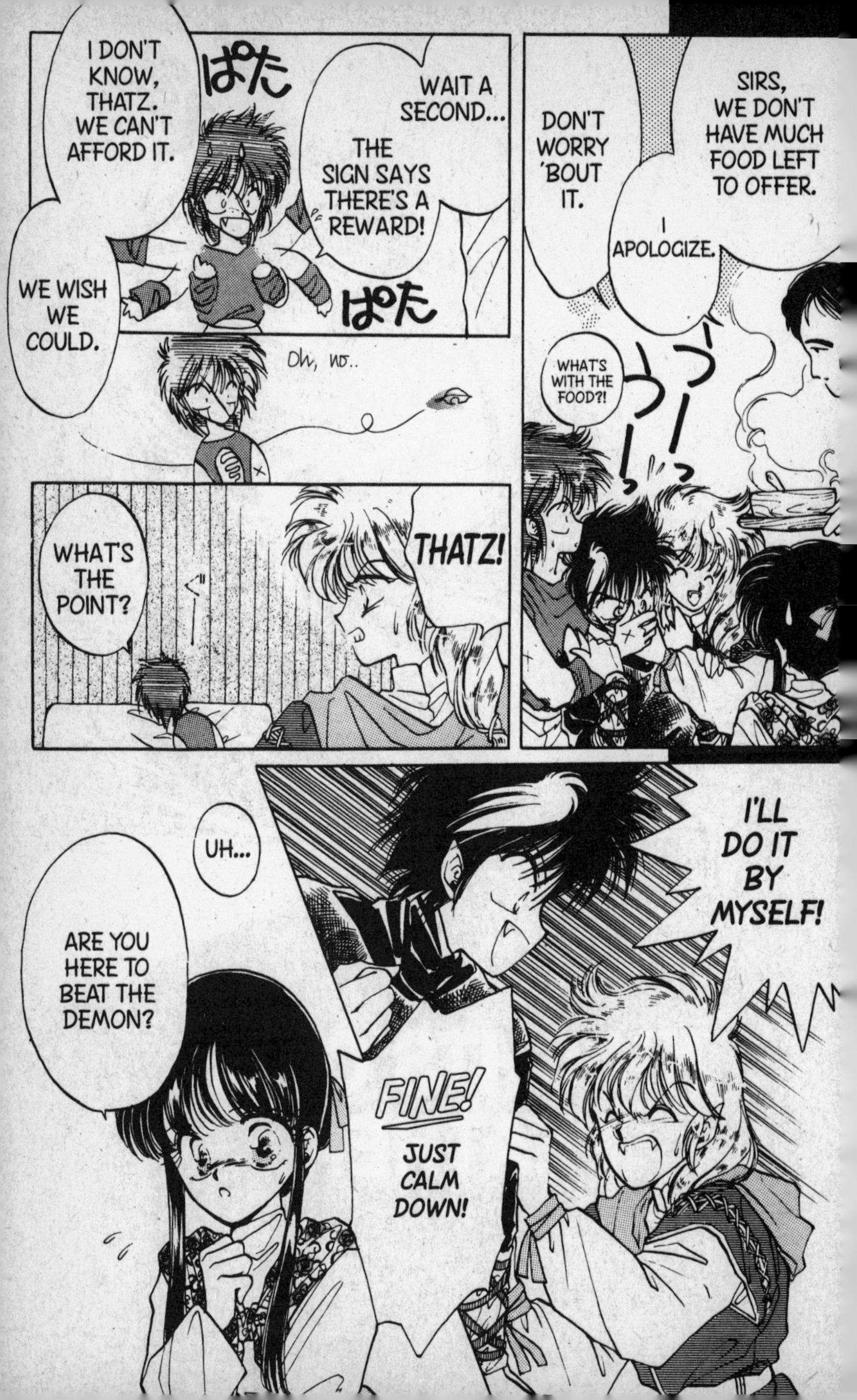
SIRS, WE DON'T HAVE MUCH FOOD LEFT TO OFFER.
I APOLOGIZE.
DON'T WORRY 'BOUT IT.
WHAT'S WITH THE FOOD?!
ぱた
WAIT A SECOND...
THE SIGN SAYS THERE'S A REWARD!
I DON'T KNOW, THATZ. WE CAN'T AFFORD IT.
ぱた
WE WISH WE COULD.
Oh, no..
THATZ!
WHAT'S THE POINT?
I'LL DO IT BY MYSELF!
FINE!
JUST CALM DOWN!
UH...
ARE YOU HERE TO BEAT THE DEMON?

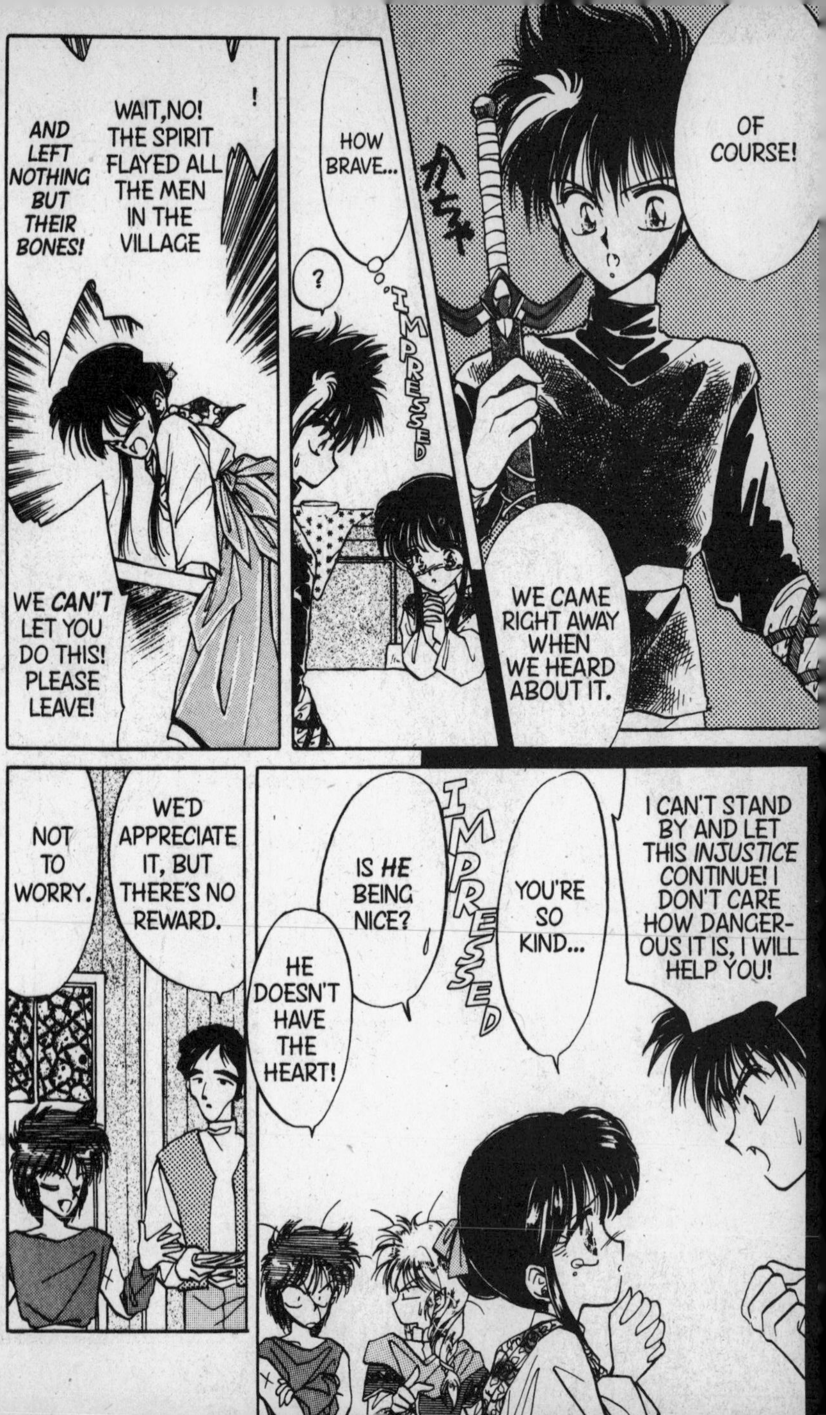
OF COURSE!
WE CAME RIGHT AWAY WHEN WE HEARD ABOUT IT.
HOW BRAVE...
?
IMPRESSED
!
WAIT,NO! THE SPIRIT FLAYED ALL THE MEN IN THE VILLAGE
AND LEFT NOTHING BUT THEIR BONES!
WE CAN'T LET YOU DO THIS! PLEASE LEAVE!
I CAN'T STAND BY AND LET THIS INJUSTICE CONTINUE! I DON'T CARE HOW DANGER-OUS IT IS, I WILL HELP YOU!
YOU'RE SO KIND...
IMPRESSED
IS HE BEING NICE?
HE DOESN'T HAVE THE HEART!
WE'D APPRECIATE IT, BUT THERE'S NO REWARD.
NOT TO WORRY.

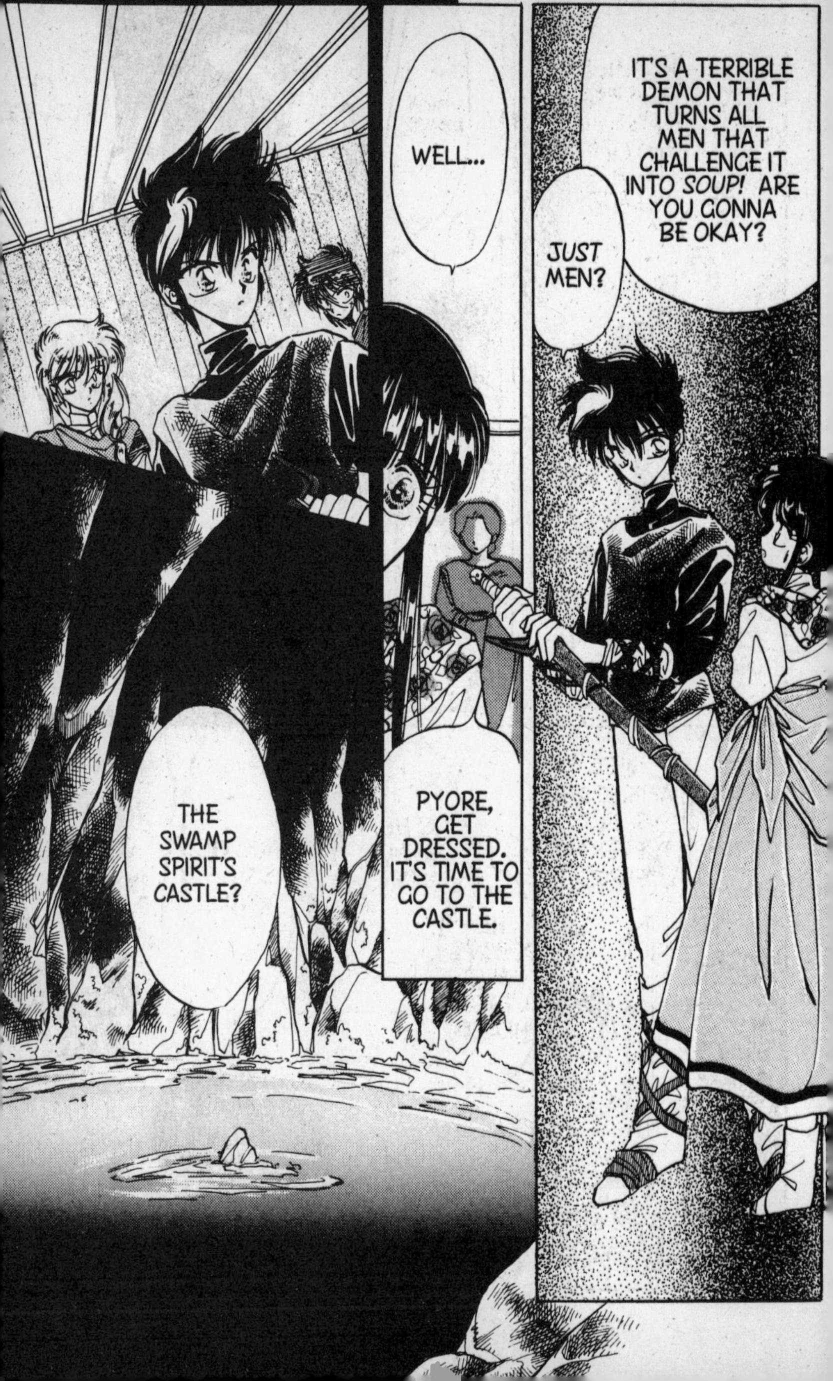
IT'S A TERRIBLE DEMON THAT TURNS ALL MEN THAT CHALLENGE IT INTO *SOUP!* ARE YOU GONNA BE OKAY?
JUST MEN?
WELL...
PYORE, GET DRESSED. IT'S TIME TO GO TO THE CASTLE.
THE SWAMP SPIRIT'S CASTLE?

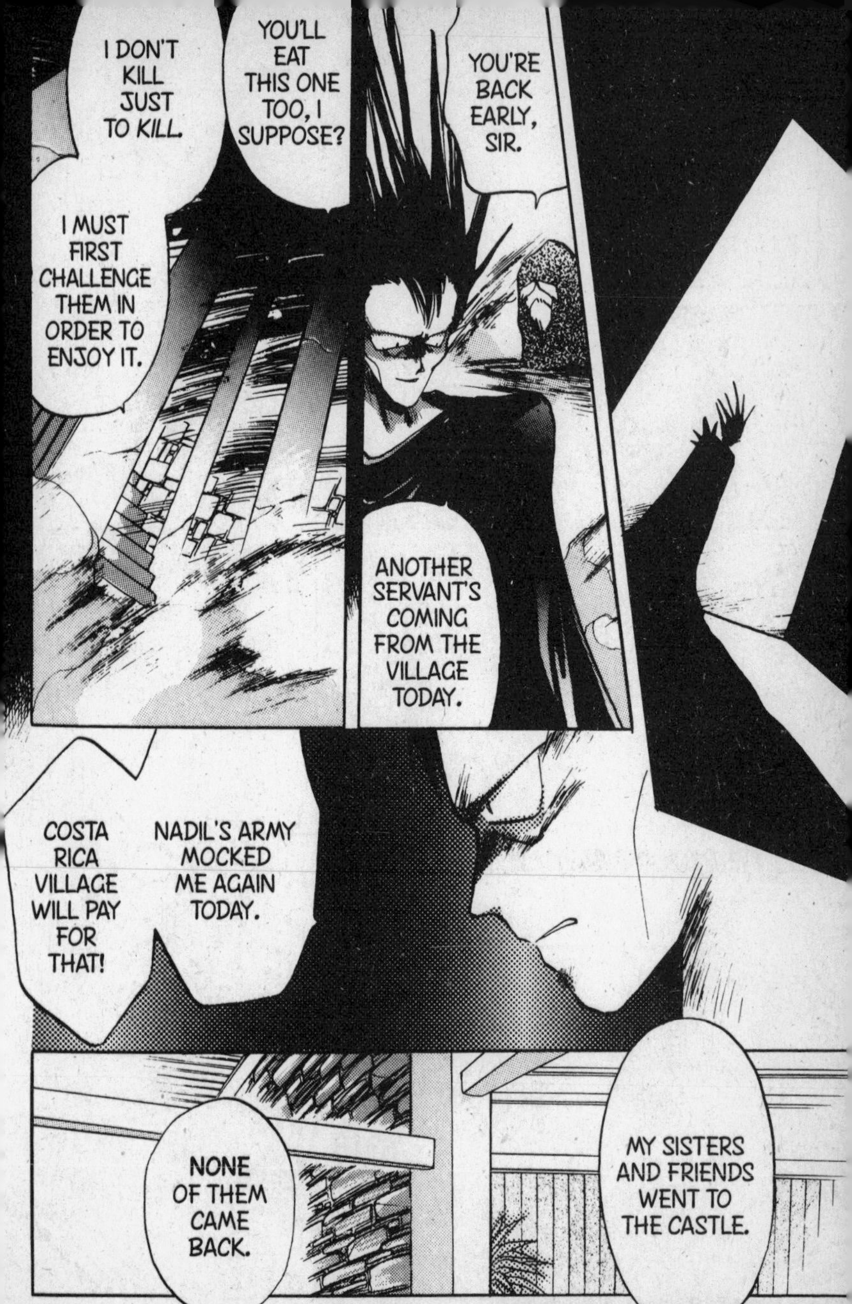
YOU'RE BACK EARLY, SIR.
ANOTHER SERVANT'S COMING FROM THE VILLAGE TODAY.
YOU'LL EAT THIS ONE TOO, I SUPPOSE?
I DON'T KILL JUST TO KILL.
I MUST FIRST CHALLENGE THEM IN ORDER TO ENJOY IT.
NADIL'S ARMY MOCKED ME AGAIN TODAY.
COSTA RICA VILLAGE WILL PAY FOR THAT!
MY SISTERS AND FRIENDS WENT TO THE CASTLE.
NONE OF THEM CAME BACK.

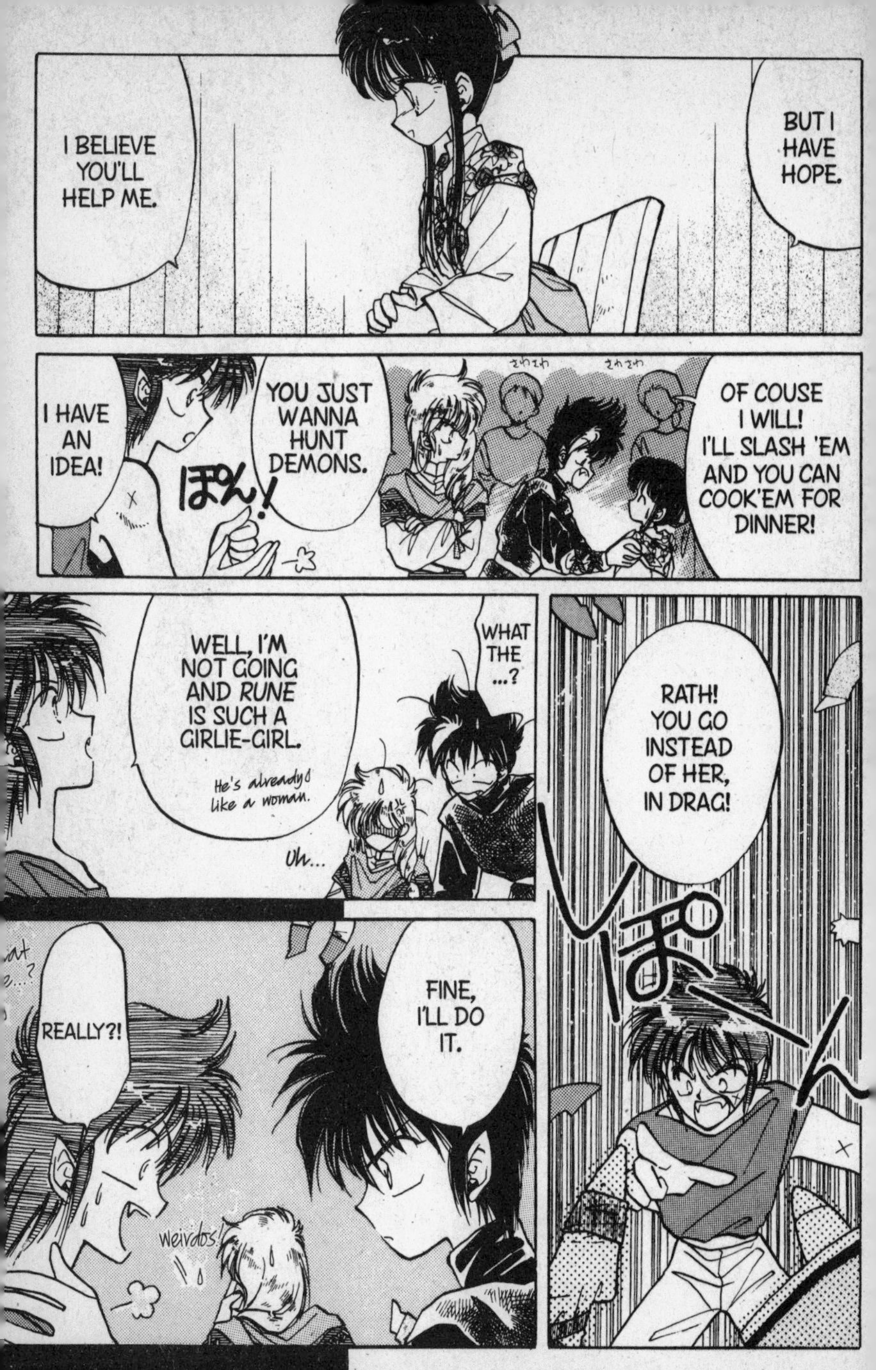
BUT I HAVE HOPE.
I BELIEVE YOU'LL HELP ME.
OF COUSE I WILL! I'LL SLASH 'EM AND YOU CAN COOK'EM FOR DINNER!
YOU JUST WANNA HUNT DEMONS.
ぽん!
I HAVE AN IDEA!
RATH! YOU GO INSTEAD OF HER, IN DRAG!
WHAT THE ...?
WELL, I'M NOT GOING AND *RUNE* IS SUCH A GIRLIE-GIRL.
He's already like a woman.
Uh...
FINE, I'LL DO IT.
REALLY?!
weirdos!

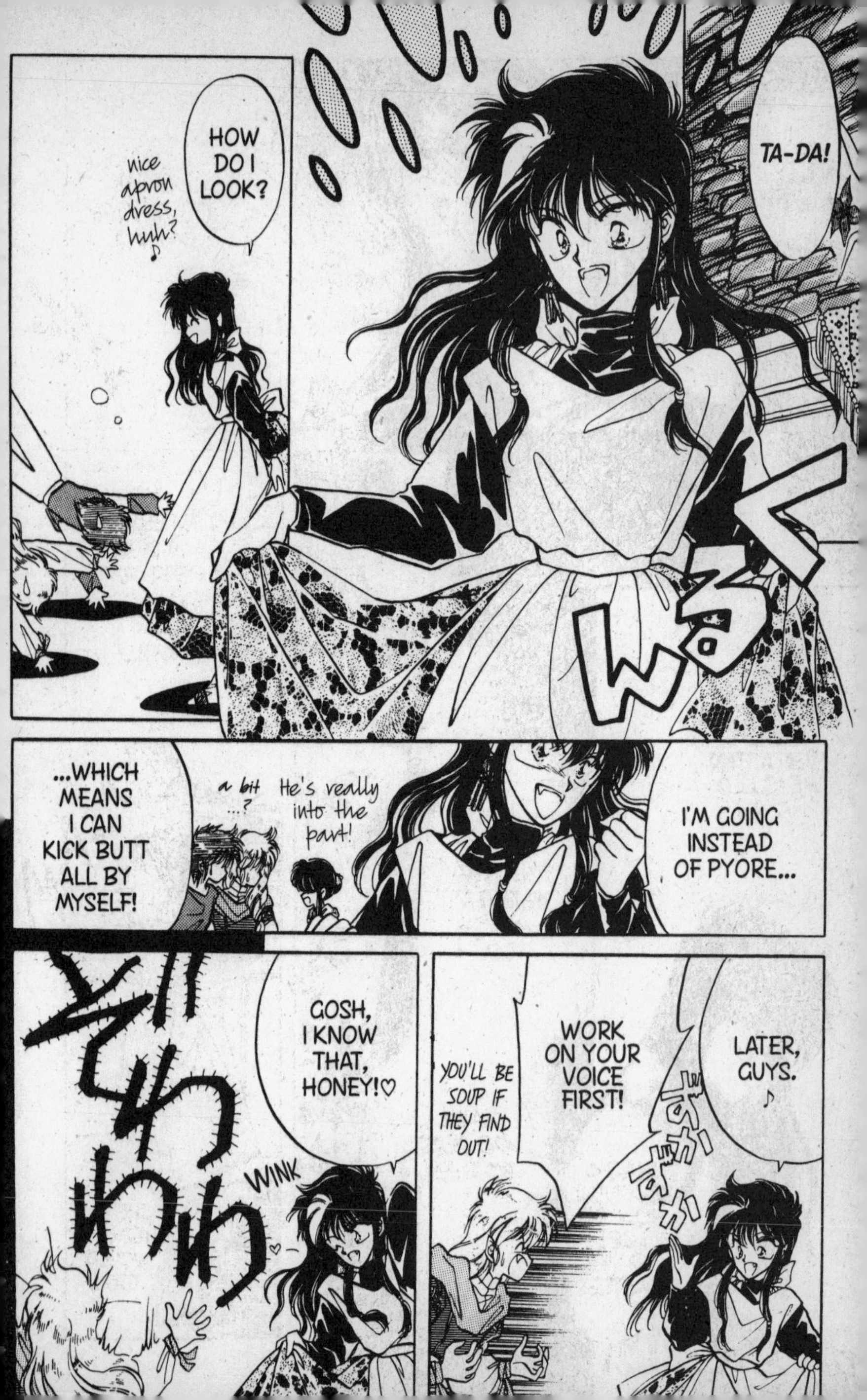
TA-DA!
HOW DO I LOOK?
nice apron dress, huh? ♪
I'M GOING INSTEAD OF PYORE...
He's really into the part!
a bit ...?
...WHICH MEANS I CAN KICK BUTT ALL BY MYSELF!
LATER, GUYS. ♪
WORK ON YOUR VOICE FIRST!
YOU'LL BE SOUP IF THEY FIND OUT!
GOSH, I KNOW THAT, HONEY!♡
WINK

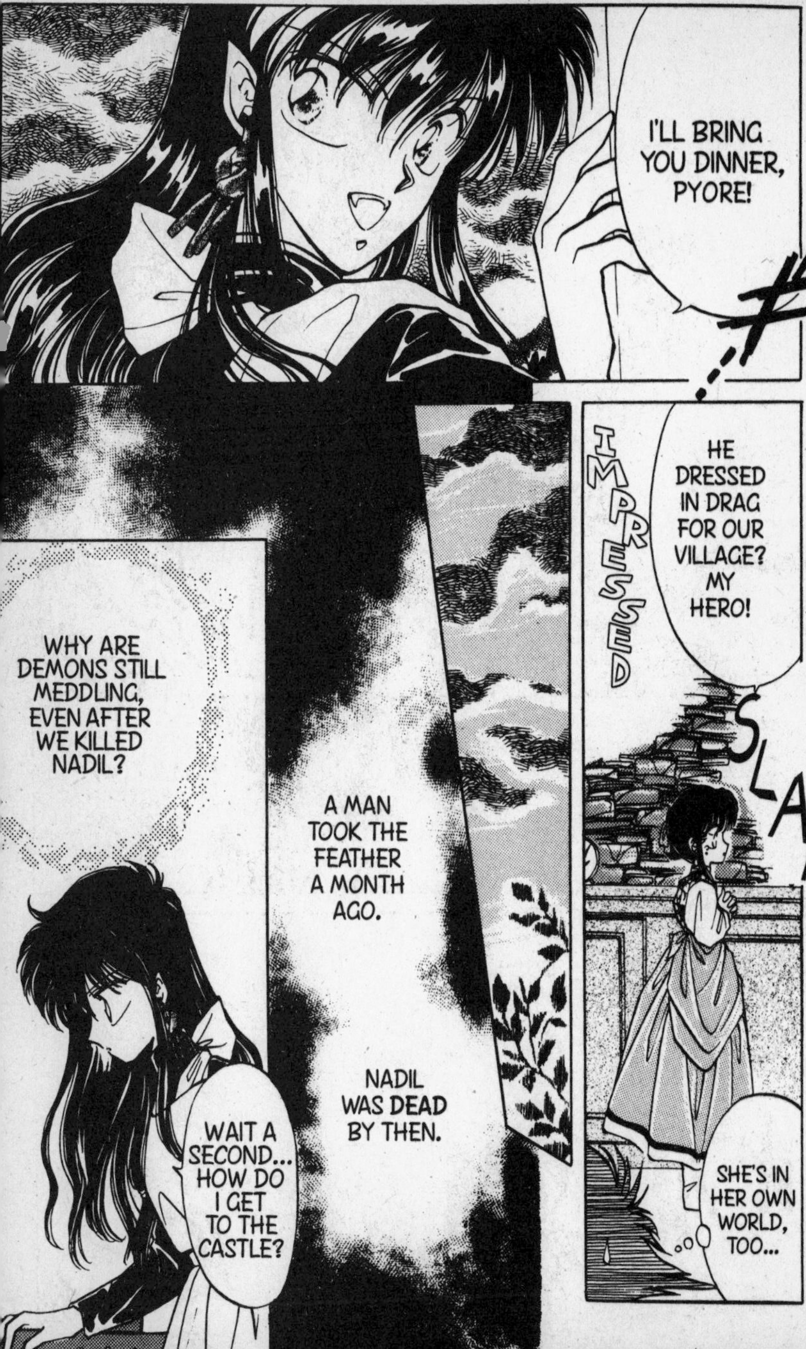
I'LL BRING YOU DINNER, PYORE!
IMPRESSED
HE DRESSED IN DRAG FOR OUR VILLAGE? MY HERO!
SLAM
SHE'S IN HER OWN WORLD, TOO...
A MAN TOOK THE FEATHER A MONTH AGO.
NADIL WAS DEAD BY THEN.
WHY ARE DEMONS STILL MEDDLING, EVEN AFTER WE KILLED NADIL?
WAIT A SECOND... HOW DO I GET TO THE CASTLE?

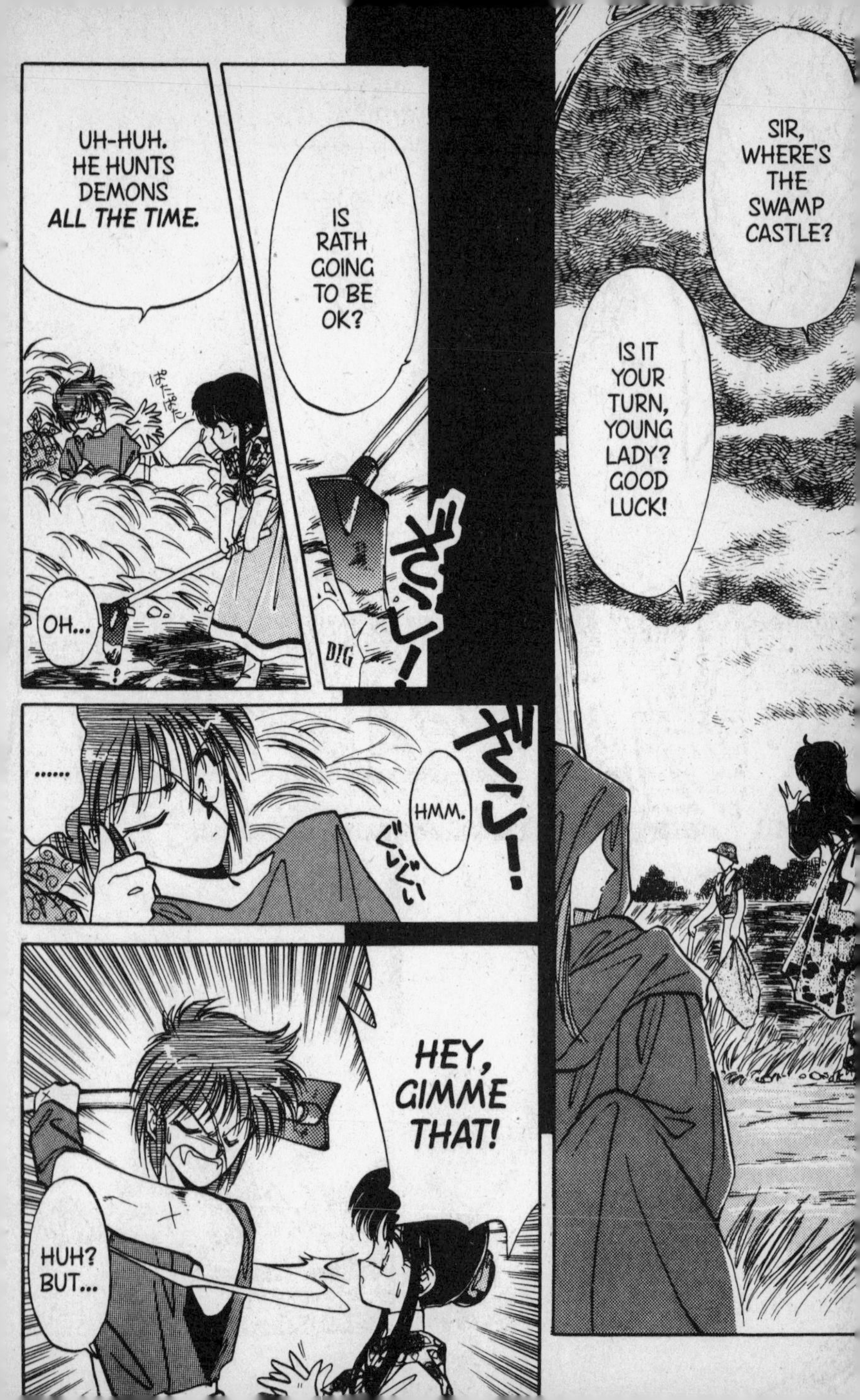
SIR, WHERE'S THE SWAMP CASTLE?
IS IT YOUR TURN, YOUNG LADY? GOOD LUCK!
IS RATH GOING TO BE OK?
DIG
UH-HUH. HE HUNTS DEMONS *ALL THE TIME.*
ぱたぱた
OH...
HMM.
ぐいぐい
......
HEY, GIMME THAT!
HUH? BUT...

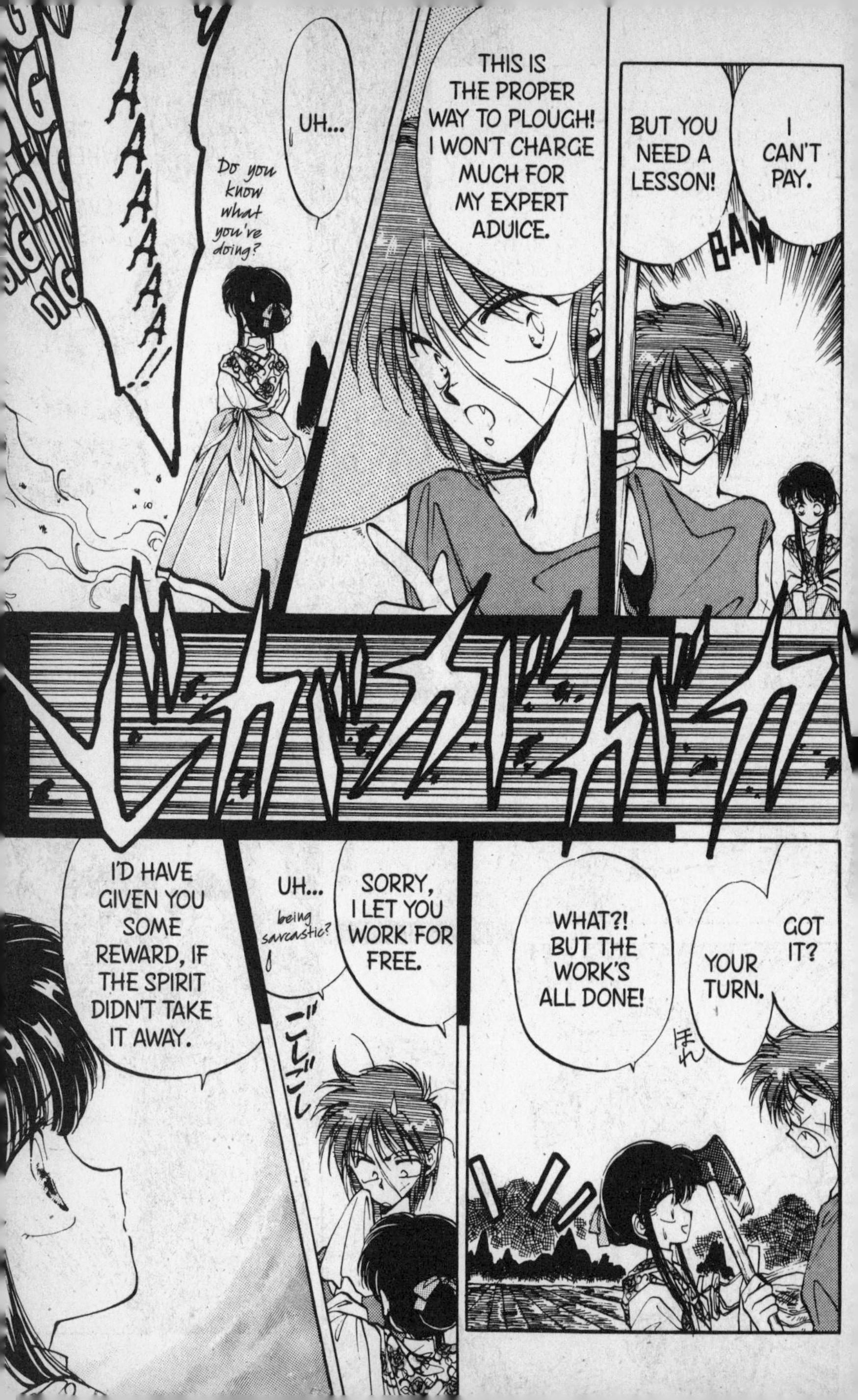
I CAN'T PAY.
BUT YOU NEED A LESSON!
BAM
THIS IS THE PROPER WAY TO PLOUGH! I WON'T CHARGE MUCH FOR MY EXPERT ADUICE.
UH...
AAAAAAA!!
Do you know what you're doing?
DIG DIG DIG
GOT IT?
YOUR TURN.
ほん
WHAT?! BUT THE WORK'S ALL DONE!
SORRY, I LET YOU WORK FOR FREE.
UH...
being sarcastic?
ごしごし
I'D HAVE GIVEN YOU SOME REWARD, IF THE SPIRIT DIDN'T TAKE IT AWAY.

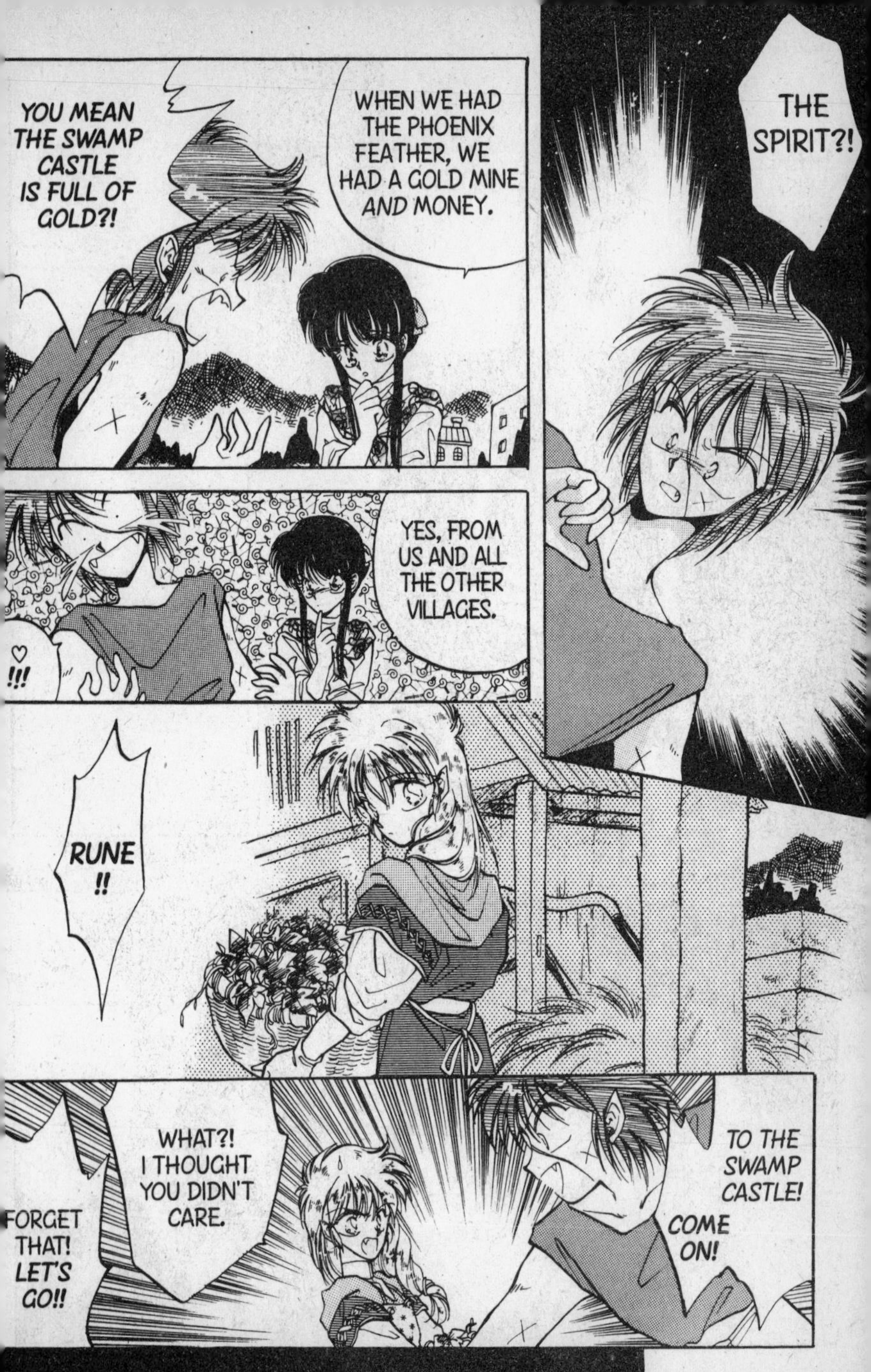
THE SPIRIT?!
WHEN WE HAD THE PHOENIX FEATHER, WE HAD A GOLD MINE AND MONEY.
YOU MEAN THE SWAMP CASTLE IS FULL OF GOLD?!
YES, FROM US AND ALL THE OTHER VILLAGES.
♥ !!!
RUNE !!
TO THE SWAMP CASTLE!
COME ON!
WHAT?! I THOUGHT YOU DIDN'T CARE.
FORGET THAT! LET'S GO!!

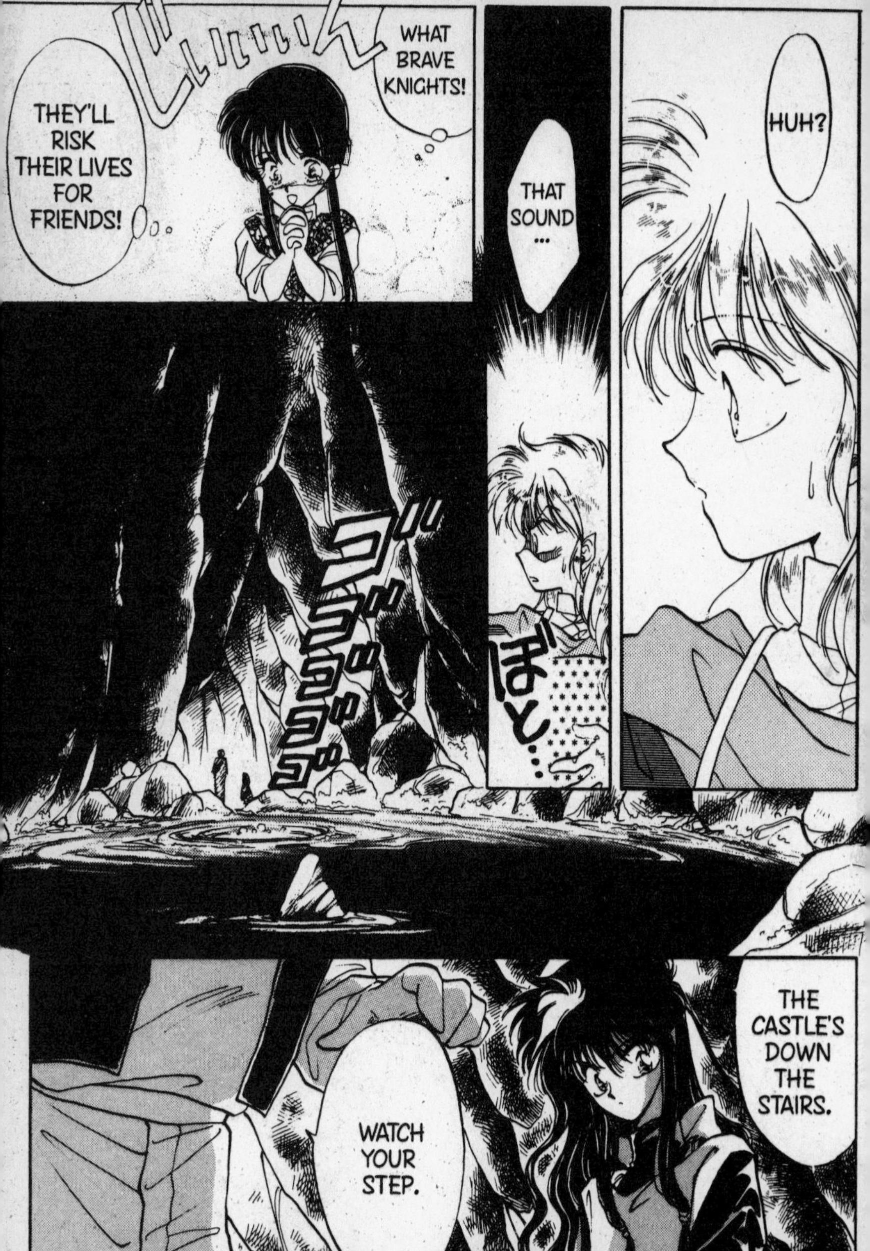
HUH?
THAT SOUND ...
WHAT BRAVE KNIGHTS!
THEY'LL RISK THEIR LIVES FOR FRIENDS!
ぽと…
THE CASTLE'S DOWN THE STAIRS.
WATCH YOUR STEP.

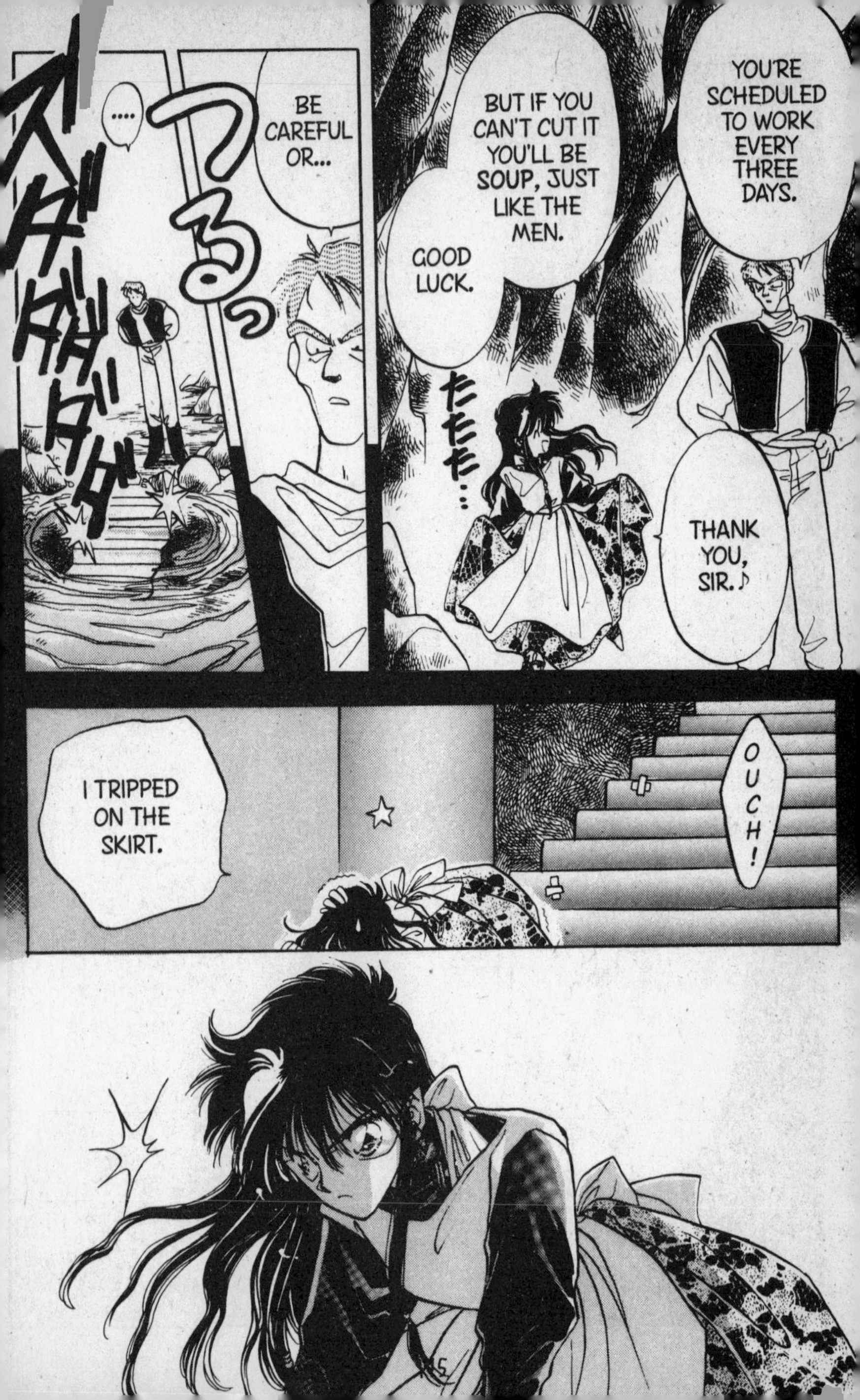
YOU'RE SCHEDULED TO WORK EVERY THREE DAYS.
THANK YOU, SIR.♪
BUT IF YOU CAN'T CUT IT YOU'LL BE SOUP, JUST LIKE THE MEN.
GOOD LUCK.
たたた…
BE CAREFUL OR...
つるっ
....
OUCH!
I TRIPPED ON THE SKIRT.

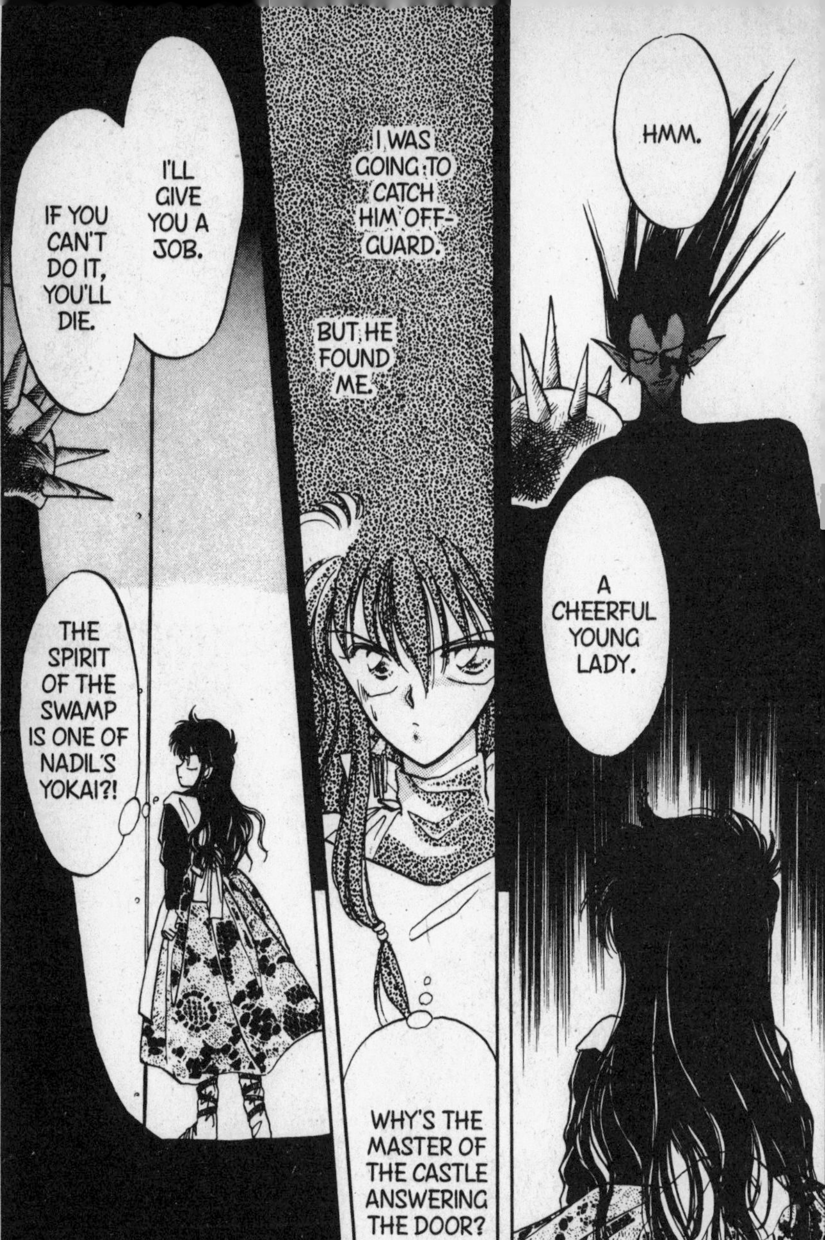
HMM.
A CHEERFUL YOUNG LADY.
I WAS GOING TO CATCH HIM OFF-GUARD.
BUT HE FOUND ME.
WHY'S THE MASTER OF THE CASTLE ANSWERING THE DOOR?
I'LL GIVE YOU A JOB.
IF YOU CAN'T DO IT, YOU'LL DIE.
THE SPIRIT OF THE SWAMP IS ONE OF NADIL'S YOKAI?!

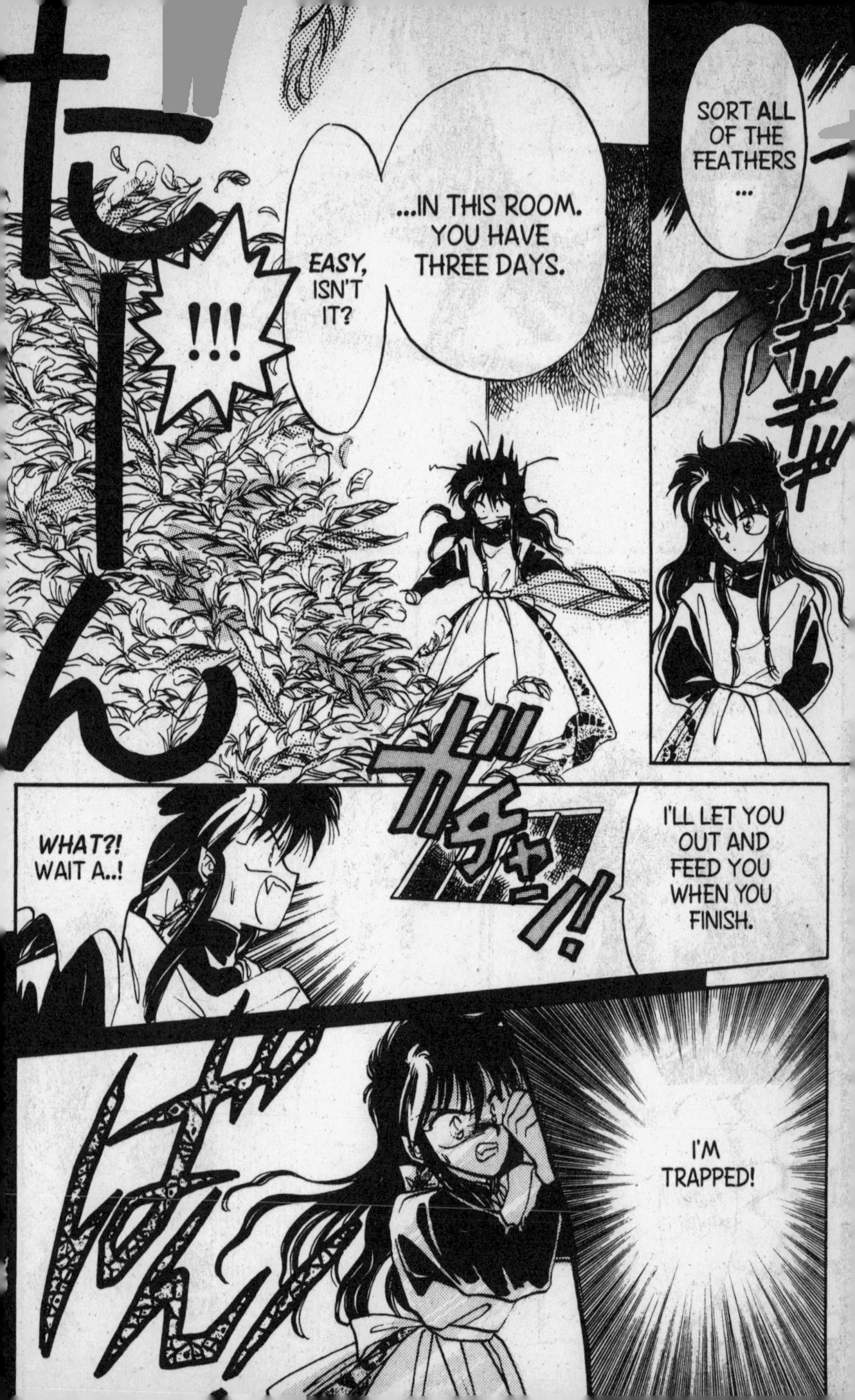
SORT ALL OF THE FEATHERS ...
...IN THIS ROOM. YOU HAVE THREE DAYS.
EASY, ISN'T IT?
!!!
I'LL LET YOU OUT AND FEED YOU WHEN YOU FINISH.
WHAT?! WAIT A..!
I'M TRAPPED!

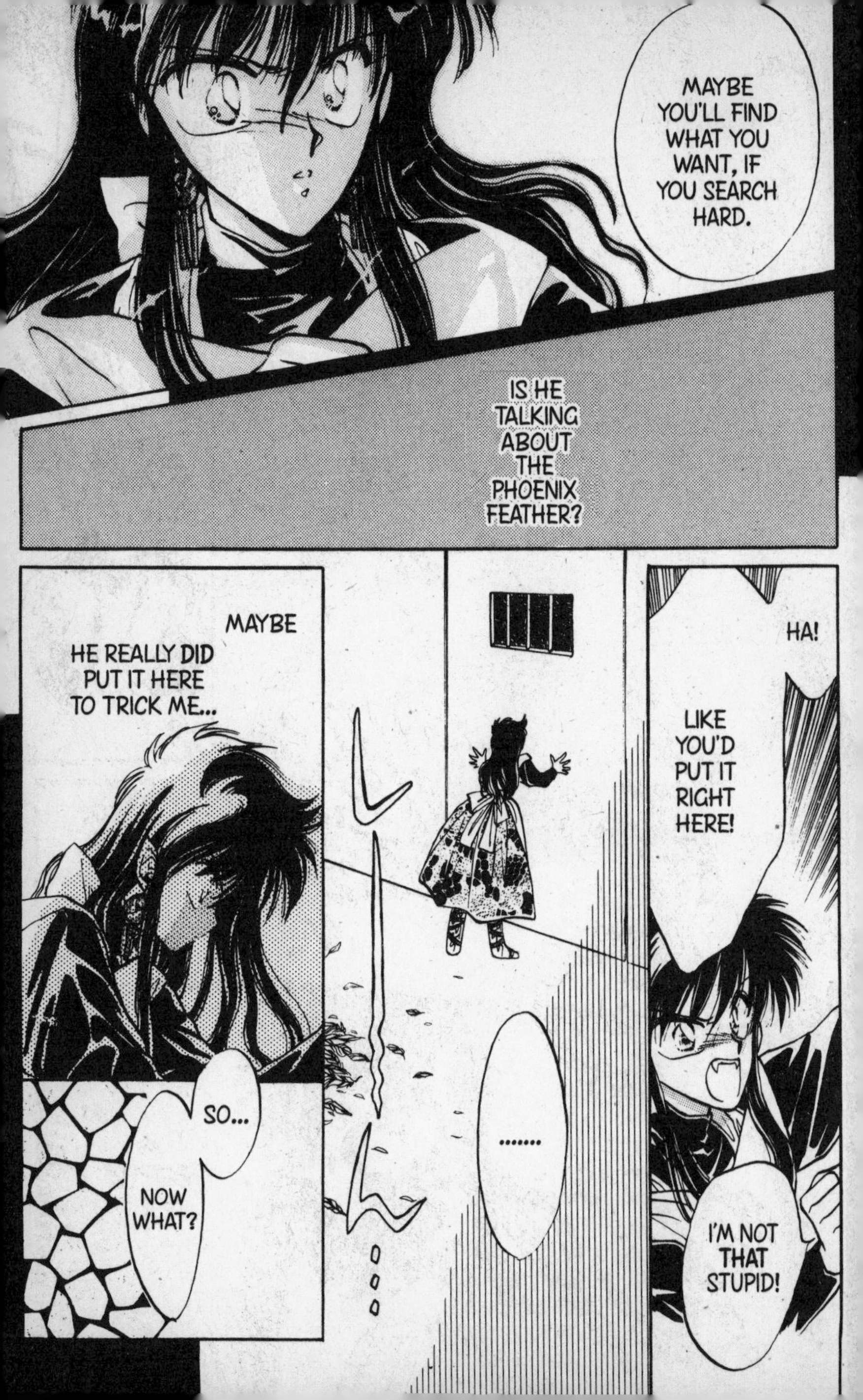
MAYBE YOU'LL FIND WHAT YOU WANT, IF YOU SEARCH HARD.
IS HE TALKING ABOUT THE PHOENIX FEATHER?
HA!
LIKE YOU'D PUT IT RIGHT HERE!
I'M NOT THAT STUPID!
....
MAYBE
HE REALLY DID PUT IT HERE TO TRICK ME...
SO...
NOW WHAT?

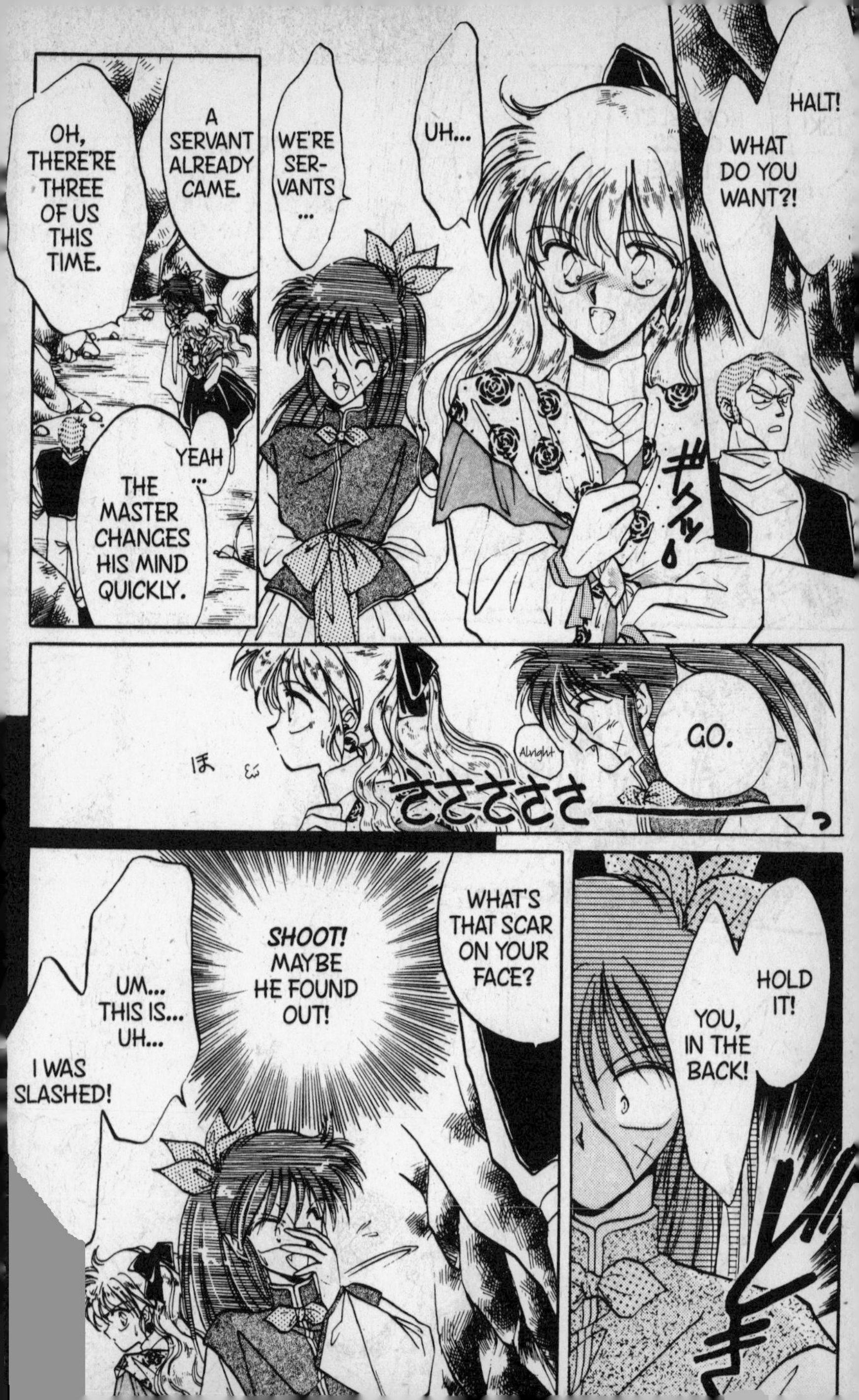
HALT!
WHAT DO YOU WANT?!
ギクッ
UH...
WE'RE SER-VANTS ...
A SERVANT ALREADY CAME.
OH, THERE'RE THREE OF US THIS TIME.
YEAH ...
THE MASTER CHANGES HIS MIND QUICKLY.
GO.
Alright
ほ
さささささ——っ
HOLD IT!
YOU, IN THE BACK!
WHAT'S THAT SCAR ON YOUR FACE?
SHOOT! MAYBE HE FOUND OUT!
UM... THIS IS... UH...
I WAS SLASHED!

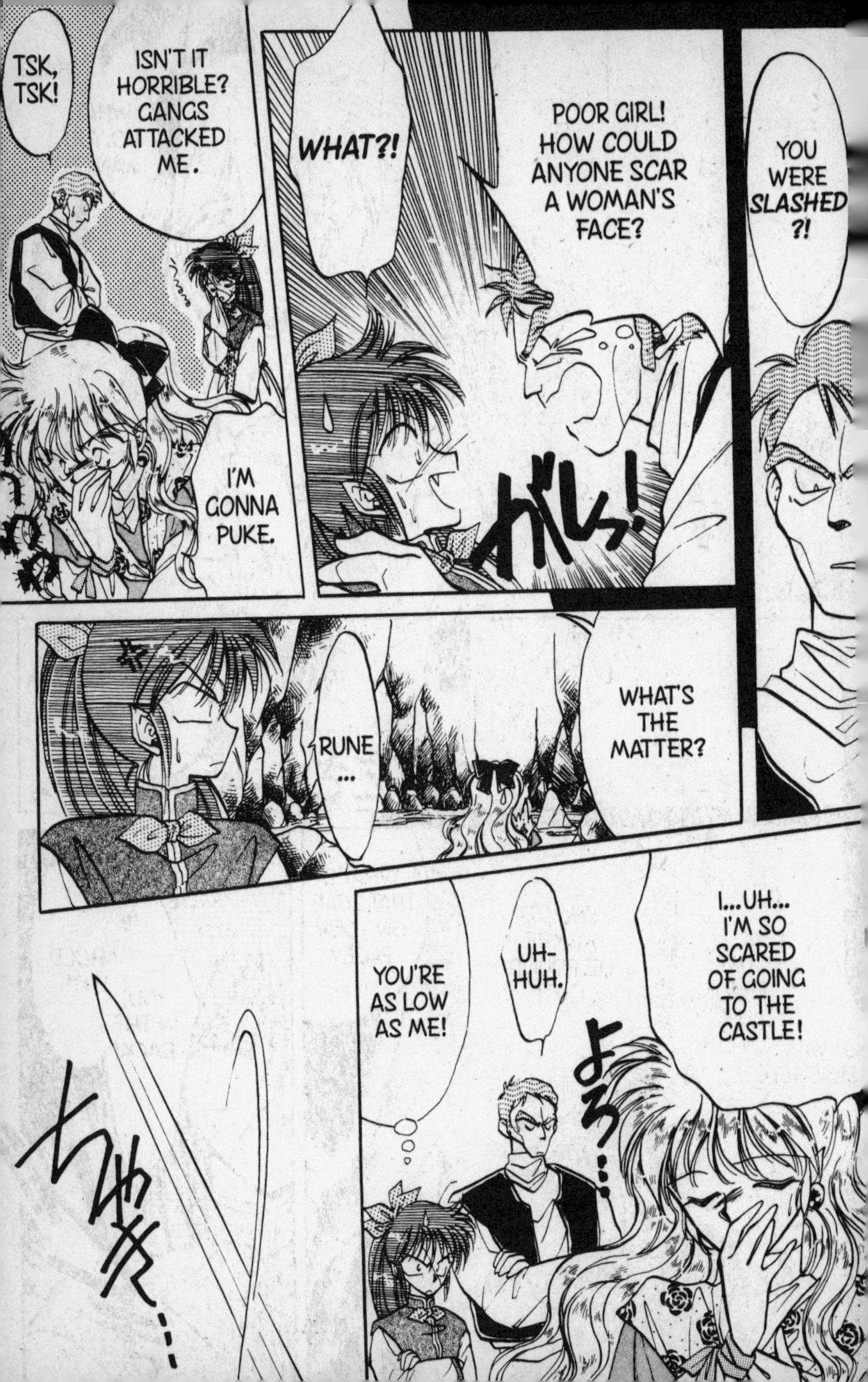
YOU WERE SLASHED?!
POOR GIRL! HOW COULD ANYONE SCAR A WOMAN'S FACE?
WHAT?!
ISN'T IT HORRIBLE? GANGS ATTACKED ME.
TSK, TSK!
I'M GONNA PUKE.
WHAT'S THE MATTER?
RUNE ...
I...UH... I'M SO SCARED OF GOING TO THE CASTLE!
UH-HUH.
YOU'RE AS LOW AS ME!
よろ…

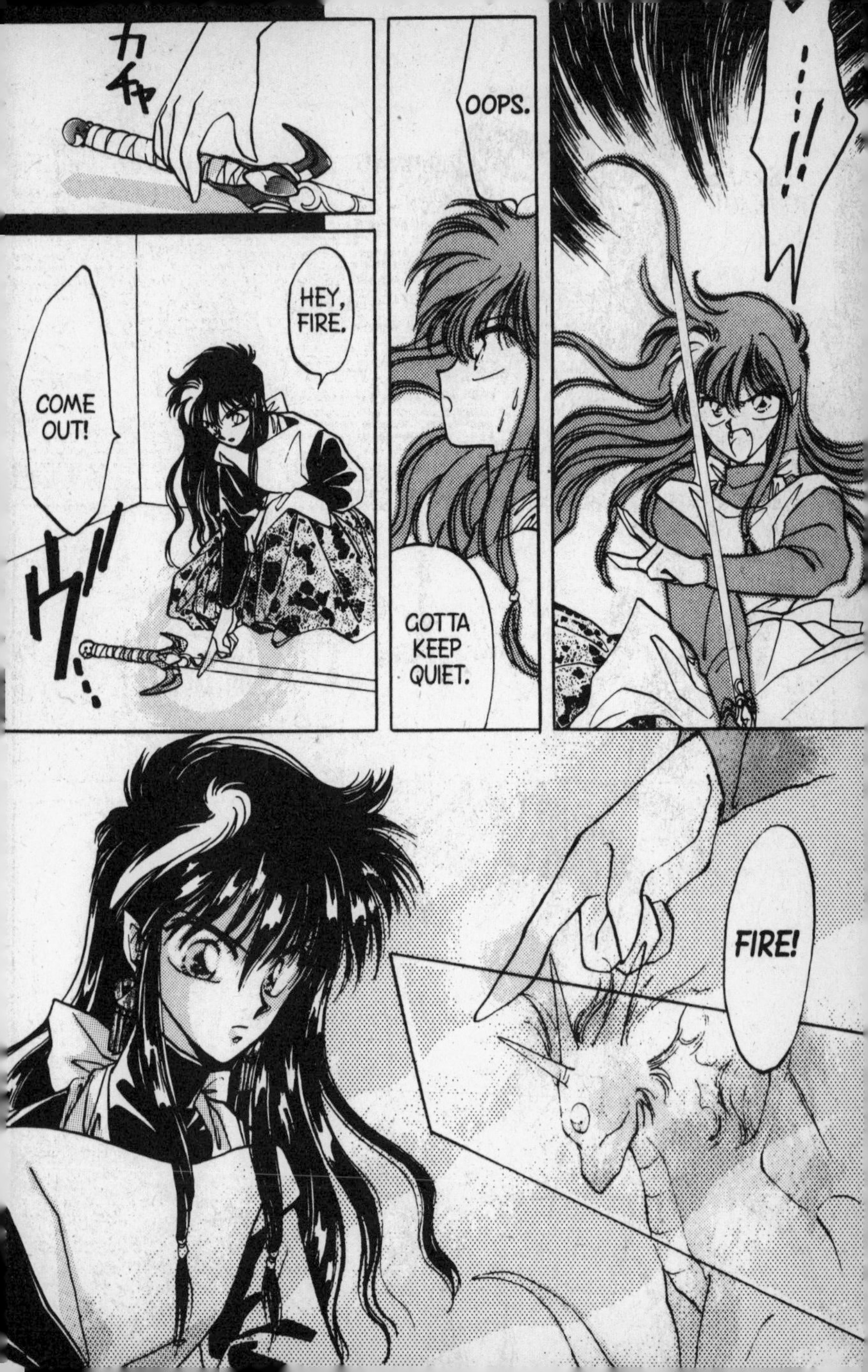
...!!
OOPS.
GOTTA KEEP QUIET.
カチャ
HEY, FIRE.
COME OUT!
ドゥ
FIRE!

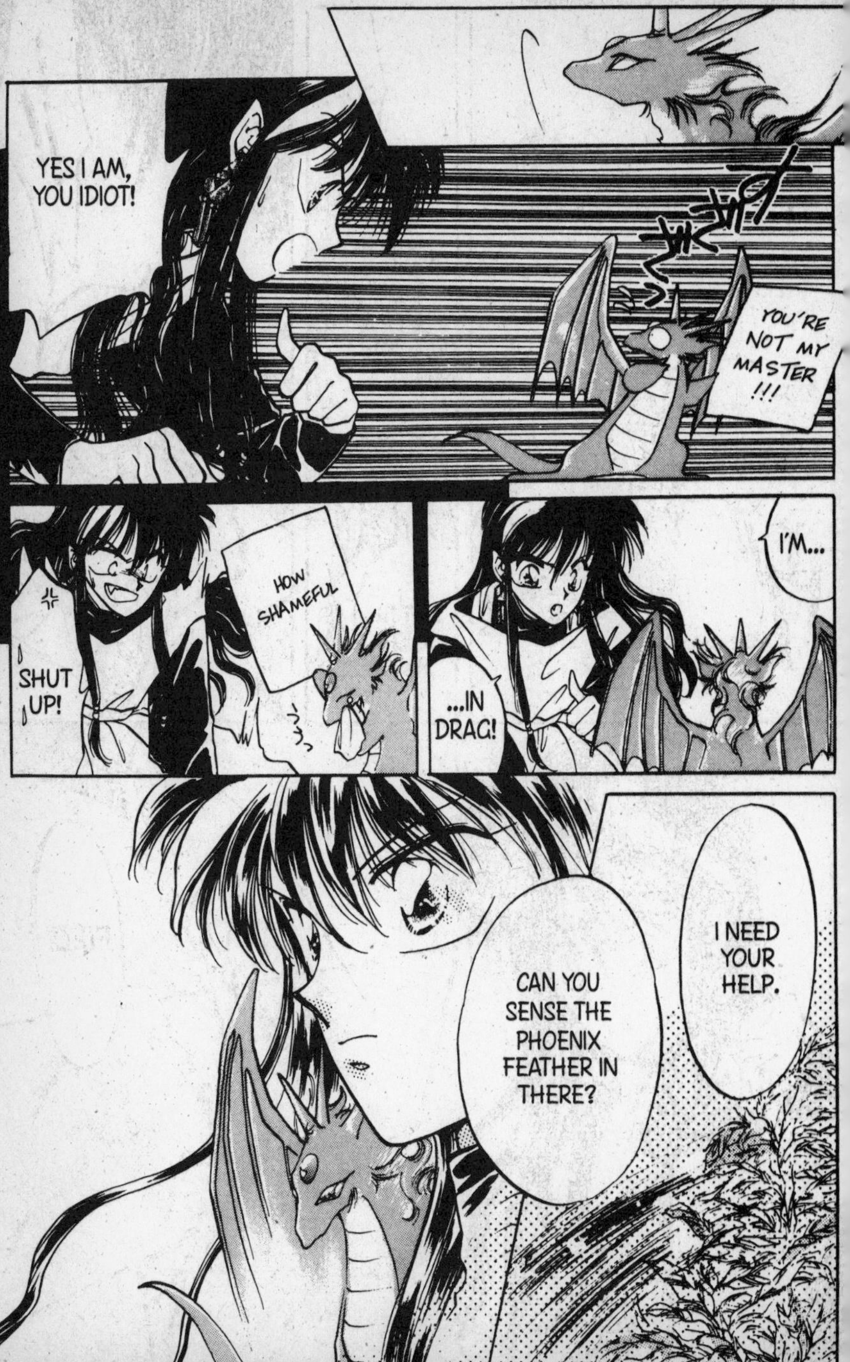
YOU'RE NOT MY MASTER!!!
YES I AM, YOU IDIOT!
I'M...
...IN DRAG!
HOW SHAMEFUL
SHUT UP!
I NEED YOUR HELP.
CAN YOU SENSE THE PHOENIX FEATHER IN THERE?

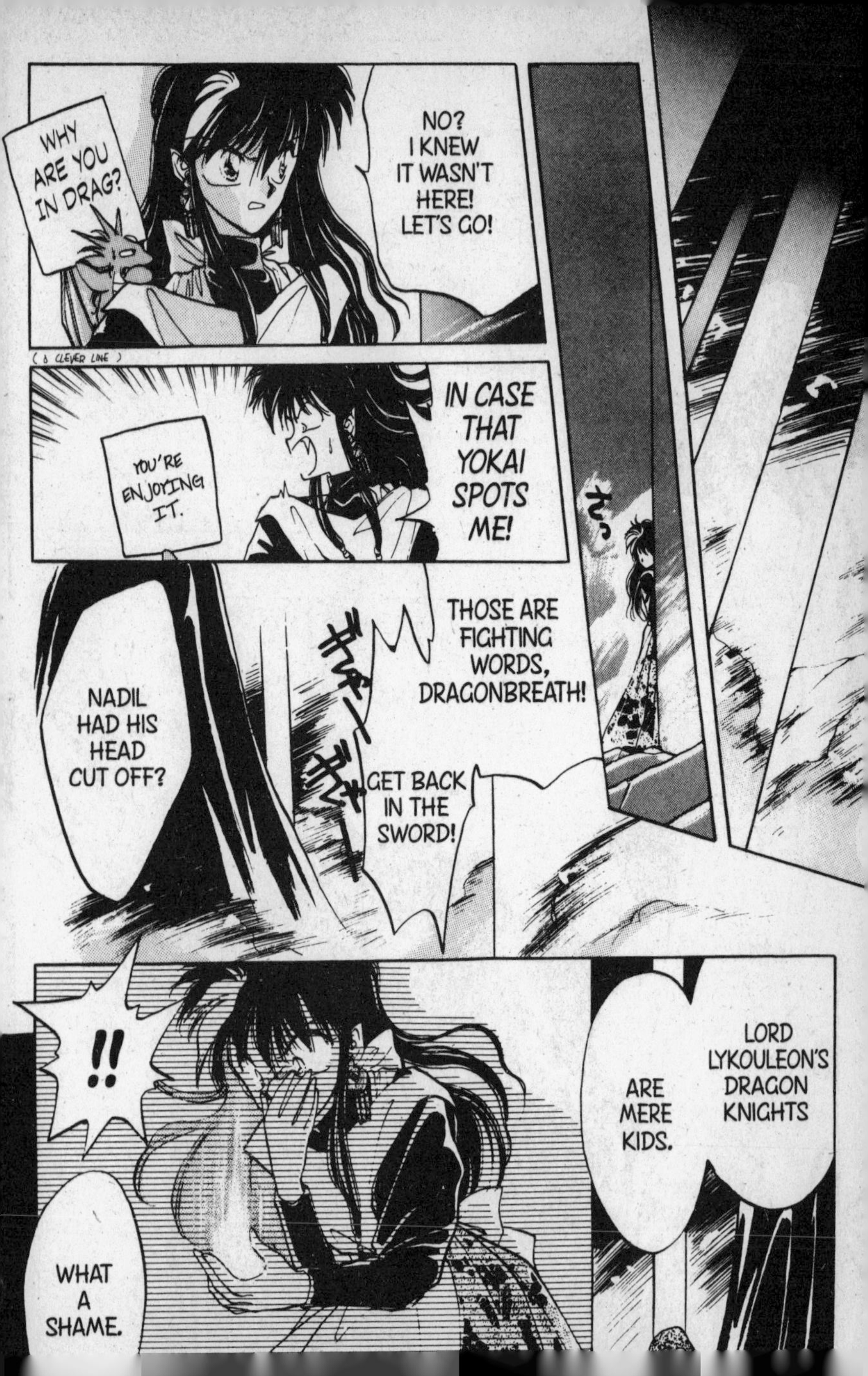
NO? I KNEW IT WASN'T HERE! LET'S GO!
WHY ARE YOU IN DRAG?
(a CLEVER LINE)
IN CASE THAT YOKAI SPOTS ME!
YOU'RE ENJOYING IT.
THOSE ARE FIGHTING WORDS, DRAGONBREATH!
GET BACK IN THE SWORD!
ギャー ギャー
NADIL HAD HIS HEAD CUT OFF?
LORD LYKOULEON'S DRAGON KNIGHTS
ARE MERE KIDS.
!!
WHAT A SHAME.

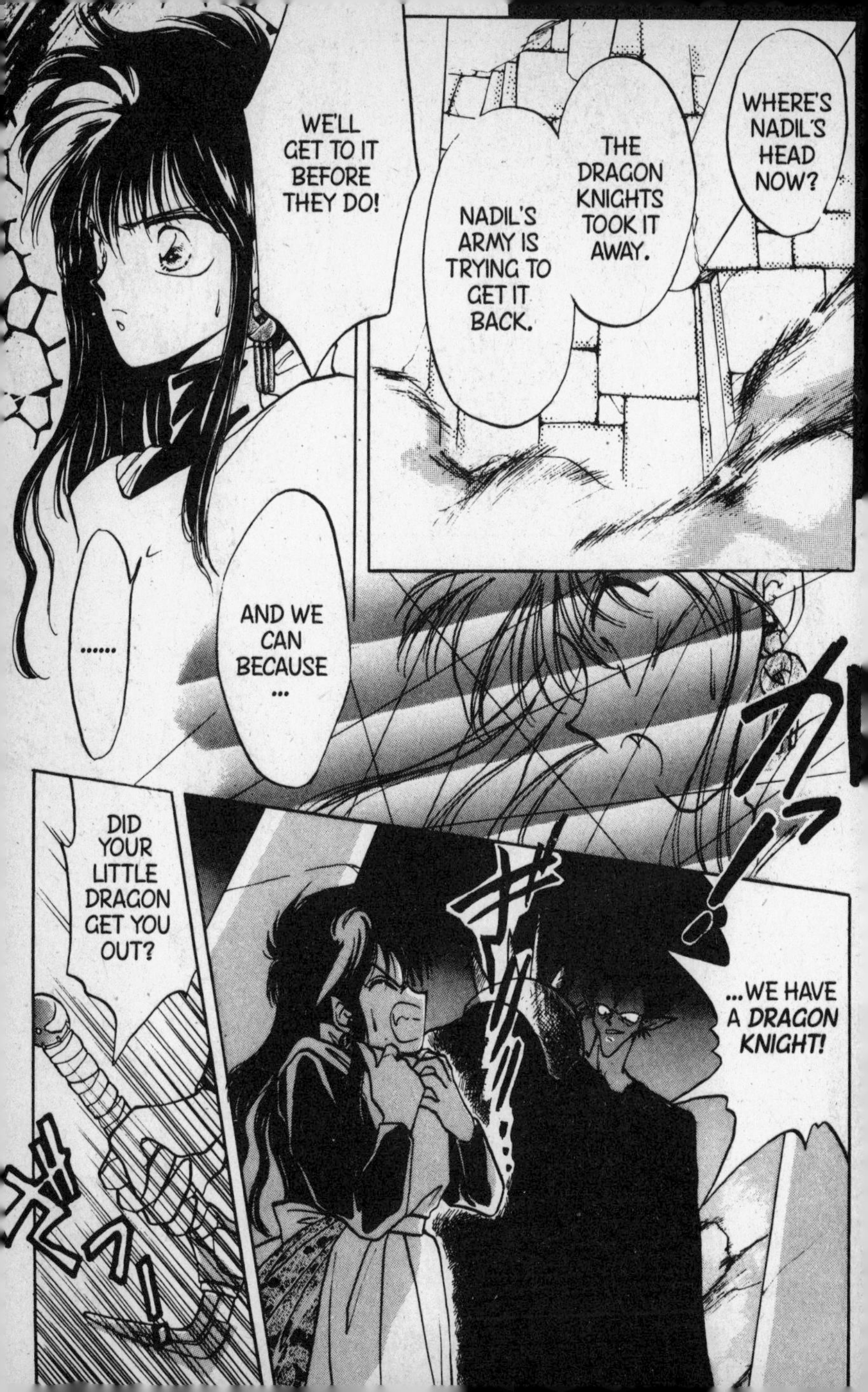
WHERE'S NADIL'S HEAD NOW?
THE DRAGON KNIGHTS TOOK IT AWAY.
NADIL'S ARMY IS TRYING TO GET IT BACK.
WE'LL GET TO IT BEFORE THEY DO!
AND WE CAN BECAUSE ...
......
...WE HAVE A *DRAGON* KNIGHT!
DID YOUR LITTLE DRAGON GET YOU OUT?

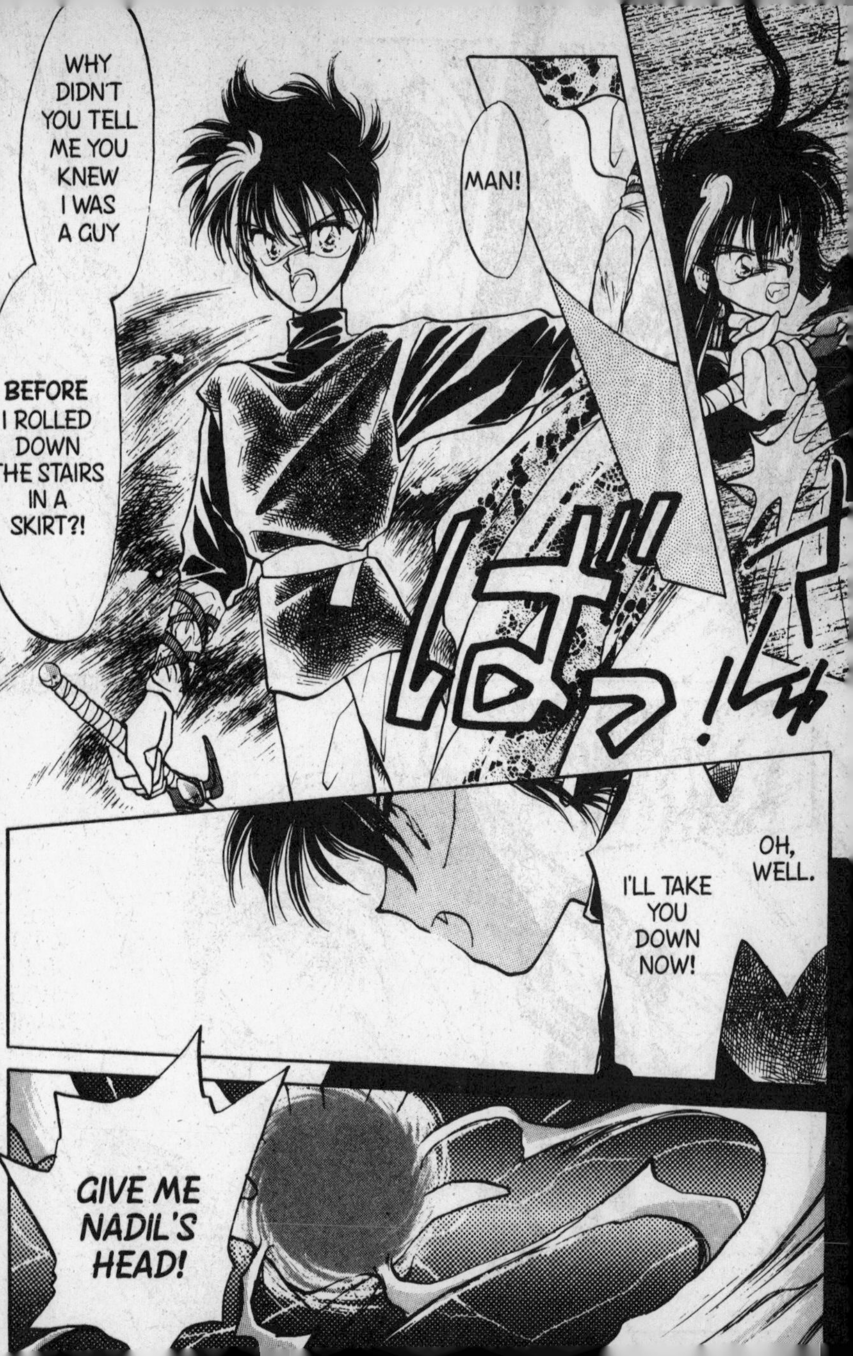
MAN!
WHY DIDN'T YOU TELL ME YOU KNEW I WAS A GUY
BEFORE I ROLLED DOWN THE STAIRS IN A SKIRT?!
ばっ!
OH, WELL.
I'LL TAKE YOU DOWN NOW!
GIVE ME NADIL'S HEAD!

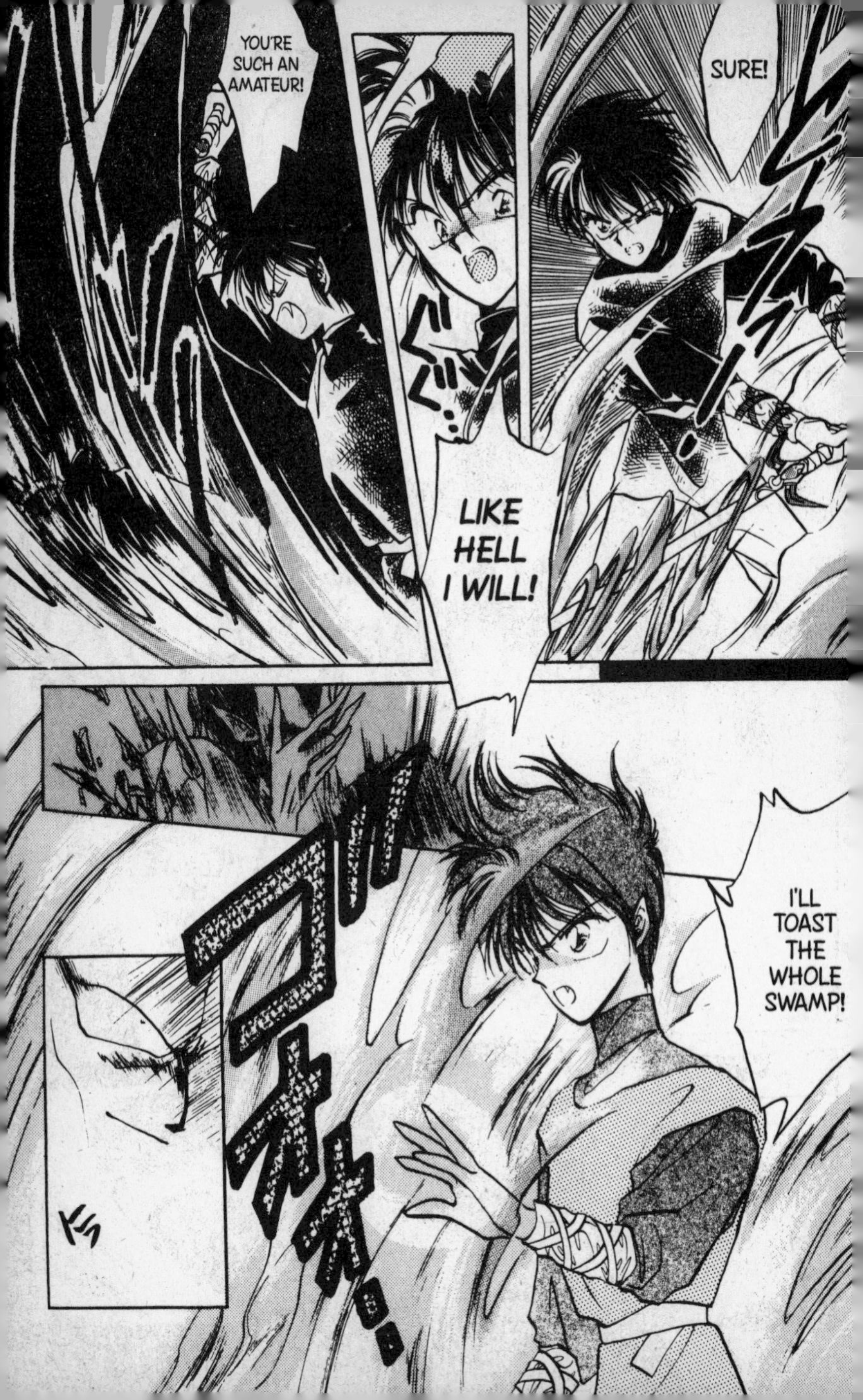
SURE!
LIKE HELL I WILL!
YOU'RE SUCH AN AMATEUR!
I'LL TOAST THE WHOLE SWAMP!

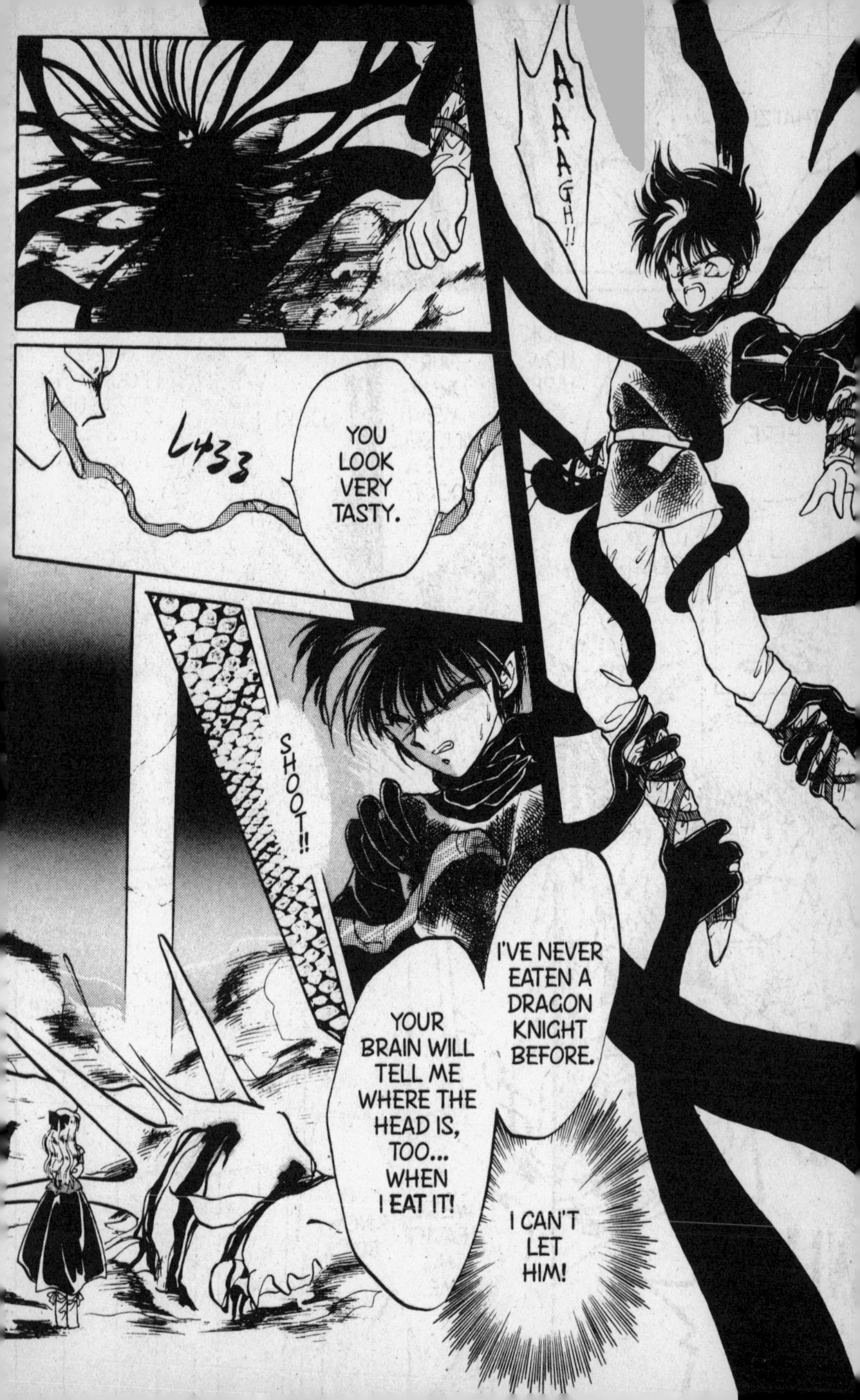
AAAAGH!!
YOU LOOK VERY TASTY.
しゅるる
SHOOT!!
I'VE NEVER EATEN A DRAGON KNIGHT BEFORE.
YOUR BRAIN WILL TELL ME WHERE THE HEAD IS, TOO... WHEN I EAT IT!
I CAN'T LET HIM!

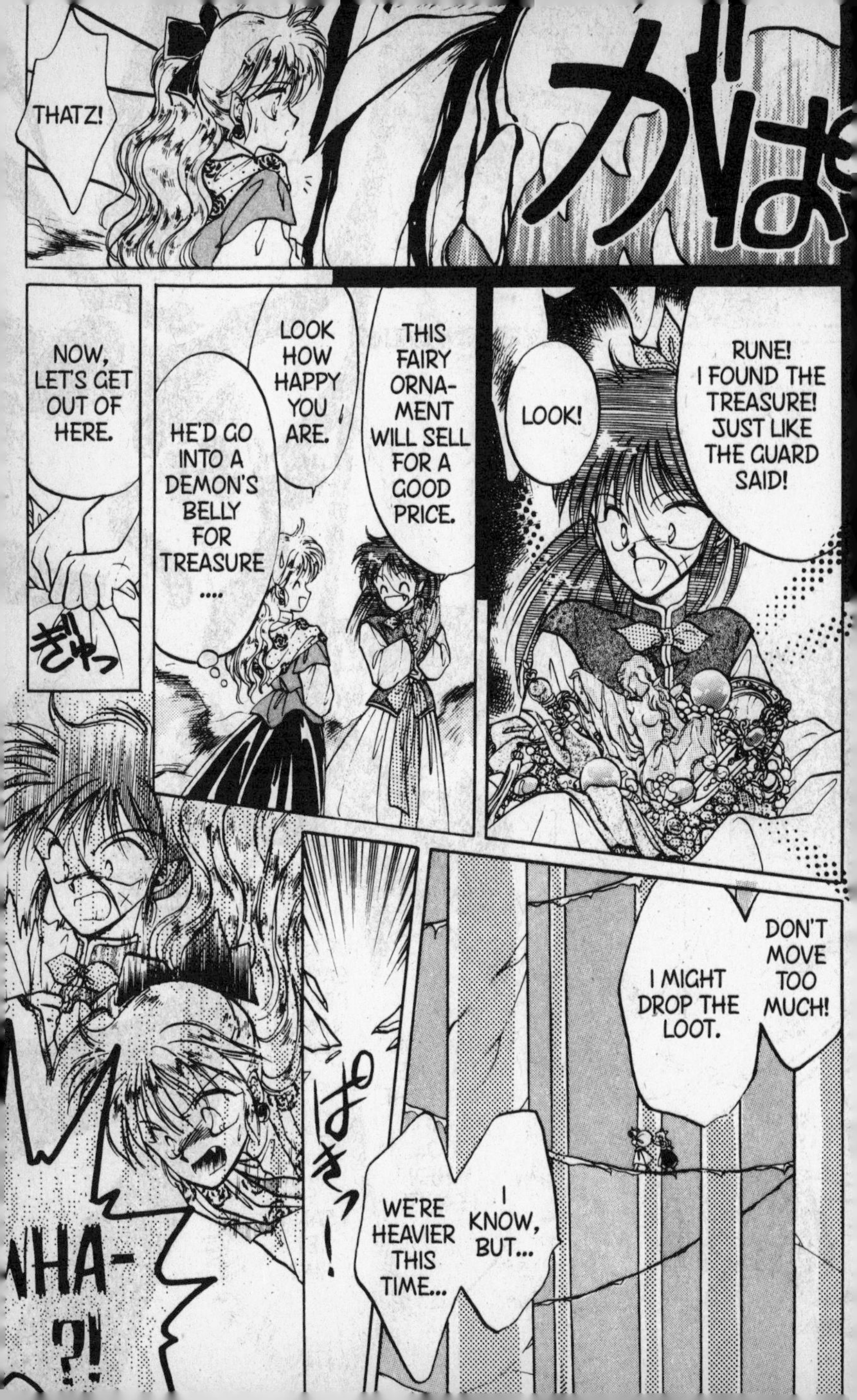
がばっ
THATZ!
RUNE! I FOUND THE TREASURE! JUST LIKE THE GUARD SAID!
LOOK!
THIS FAIRY ORNAMENT WILL SELL FOR A GOOD PRICE.
LOOK HOW HAPPY YOU ARE.
HE'D GO INTO A DEMON'S BELLY FOR TREASURE ....
NOW, LET'S GET OUT OF HERE.
ぎゅっ
DON'T MOVE TOO MUCH!
I MIGHT DROP THE LOOT.
I KNOW, BUT...
WE'RE HEAVIER THIS TIME...
ぱきっ!
NHA- ?!

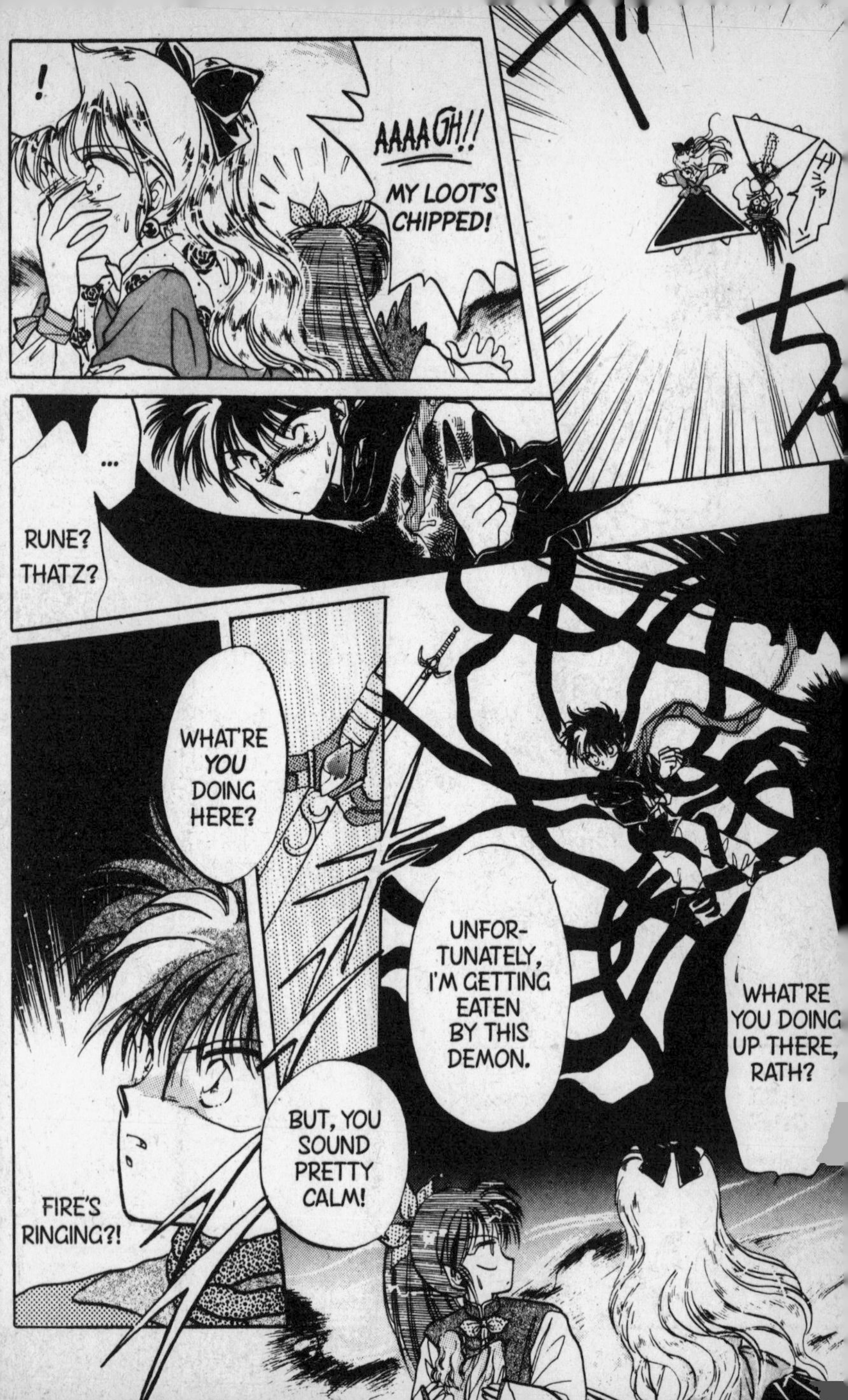
!
AAAAGH!!
MY LOOT'S CHIPPED!
...
RUNE? THATZ?
WHAT'RE YOU DOING UP THERE, RATH?
UNFOR-TUNATELY, I'M GETTING EATEN BY THIS DEMON.
BUT, YOU SOUND PRETTY CALM!
WHAT'RE YOU DOING HERE?
FIRE'S RINGING?!

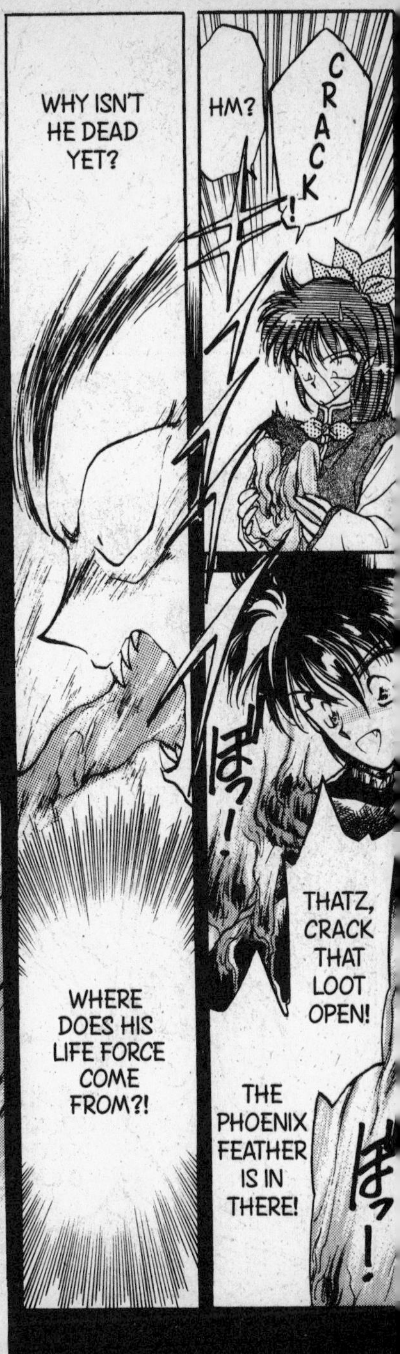
HM?
CRACK
!
ぽっ!
THATZ, CRACK THAT LOOT OPEN!
THE PHOENIX FEATHER IS IN THERE!
ぽっ!
WHY ISN'T HE DEAD YET?
WHERE DOES HIS LIFE FORCE COME FROM?!
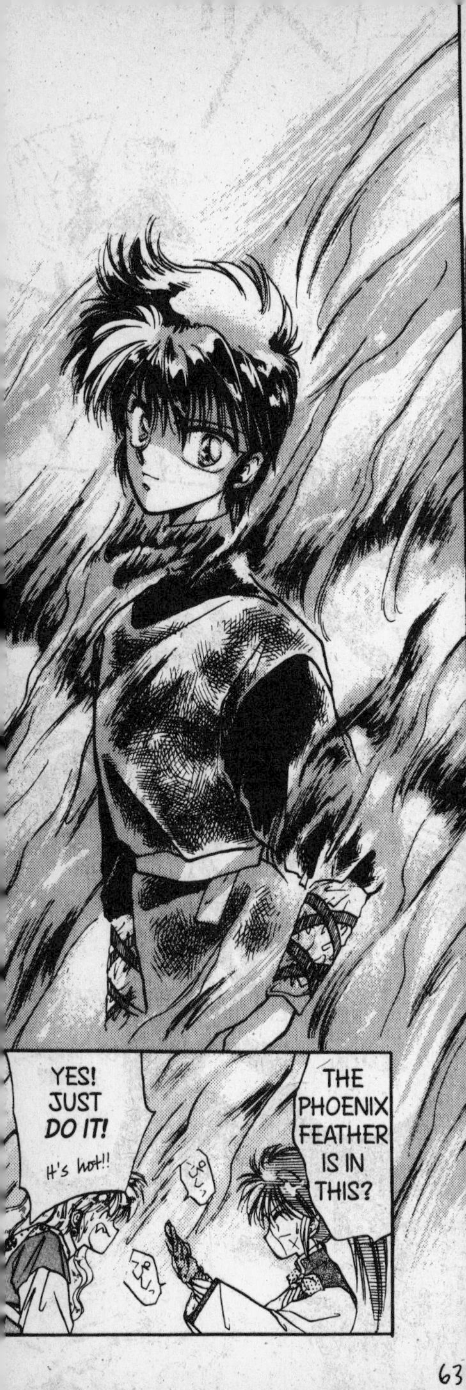
THE PHOENIX FEATHER IS IN THIS?
YES! JUST *DO IT!*
It's hot!!

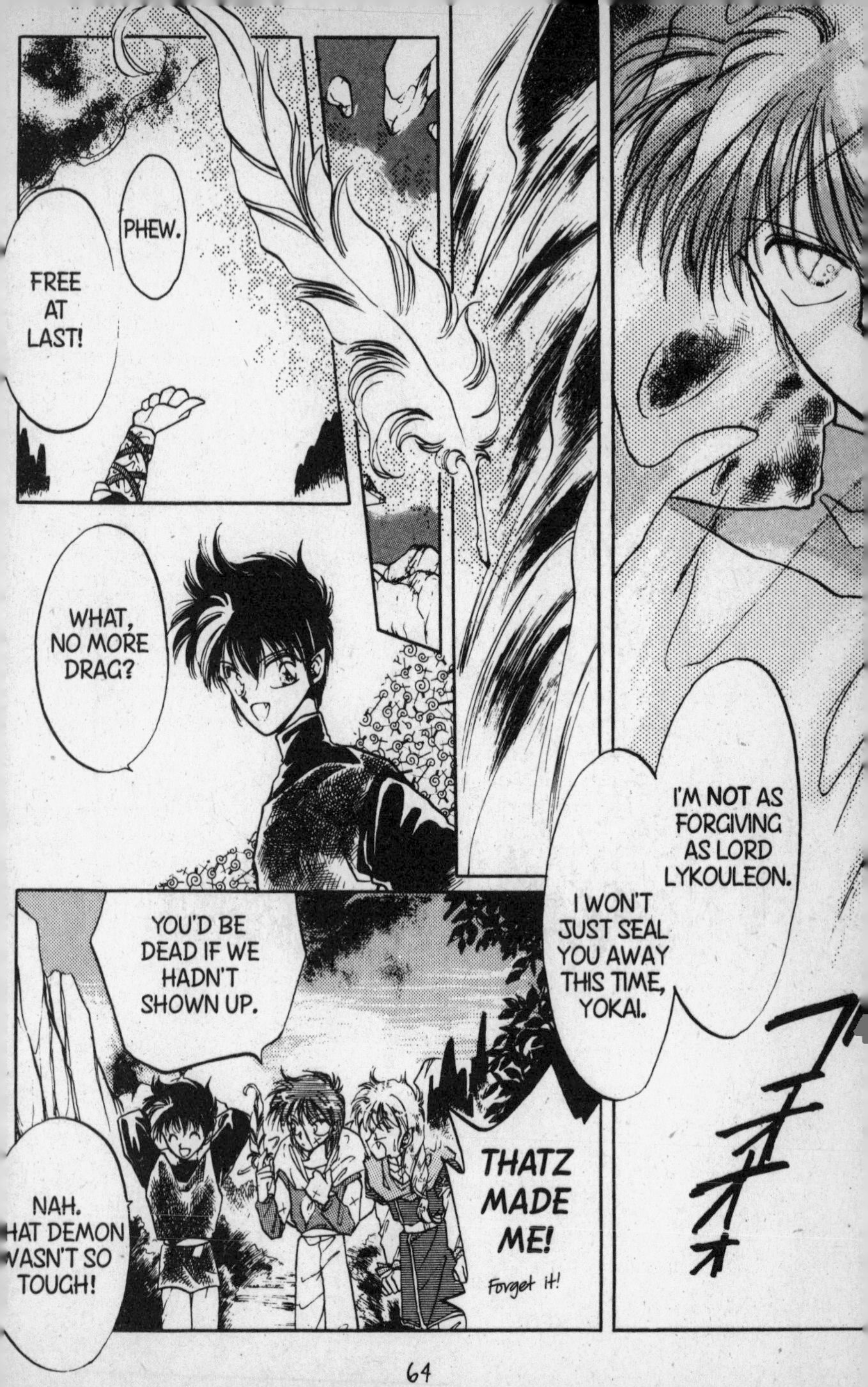

I'M NOT AS FORGIVING AS LORD LYKOULEON.
I WON'T JUST SEAL YOU AWAY THIS TIME, YOKAI.
PHEW.
FREE AT LAST!
WHAT, NO MORE DRAG?
YOU'D BE DEAD IF WE HADN'T SHOWN UP.
THATZ MADE ME!
Forget it!
NAH. HAT DEMON VASN'T SO TOUGH!

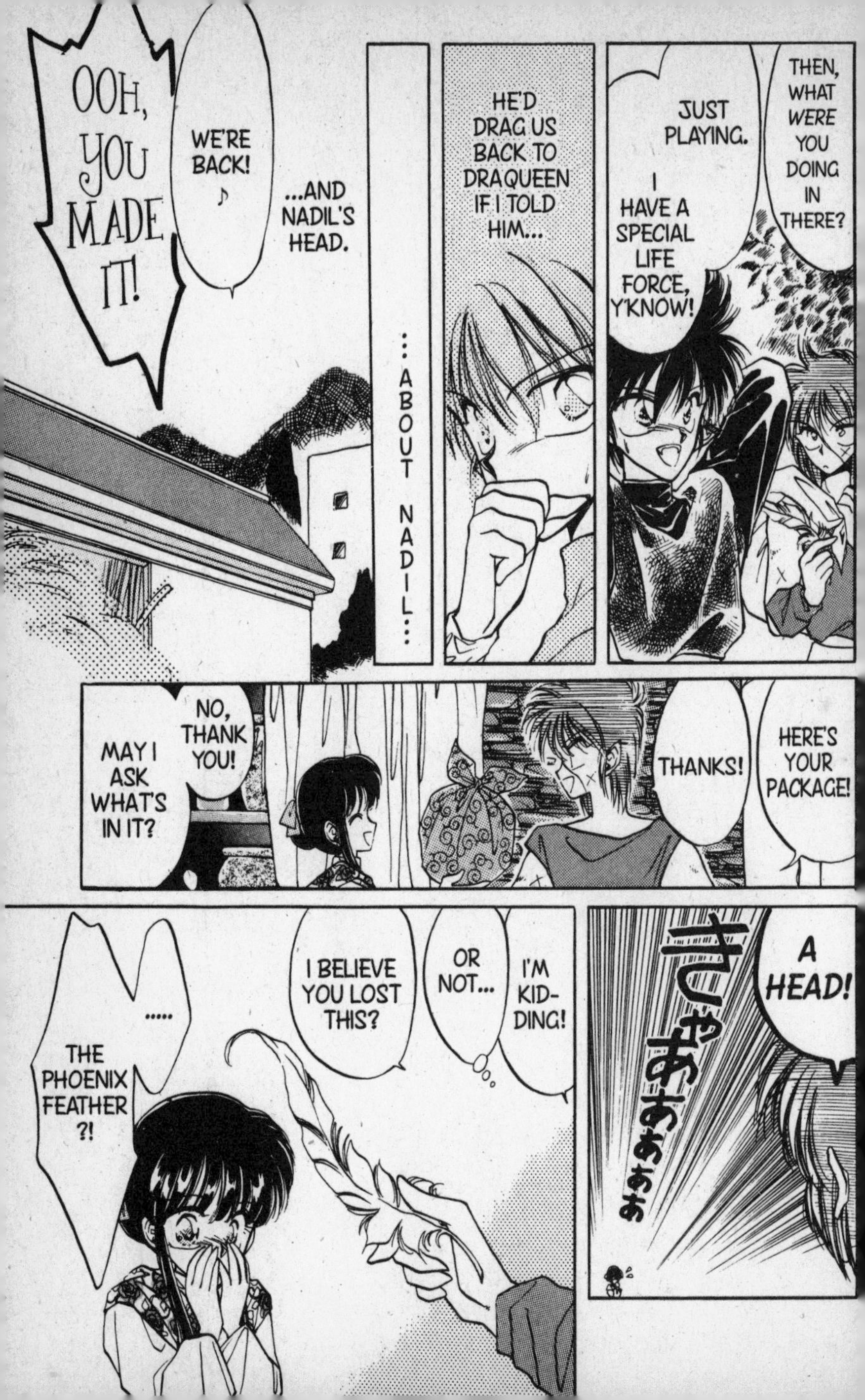
THEN, WHAT WERE YOU DOING IN THERE?
JUST PLAYING.
I HAVE A SPECIAL LIFE FORCE, Y'KNOW!
HE'D DRAG US BACK TO DRAQUEEN IF I TOLD HIM...
...ABOUT NADIL...
...AND NADIL'S HEAD.
WE'RE BACK! ♪
OOH, YOU MADE IT!
HERE'S YOUR PACKAGE!
THANKS!
NO, THANK YOU!
MAY I ASK WHAT'S IN IT?
A HEAD!
きゃああああああ
I'M KID-DING!
OR NOT...
I BELIEVE YOU LOST THIS?
......
THE PHOENIX FEATHER?!

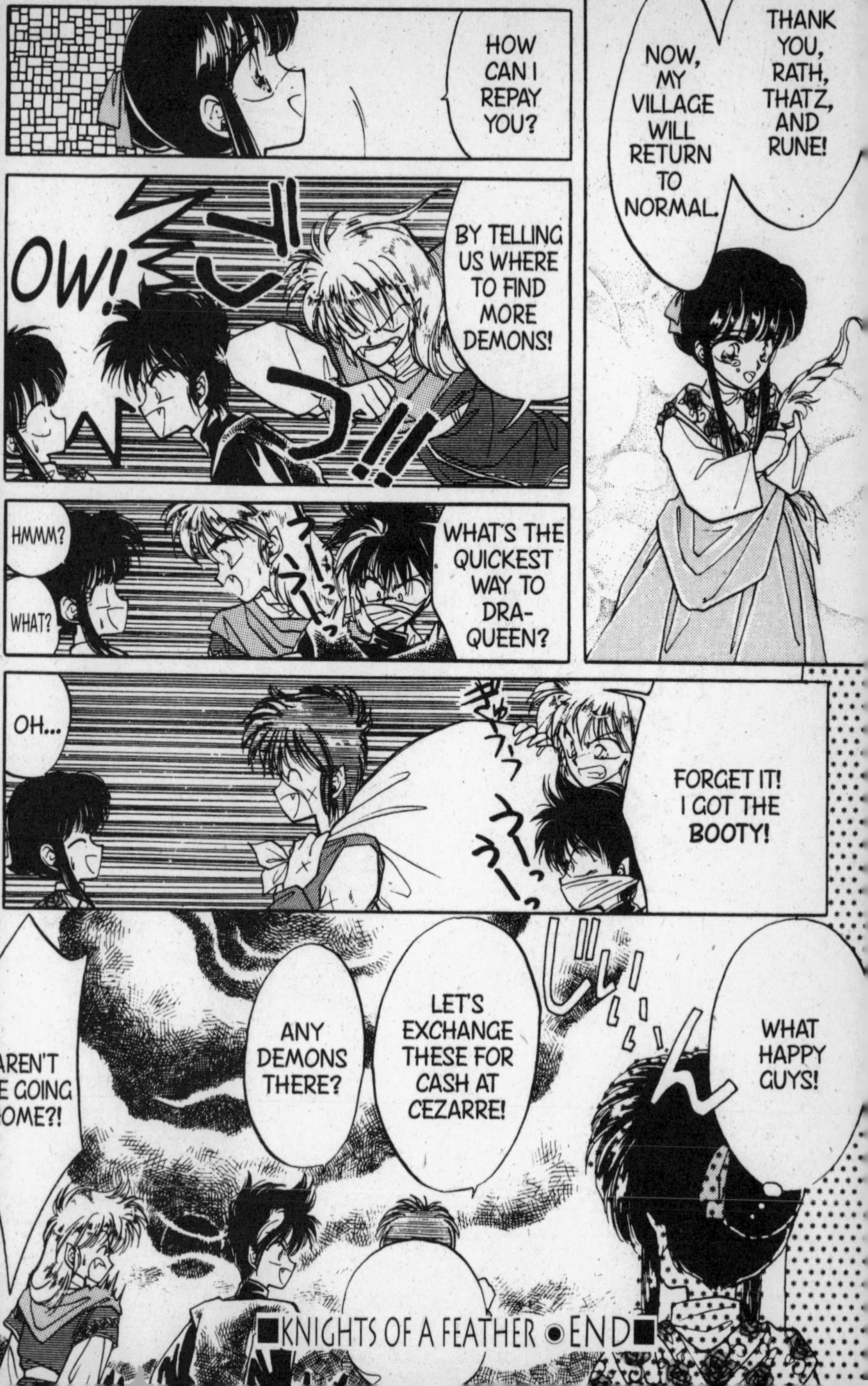
THANK YOU, RATH, THATZ, AND RUNE!
NOW, MY VILLAGE WILL RETURN TO NORMAL.
HOW CAN I REPAY YOU?
BY TELLING US WHERE TO FIND MORE DEMONS!
OW!
WHAT'S THE QUICKEST WAY TO DRA-QUEEN?
HMMM?
WHAT?
FORGET IT! I GOT THE BOOTY!
OH...
WHAT HAPPY GUYS!
LET'S EXCHANGE THESE FOR CASH AT CEZARRE!
ANY DEMONS THERE?
AREN'T E GOING OME?!
KNIGHTS OF A FEATHER • END

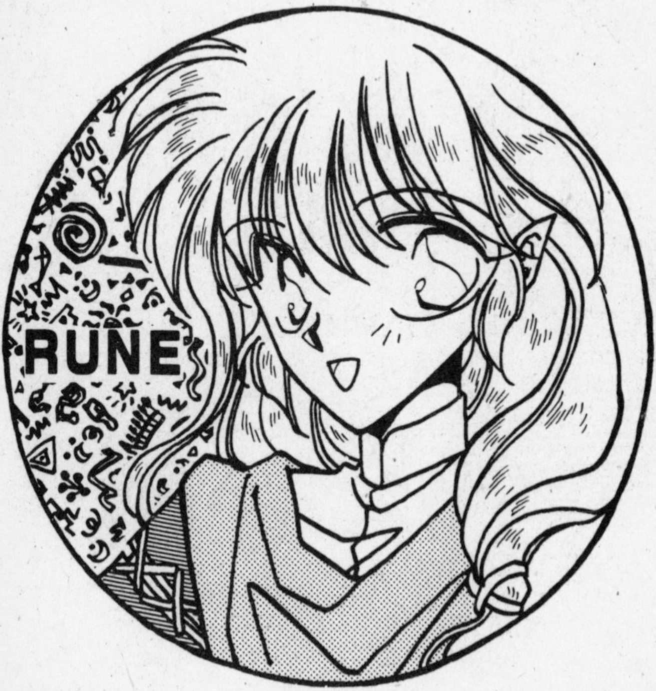
RUNE

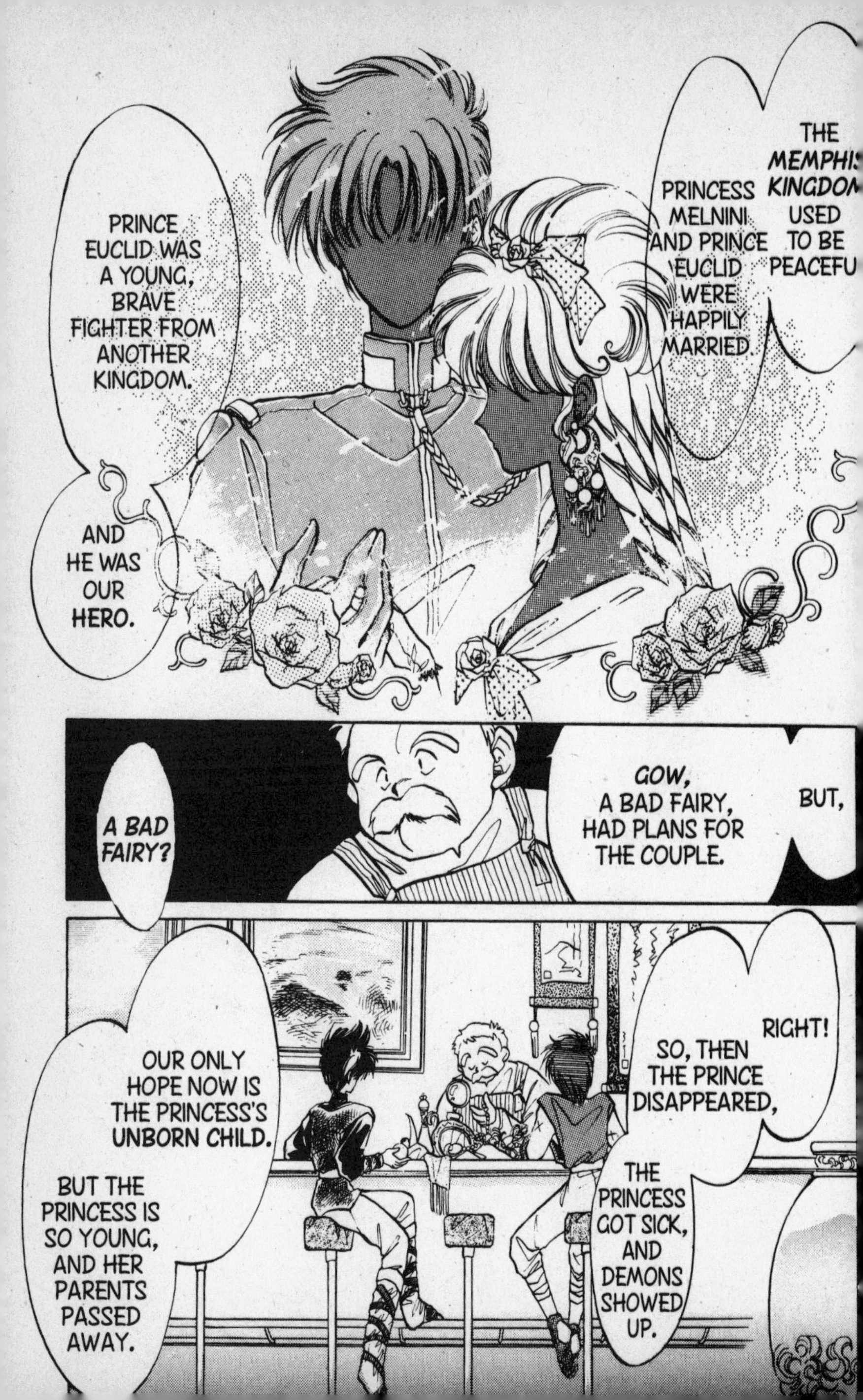
THE MEMPHIS KINGDOM USED TO BE PEACEFU
PRINCESS MELNINI AND PRINCE EUCLID WERE HAPPILY MARRIED
PRINCE EUCLID WAS A YOUNG, BRAVE FIGHTER FROM ANOTHER KINGDOM.
AND HE WAS OUR HERO.
BUT,
GOW, A BAD FAIRY, HAD PLANS FOR THE COUPLE.
A BAD FAIRY?
RIGHT!
SO, THEN THE PRINCE DISAPPEARED,
THE PRINCESS GOT SICK, AND DEMONS SHOWED UP.
OUR ONLY HOPE NOW IS THE PRINCESS'S UNBORN CHILD.
BUT THE PRINCESS IS SO YOUNG, AND HER PARENTS PASSED AWAY.

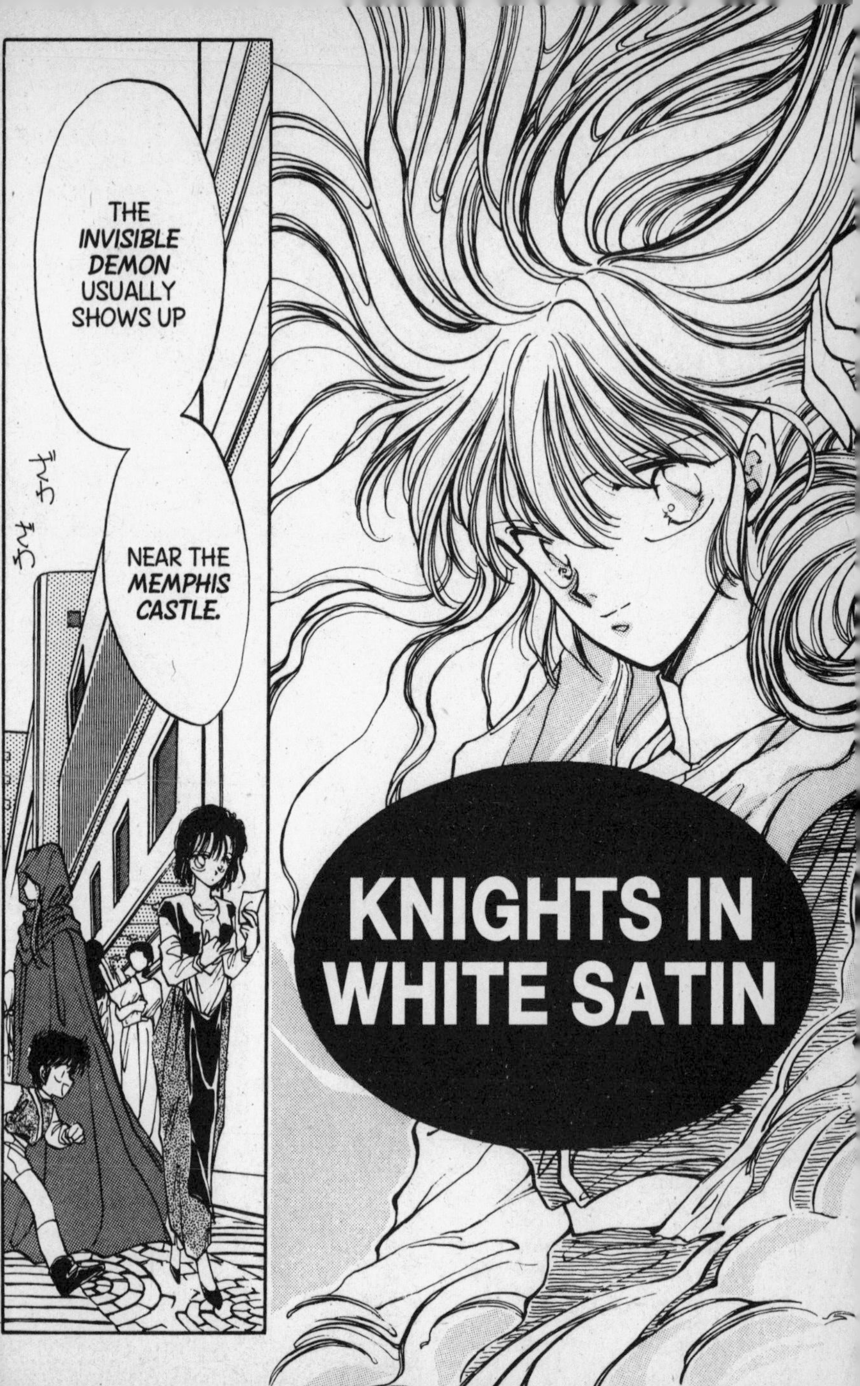
KNIGHTS IN WHITE SATIN
THE INVISIBLE DEMON USUALLY SHOWS UP
NEAR THE MEMPHIS CASTLE.

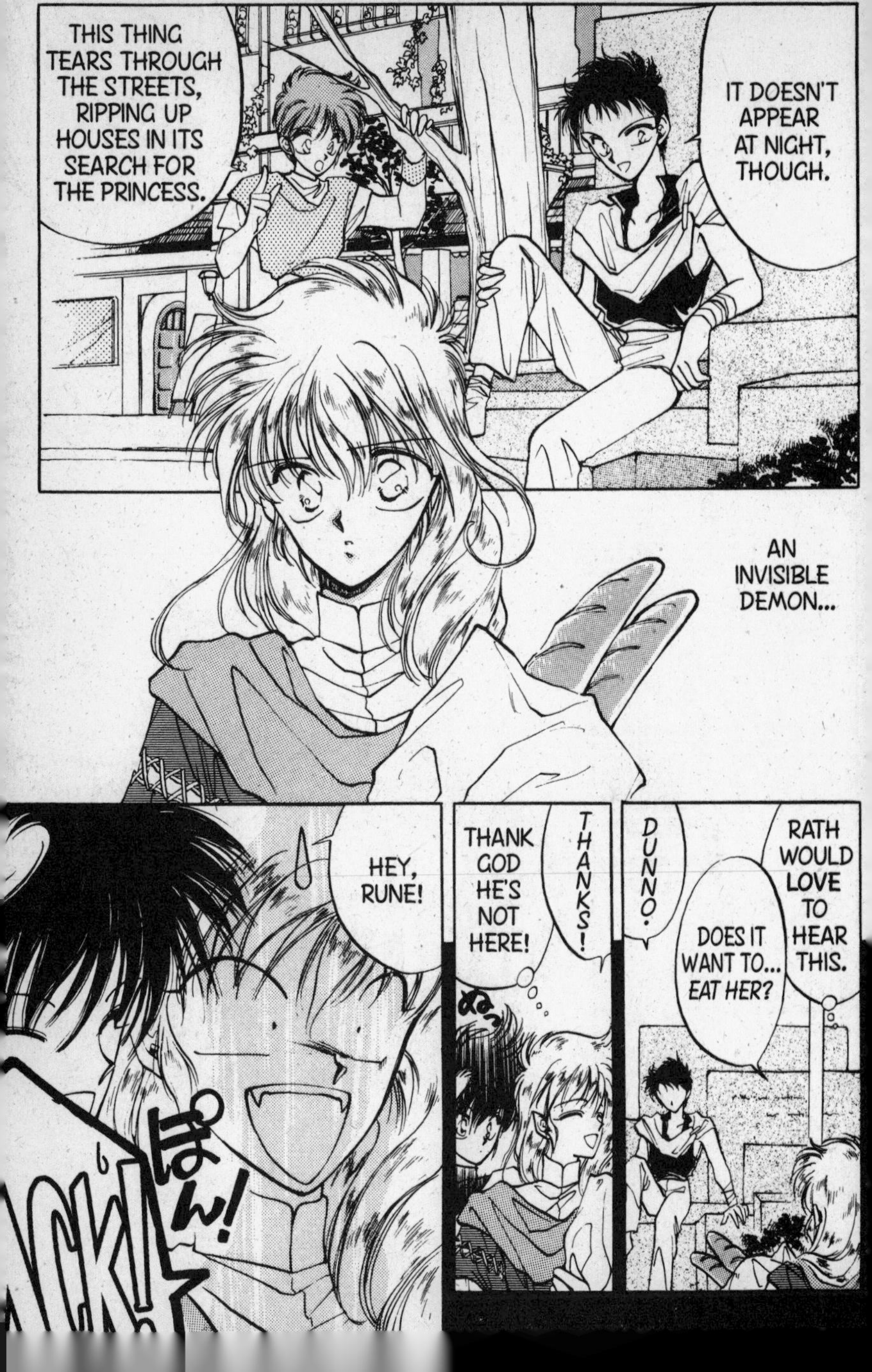
IT DOESN'T APPEAR AT NIGHT, THOUGH.
THIS THING TEARS THROUGH THE STREETS, RIPPING UP HOUSES IN ITS SEARCH FOR THE PRINCESS.
AN INVISIBLE DEMON...
DOES IT WANT TO... *EAT HER?*
DUNNO.
RATH WOULD LOVE TO HEAR THIS.
THANKS!
THANK GOD HE'S NOT HERE!
ぬっ
HEY, RUNE!
ぱん!

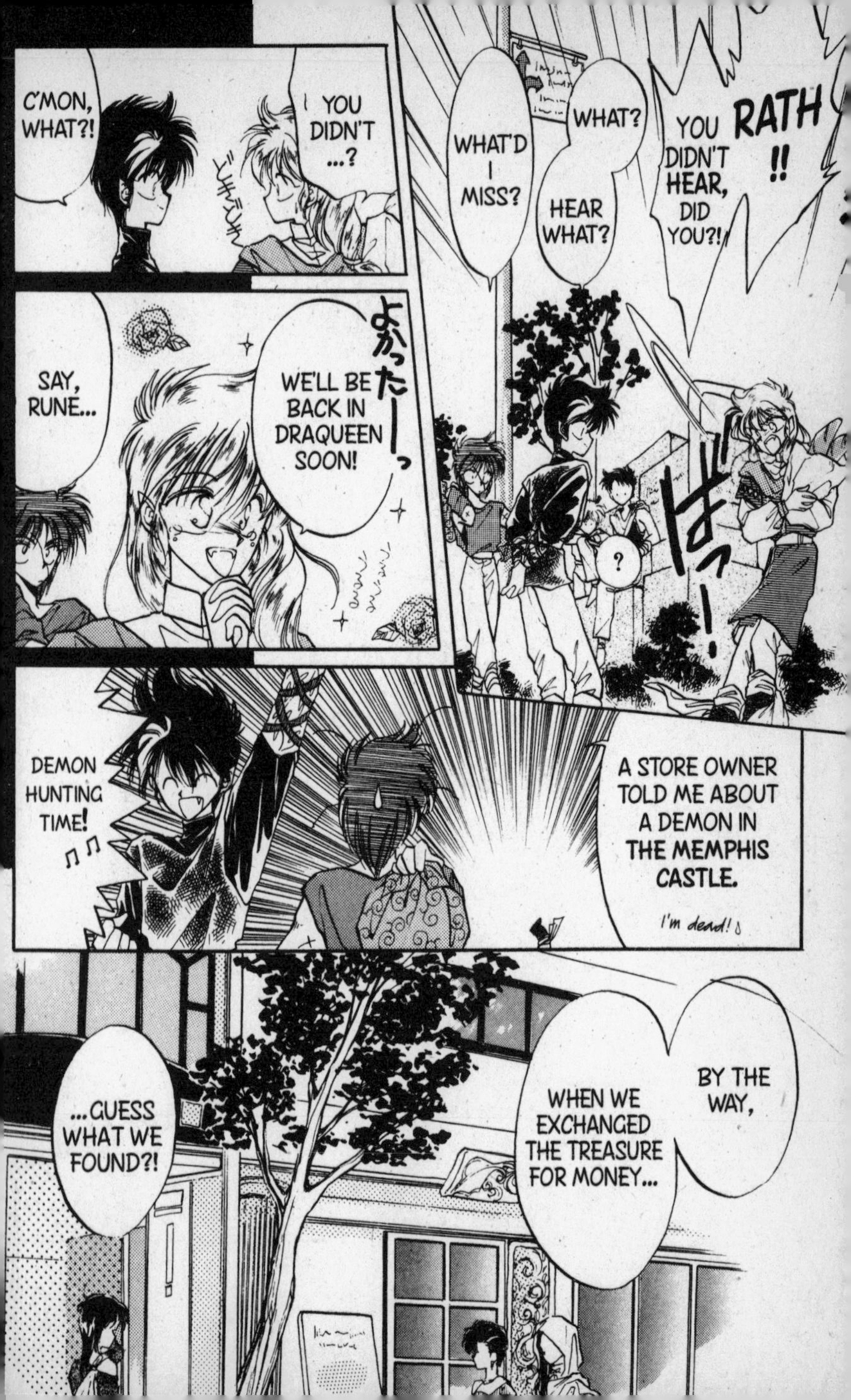
RATH !!
YOU DIDN'T HEAR, DID YOU?!
WHAT?
HEAR WHAT?
WHAT'D I MISS?
ばっ!
?
YOU DIDN'T ...?
C'MON, WHAT?!
よかったーっ
WE'LL BE BACK IN DRAQUEEN SOON!
SAY, RUNE...
A STORE OWNER TOLD ME ABOUT A DEMON IN THE MEMPHIS CASTLE.
I'm dead!
DEMON HUNTING TIME!
BY THE WAY,
WHEN WE EXCHANGED THE TREASURE FOR MONEY...
...GUESS WHAT WE FOUND?!

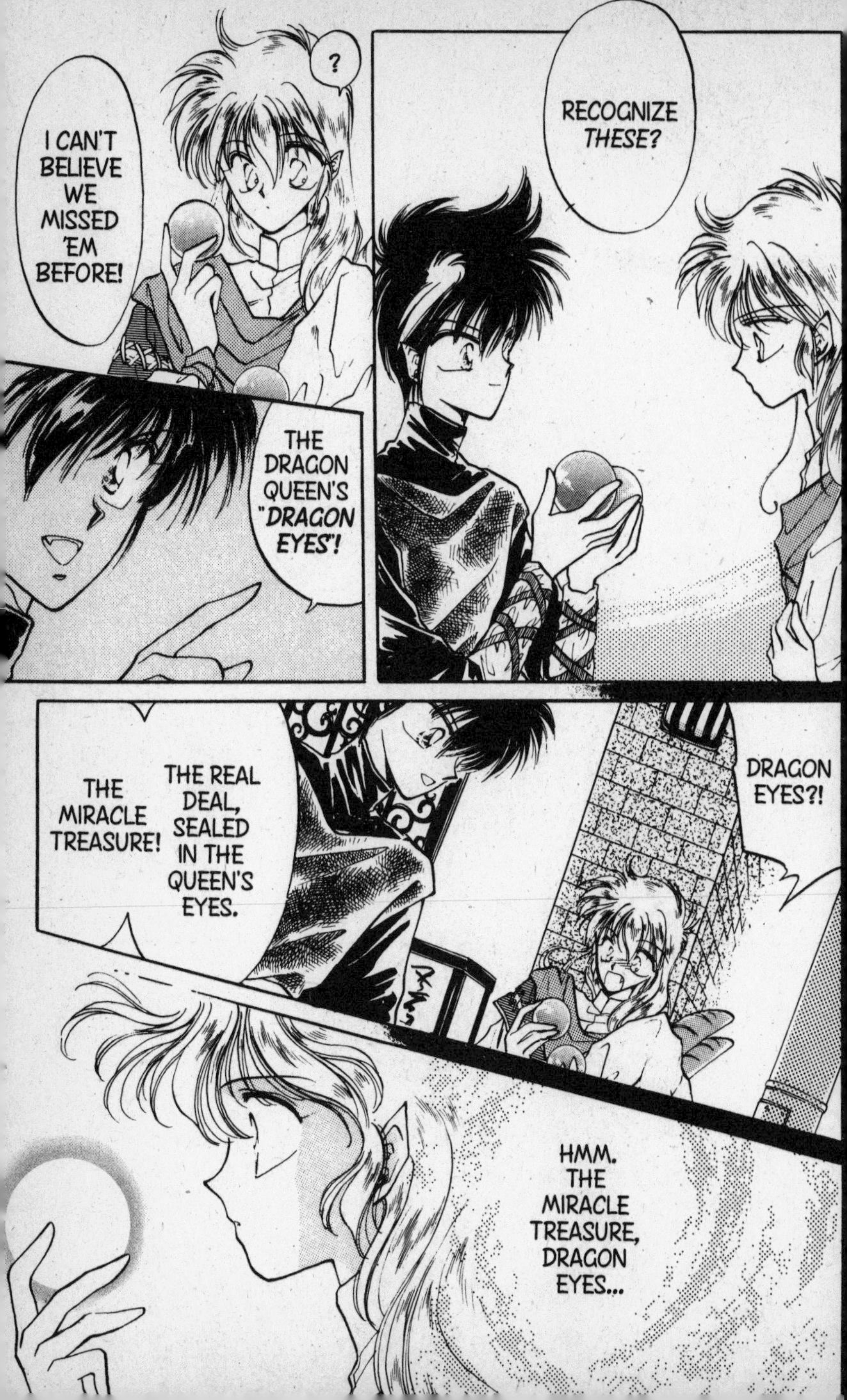
RECOGNIZE THESE?
?
I CAN'T BELIEVE WE MISSED 'EM BEFORE!
THE DRAGON QUEEN'S "DRAGON EYES"!
DRAGON EYES?!
THE REAL DEAL, SEALED IN THE QUEEN'S EYES.
THE MIRACLE TREASURE!
HMM. THE MIRACLE TREASURE, DRAGON EYES...

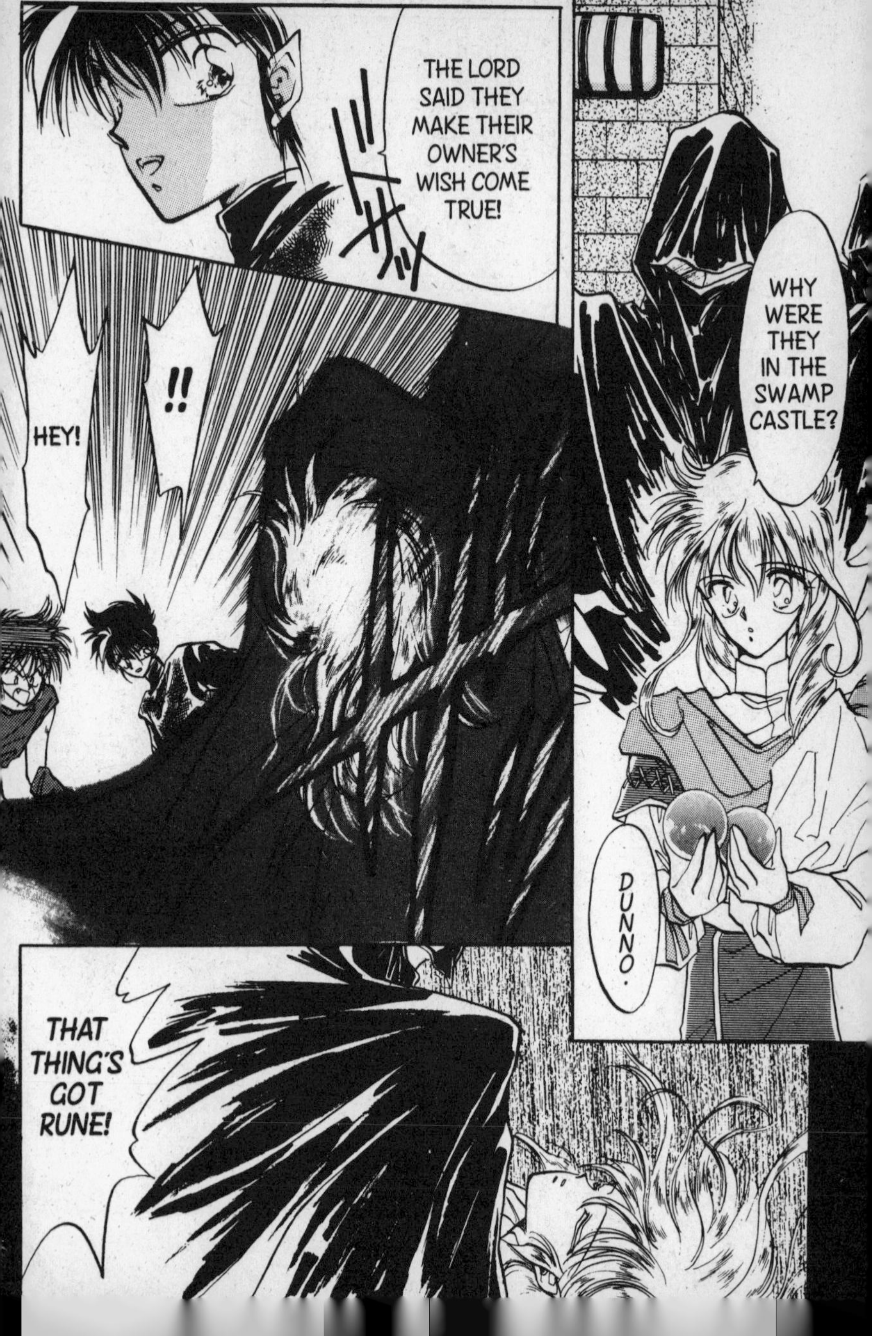
WHY WERE THEY IN THE SWAMP CASTLE?
DUNNO.
THE LORD SAID THEY MAKE THEIR OWNER'S WISH COME TRUE!
!!
HEY!
THAT THING'S GOT RUNE!

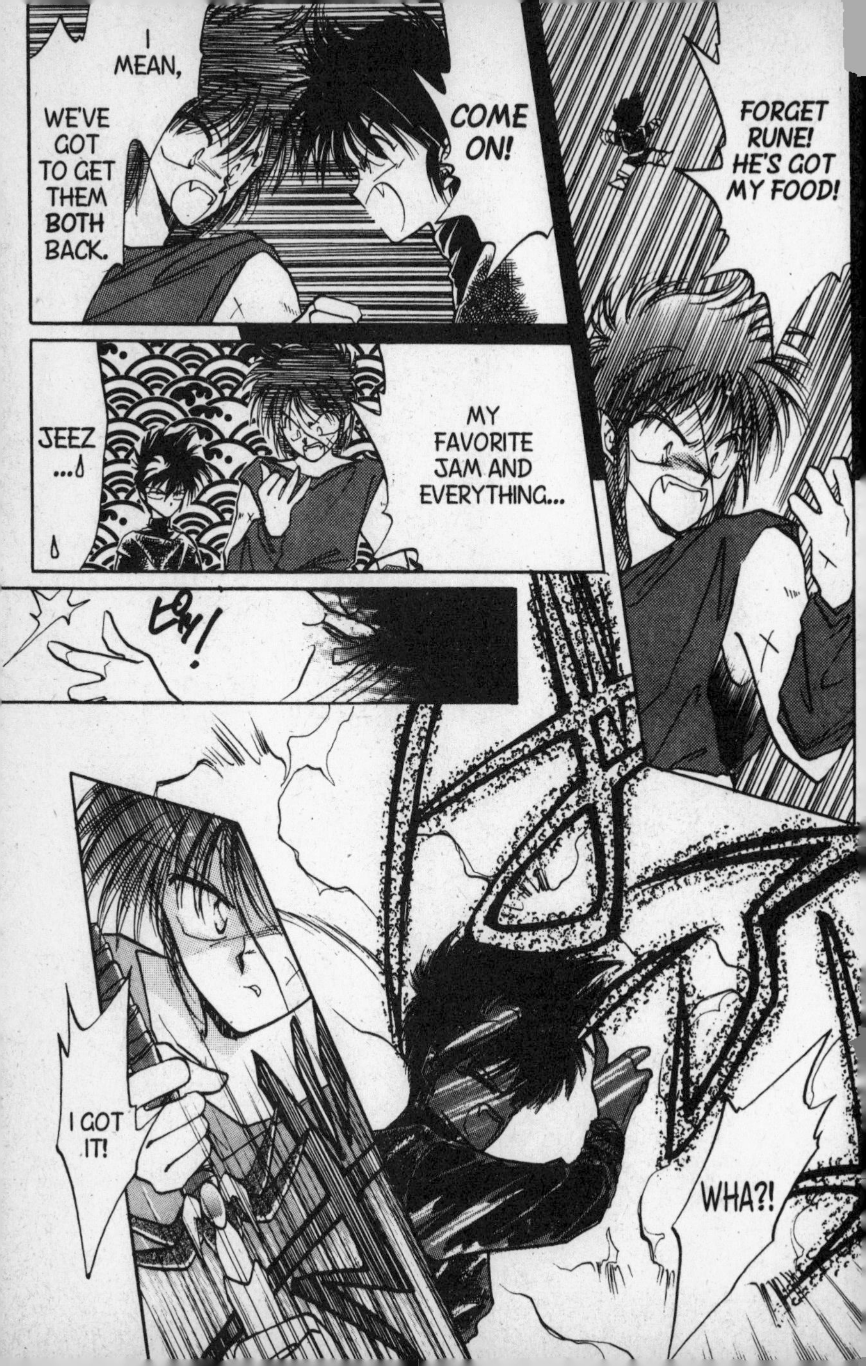
FORGET RUNE! HE'S GOT MY FOOD!
COME ON!
I MEAN,
WE'VE GOT TO GET THEM BOTH BACK.
MY FAVORITE JAM AND EVERYTHING...
JEEZ ...
ピク!
WHA?!
I GOT IT!

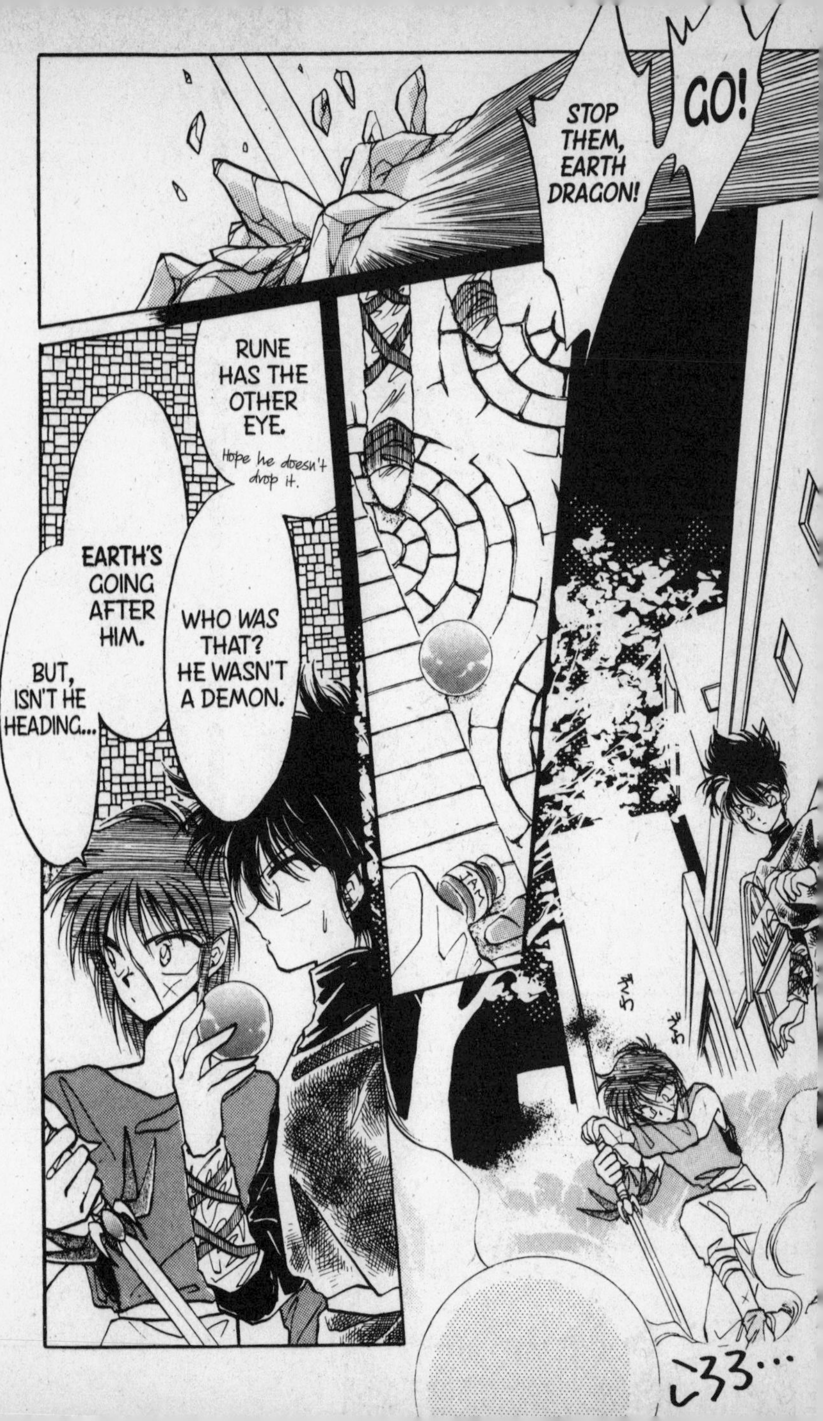
GO!
STOP THEM, EARTH DRAGON!
JAM
RUNE HAS THE OTHER EYE.
Hope he doesn't drop it.
WHO WAS THAT? HE WASN'T A DEMON.
EARTH'S GOING AFTER HIM.
BUT, ISN'T HE HEADING...

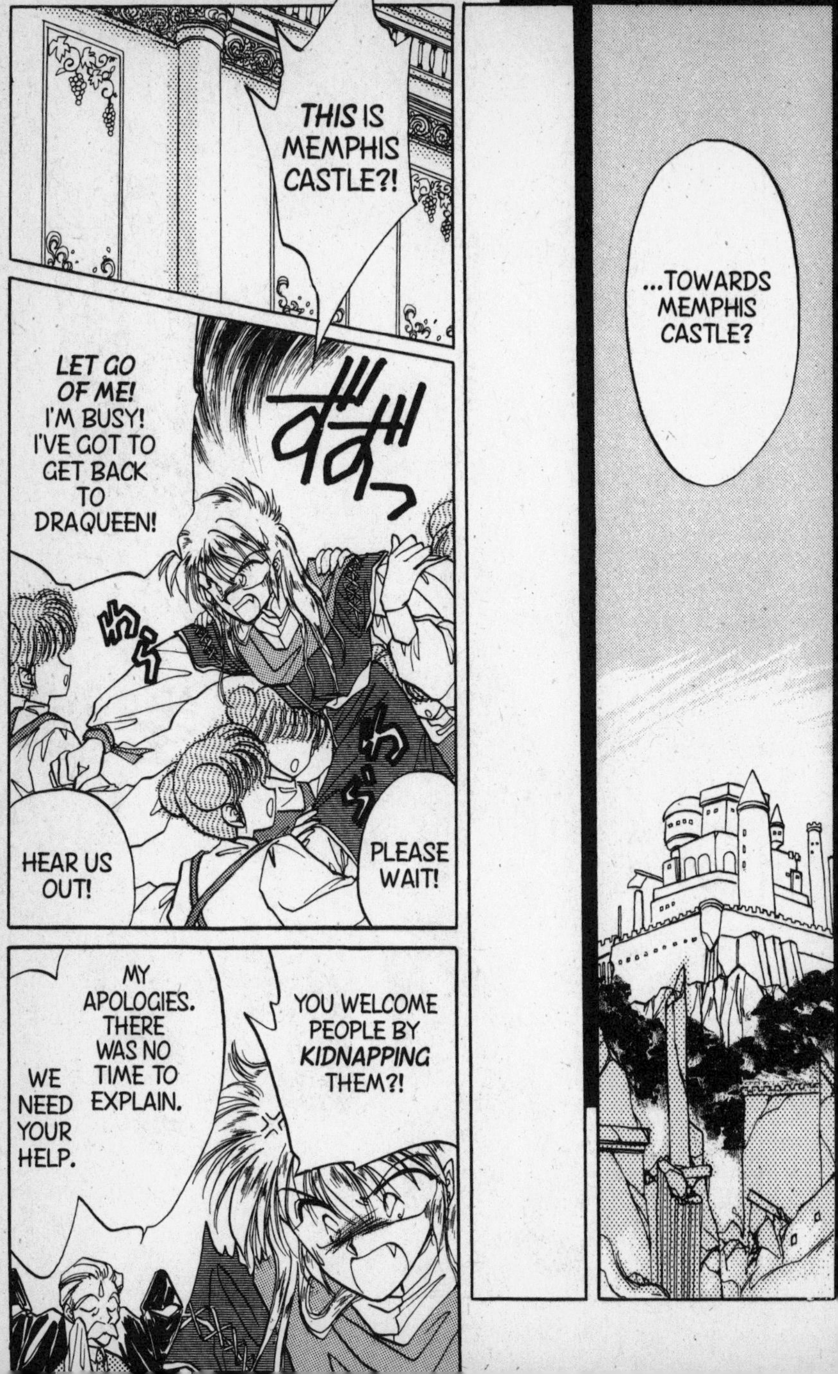
...TOWARDS MEMPHIS CASTLE?
THIS IS MEMPHIS CASTLE?!
LET GO OF ME! I'M BUSY! I'VE GOT TO GET BACK TO DRAQUEEN!
ずずっ
PLEASE WAIT!
HEAR US OUT!
YOU WELCOME PEOPLE BY KIDNAPPING THEM?!
MY APOLOGIES. THERE WAS NO TIME TO EXPLAIN.
WE NEED YOUR HELP.

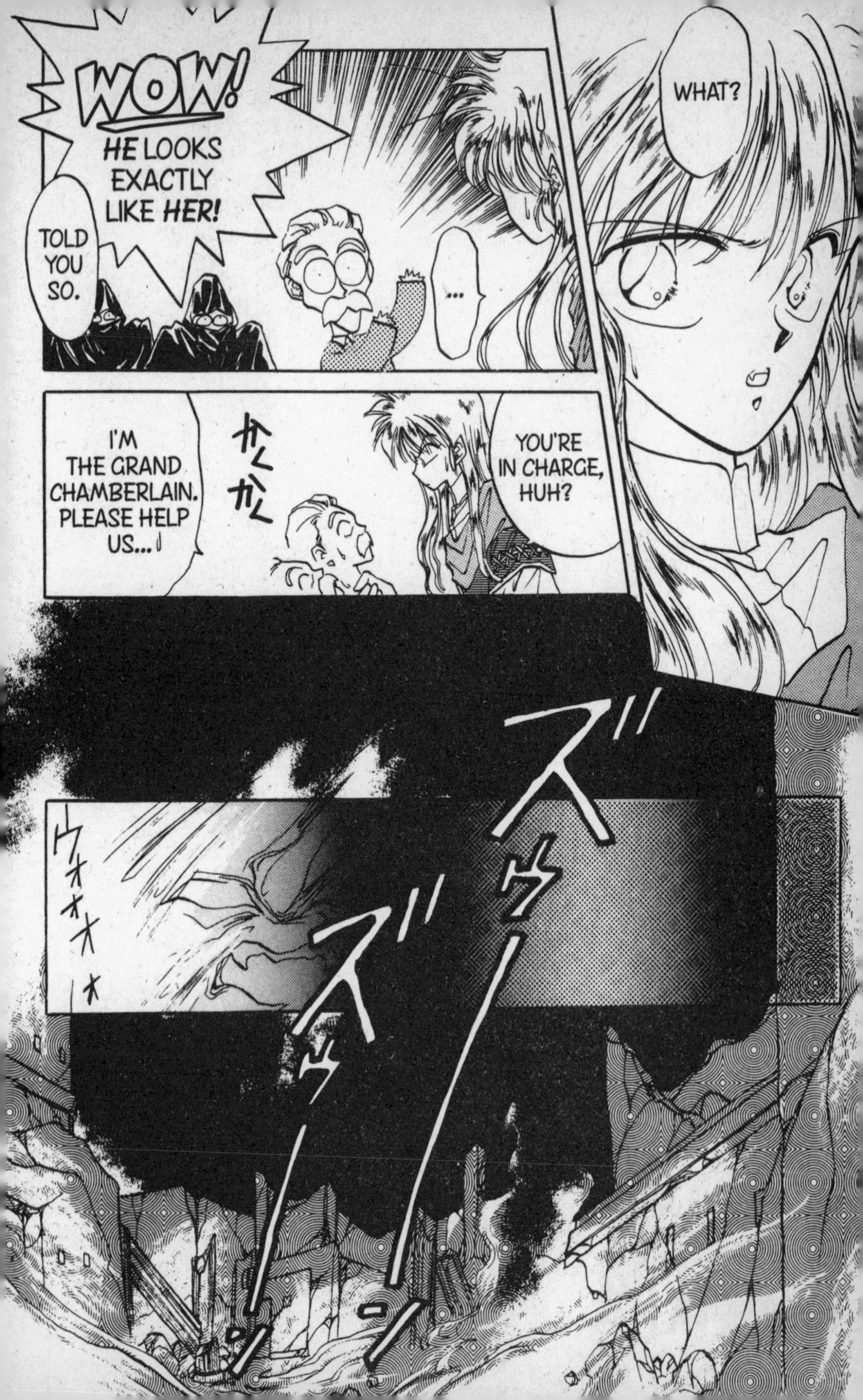
WHAT?
...
WOW! HE LOOKS EXACTLY LIKE HER!
TOLD YOU SO.
YOU'RE IN CHARGE, HUH?
かくかく
I'M THE GRAND CHAMBERLAIN. PLEASE HELP US...
ズゥー
ズゥー
ウォォォォ

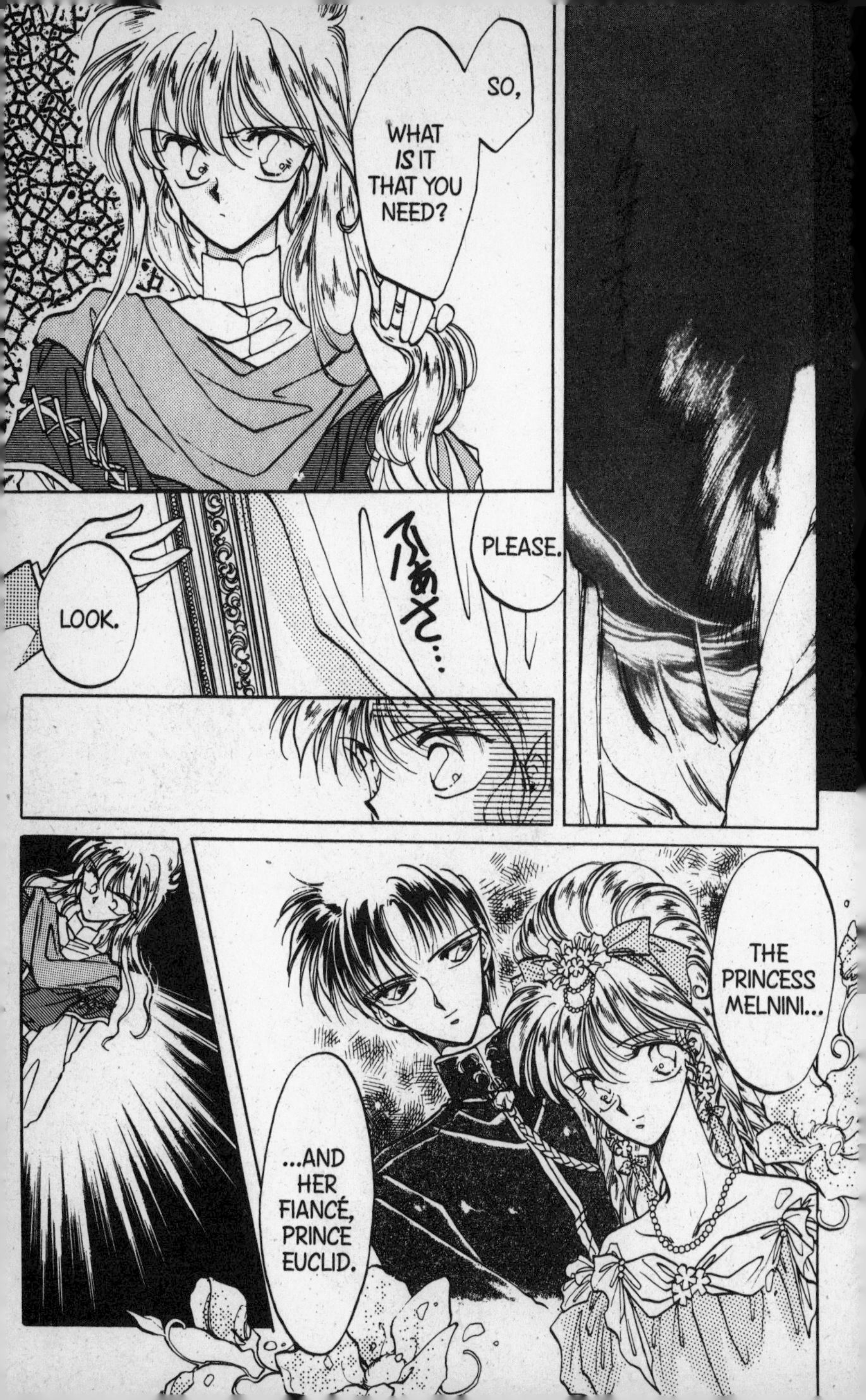
SO, WHAT *IS* IT THAT YOU NEED?
PLEASE.
ふあさ…
LOOK.
THE PRINCESS MELNINI...
...AND HER FIANCÉ, PRINCE EUCLID.

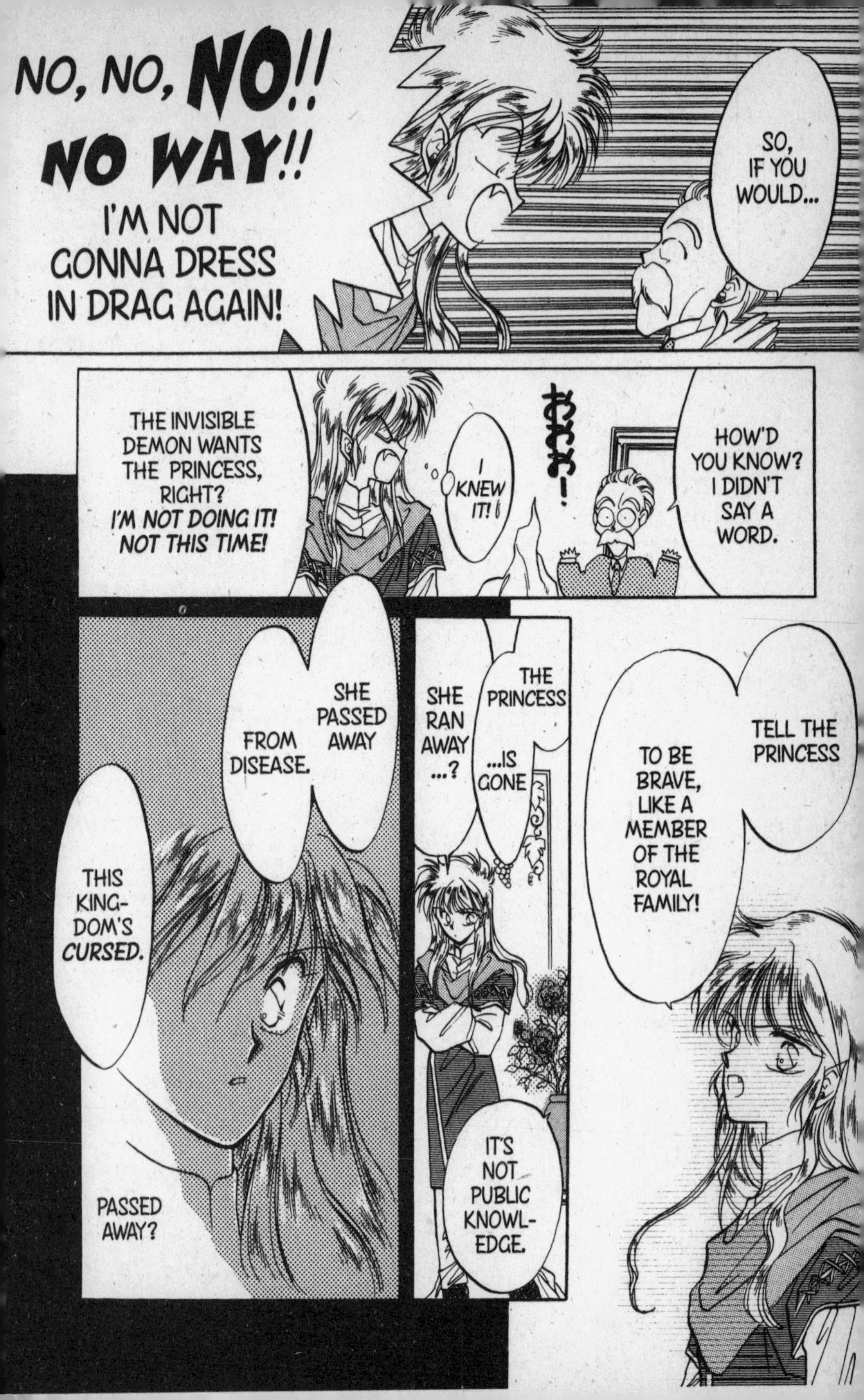
SO, IF YOU WOULD...
NO, NO, **NO!! NO WAY!!**
I'M NOT GONNA DRESS IN DRAG AGAIN!
HOW'D YOU KNOW? I DIDN'T SAY A WORD.
I KNEW IT!
THE INVISIBLE DEMON WANTS THE PRINCESS, RIGHT? *I'M NOT DOING IT! NOT THIS TIME!*
TELL THE PRINCESS TO BE BRAVE, LIKE A MEMBER OF THE ROYAL FAMILY!
THE PRINCESS ...IS GONE
SHE RAN AWAY ...?
IT'S NOT PUBLIC KNOWL-EDGE.
SHE PASSED AWAY FROM DISEASE.
THIS KING-DOM'S *CURSED.*
PASSED AWAY?

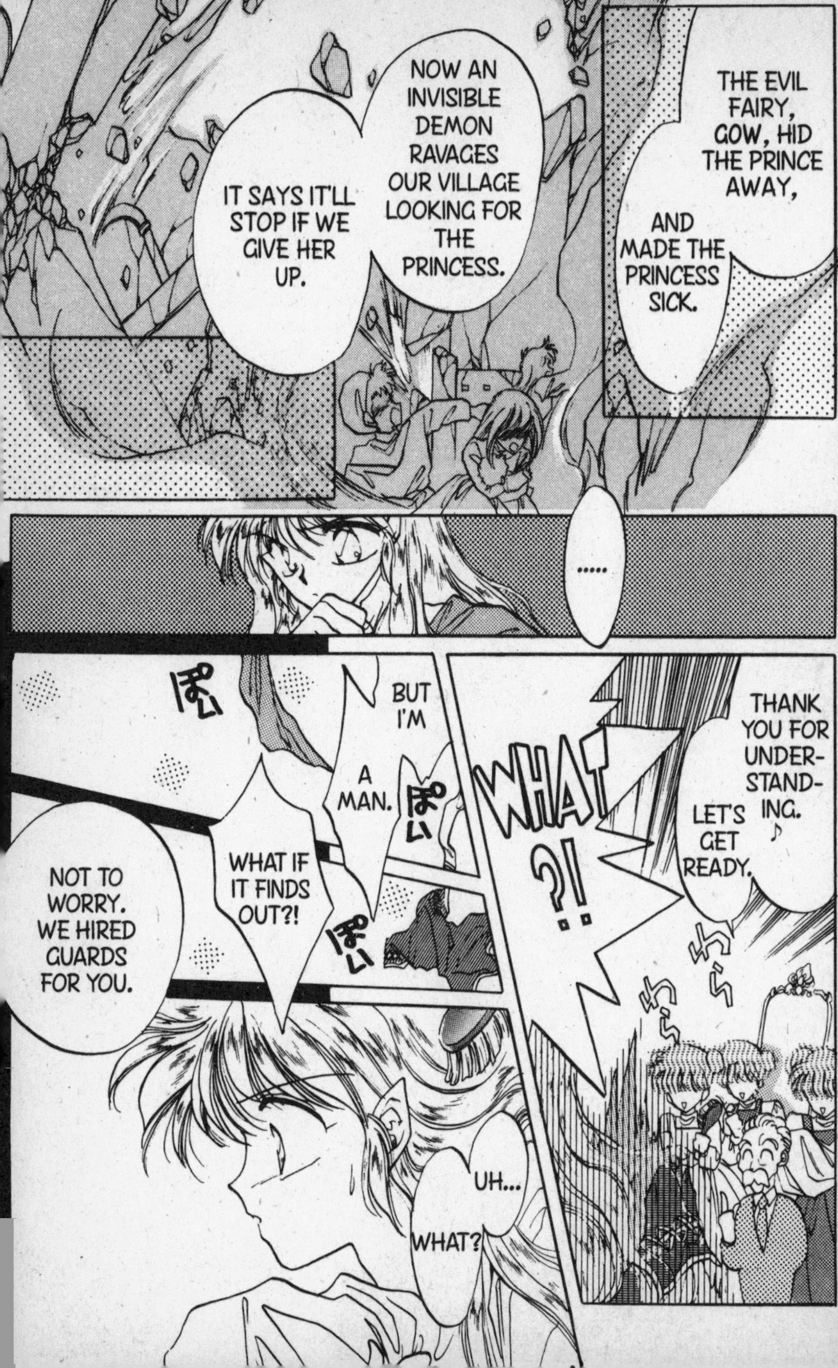
THE EVIL FAIRY, GOW, HID THE PRINCE AWAY,
AND MADE THE PRINCESS SICK.
NOW AN INVISIBLE DEMON RAVAGES OUR VILLAGE LOOKING FOR THE PRINCESS.
IT SAYS IT'LL STOP IF WE GIVE HER UP.
.....
THANK YOU FOR UNDERSTANDING. ♪
LET'S GET READY.
WHAT ?!
わら わら
BUT I'M
A MAN.
ぽい
ぽい
ぽい
WHAT IF IT FINDS OUT?!
NOT TO WORRY. WE HIRED GUARDS FOR YOU.
UH...
WHAT?

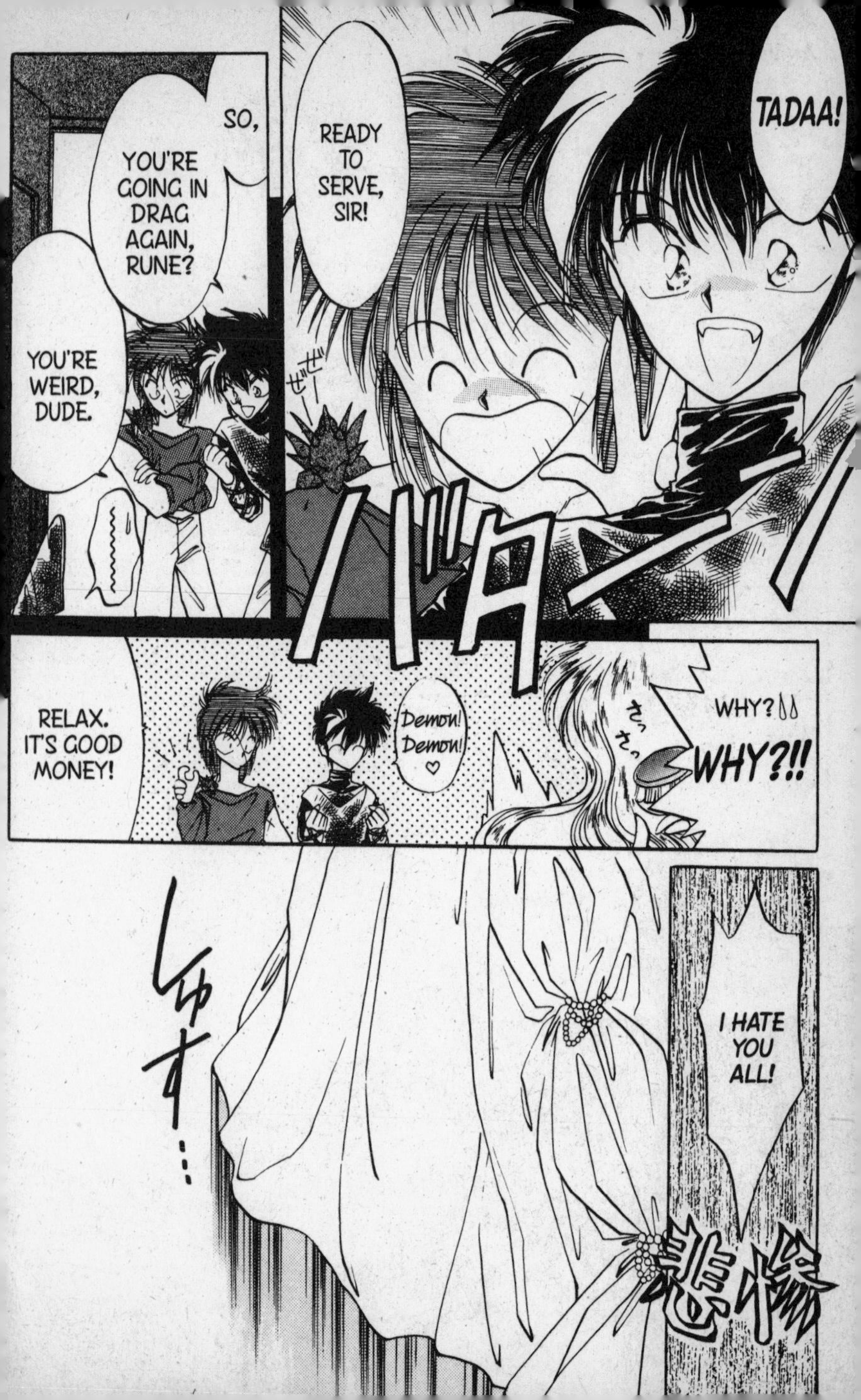
TADAA!
READY TO SERVE, SIR!
SO, YOU'RE GOING IN DRAG AGAIN, RUNE?
YOU'RE WEIRD, DUDE.
バタン
WHY? WHY?!!
Demon! Demon! ♡
RELAX. IT'S GOOD MONEY!
I HATE YOU ALL!

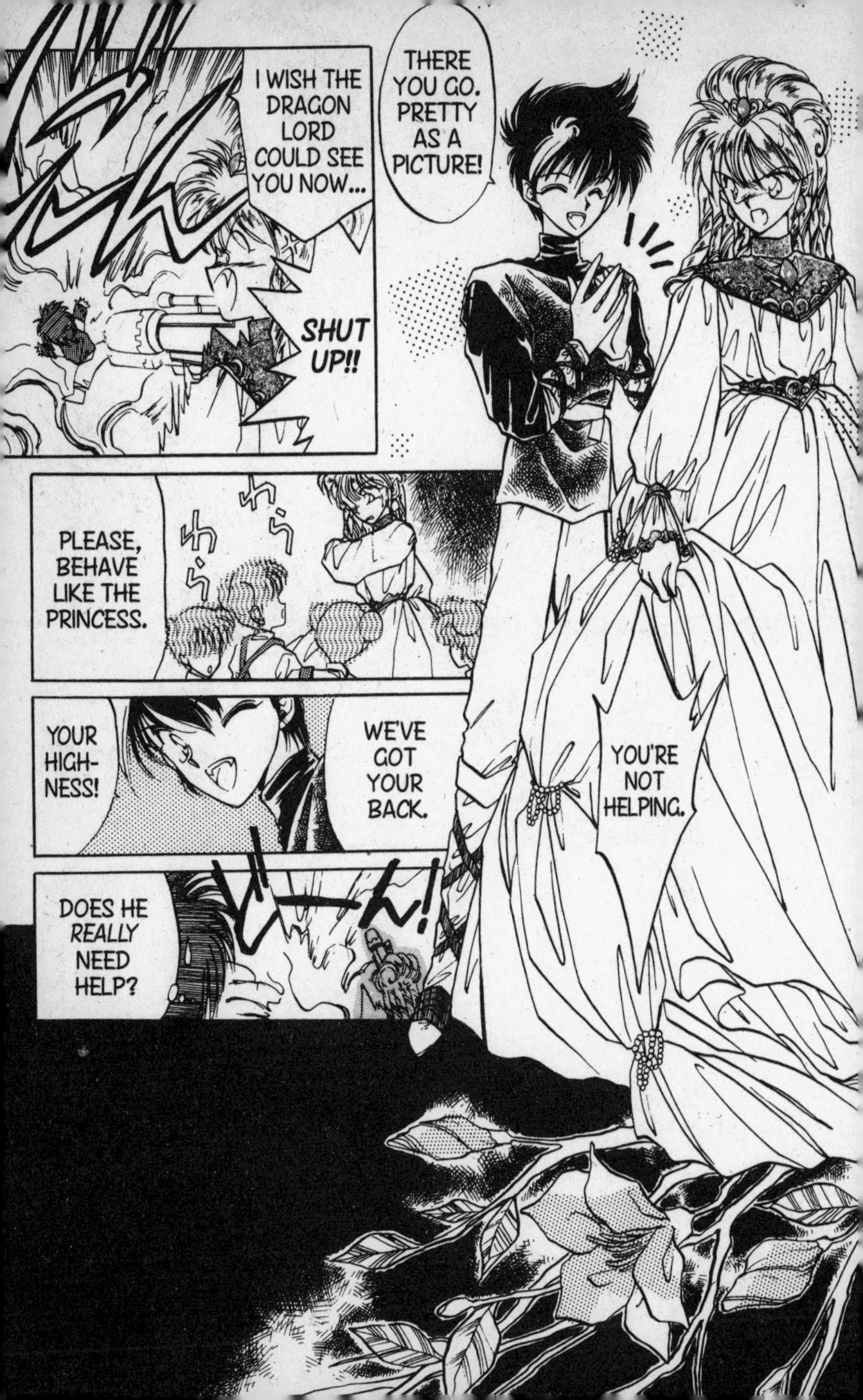

THERE YOU GO. PRETTY AS A PICTURE!
YOU'RE NOT HELPING.
I WISH THE DRAGON LORD COULD SEE YOU NOW...
SHUT UP!!
PLEASE, BEHAVE LIKE THE PRINCESS.
わらわら
YOUR HIGH-NESS!
WE'VE GOT YOUR BACK.
DOES HE REALLY NEED HELP?
どーん!

WAIT HERE?

BUT I THOUGHT THE DEMON DOESN'T SHOW UP AT NIGHT.

THE INVISIBLE DEMON REQUESTED IT.

THANKS FOR YOUR HELP, CHAMBERLAIN. WE'LL TAKE IT FROM HERE!

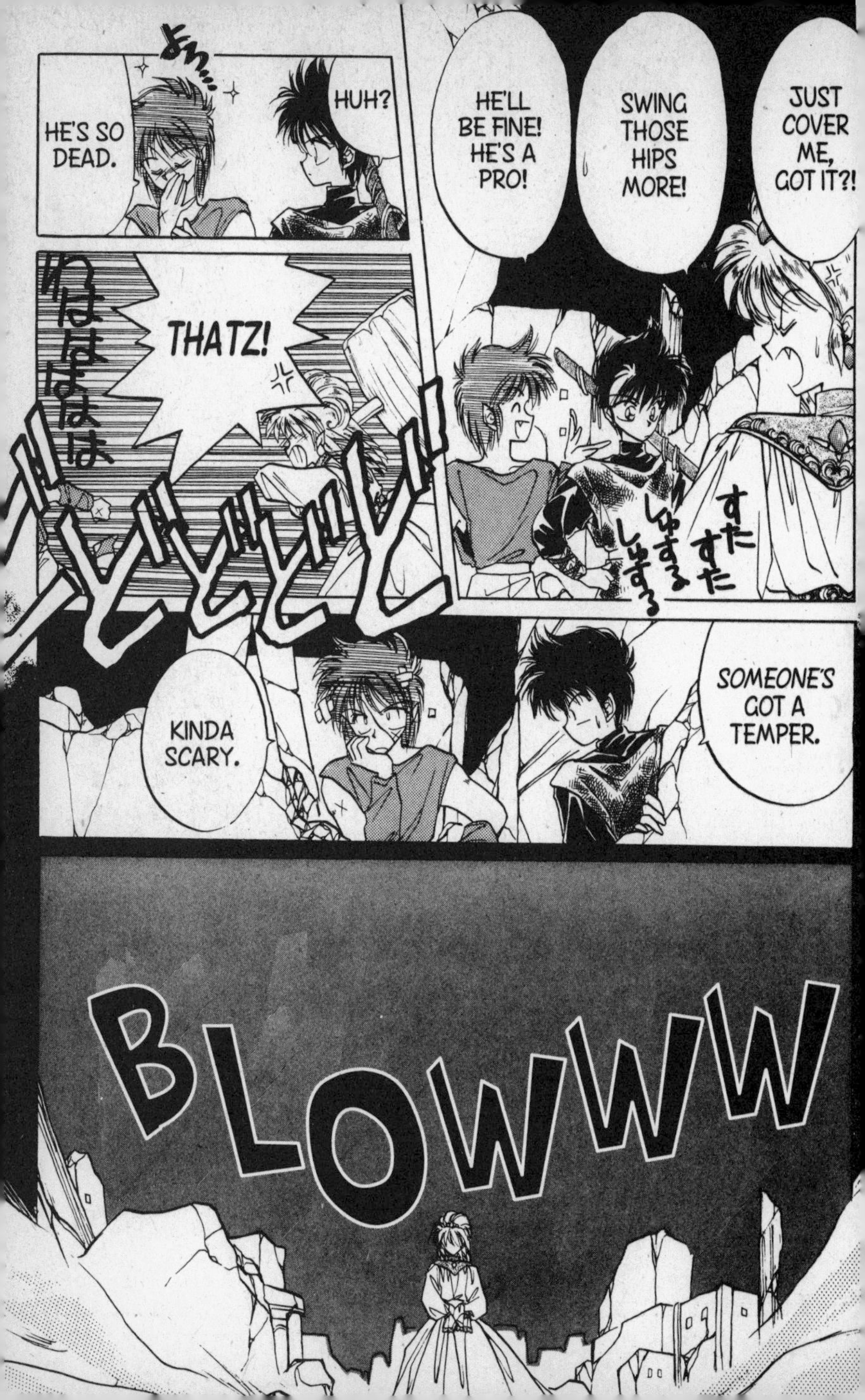
JUST COVER ME, GOT IT?!
SWING THOSE HIPS MORE!
HE'LL BE FINE! HE'S A PRO!
すたすた
しゅするしゅする
HUH?
HE'S SO DEAD.
THATZ!
SOMEONE'S GOT A TEMPER.
KINDA SCARY.
BLOWWW

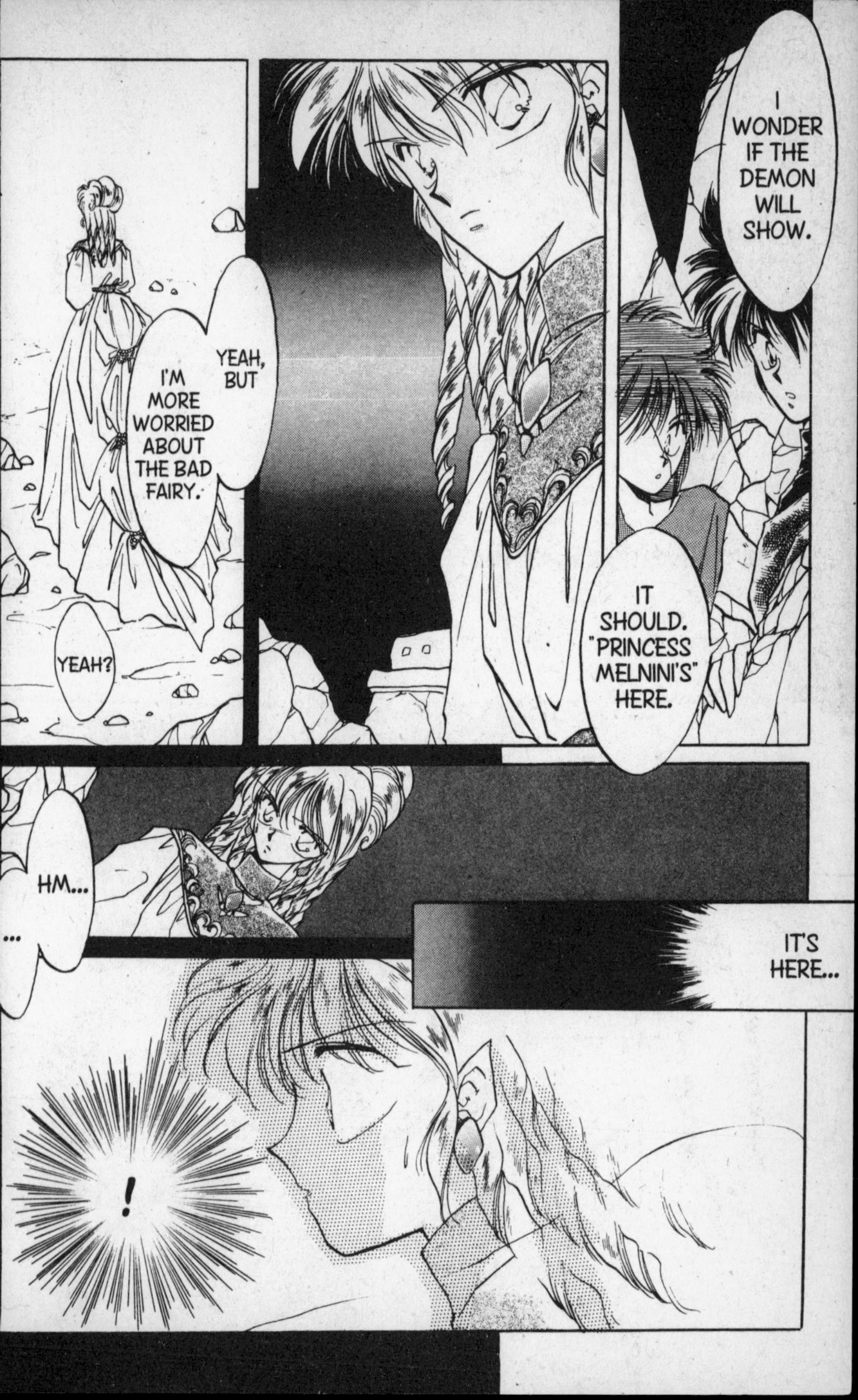

I WONDER IF THE DEMON WILL SHOW.
IT SHOULD. "PRINCESS MELNINI'S" HERE.
YEAH, BUT I'M MORE WORRIED ABOUT THE BAD FAIRY.
YEAH?
HM... ...
IT'S HERE...
!

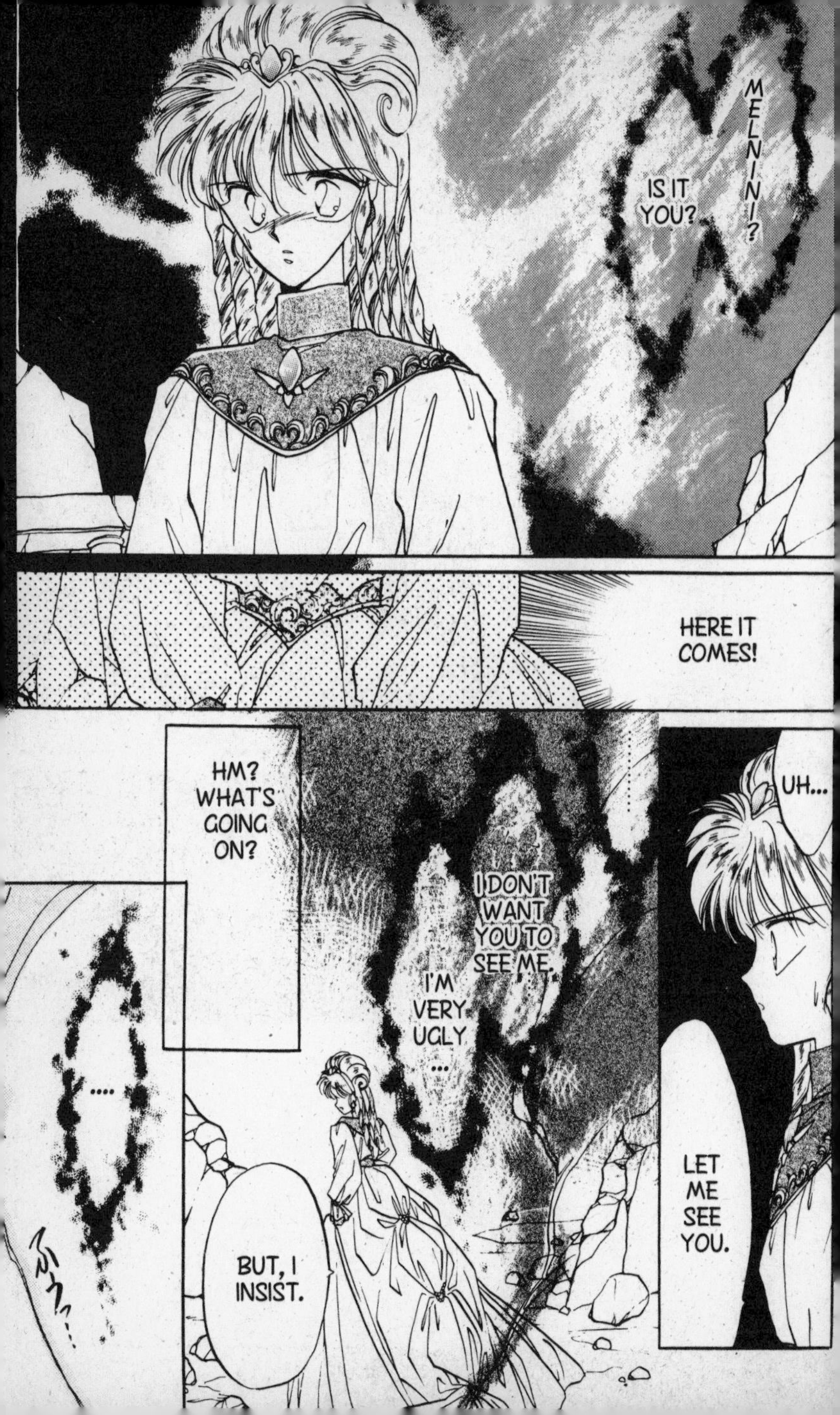
MELNINI?
IS IT YOU?
HERE IT COMES!
UH...
LET ME SEE YOU.
I DON'T WANT YOU TO SEE ME.
I'M VERY UGLY...
BUT, I INSIST.
HM? WHAT'S GOING ON?
....

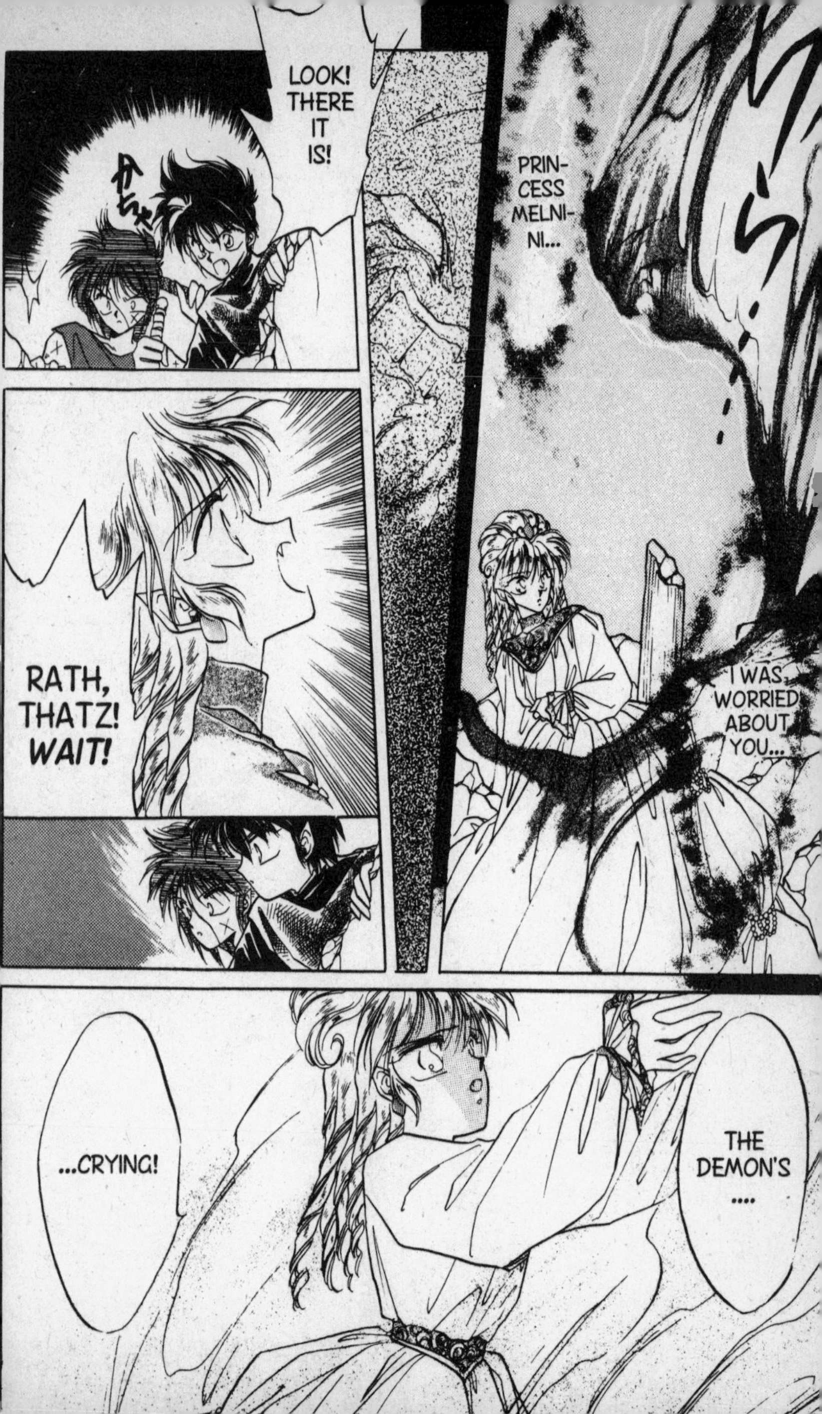
PRIN-
CESS
MELNI-
NI...
I WAS
WORRIED
ABOUT
YOU...
LOOK!
THERE
IT
IS!
RATH,
THATZ!
WAIT!
THE
DEMON'S
....
...CRYING!

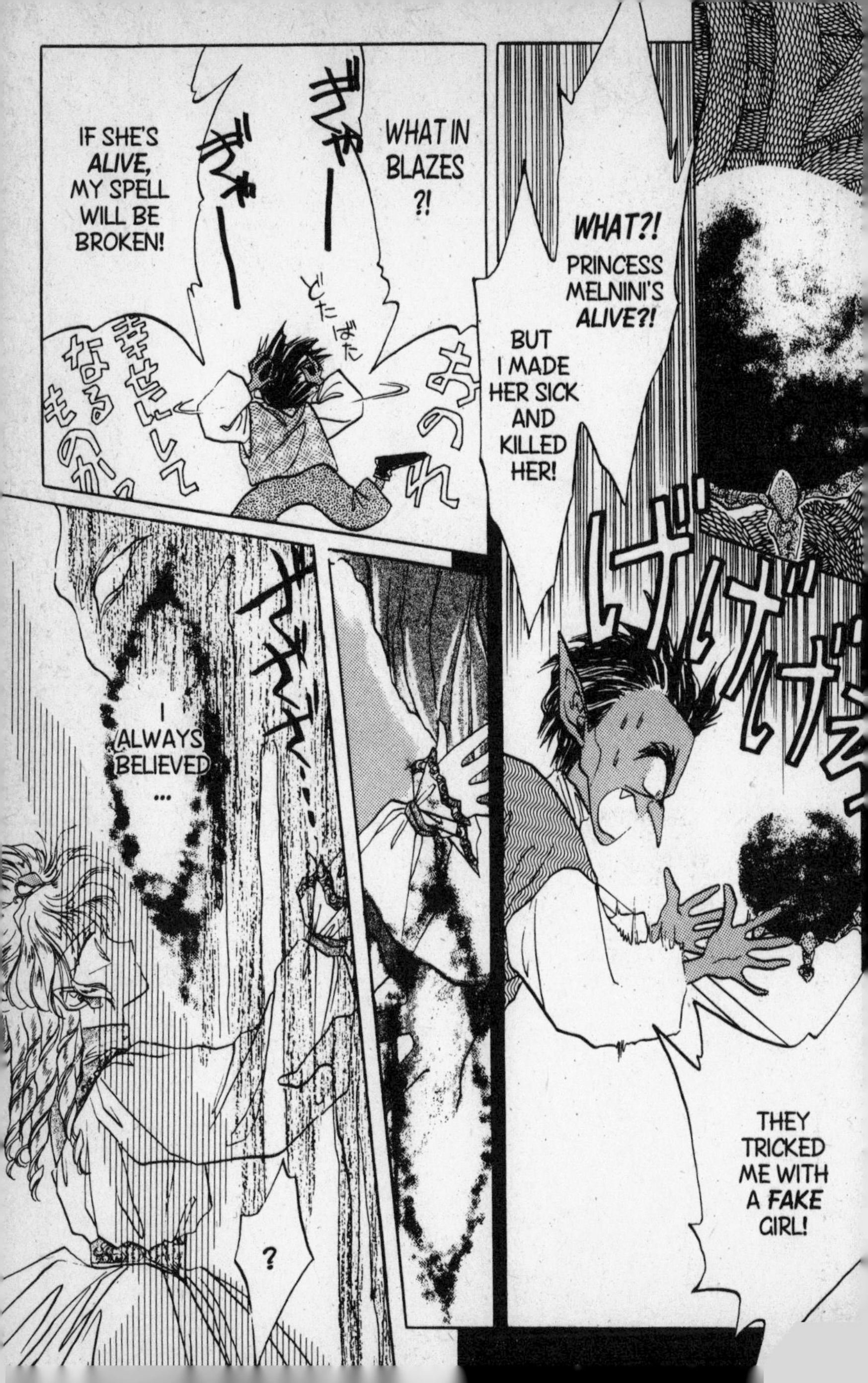
WHAT?!
PRINCESS MELNINI'S ALIVE?!
BUT I MADE HER SICK AND KILLED HER!
THEY TRICKED ME WITH A FAKE GIRL!
WHAT IN BLAZES ?!
ぎゃー
ぎゃー
どたばた
おのれ
IF SHE'S ALIVE, MY SPELL WILL BE BROKEN!
?
I ALWAYS BELIEVED ...

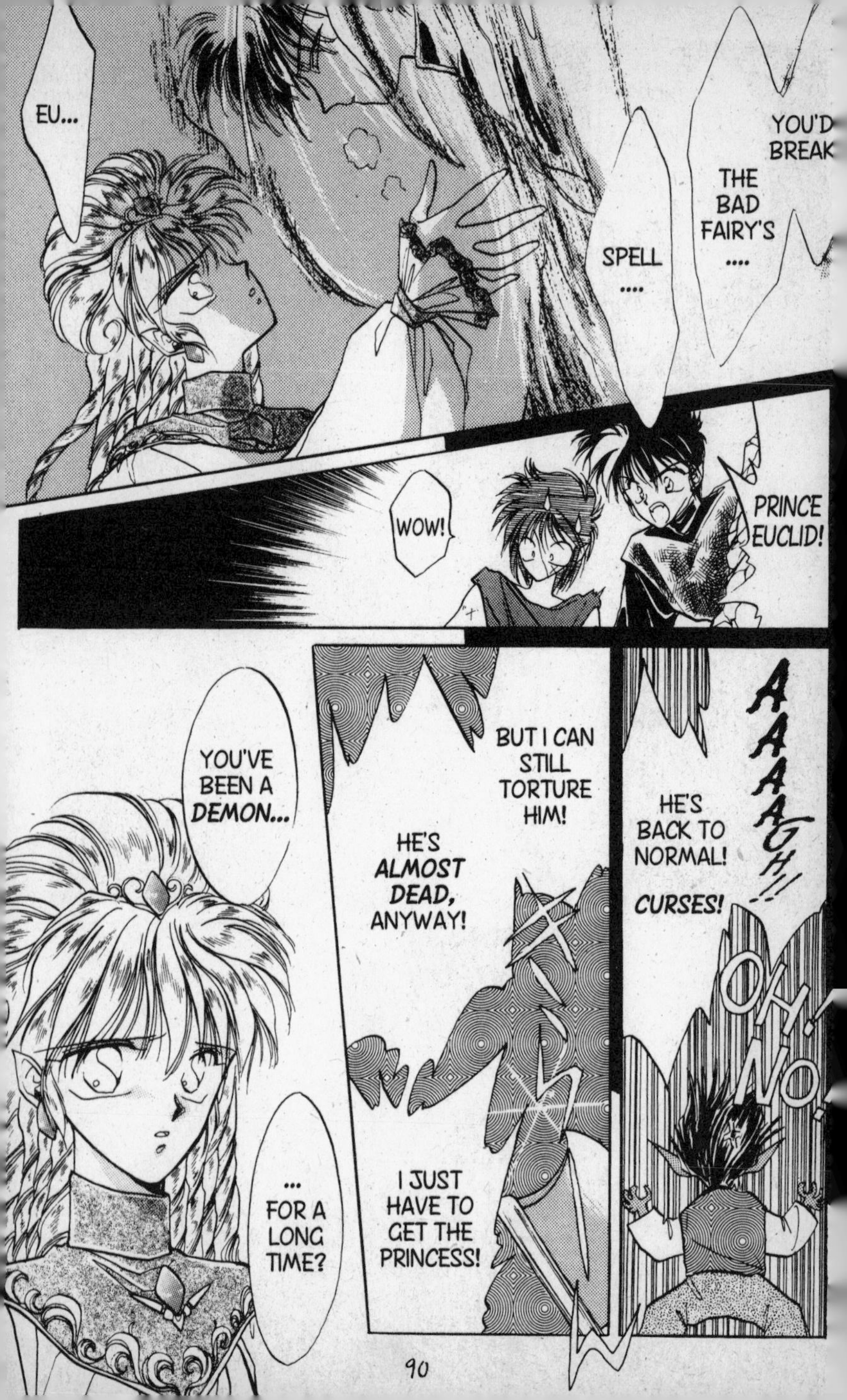
YOU'D BREAK THE BAD FAIRY'S ....
SPELL ....
EU...
PRINCE EUCLID!
WOW!
AAAAAGH!!
HE'S BACK TO NORMAL!
CURSES!
OH! NO!
BUT I CAN STILL TORTURE HIM!
HE'S *ALMOST DEAD*, ANYWAY!
I JUST HAVE TO GET THE PRINCESS!
YOU'VE BEEN A *DEMON...*
... FOR A LONG TIME?

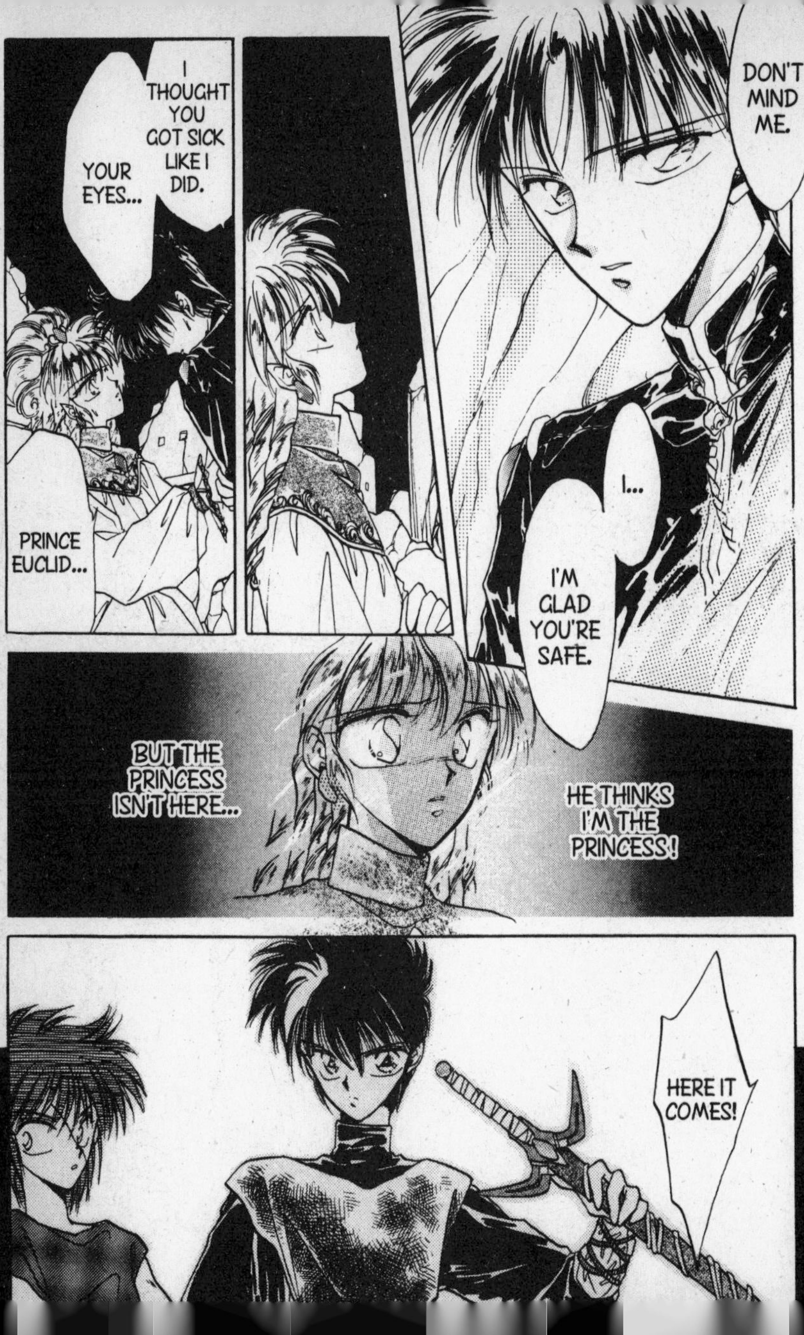
DON'T MIND ME.
I...
I'M GLAD YOU'RE SAFE.
I THOUGHT YOU GOT SICK LIKE I DID.
YOUR EYES...
PRINCE EUCLID...
HE THINKS I'M THE PRINCESS!
BUT THE PRINCESS ISN'T HERE...
HERE IT COMES!

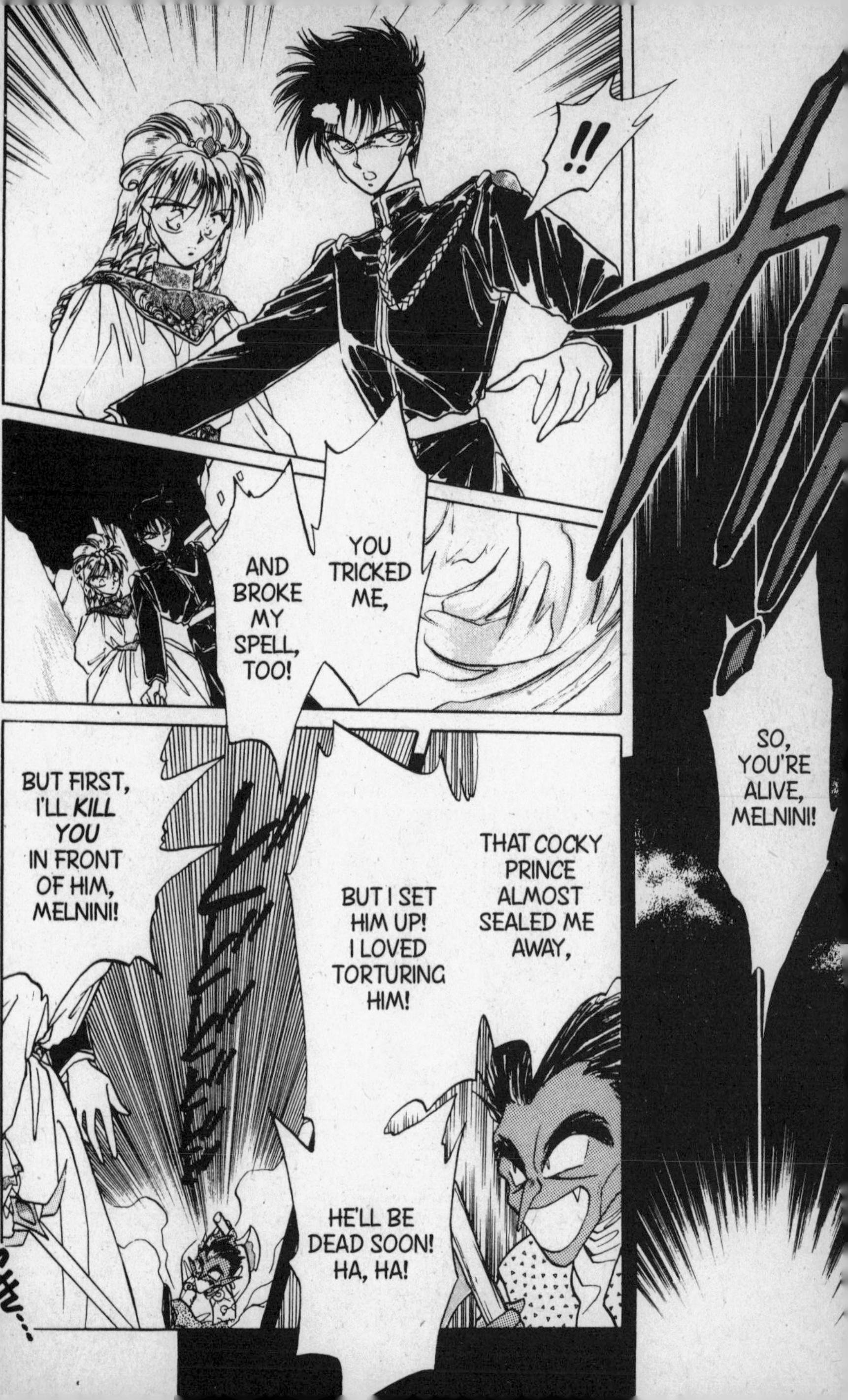
!!
SO, YOU'RE ALIVE, MELNINI!
YOU TRICKED ME, AND BROKE MY SPELL, TOO!
THAT COCKY PRINCE ALMOST SEALED ME AWAY,
BUT I SET HIM UP! I LOVED TORTURING HIM!
HE'LL BE DEAD SOON! HA, HA!
BUT FIRST, I'LL *KILL YOU* IN FRONT OF HIM, MELNINI!
SHU...

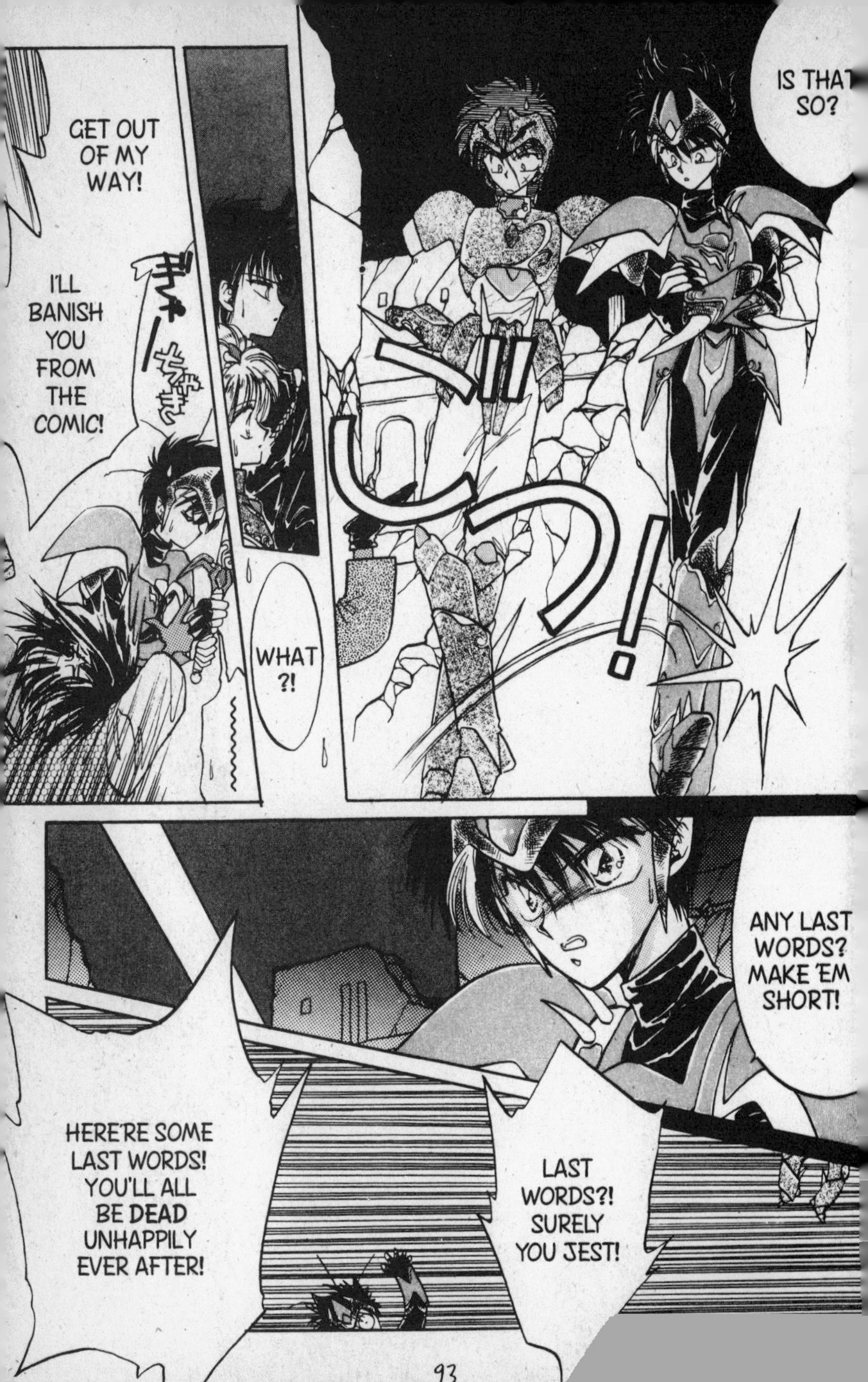
IS THAT SO?
WHAT?!
GET OUT OF MY WAY!
I'LL BANISH YOU FROM THE COMIC!
ANY LAST WORDS? MAKE 'EM SHORT!
LAST WORDS?! SURELY YOU JEST!
HERE'RE SOME LAST WORDS! YOU'LL ALL BE DEAD UNHAPPILY EVER AFTER!

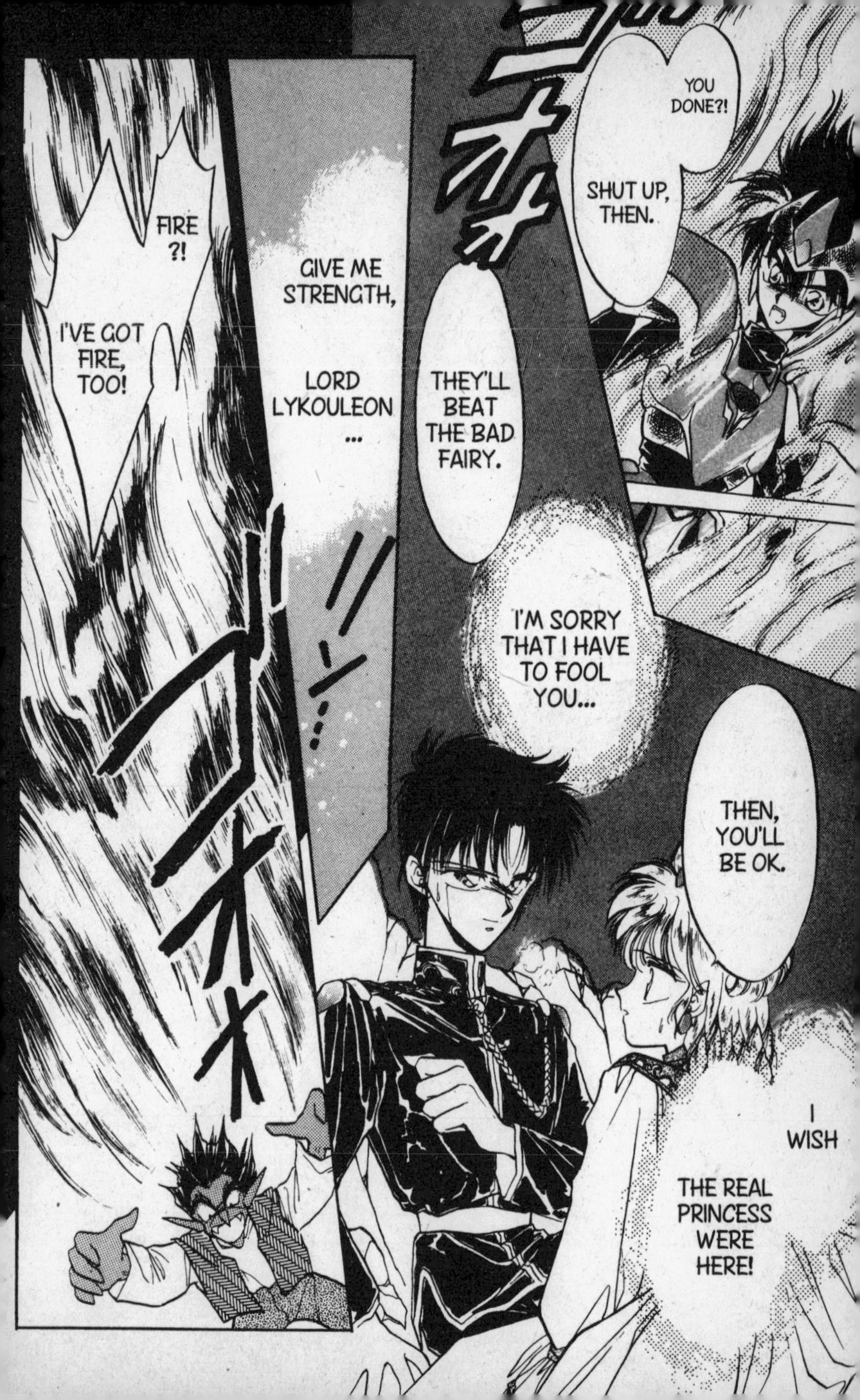
YOU DONE?!
SHUT UP, THEN.
THEY'LL BEAT THE BAD FAIRY.
THEN, YOU'LL BE OK.
I'M SORRY THAT I HAVE TO FOOL YOU...
I WISH
THE REAL PRINCESS WERE HERE!
GIVE ME STRENGTH,
LORD LYKOULEON ...
FIRE ?!
I'VE GOT FIRE, TOO!

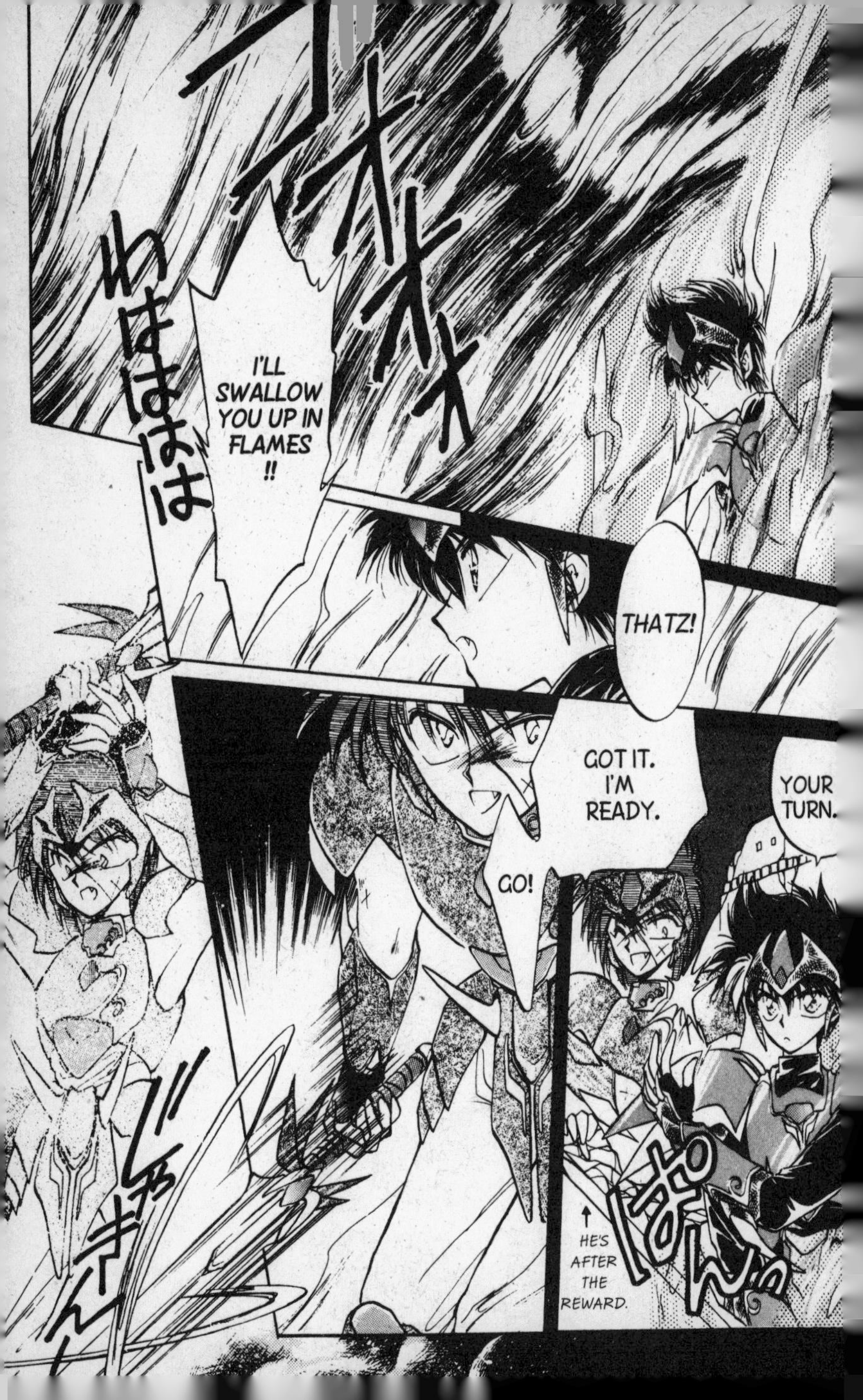
オオォ
わはははは
I'LL SWALLOW YOU UP IN FLAMES !!
THATZ!
YOUR TURN.
ぽん
↑ HE'S AFTER THE REWARD.
GOT IT. I'M READY.
GO!

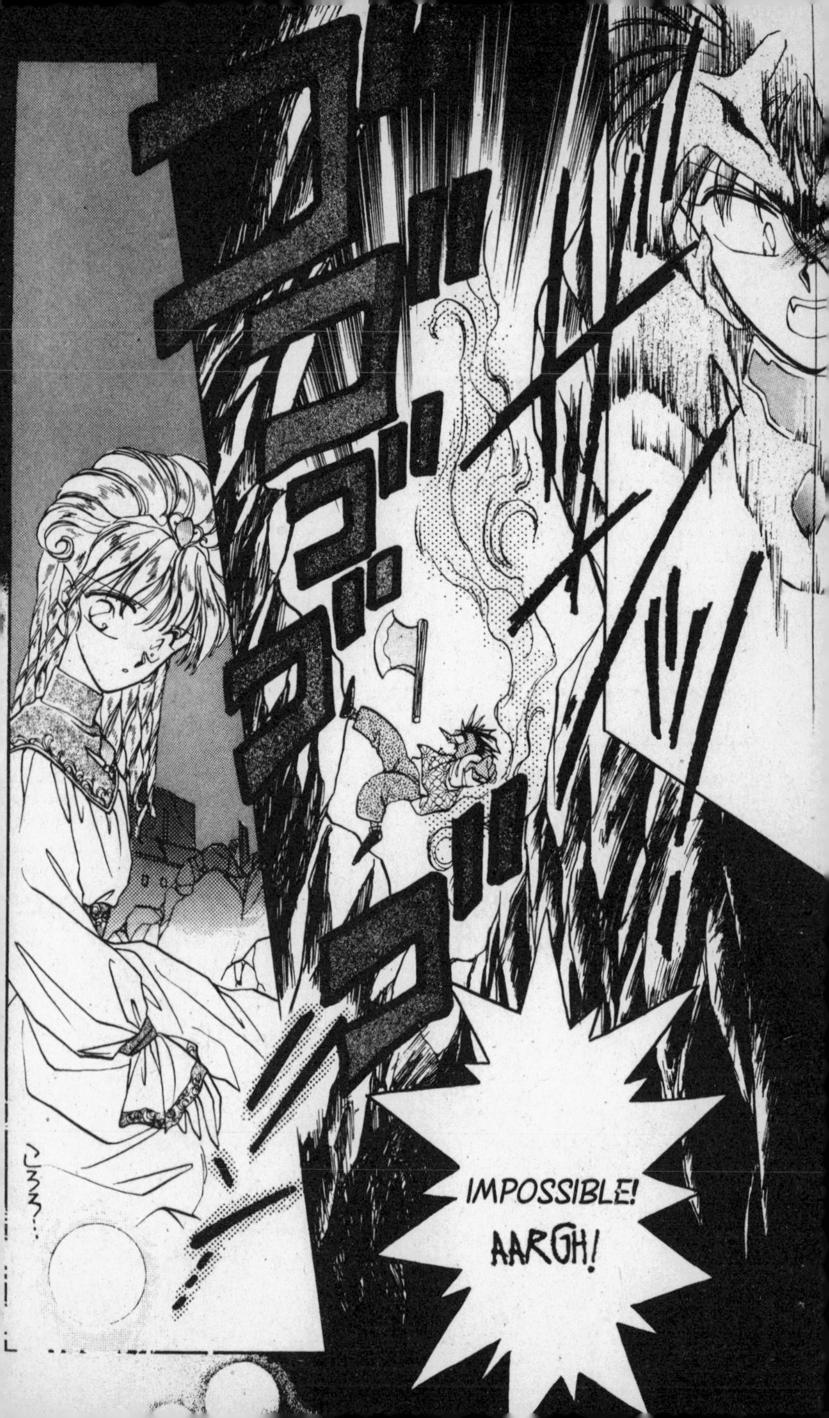
IMPOSSIBLE! AARGH!
UMM...

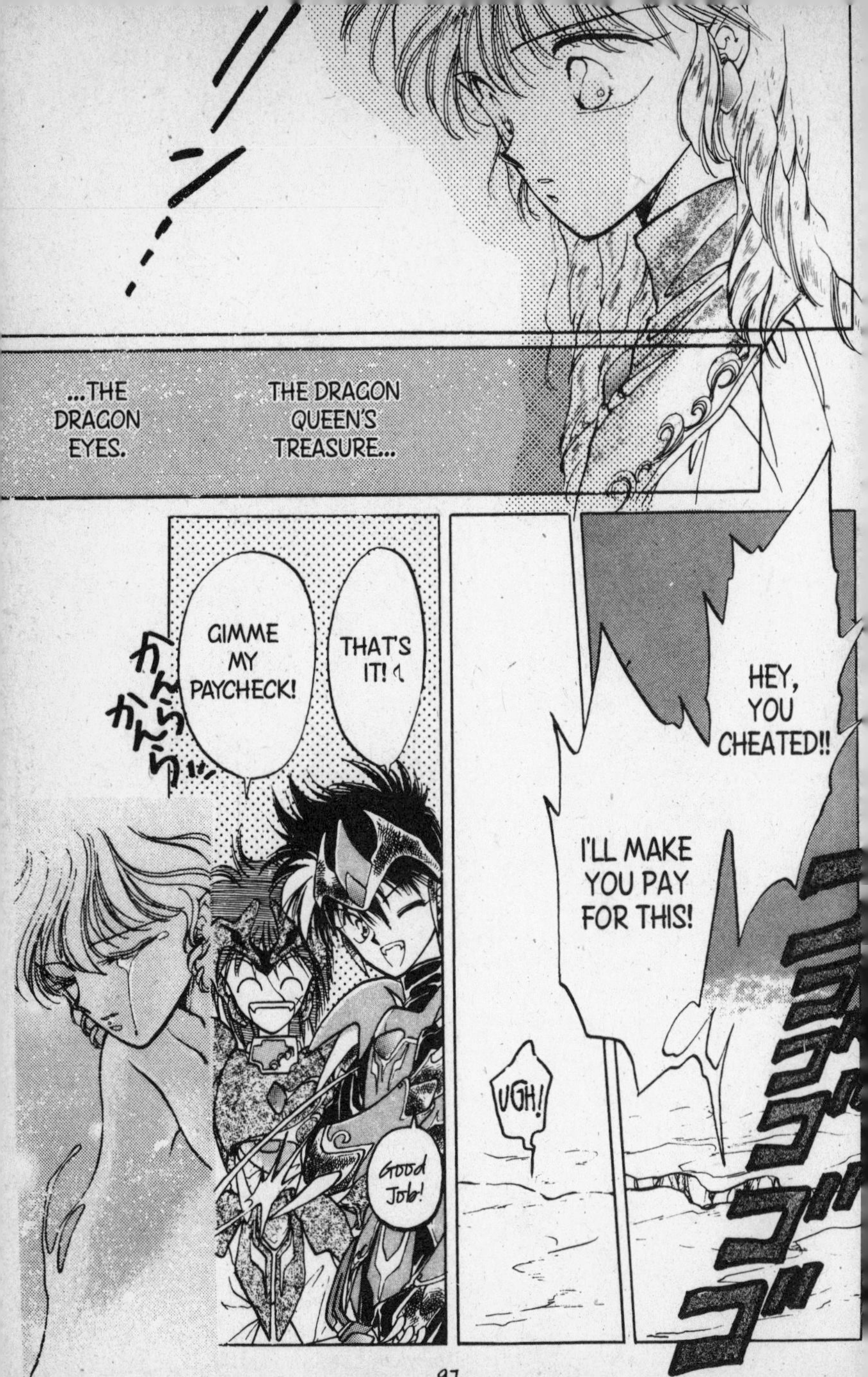
THE DRAGON QUEEN'S TREASURE...
...THE DRAGON EYES.
HEY, YOU CHEATED!!
I'LL MAKE YOU PAY FOR THIS!
UGH!
THAT'S IT!
GIMME MY PAYCHECK!
Good Job!

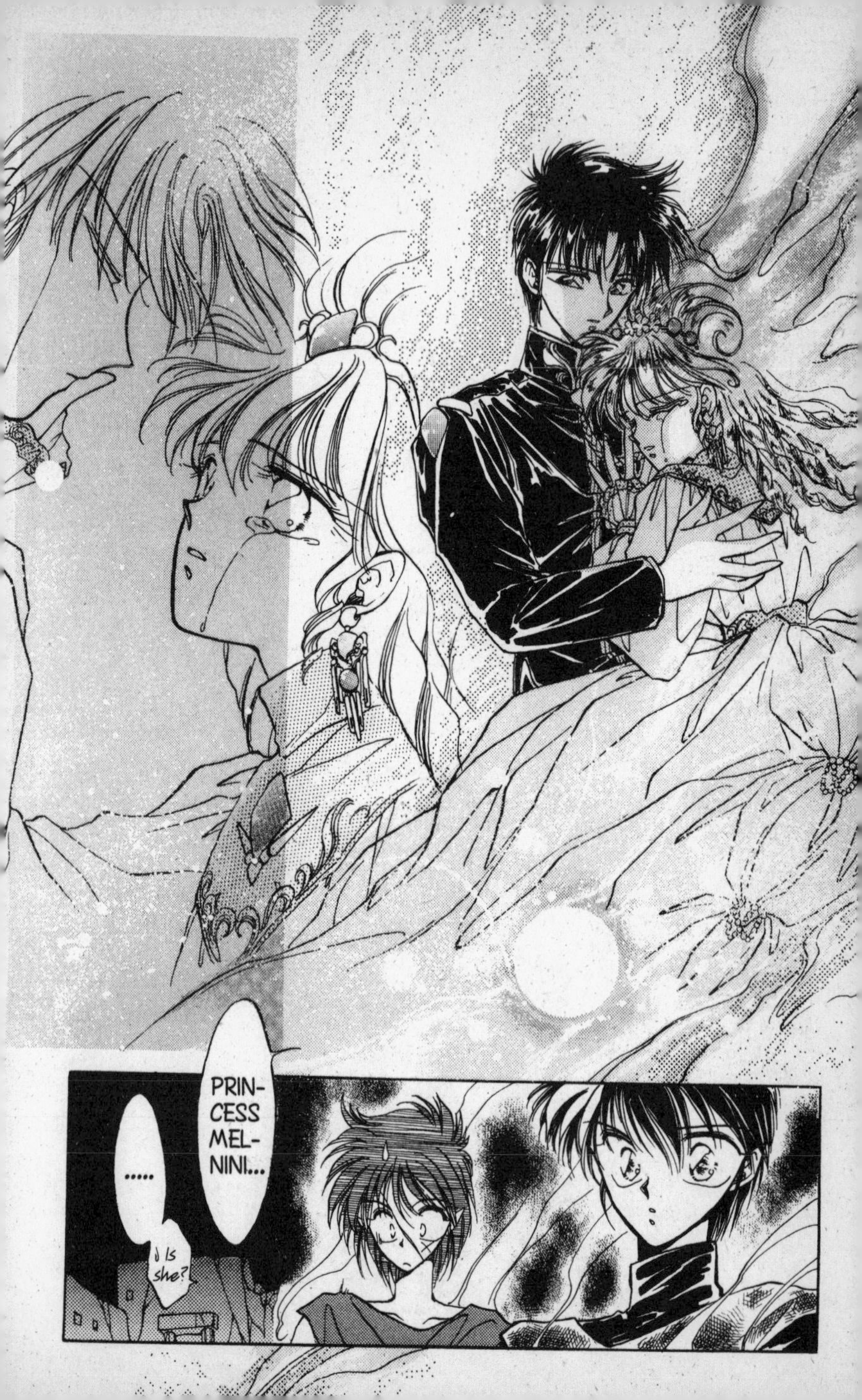
PRIN-
CESS
MEL-
NINI...
......
Is
she?

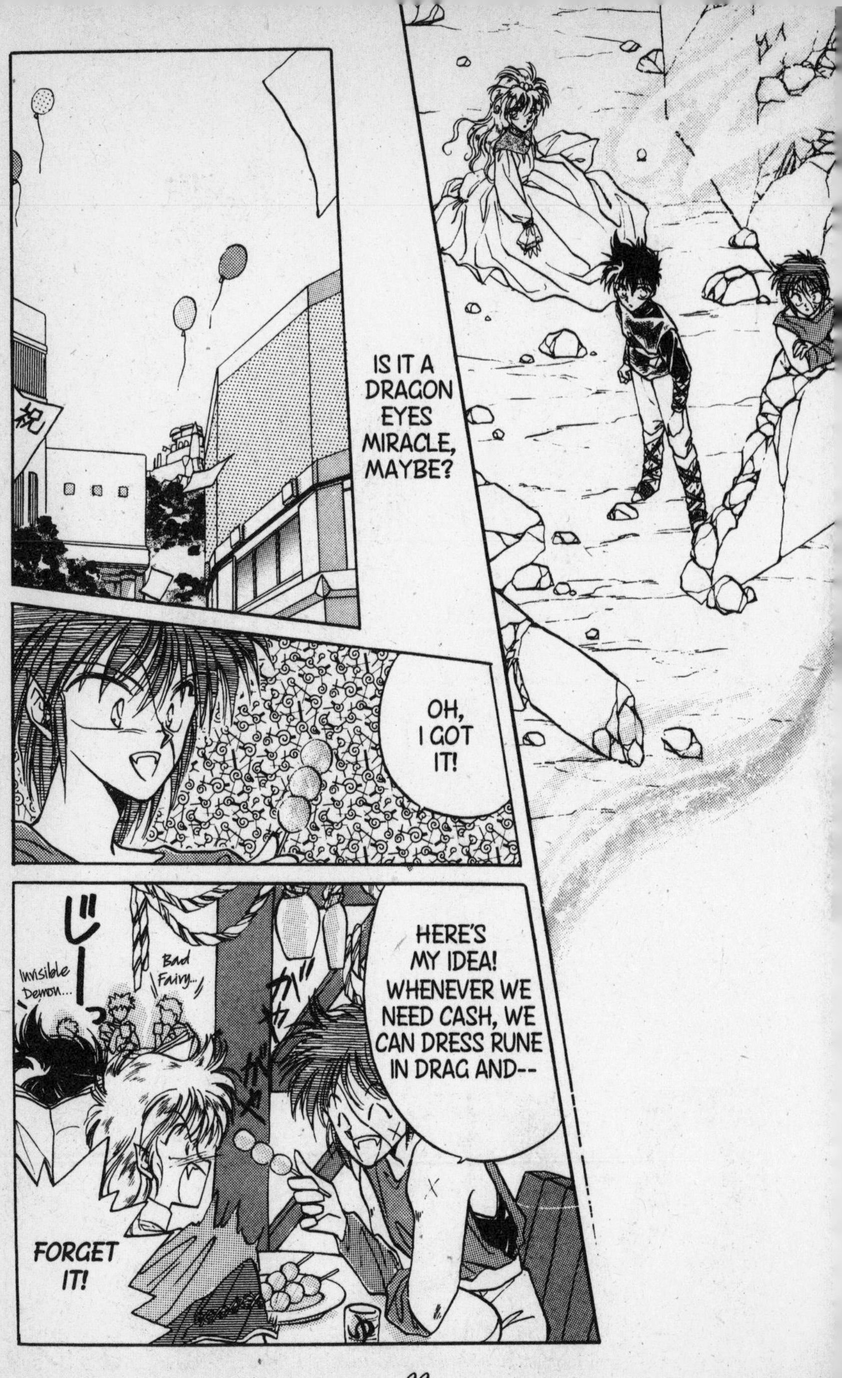
IS IT A DRAGON EYES MIRACLE, MAYBE?
祝
OH, I GOT IT!
HERE'S MY IDEA! WHENEVER WE NEED CASH, WE CAN DRESS RUNE IN DRAG AND--
Bad Fairy...
Invisible Demon...
じー
FORGET IT!

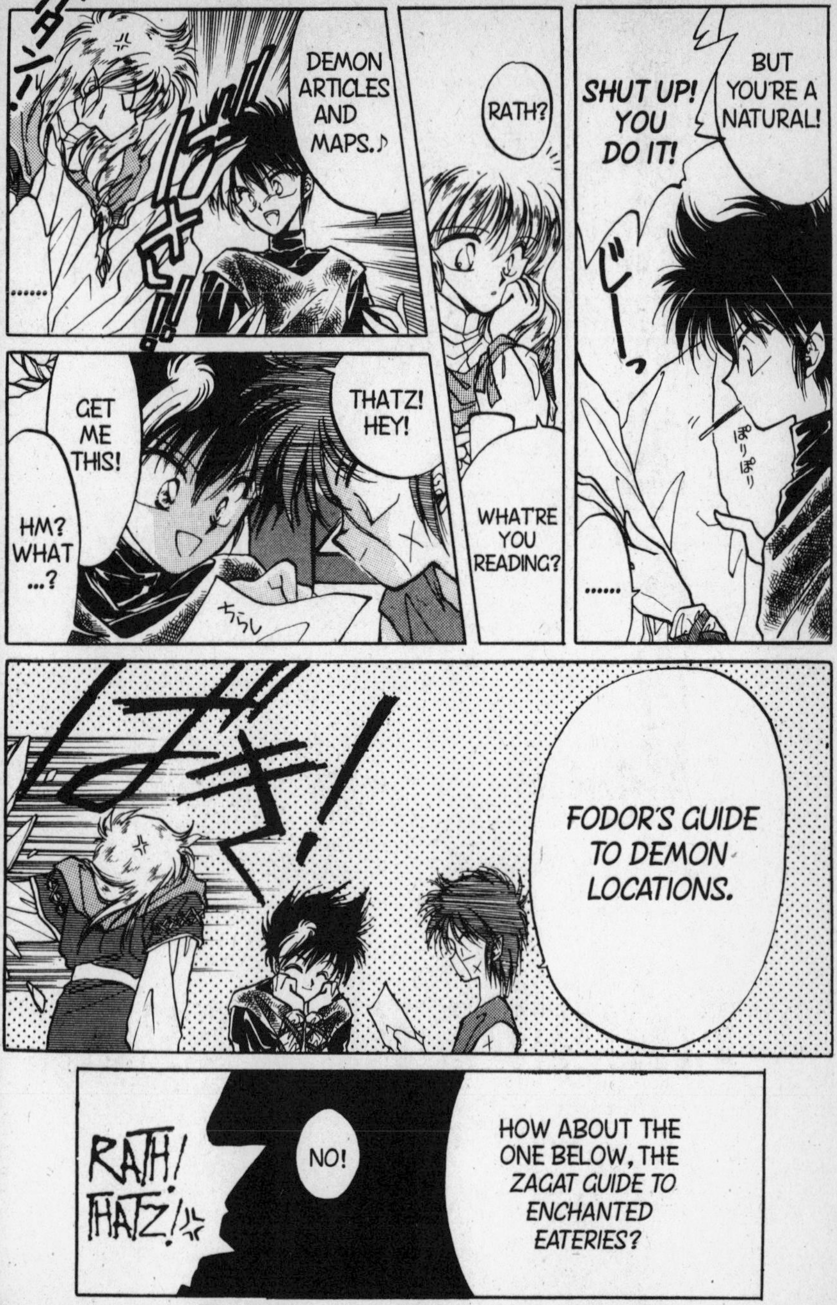
BUT YOU'RE A NATURAL!
SHUT UP! YOU DO IT!
ぽりぽり
......
RATH?
WHAT'RE YOU READING?
DEMON ARTICLES AND MAPS.♪
......
THATZ! HEY!
GET ME THIS!
HM? WHAT ...?
ちらし
FODOR'S GUIDE TO DEMON LOCATIONS.
HOW ABOUT THE ONE BELOW, THE ZAGAT GUIDE TO ENCHANTED EATERIES?
NO!
RATH! THATZ!

■KNIGHTS IN WHITE SATIN ◉END■

FINDERS KEEPERS

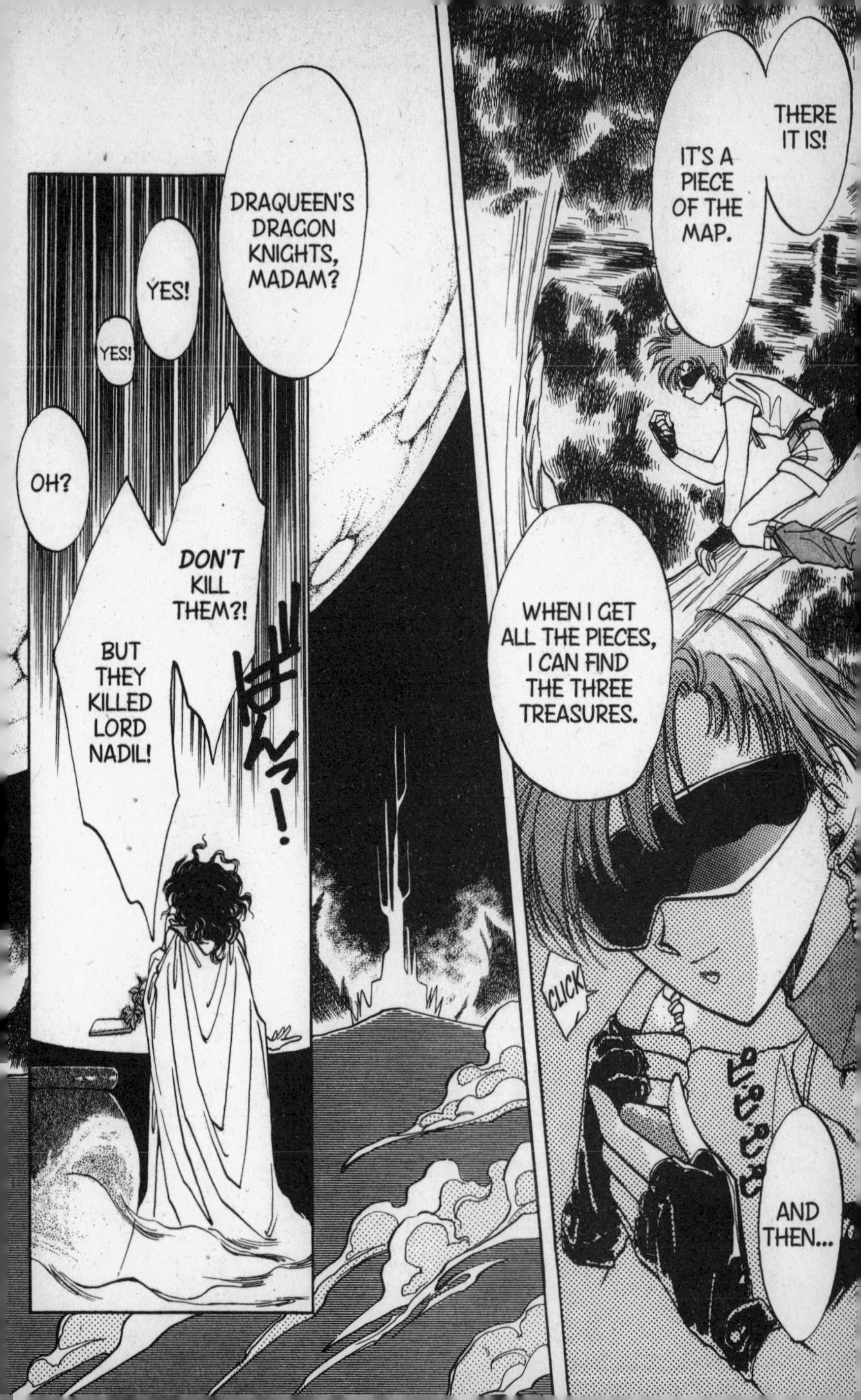
THERE IT IS!
IT'S A PIECE OF THE MAP.
WHEN I GET ALL THE PIECES, I CAN FIND THE THREE TREASURES.
CLICK
AND THEN...
DRAQUEEN'S DRAGON KNIGHTS, MADAM?
YES!
YES!
OH?
DON'T KILL THEM?!
BUT THEY KILLED LORD NADIL!

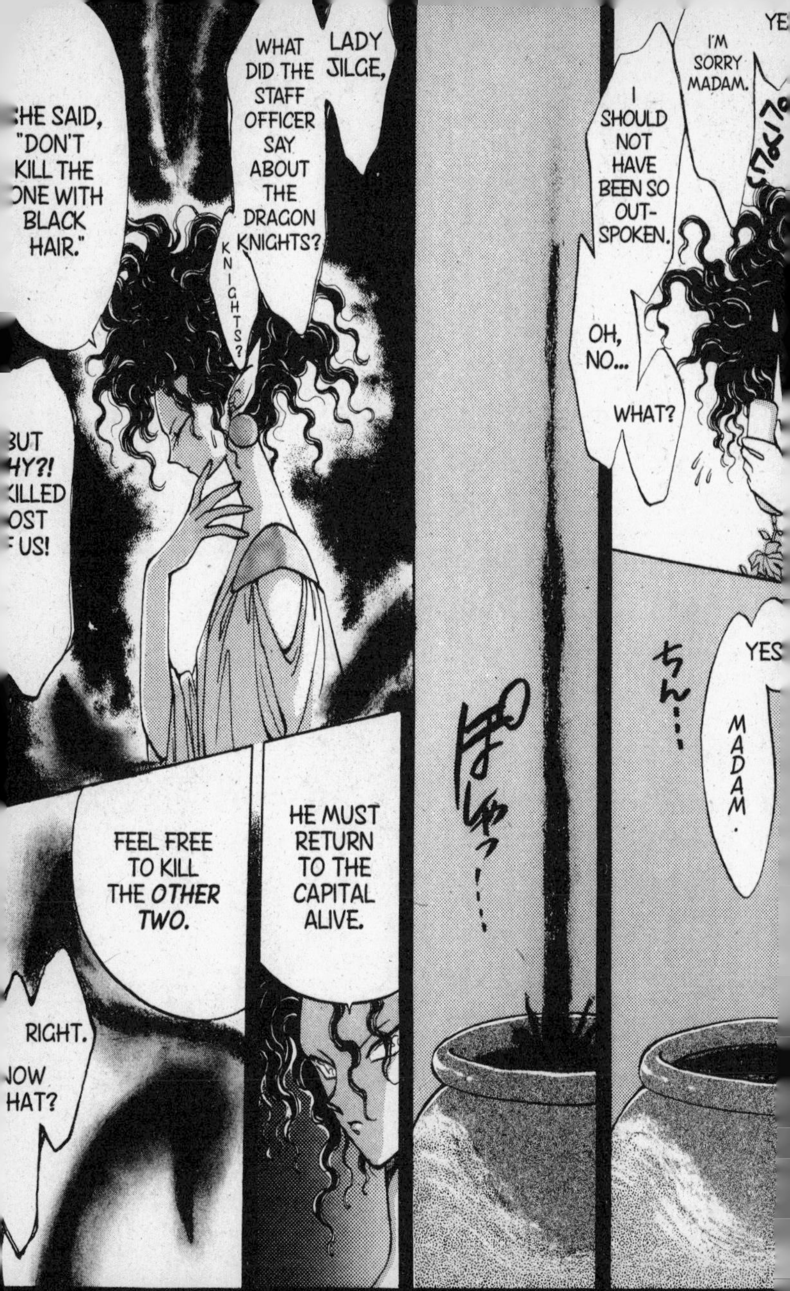
YE
I'M SORRY MADAM.
I SHOULD NOT HAVE BEEN SO OUT-SPOKEN.
WHAT?
OH, NO...
YES MADAM.
ちん…
ぱしゅっ…
LADY JILGE,
WHAT DID THE STAFF OFFICER SAY ABOUT THE DRAGON KNIGHTS?
KNIGHTS?
HE SAID, "DON'T KILL THE ONE WITH BLACK HAIR."
BUT HY?! KILLED OST F US!
HE MUST RETURN TO THE CAPITAL ALIVE.
FEEL FREE TO KILL THE *OTHER* TWO.
RIGHT.
NOW HAT?

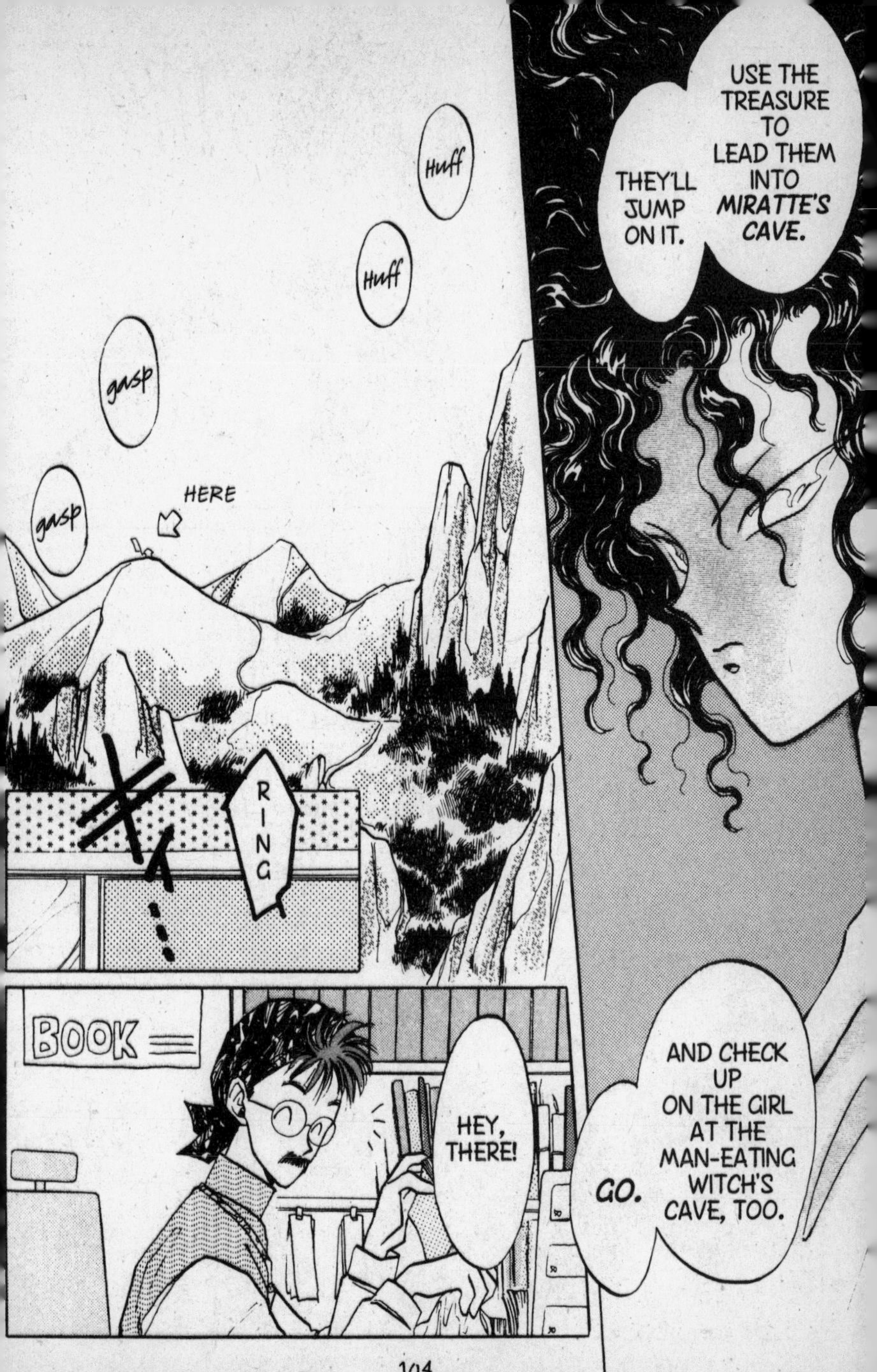
USE THE TREASURE TO LEAD THEM INTO *MIRATTE'S CAVE.*
THEY'LL JUMP ON IT.
AND CHECK UP ON THE GIRL AT THE MAN-EATING WITCH'S CAVE, TOO.
GO.
Huff
Huff
gasp
HERE
gasp
RING
HEY, THERE!

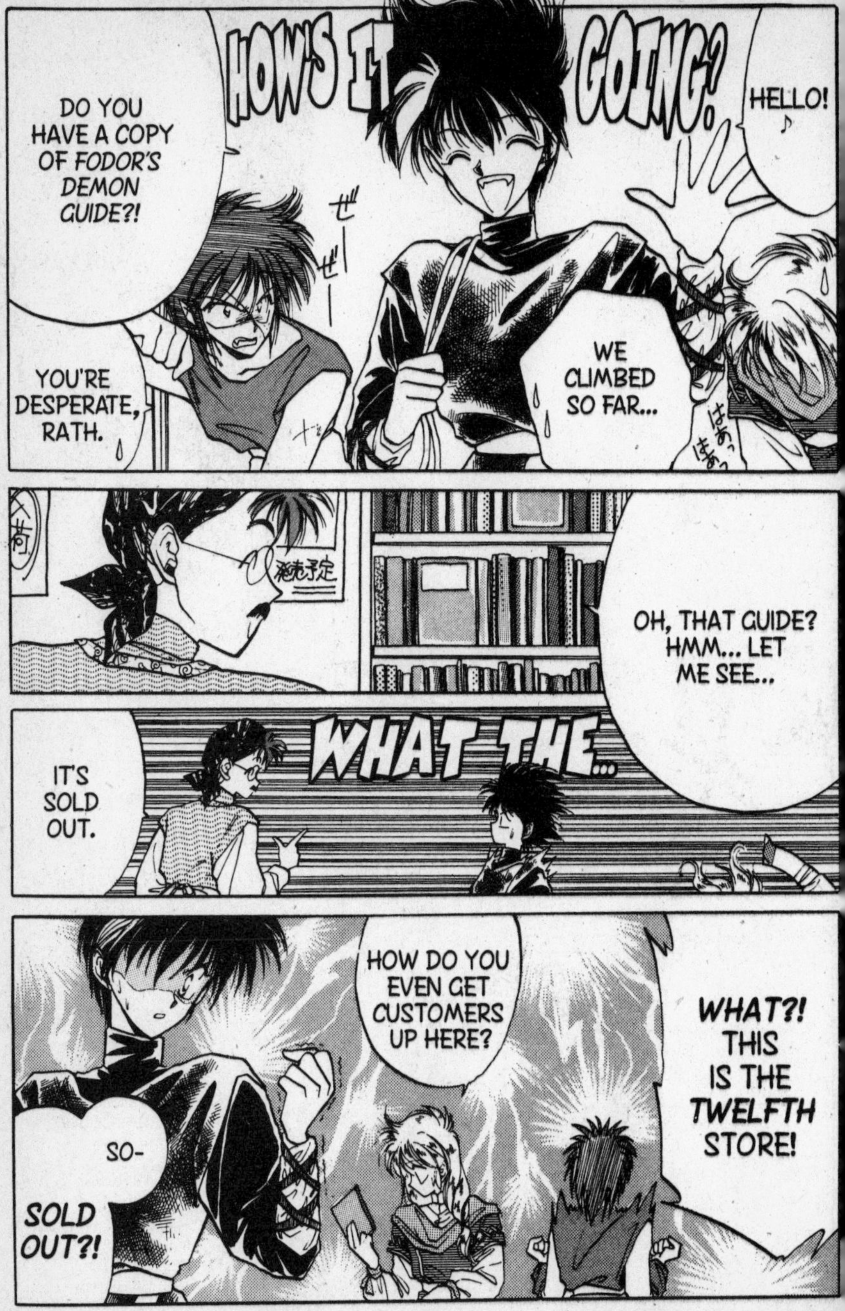

HELLO! ♪
HOW'S IT GOING?
DO YOU HAVE A COPY OF *FODOR'S DEMON GUIDE*?!
ゼー ゼー
WE CLIMBED SO FAR...
はあっ はあっ
YOU'RE DESPERATE, RATH.
OH, THAT GUIDE? HMM... LET ME SEE...
発売予定
WHAT THE...
IT'S SOLD OUT.
WHAT?! THIS IS THE ***TWELFTH*** STORE!
HOW DO YOU EVEN GET CUSTOMERS UP HERE?
SO-
SOLD OUT?!

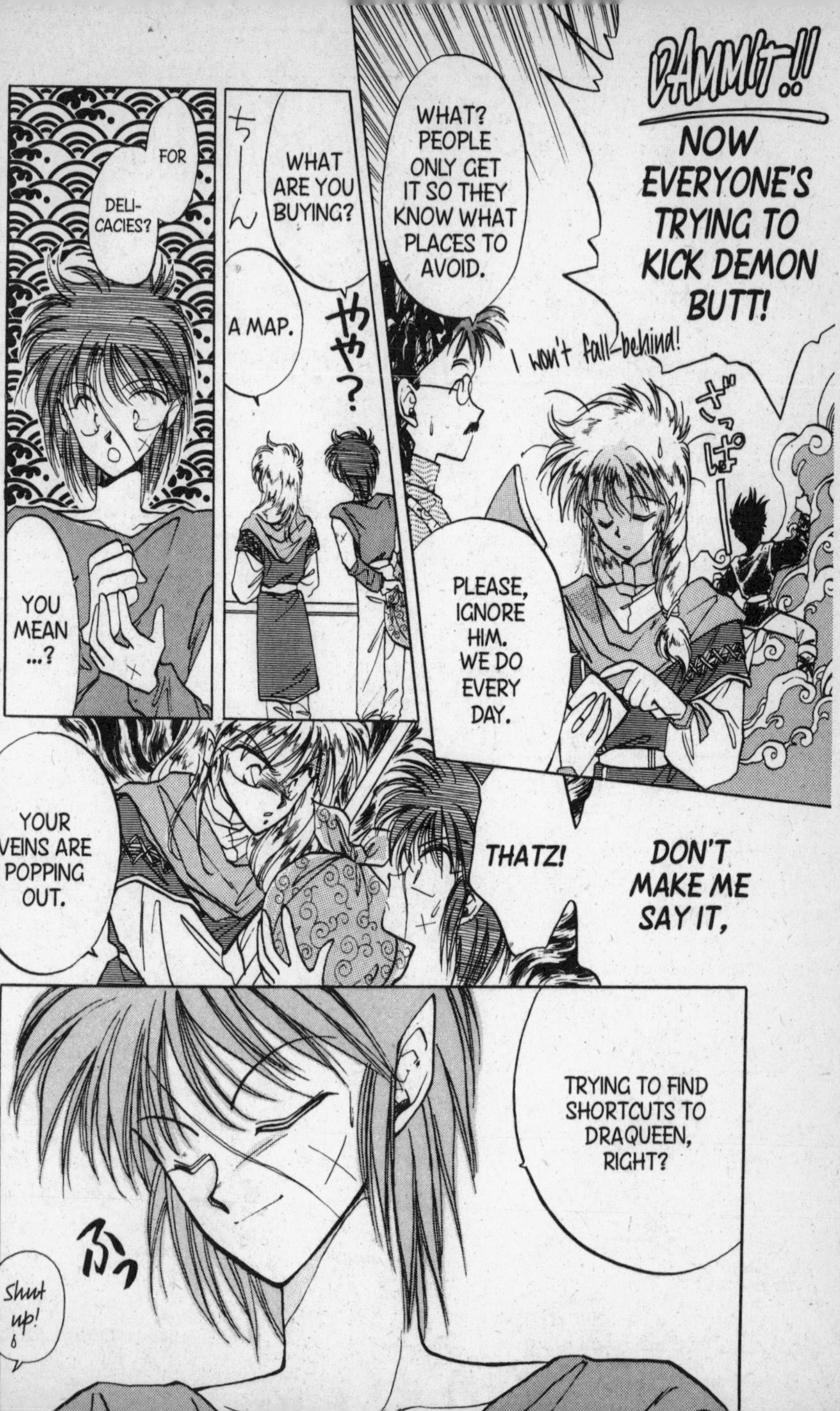
DAMMIT!!
NOW EVERYONE'S TRYING TO KICK DEMON BUTT!
I won't fall behind!
ざっぱー
WHAT? PEOPLE ONLY GET IT SO THEY KNOW WHAT PLACES TO AVOID.
PLEASE, IGNORE HIM. WE DO EVERY DAY.
ちーん
WHAT ARE YOU BUYING?
A MAP.
やや？
FOR DELI-CACIES?
YOU MEAN ...?
DON'T MAKE ME SAY IT,
THATZ!
YOUR VEINS ARE POPPING OUT.
TRYING TO FIND SHORTCUTS TO DRAQUEEN, RIGHT?
ふっ
Shut up!

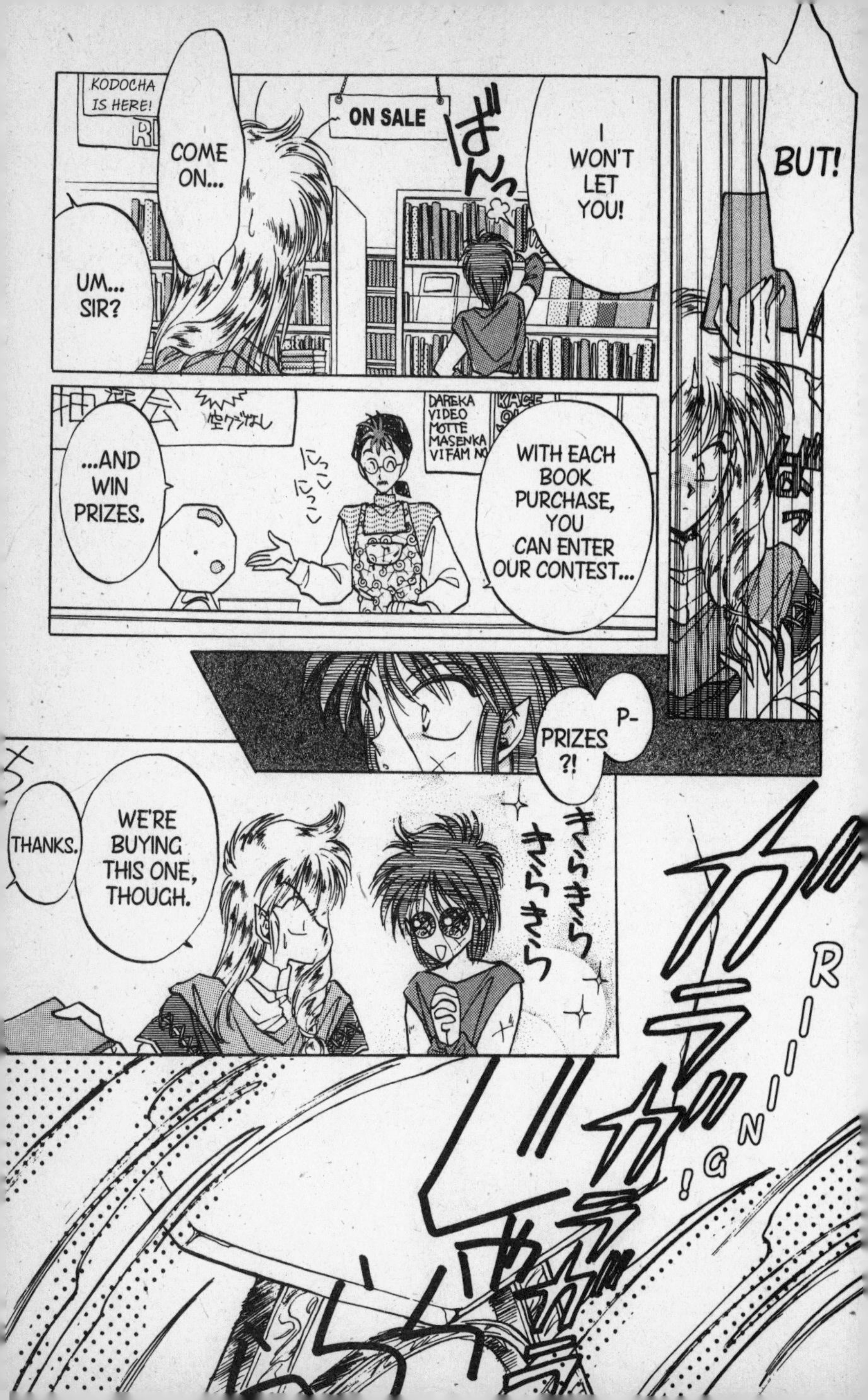
BUT!
ばっ
ばんっ
I WON'T LET YOU!
ON SALE
KODOCHA IS HERE!
COME ON...
UM... SIR?
WITH EACH BOOK PURCHASE, YOU CAN ENTER OUR CONTEST...
DAREKA VIDEO MOTTE MASENKA VIFAM NO
にっこにっこ
...AND WIN PRIZES.
P- PRIZES?!
きらきらきらきら
WE'RE BUYING THIS ONE, THOUGH.
THANKS.
RIIIING!

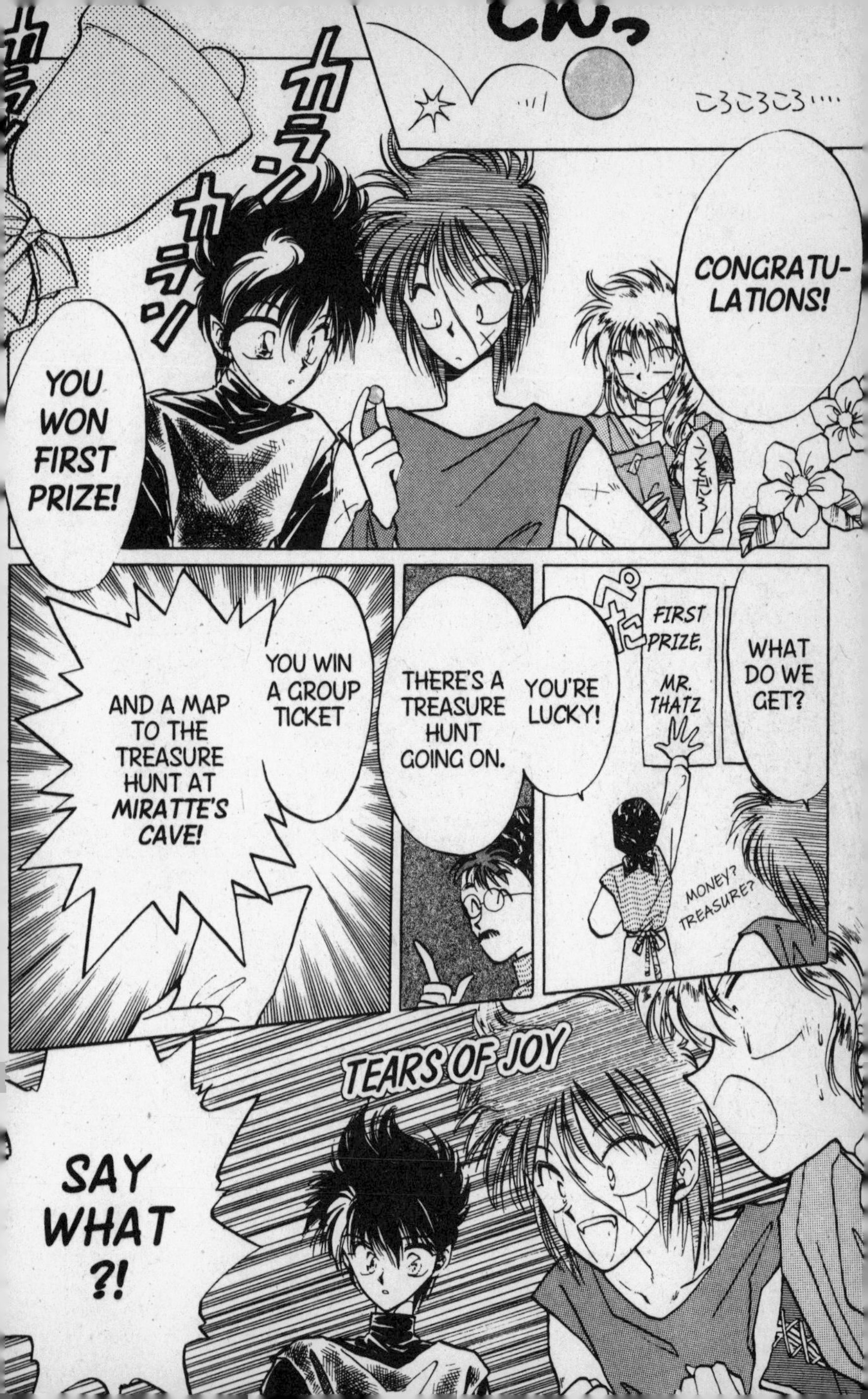
ころころころ…
カラーン カラーン
CONGRATU-LATIONS!
YOU WON FIRST PRIZE!
WHAT DO WE GET?
MONEY? TREASURE?
FIRST PRIZE, MR. THATZ
ぺた
YOU'RE LUCKY!
THERE'S A TREASURE HUNT GOING ON.
YOU WIN A GROUP TICKET
AND A MAP TO THE TREASURE HUNT AT MIRATTE'S CAVE!
TEARS OF JOY
SAY WHAT ?!

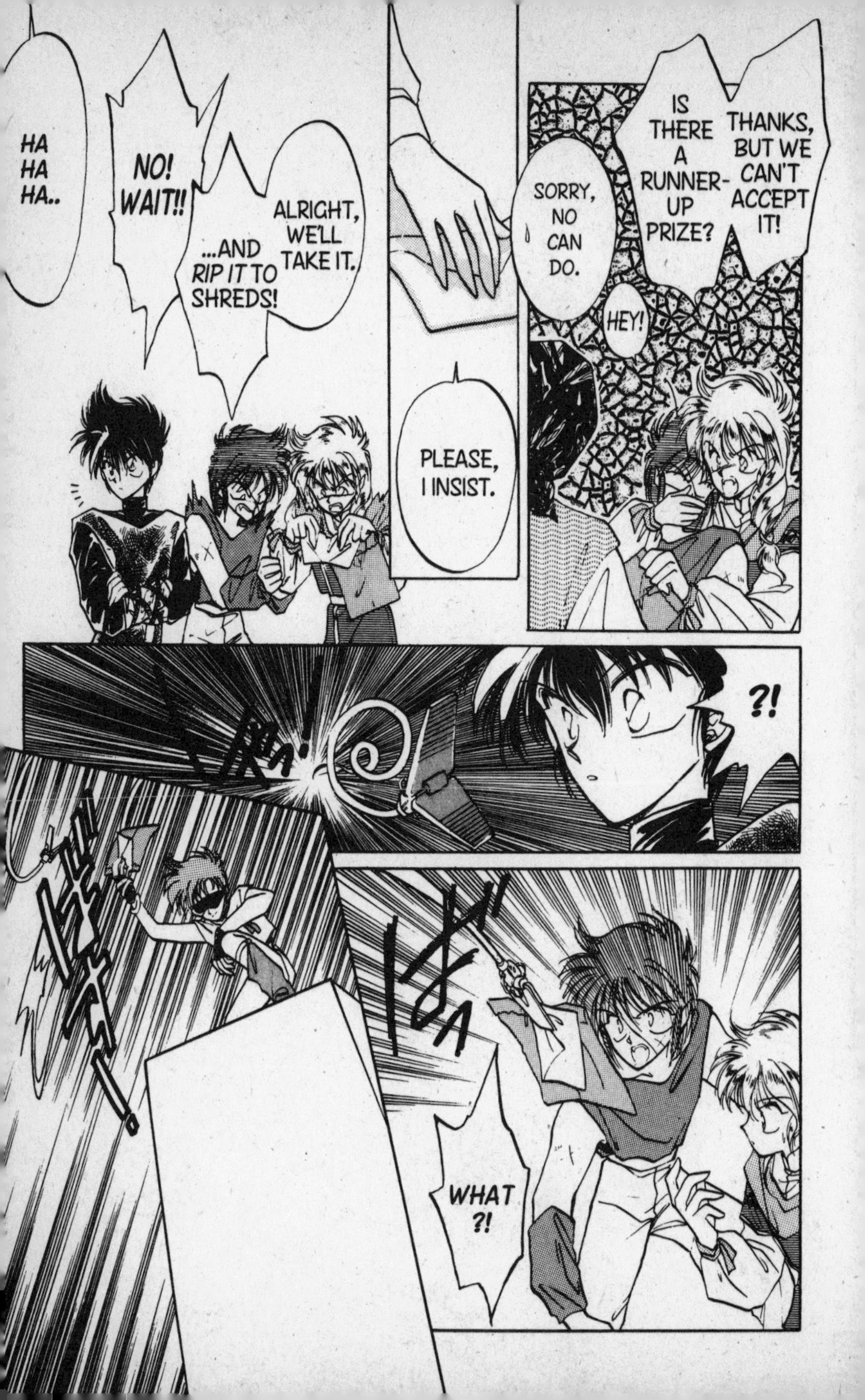
THANKS, BUT WE CAN'T ACCEPT IT!
IS THERE A RUNNER-UP PRIZE?
SORRY, NO CAN DO.
HEY!
PLEASE, I INSIST.
ALRIGHT, WE'LL TAKE IT.
...AND RIP IT TO SHREDS!
NO! WAIT!!
HA HA HA..
?!
WHAT ?!

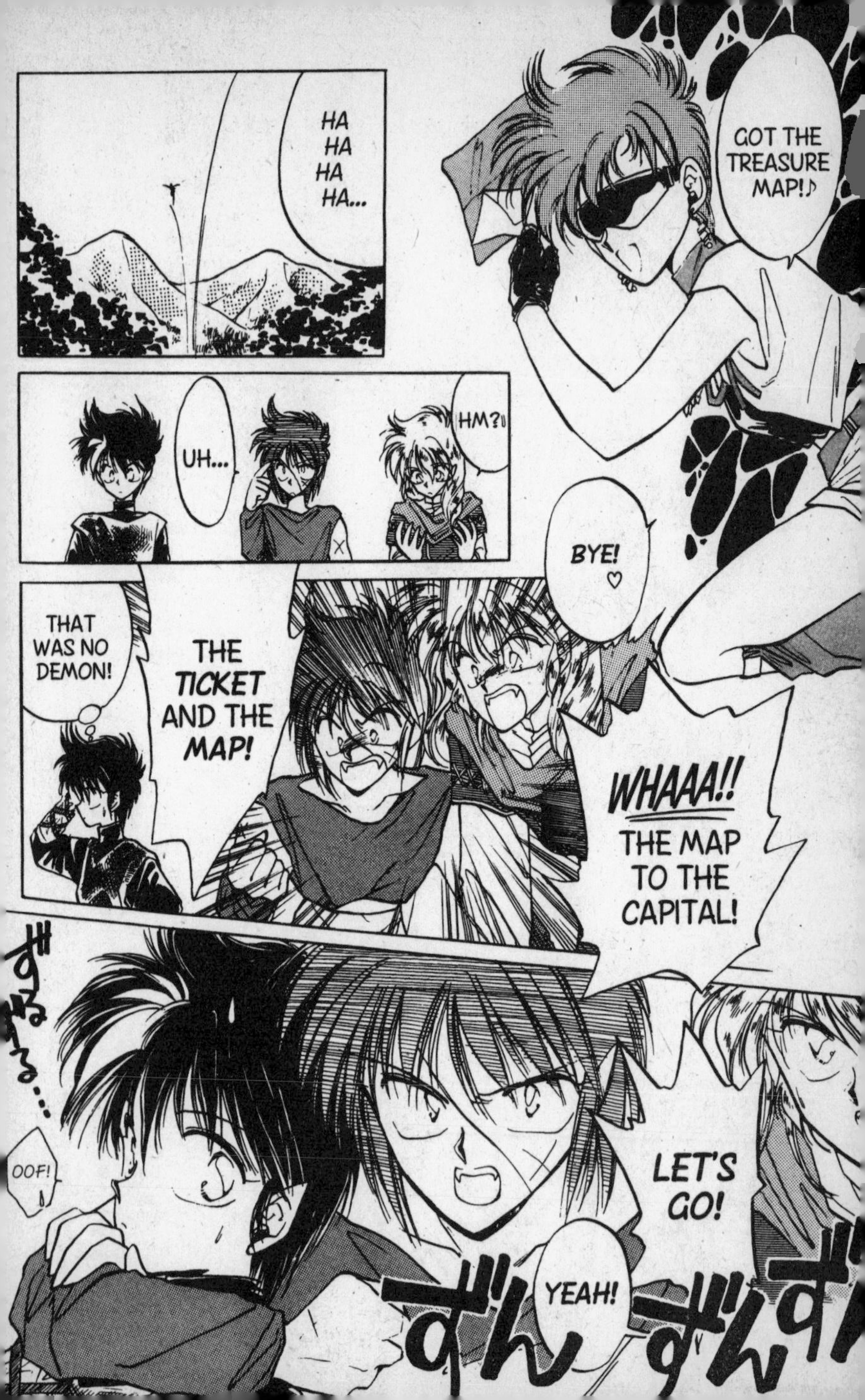
GOT THE TREASURE MAP!♪
BYE! ♡
HA HA HA HA...
HM?!
UH...
WHAAA!! THE MAP TO THE CAPITAL!
THE TICKET AND THE MAP!
THAT WAS NO DEMON!
LET'S GO!
YEAH!
OOF!
ずん ずん ず

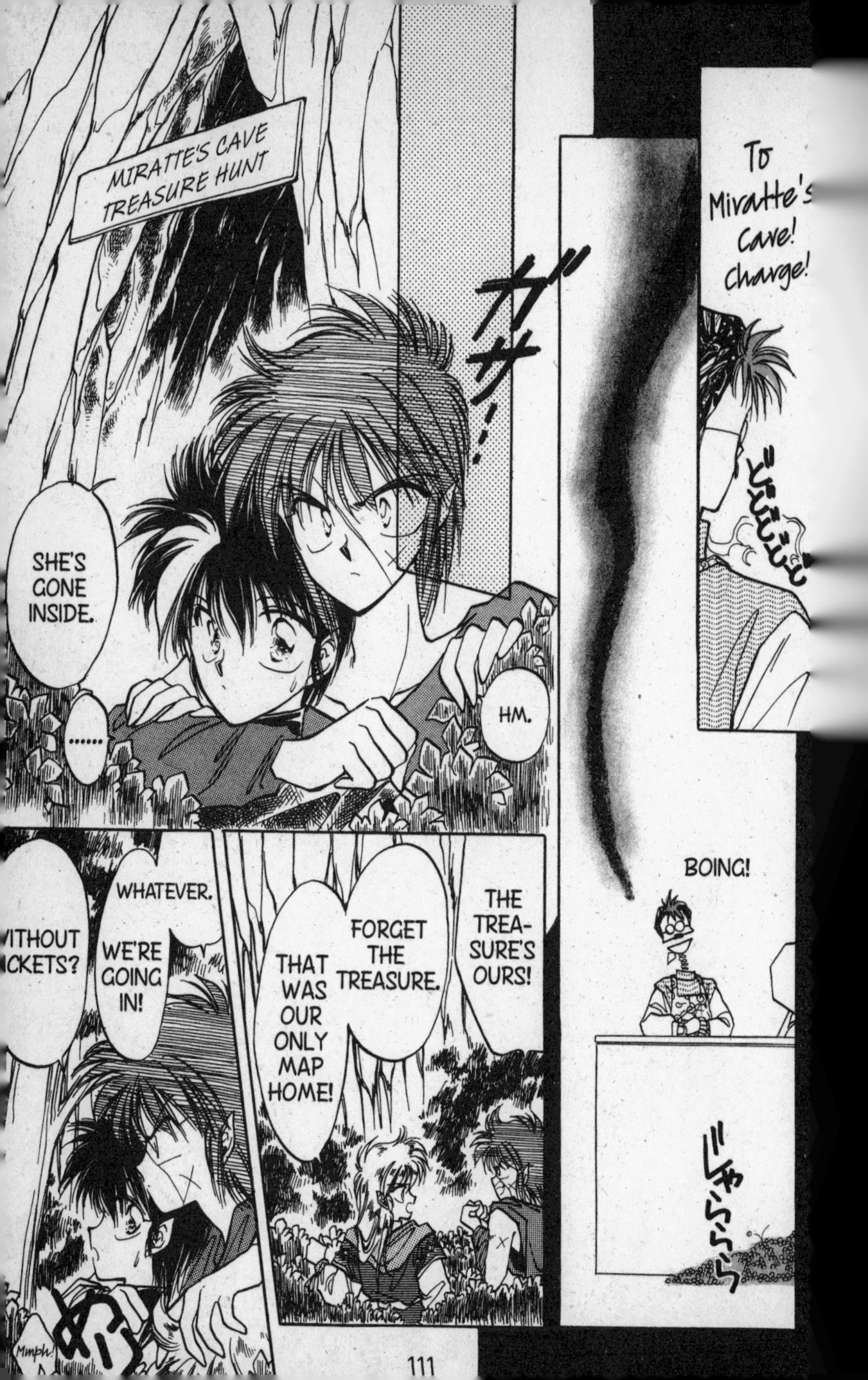
To Miratte's Cave! Charge!
どどどど
BOING!
じゃららら
MIRATTE'S CAVE TREASURE HUNT
ガサ
SHE'S GONE INSIDE.
......
HM.
THE TREA-SURE'S OURS!
FORGET THE TREASURE.
THAT WAS OUR ONLY MAP HOME!
WHATEVER.
WE'RE GOING IN!
ITHOUT CKETS?
Mmph!

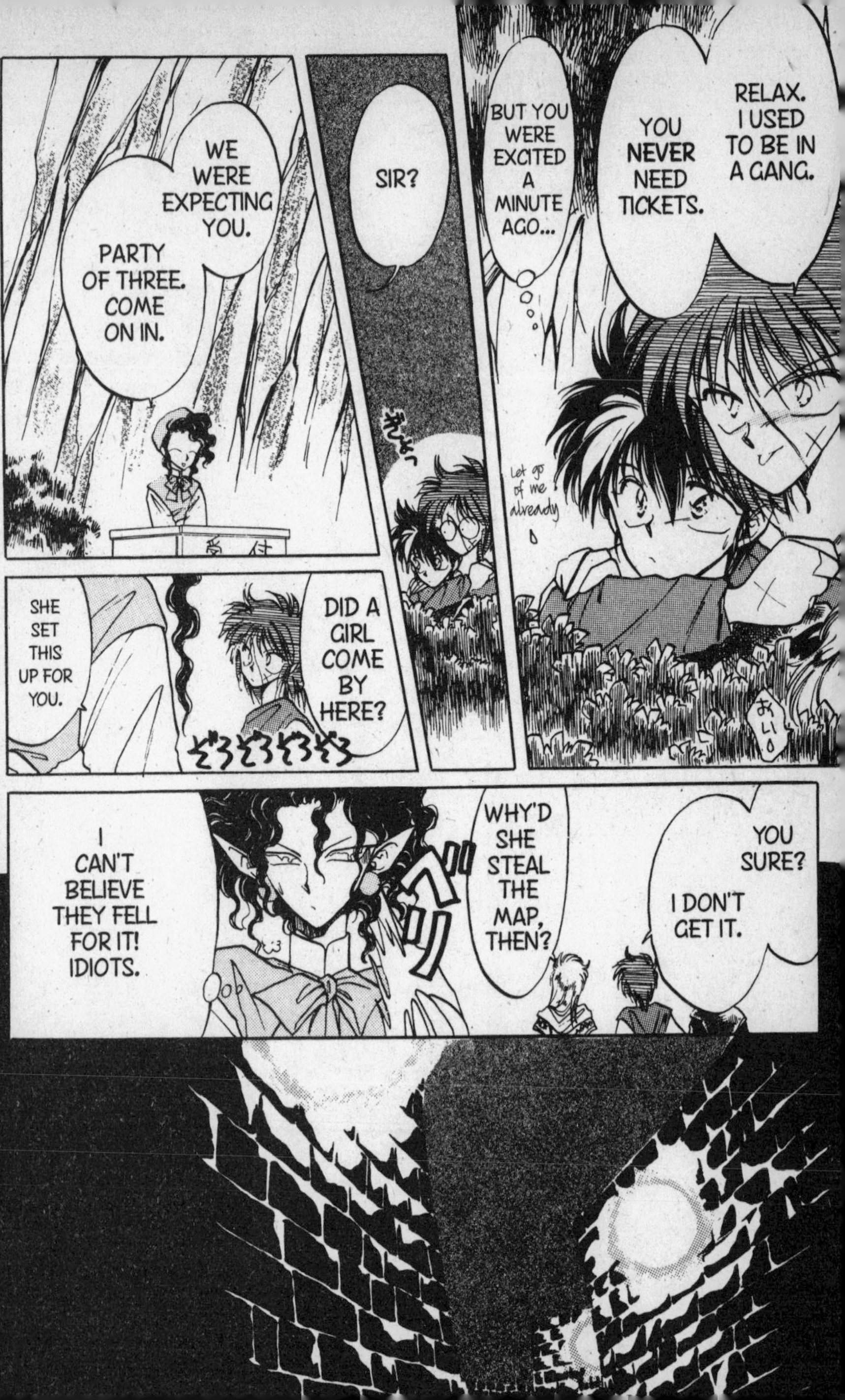

RELAX. I USED TO BE IN A GANG.
YOU NEVER NEED TICKETS.
BUT YOU WERE EXCITED A MINUTE AGO...
Let go of me already
おい
SIR?
ぎょっ
WE WERE EXPECTING YOU.
PARTY OF THREE. COME ON IN.
DID A GIRL COME BY HERE?
SHE SET THIS UP FOR YOU.
YOU SURE?
I DON'T GET IT.
WHY'D SHE STEAL THE MAP, THEN?
I CAN'T BELIEVE THEY FELL FOR IT! IDIOTS.

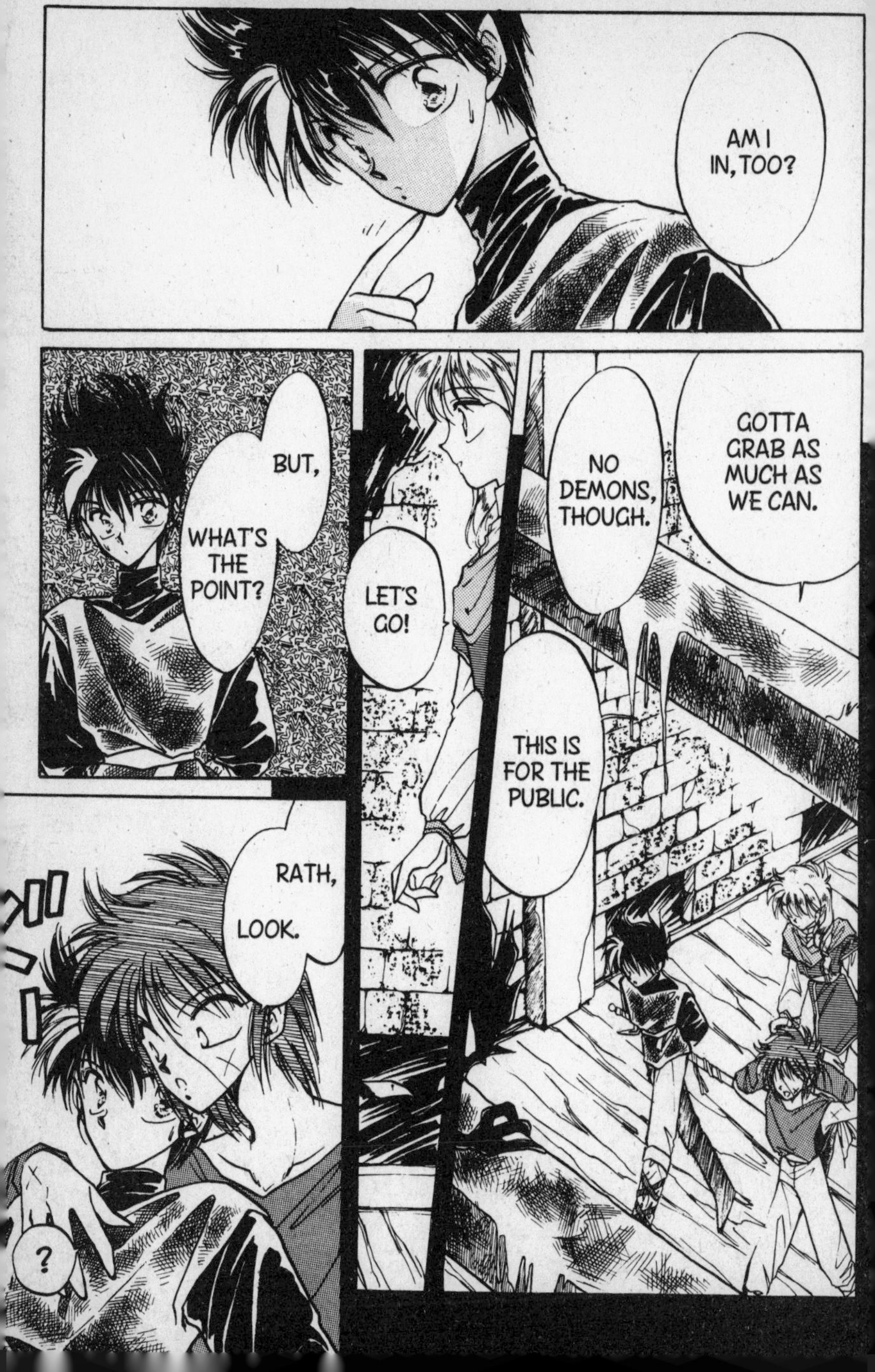
AM I IN, TOO?
GOTTA GRAB AS MUCH AS WE CAN.
NO DEMONS, THOUGH.
THIS IS FOR THE PUBLIC.
LET'S GO!
BUT, WHAT'S THE POINT?
RATH, LOOK.
?

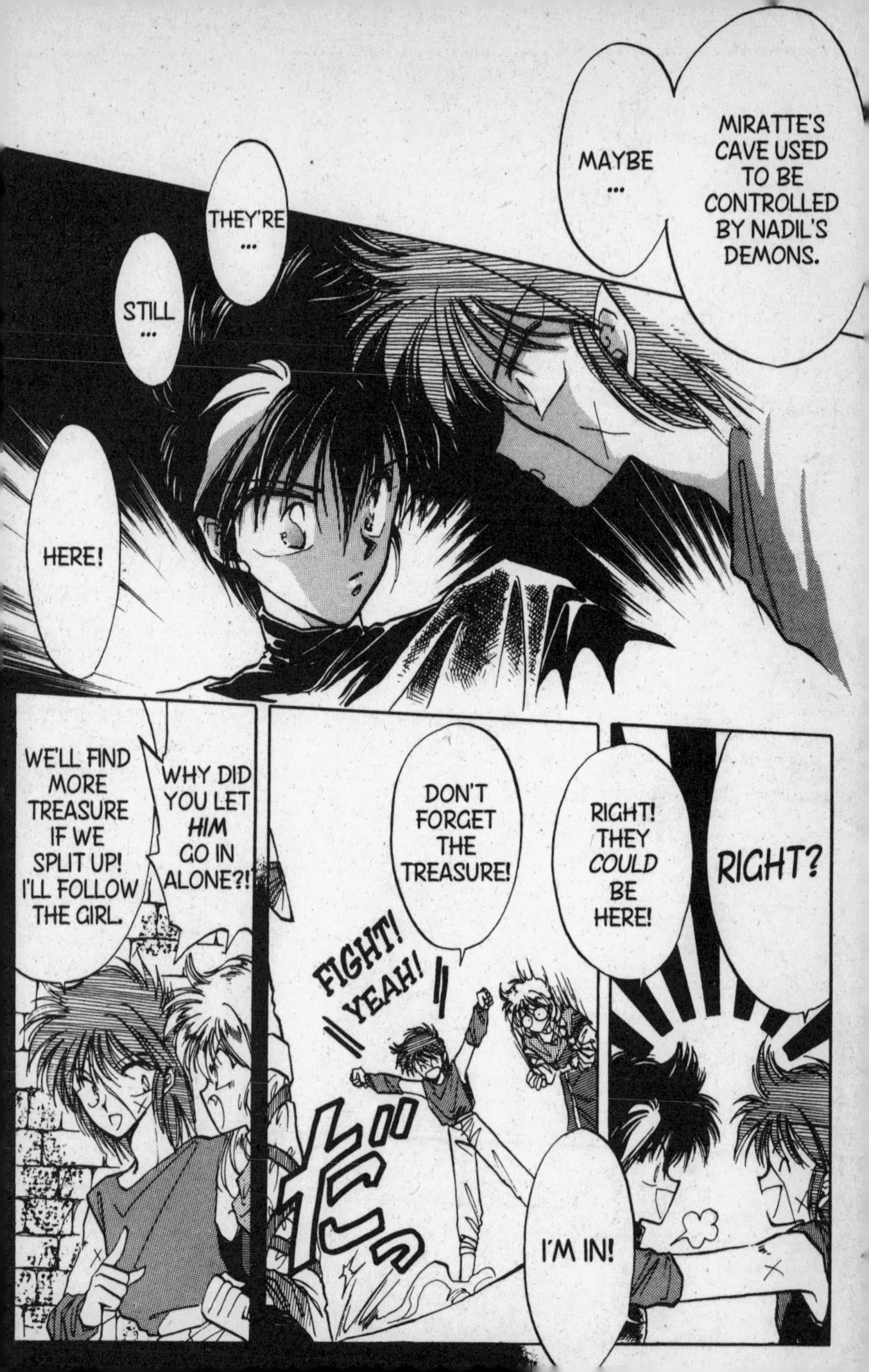
MIRATTE'S CAVE USED TO BE CONTROLLED BY NADIL'S DEMONS.
MAYBE ...
THEY'RE ...
STILL ...
HERE!
RIGHT?
RIGHT! THEY COULD BE HERE!
I'M IN!
DON'T FORGET THE TREASURE!
FIGHT! YEAH!
WHY DID YOU LET HIM GO IN ALONE?!
WE'LL FIND MORE TREASURE IF WE SPLIT UP! I'LL FOLLOW THE GIRL.

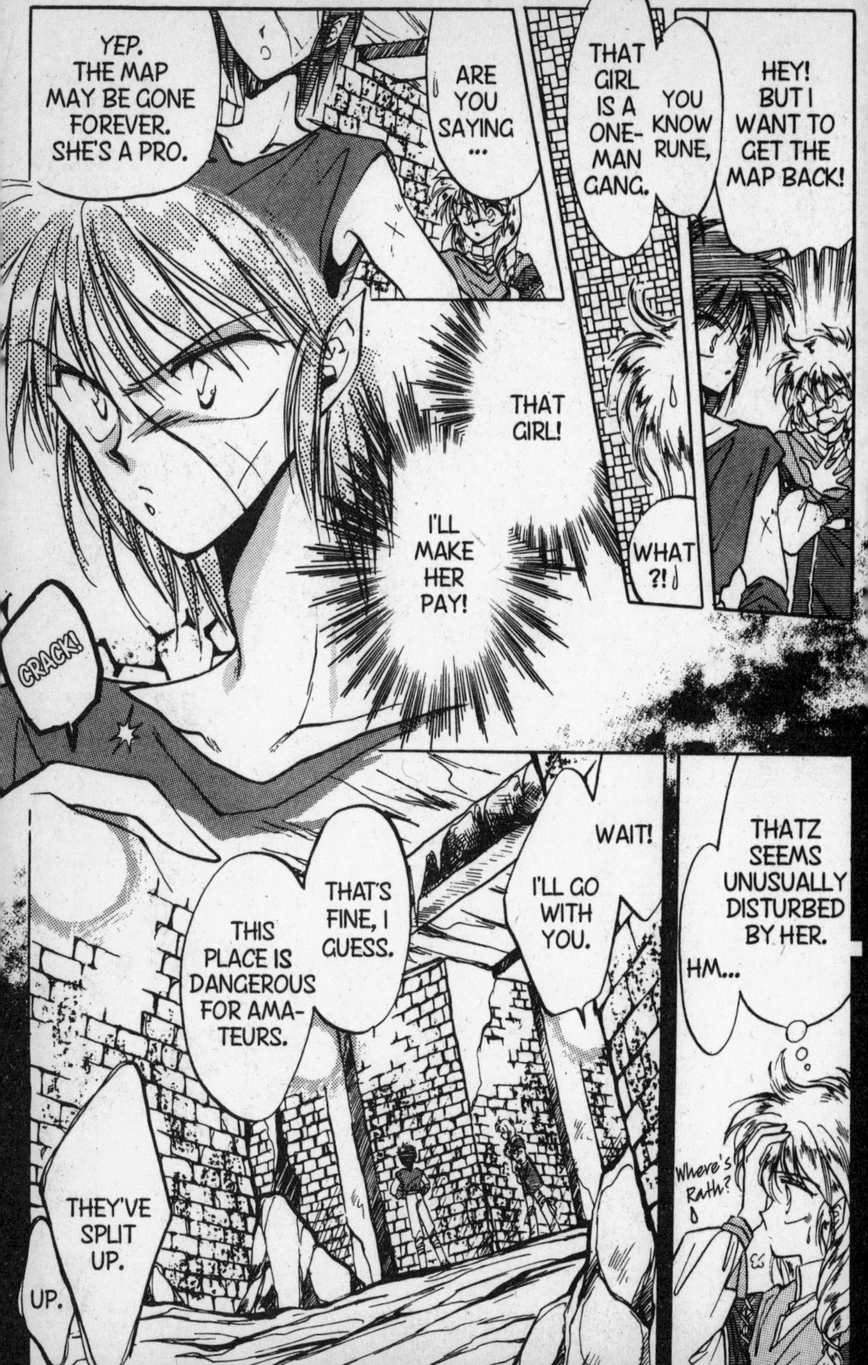
HEY! BUT I WANT TO GET THE MAP BACK!
YOU KNOW RUNE,
THAT GIRL IS A ONE-MAN GANG.
WHAT?!
ARE YOU SAYING...
YEP. THE MAP MAY BE GONE FOREVER. SHE'S A PRO.
THAT GIRL!
I'LL MAKE HER PAY!
CRACK!
THATZ SEEMS UNUSUALLY DISTURBED BY HER.
HM...
Where's Rath?
WAIT!
I'LL GO WITH YOU.
THAT'S FINE, I GUESS.
THIS PLACE IS DANGEROUS FOR AMA-TEURS.
THEY'VE SPLIT UP.
UP.

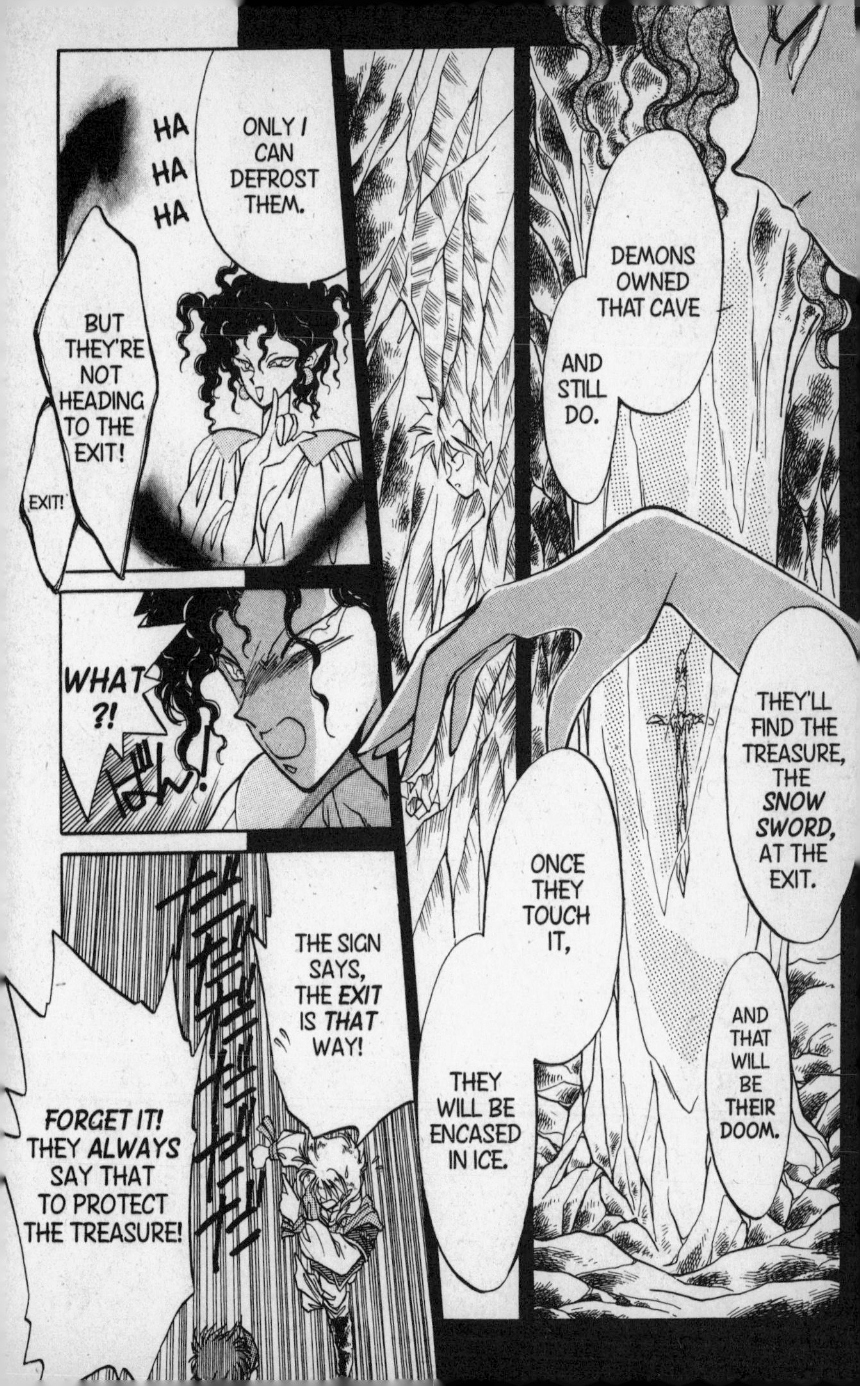

DEMONS OWNED THAT CAVE
AND STILL DO.
THEY'LL FIND THE TREASURE, THE *SNOW SWORD,* AT THE EXIT.
ONCE THEY TOUCH IT,
THEY WILL BE ENCASED IN ICE.
AND THAT WILL BE THEIR DOOM.
ONLY I CAN DEFROST THEM.
HA HA HA
BUT THEY'RE NOT HEADING TO THE EXIT!
EXIT!
WHAT?!
ばん!
THE SIGN SAYS, THE *EXIT* IS *THAT* WAY!
FORGET IT! THEY *ALWAYS* SAY THAT TO PROTECT THE TREASURE!

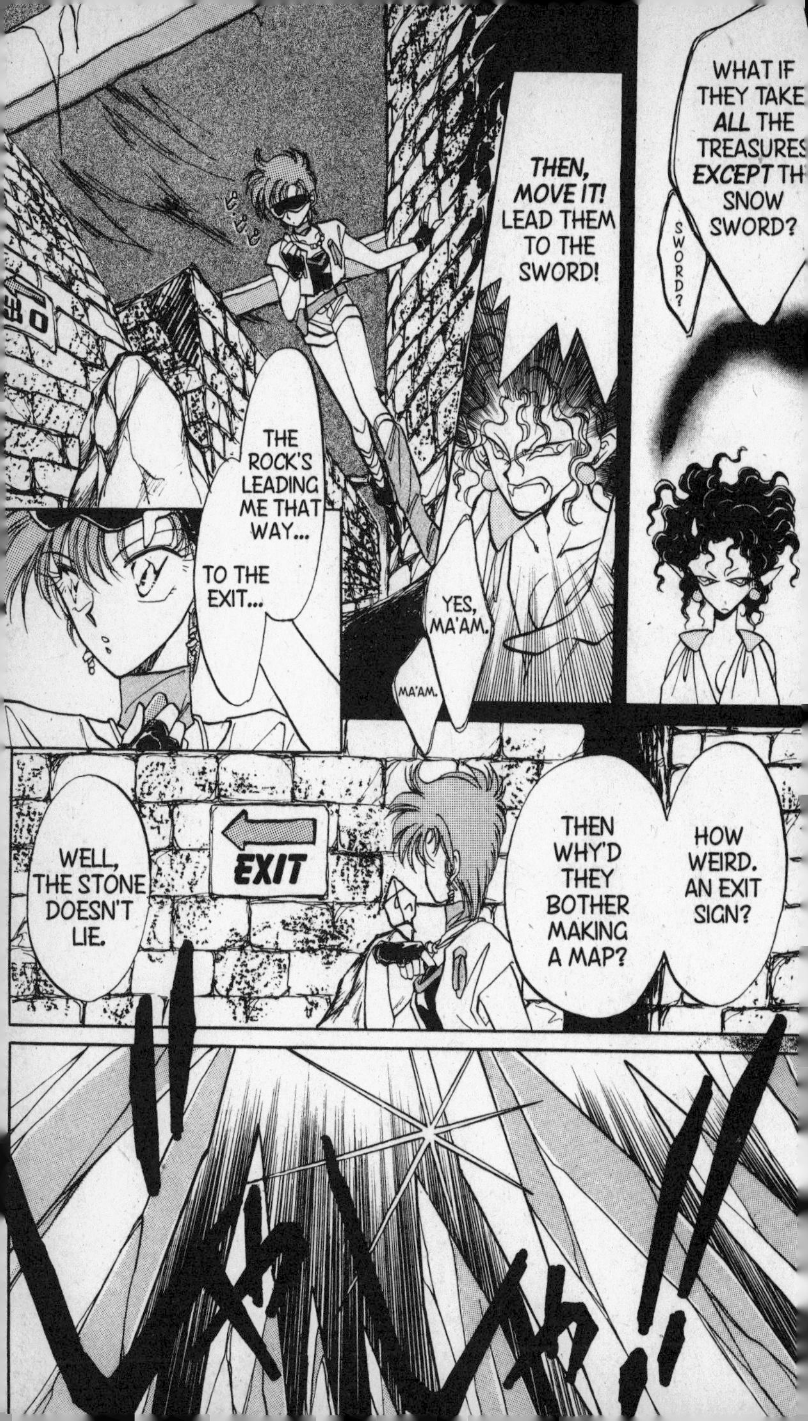
WHAT IF THEY TAKE ALL THE TREASURES EXCEPT TH SNOW SWORD?
SWORD?
THEN, MOVE IT! LEAD THEM TO THE SWORD!
YES, MA'AM.
MA'AM.
THE ROCK'S LEADING ME THAT WAY...
TO THE EXIT...
HOW WEIRD. AN EXIT SIGN?
THEN WHY'D THEY BOTHER MAKING A MAP?
EXIT
WELL, THE STONE DOESN'T LIE.

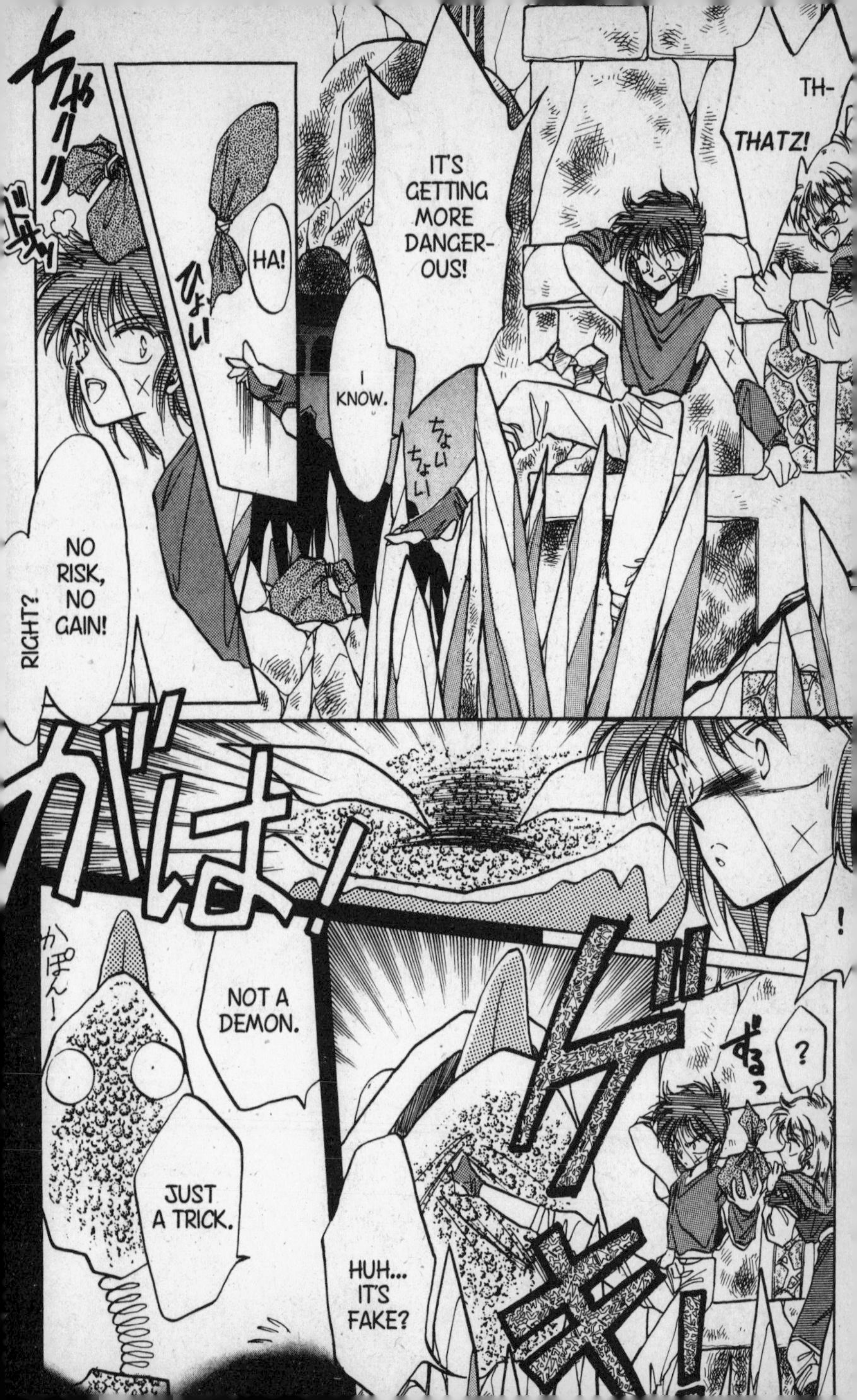
TH-
THATZ!
IT'S GETTING MORE DANGER-OUS!
I KNOW.
ちょい ちょい
ひょい
HA!
ちゃりり
NO RISK, NO GAIN!
RIGHT?
がしゃ!
!
?
ずるっ
HUH... IT'S FAKE?
かぽん!
NOT A DEMON.
JUST A TRICK.

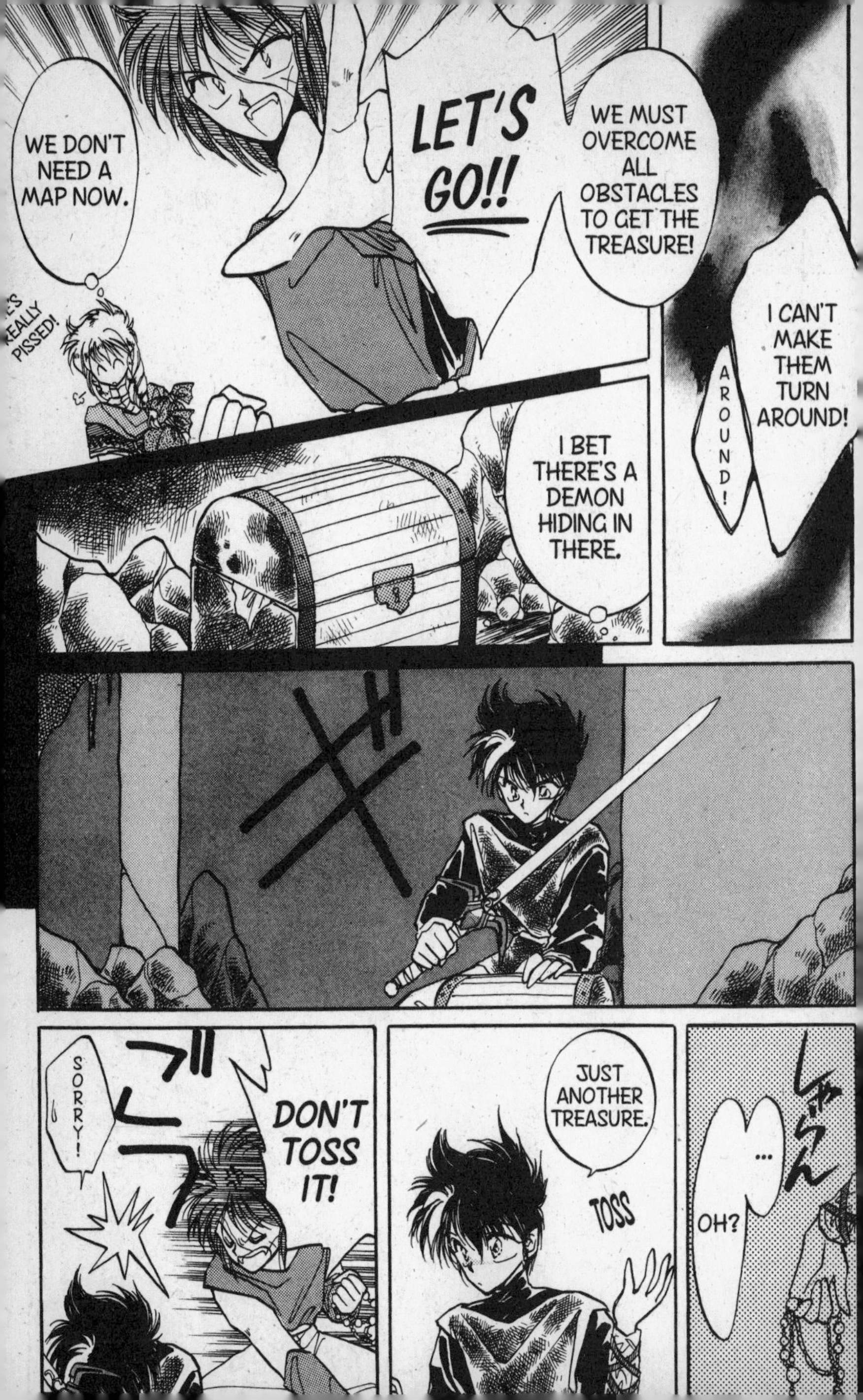
I CAN'T MAKE THEM TURN AROUND!
AROUND!
WE MUST OVERCOME ALL OBSTACLES TO GET THE TREASURE!
LET'S GO!!
WE DON'T NEED A MAP NOW.
E'S REALLY PISSED!
I BET THERE'S A DEMON HIDING IN THERE.
しゃらん
...
OH?
JUST ANOTHER TREASURE.
TOSS
DON'T TOSS IT!
SORRY!

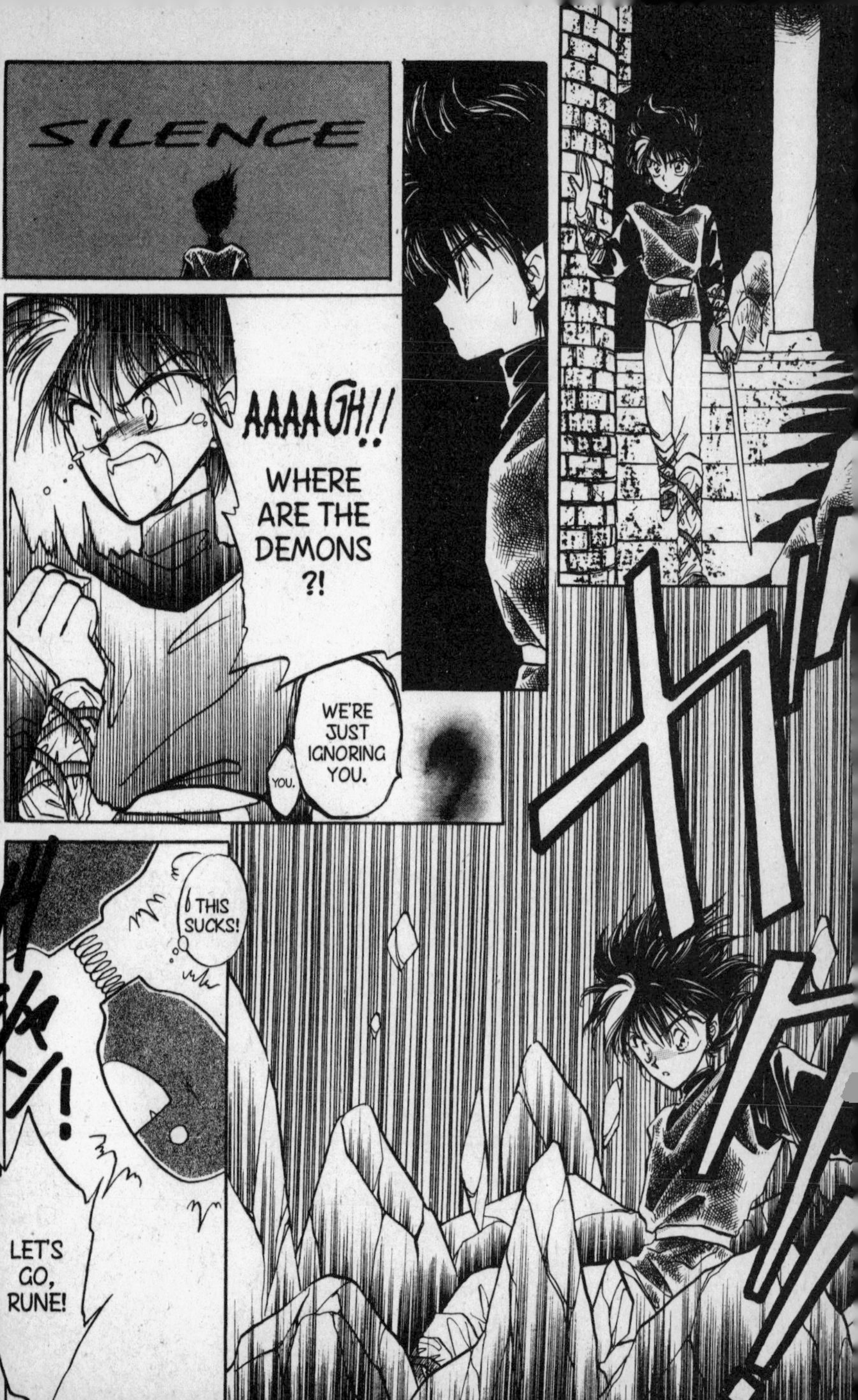
SILENCE
AAAAGH!!
WHERE ARE THE DEMONS ?!
WE'RE JUST IGNORING YOU.
YOU.
THIS SUCKS!
LET'S GO, RUNE!

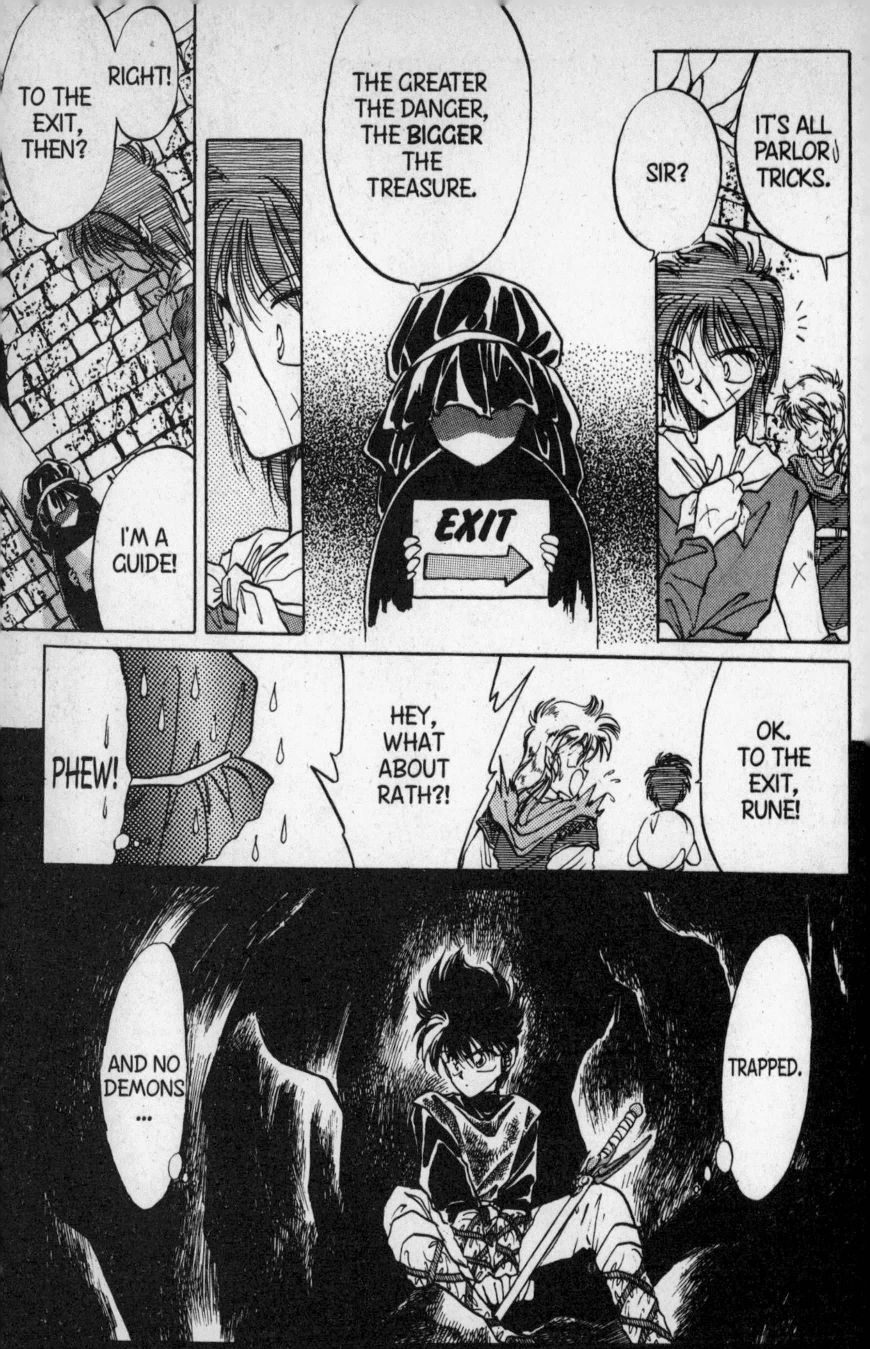
IT'S ALL PARLOR TRICKS.
SIR?
THE GREATER THE DANGER, THE BIGGER THE TREASURE.
EXIT
RIGHT!
TO THE EXIT, THEN?
I'M A GUIDE!
OK. TO THE EXIT, RUNE!
HEY, WHAT ABOUT RATH?!
PHEW!
TRAPPED.
AND NO DEMONS ...

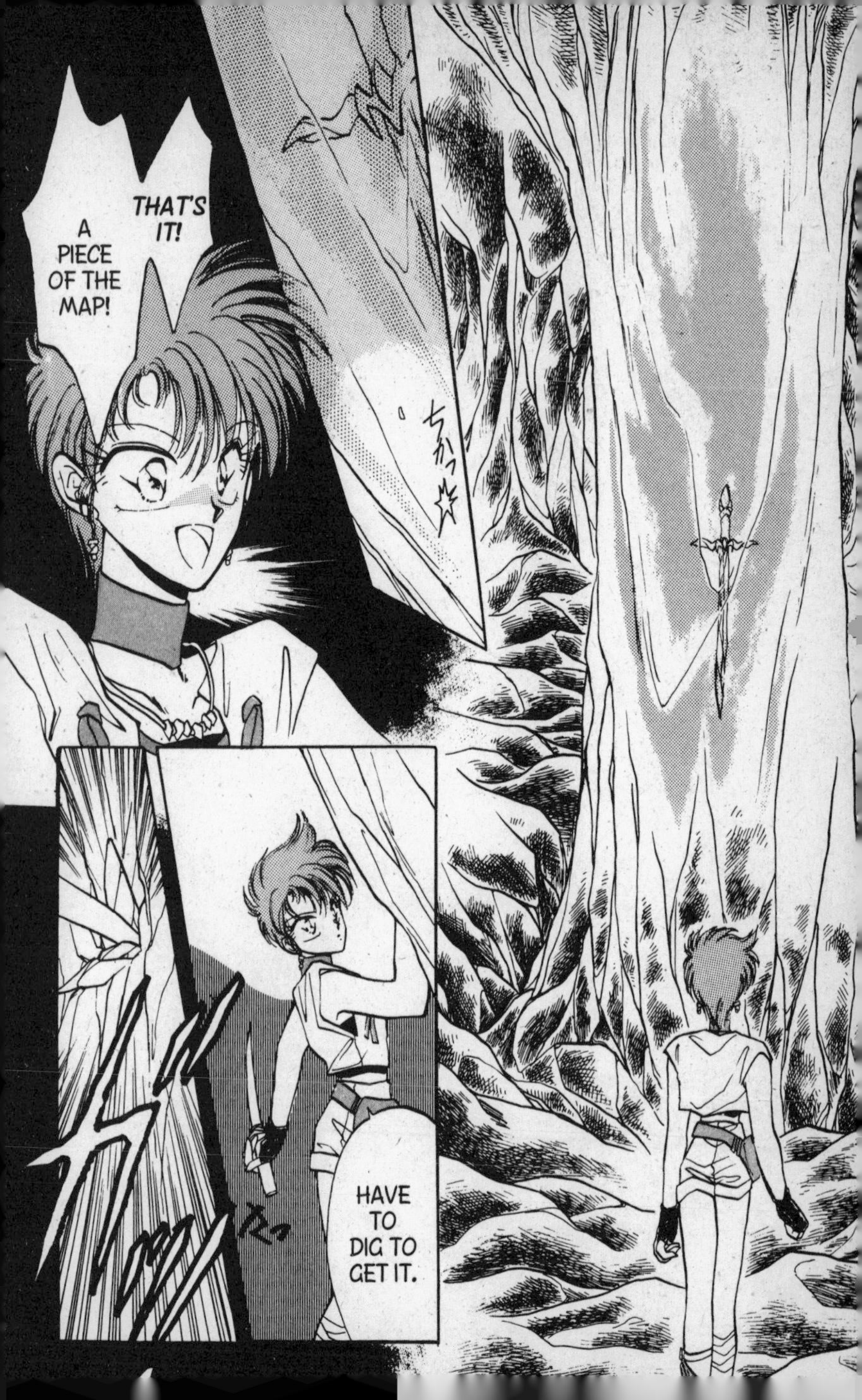
ちかっ
THAT'S IT!
A PIECE OF THE MAP!
HAVE TO DIG TO GET IT.

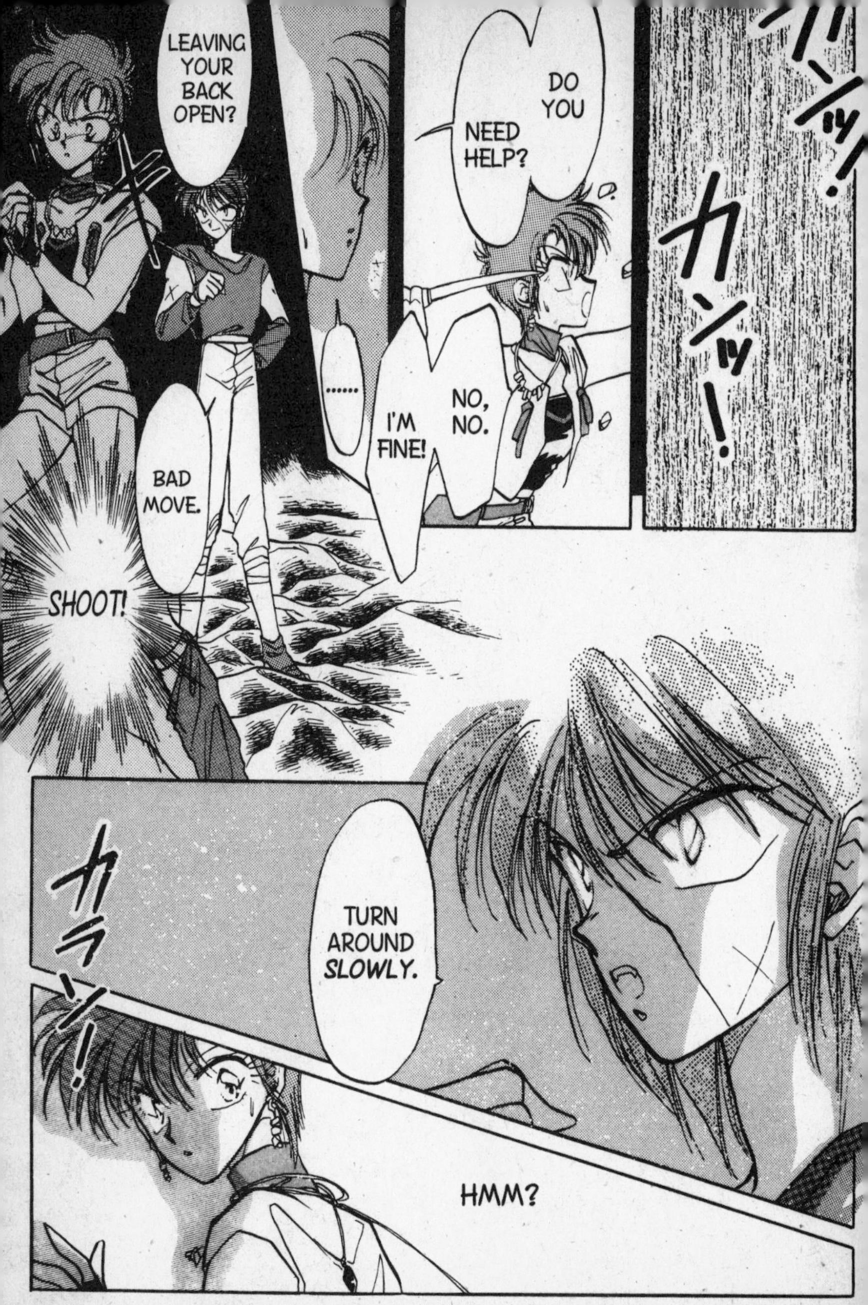
カンッー!
DO YOU NEED HELP?
NO, NO. I'M FINE!
......
LEAVING YOUR BACK OPEN?
BAD MOVE.
SHOOT!
TURN AROUND SLOWLY.
HMM?
カラン!

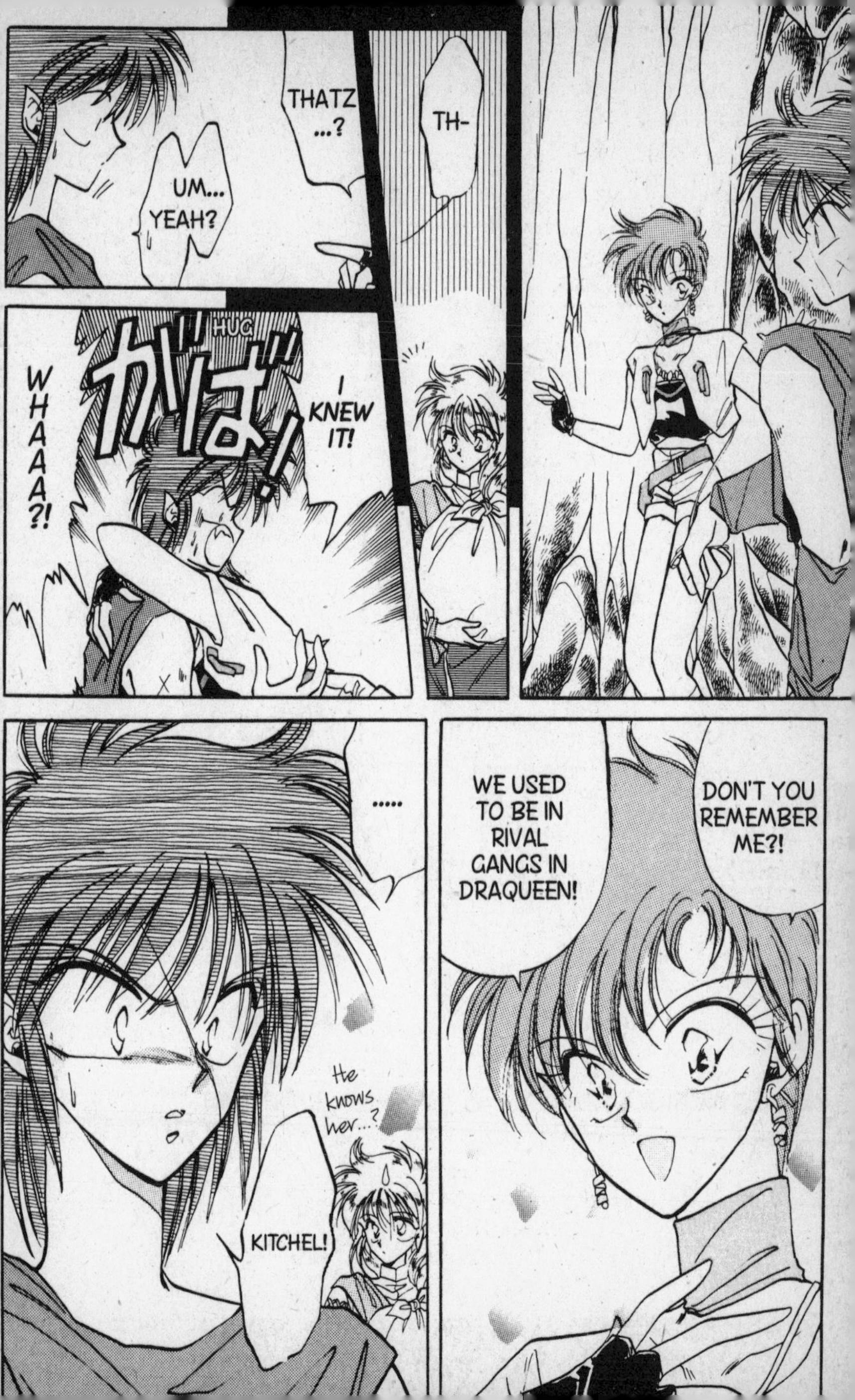
TH-
THATZ ...?
UM... YEAH?
I KNEW IT!
かば！
HUG
WHAAAA?!
DON'T YOU REMEMBER ME?!
WE USED TO BE IN RIVAL GANGS IN DRAQUEEN!
.....
He knows her...?
KITCHEL!

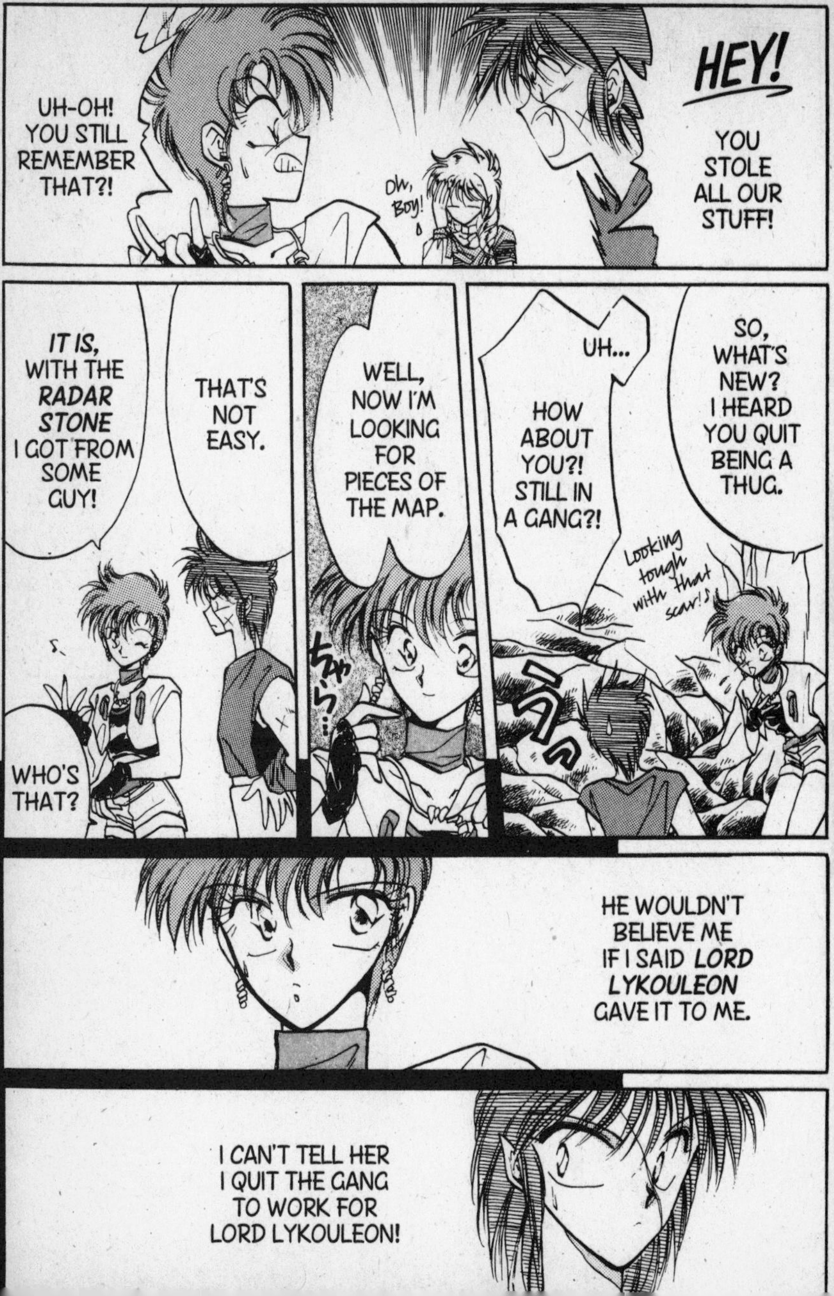
HEY!
YOU STOLE ALL OUR STUFF!
Oh, Boy!
UH-OH! YOU STILL REMEMBER THAT?!
SO, WHAT'S NEW? I HEARD YOU QUIT BEING A THUG.
UH...
HOW ABOUT YOU?! STILL IN A GANG?!
Looking tough with that scar!♪
WELL, NOW I'M LOOKING FOR PIECES OF THE MAP.
ちゃら…
THAT'S NOT EASY.
IT IS, WITH THE RADAR STONE I GOT FROM SOME GUY!
WHO'S THAT?
HE WOULDN'T BELIEVE ME IF I SAID LORD LYKOULEON GAVE IT TO ME.
I CAN'T TELL HER I QUIT THE GANG TO WORK FOR LORD LYKOULEON!

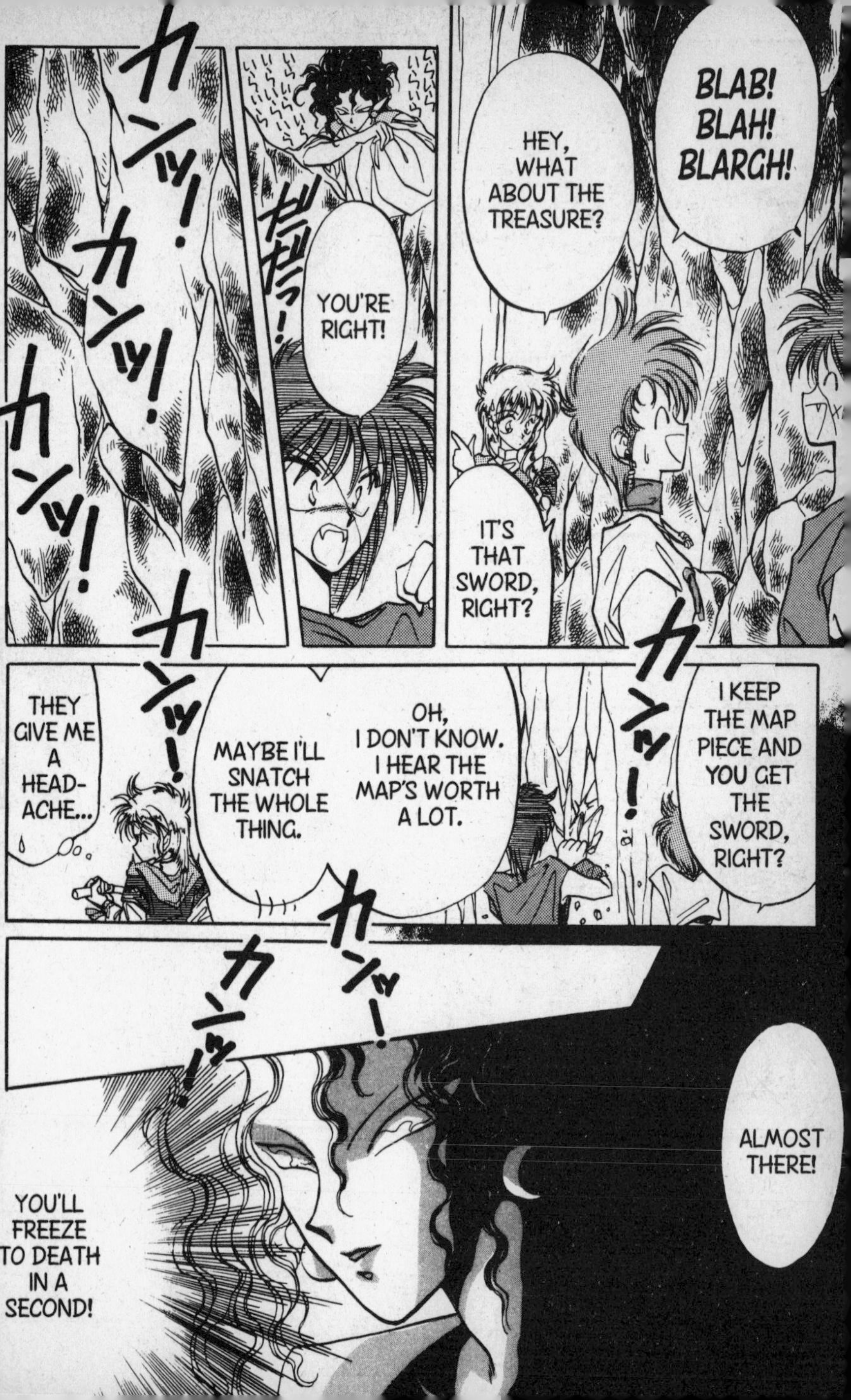
BLAB! BLAH! BLARGH!
HEY, WHAT ABOUT THE TREASURE?
IT'S THAT SWORD, RIGHT?
YOU'RE RIGHT!
カンッ! カンッ! カンッ!
I KEEP THE MAP PIECE AND YOU GET THE SWORD, RIGHT?
OH, I DON'T KNOW. I HEAR THE MAP'S WORTH A LOT.
MAYBE I'LL SNATCH THE WHOLE THING.
THEY GIVE ME A HEAD-ACHE...
ALMOST THERE!
YOU'LL FREEZE TO DEATH IN A SECOND!

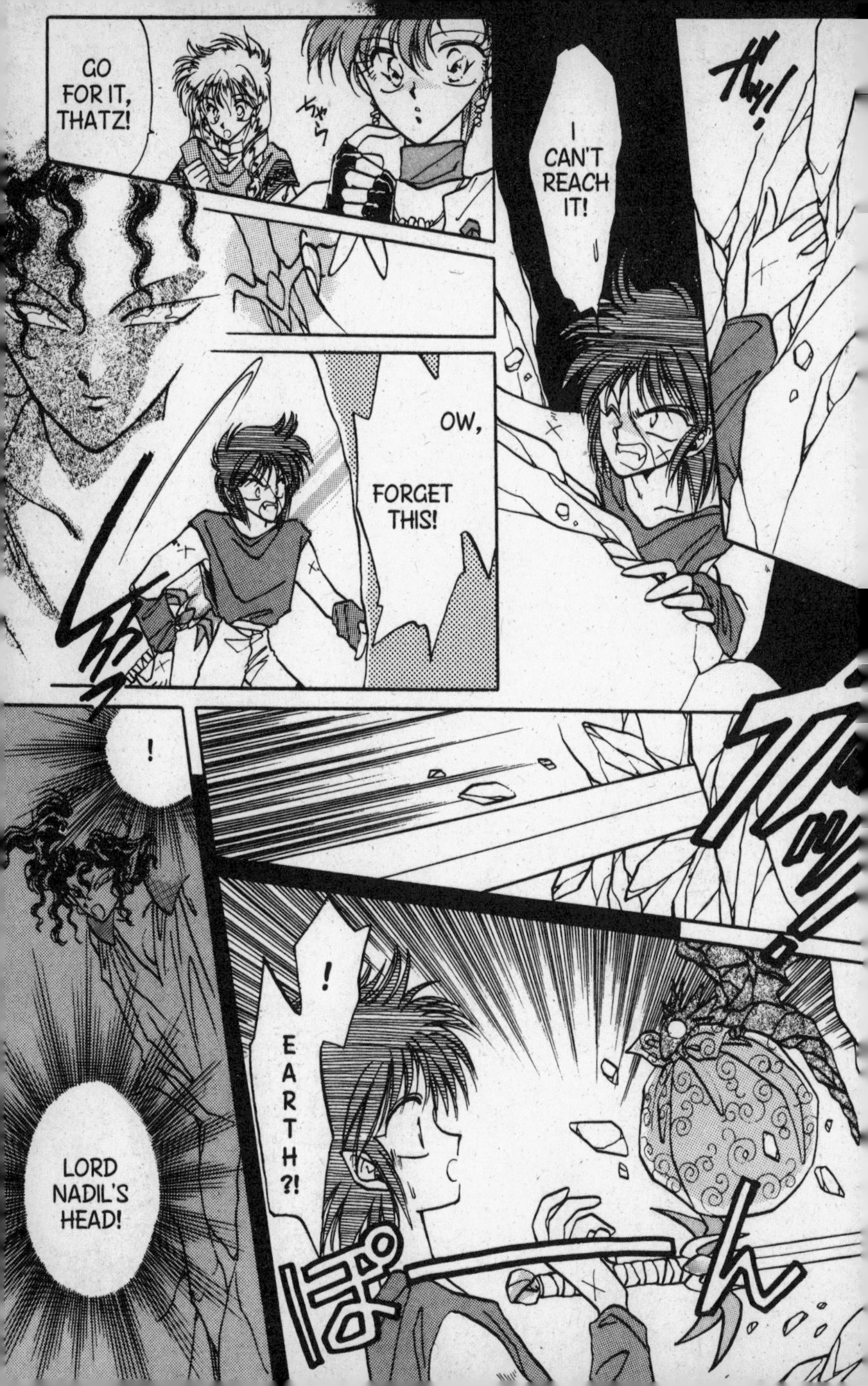
I CAN'T REACH IT!
GO FOR IT, THATZ!
OW, FORGET THIS!
!
EARTH?!
!
LORD NADIL'S HEAD!

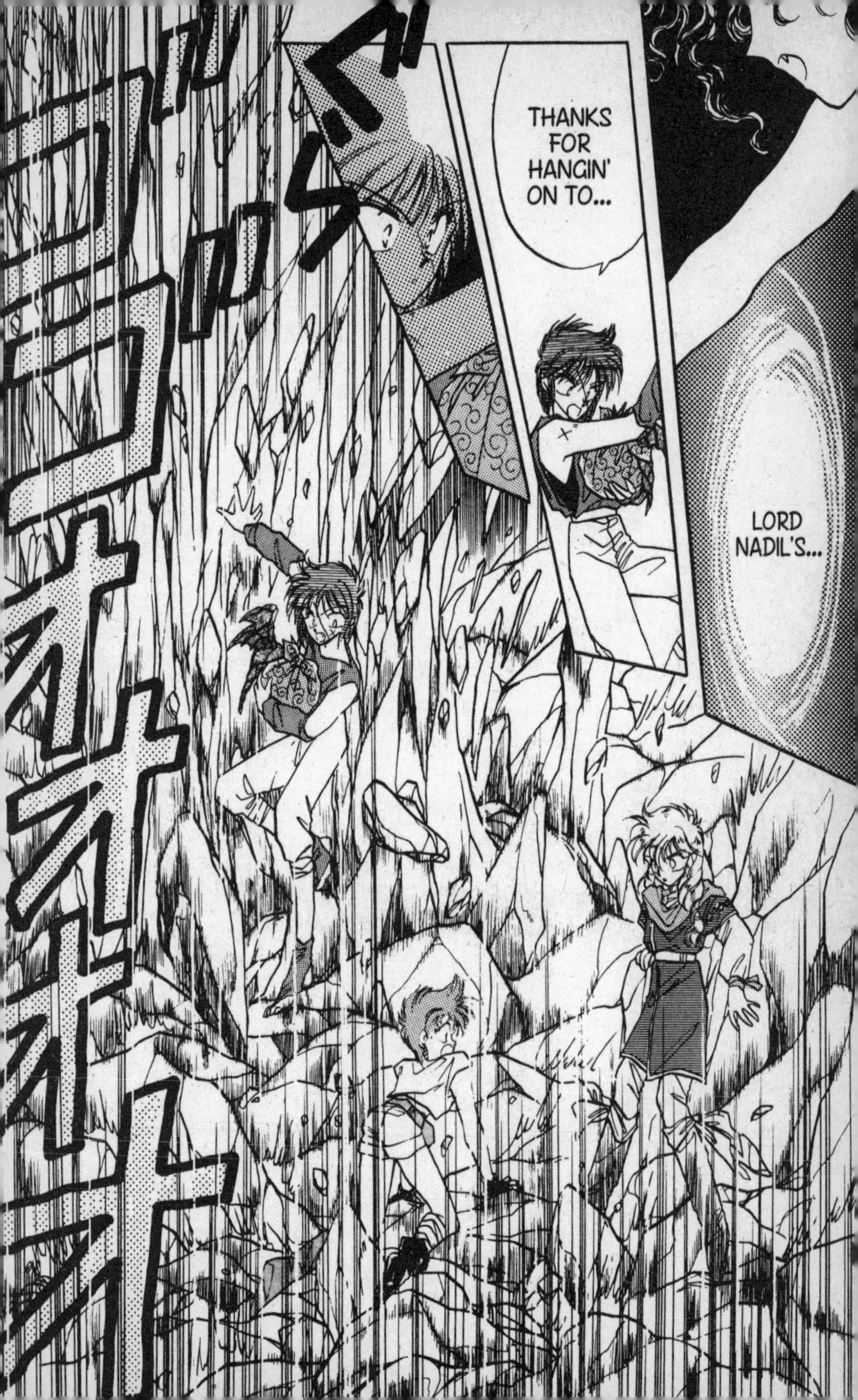
THANKS FOR HANGIN' ON TO...
LORD NADIL'S...

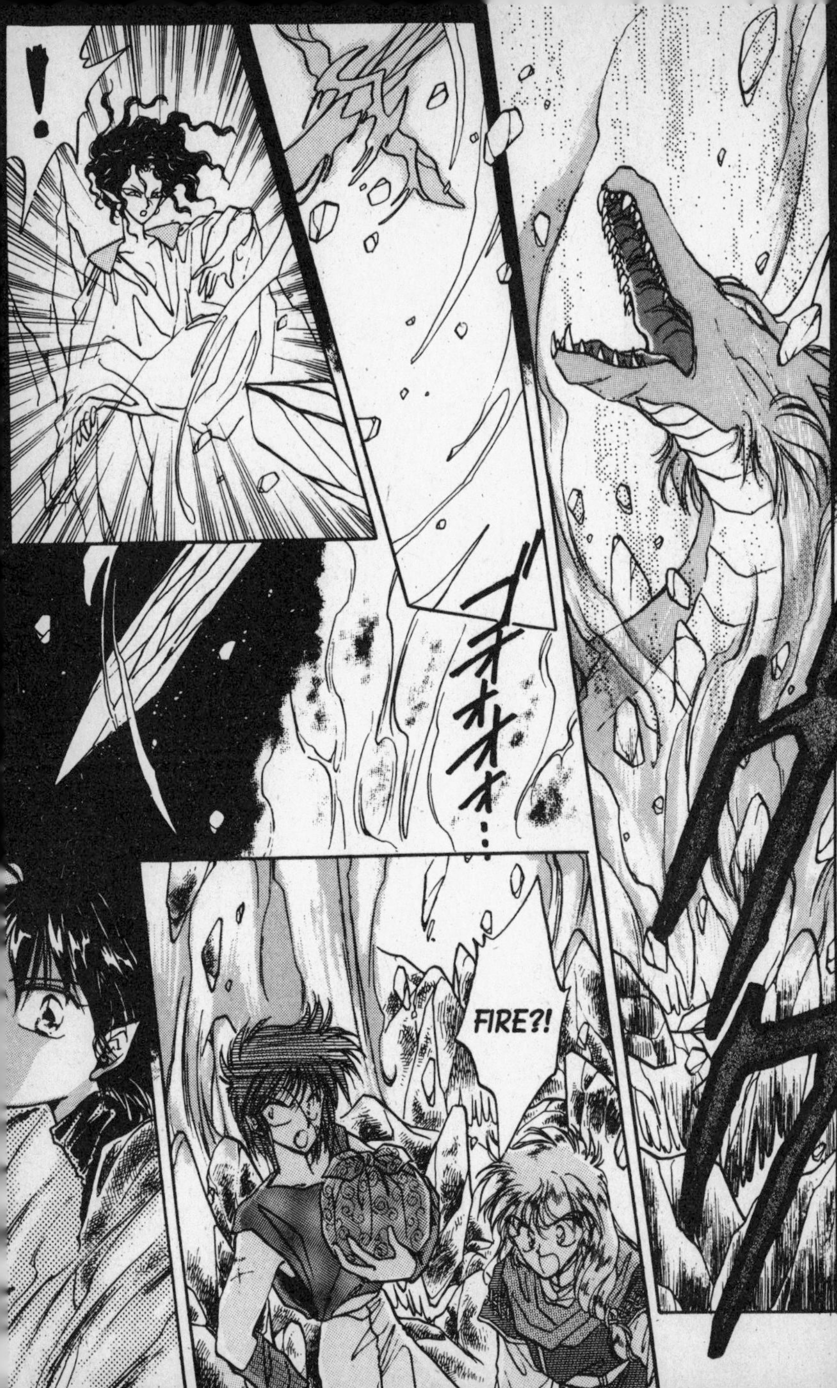

!
ゴオオオオ…
FIRE?!

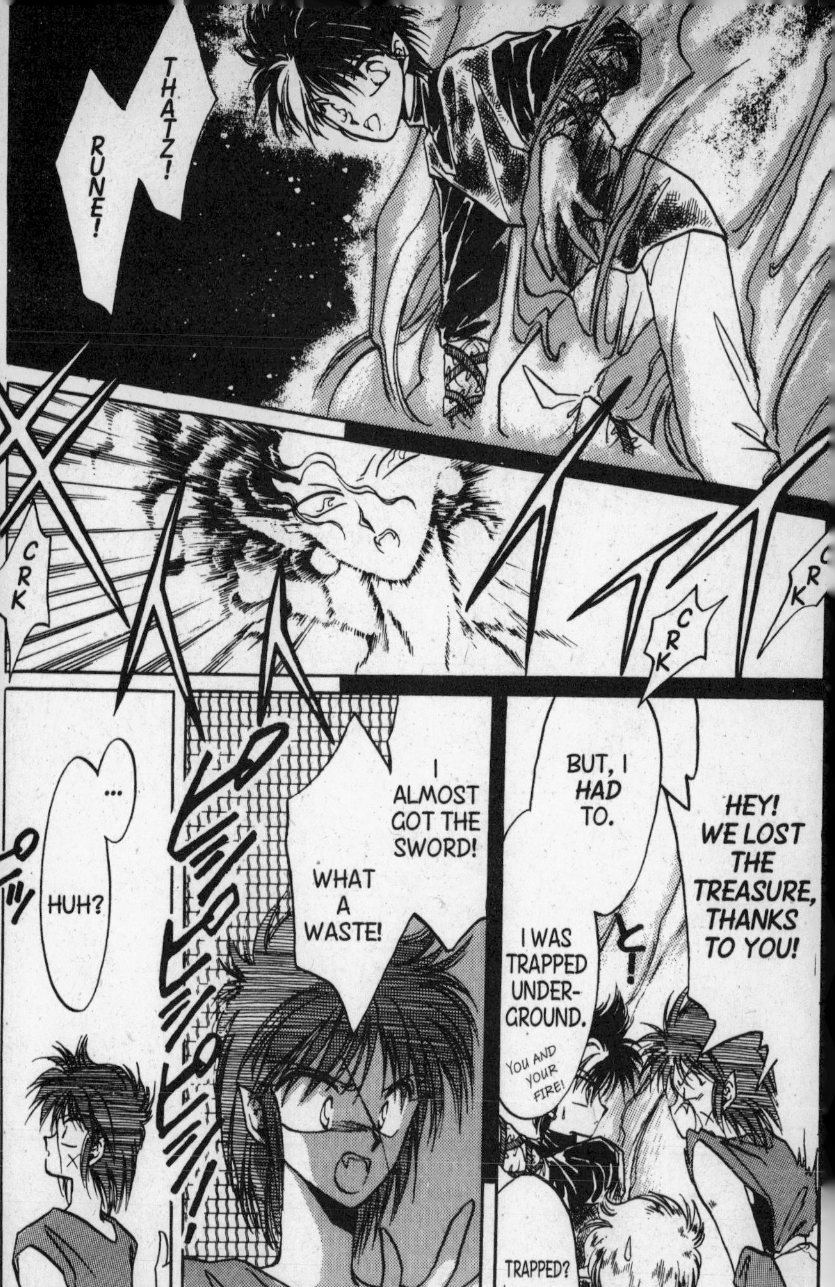
THATZ!
RUNE!
CRK
CRK
CRK
CRK
HEY! WE LOST THE TREASURE, THANKS TO YOU!
BUT, I HAD TO.
I WAS TRAPPED UNDERGROUND.
YOU AND YOUR FIRE!
TRAPPED?
I ALMOST GOT THE SWORD!
WHAT A WASTE!
...
HUH?

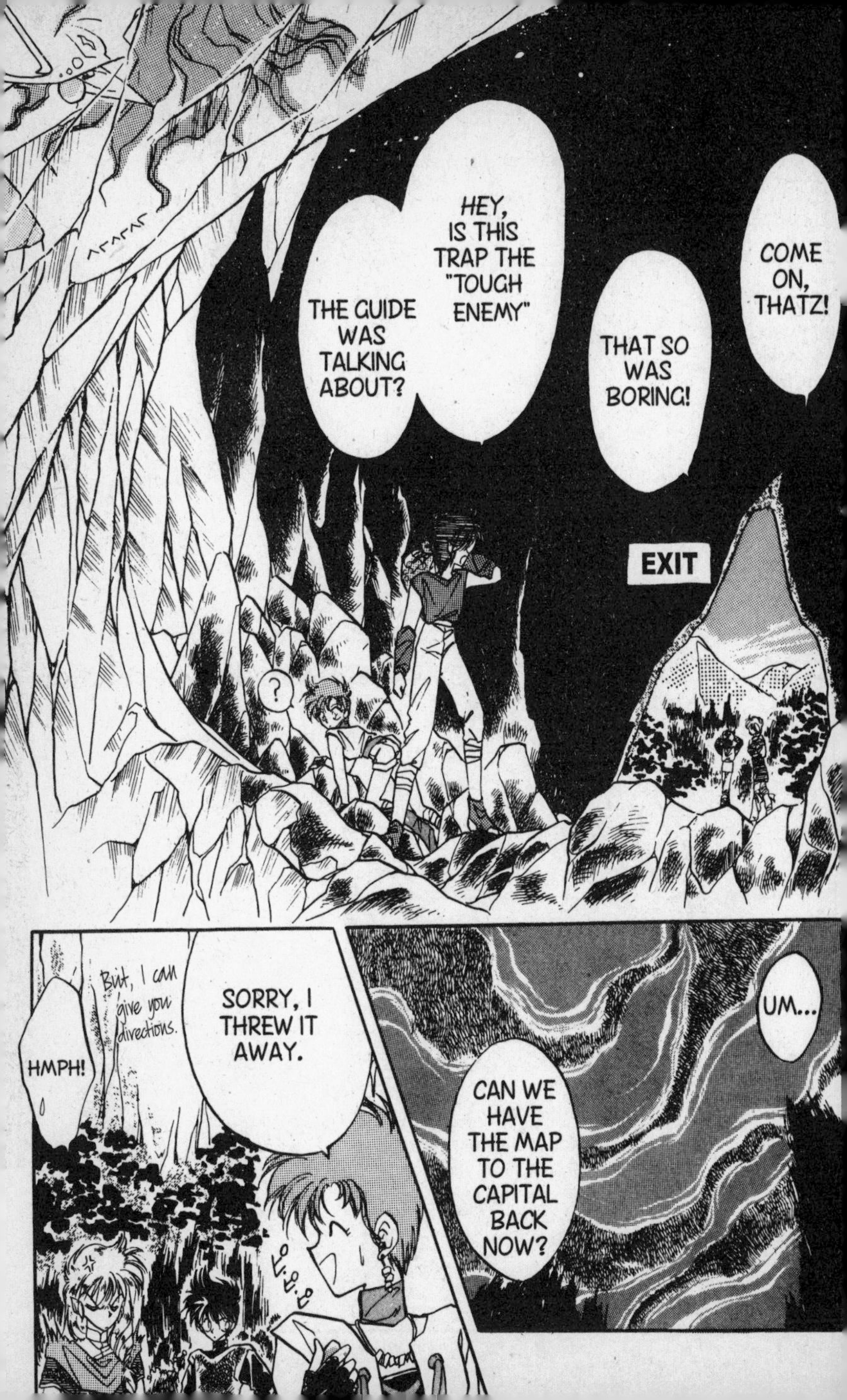
COME ON, THATZ!
THAT SO WAS BORING!
HEY, IS THIS TRAP THE "TOUGH ENEMY"
THE GUIDE WAS TALKING ABOUT?
?
EXIT
UM...
CAN WE HAVE THE MAP TO THE CAPITAL BACK NOW?
SORRY, I THREW IT AWAY.
But, I can give you directions.
HMPH!

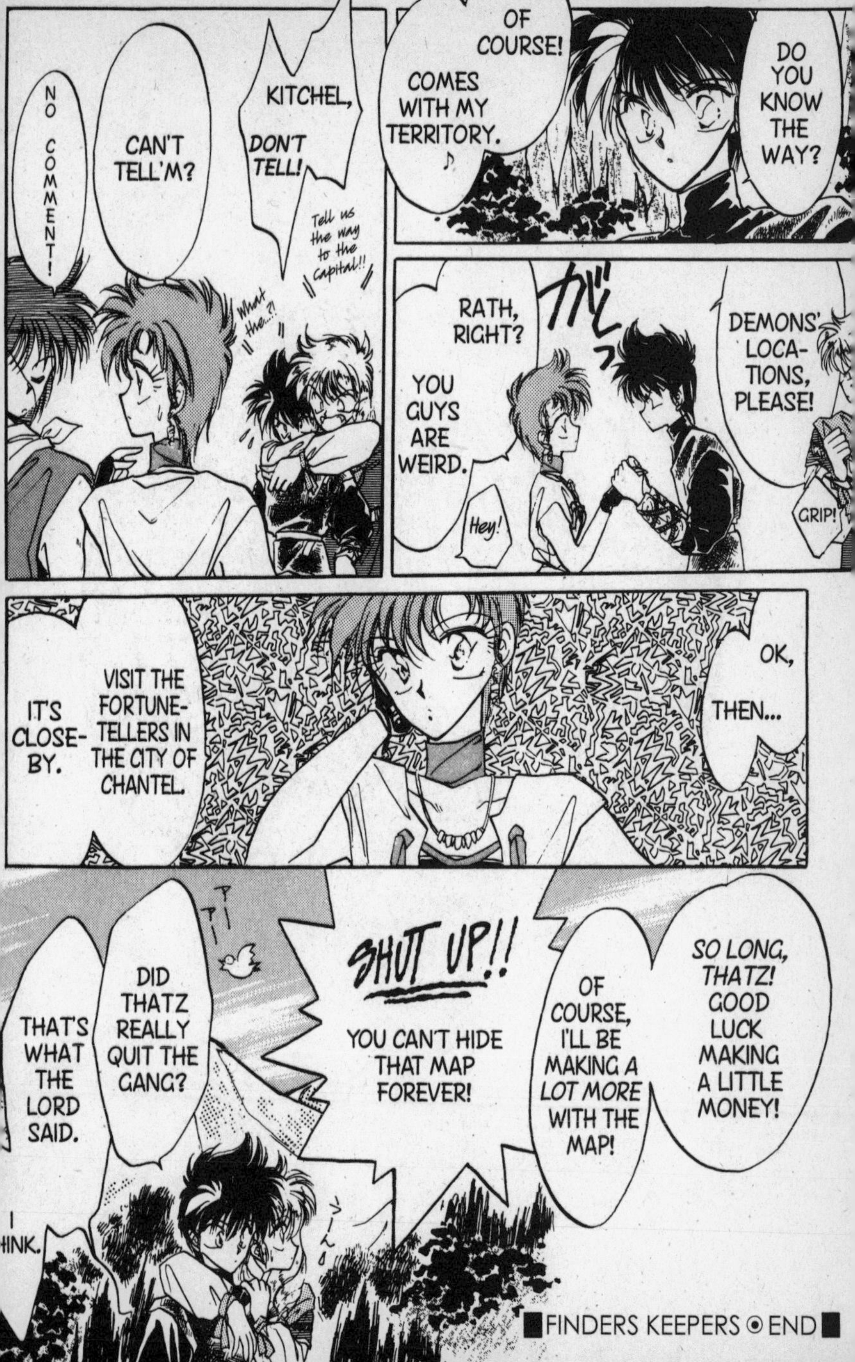
DO YOU KNOW THE WAY?
OF COURSE! COMES WITH MY TERRITORY. ♪
DEMONS' LOCATIONS, PLEASE!
GRIP!
RATH, RIGHT?
YOU GUYS ARE WEIRD.
Hey!
KITCHEL, DON'T TELL!
Tell us the way to the capital!!
What the...?!
CAN'T TELL'M?
NO COMMENT!
OK, THEN...
VISIT THE FORTUNE-TELLERS IN THE CITY OF CHANTEL.
IT'S CLOSE-BY.
SO LONG, THATZ! GOOD LUCK MAKING A LITTLE MONEY!
OF COURSE, I'LL BE MAKING A LOT MORE WITH THE MAP!
SHUT UP!!
YOU CAN'T HIDE THAT MAP FOREVER!
DID THATZ REALLY QUIT THE GANG?
THAT'S WHAT THE LORD SAID.
I HINK.

■FINDERS KEEPERS ⊙ END■

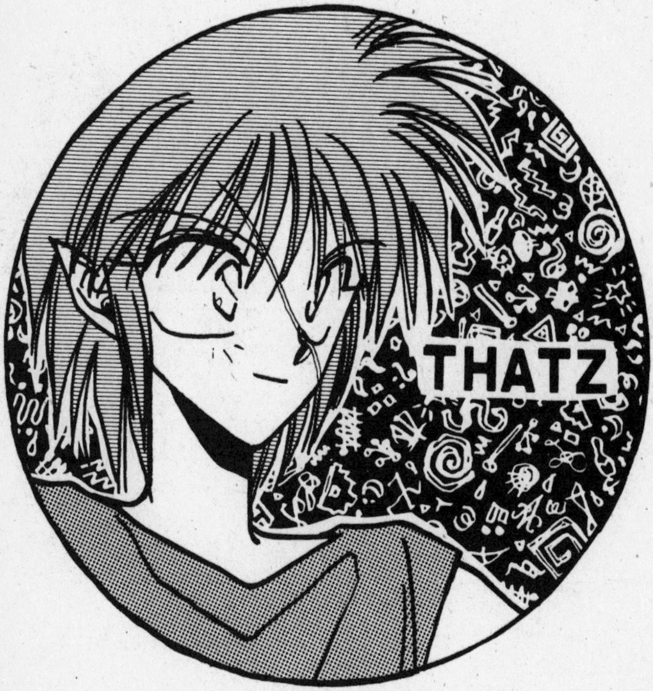
THATZ

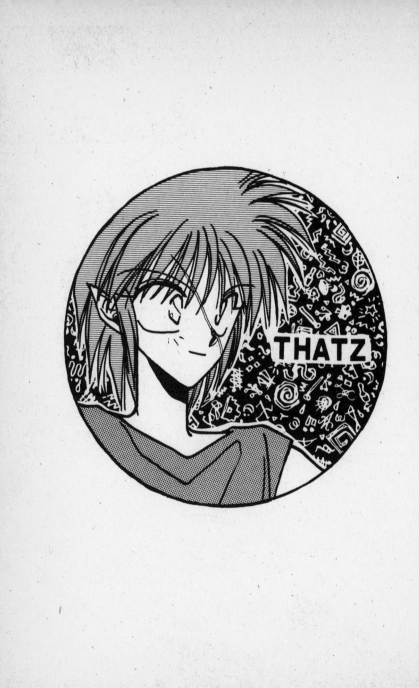

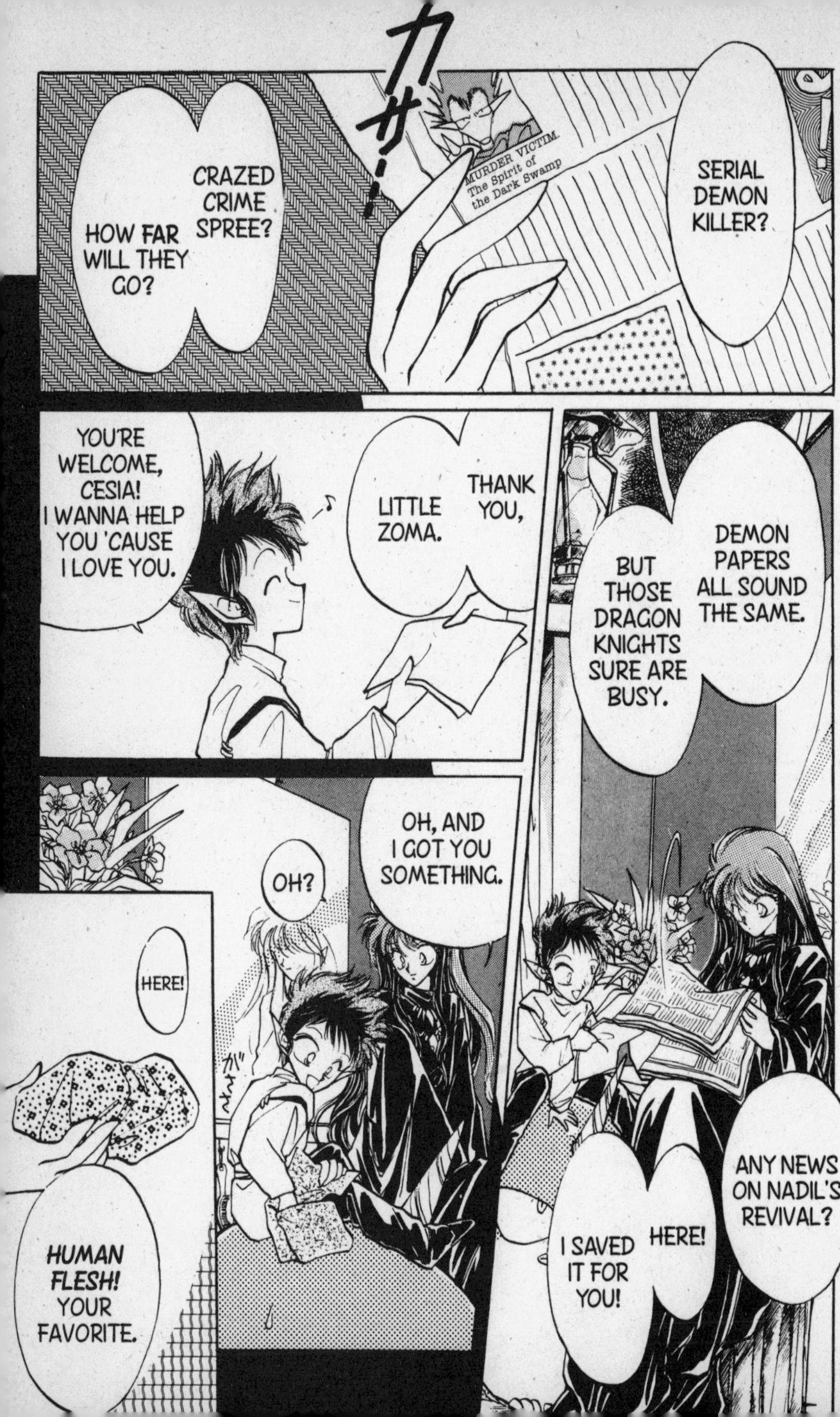
カサ
SERIAL DEMON KILLER?
MURDER VICTIM The Spirit of the Dark Swamp
CRAZED CRIME SPREE?
HOW FAR WILL THEY GO?
DEMON PAPERS ALL SOUND THE SAME.
BUT THOSE DRAGON KNIGHTS SURE ARE BUSY.
ANY NEWS ON NADIL'S REVIVAL?
HERE!
I SAVED IT FOR YOU!
THANK YOU, LITTLE ZOMA.
YOU'RE WELCOME, CESIA! I WANNA HELP YOU 'CAUSE I LOVE YOU.
OH, AND I GOT YOU SOMETHING.
OH?
HERE!
HUMAN FLESH! YOUR FAVORITE.

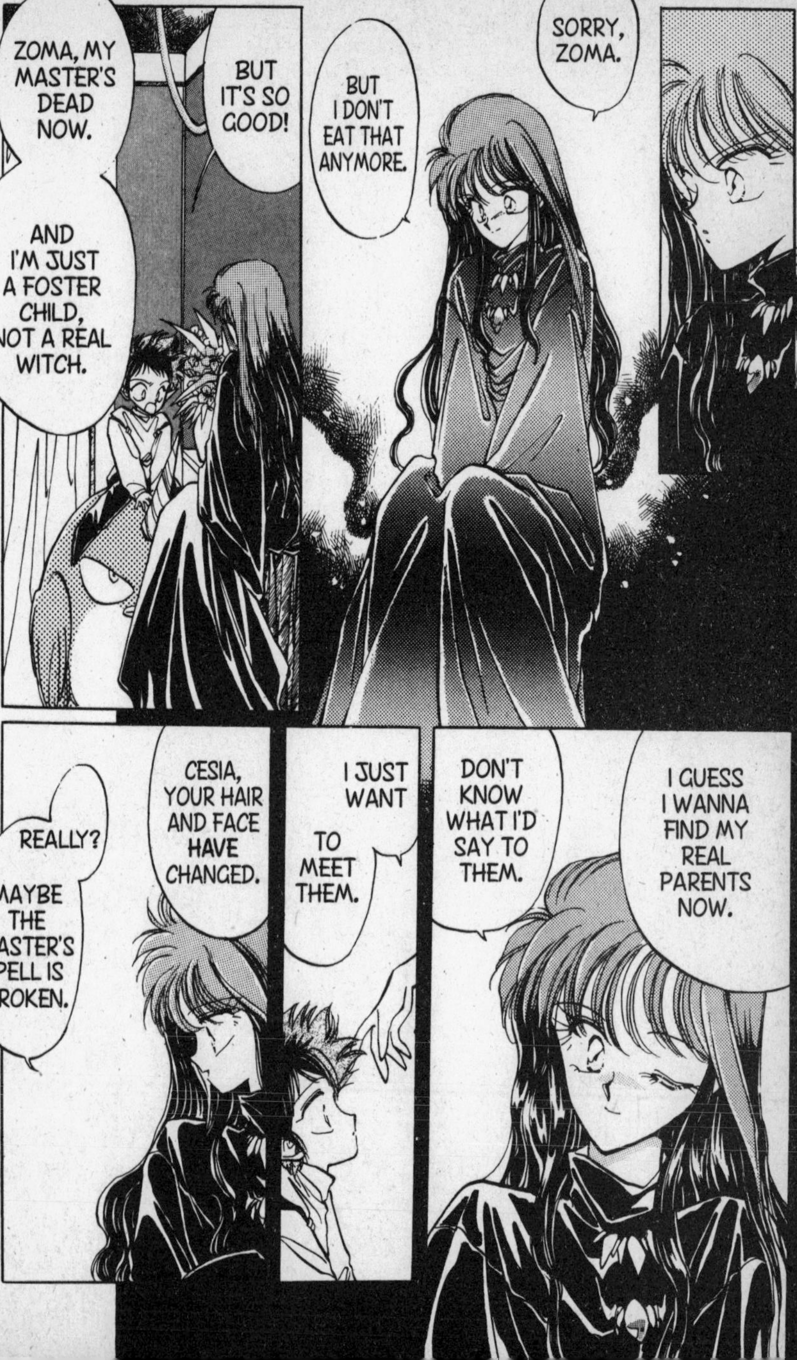
SORRY, ZOMA.
BUT I DON'T EAT THAT ANYMORE.
BUT IT'S SO GOOD!
ZOMA, MY MASTER'S DEAD NOW.
AND I'M JUST A FOSTER CHILD, NOT A REAL WITCH.
I GUESS I WANNA FIND MY REAL PARENTS NOW.
DON'T KNOW WHAT I'D SAY TO THEM.
I JUST WANT
TO MEET THEM.
CESIA, YOUR HAIR AND FACE HAVE CHANGED.
REALLY?
MAYBE THE MASTER'S SPELL IS BROKEN.

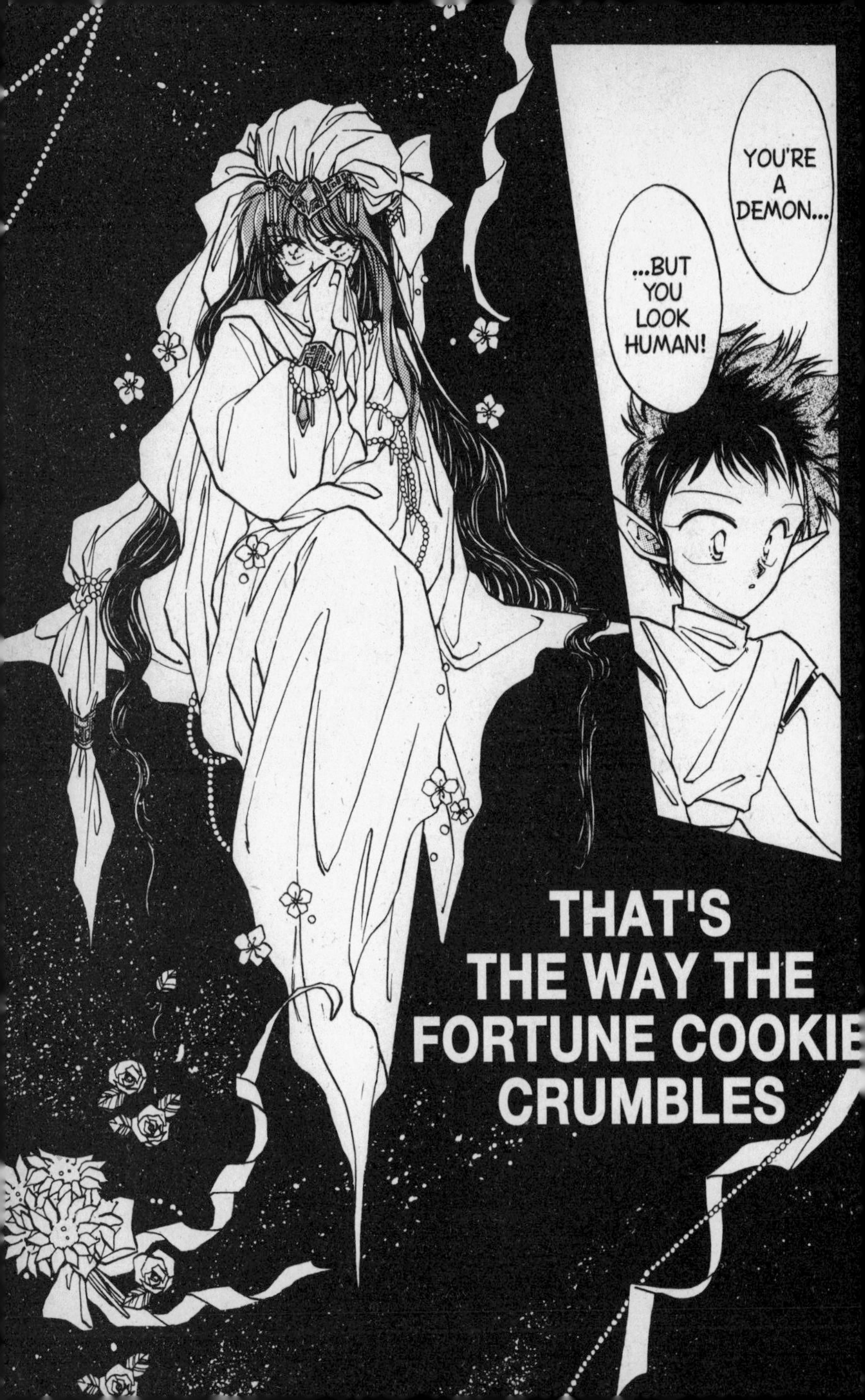
YOU'RE A DEMON...
...BUT YOU LOOK HUMAN!
THAT'S THE WAY THE FORTUNE COOKIE CRUMBLES

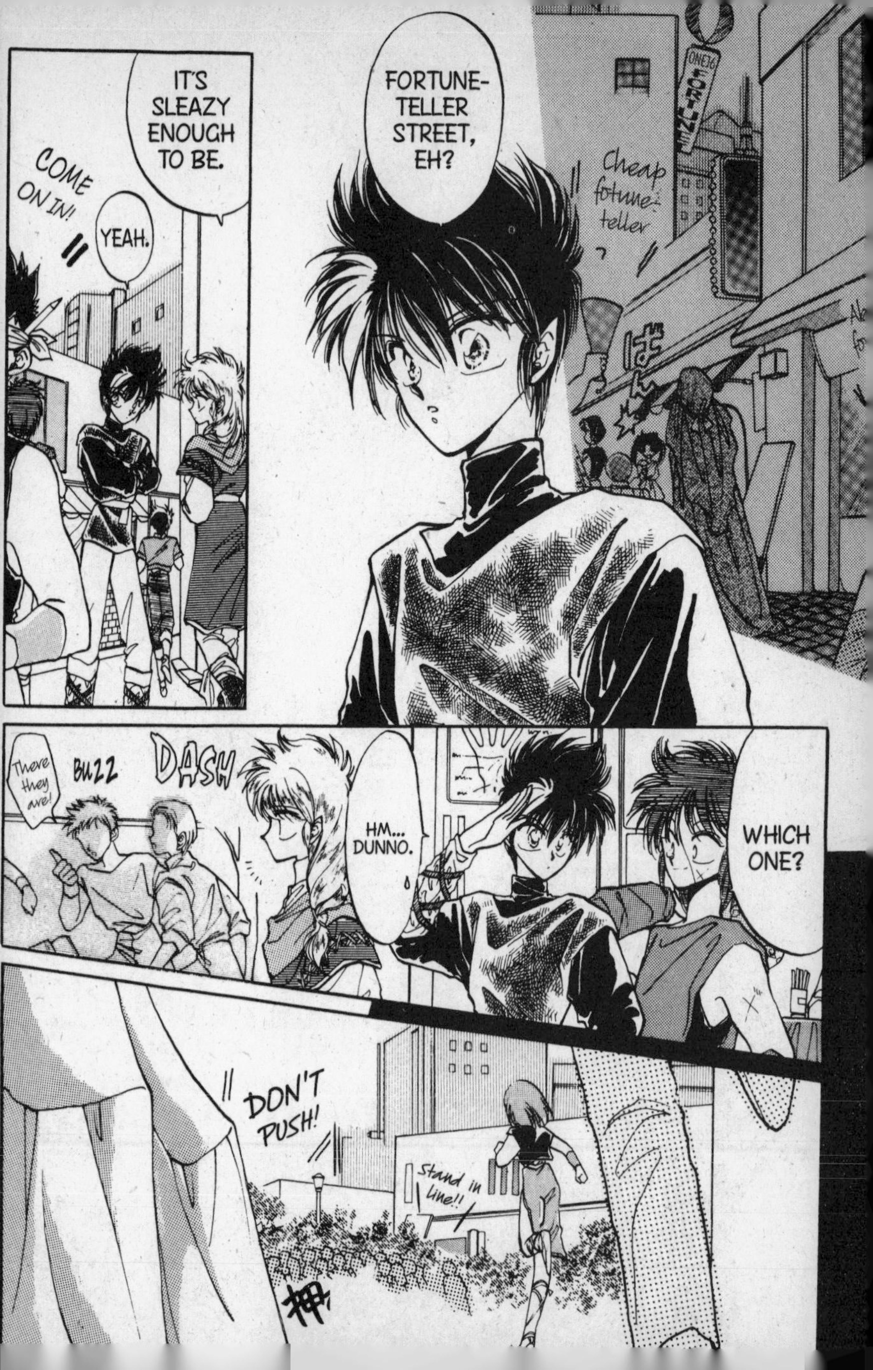
FORTUNE-TELLER STREET, EH?
FORTUNE
Cheap fortune-teller
IT'S SLEAZY ENOUGH TO BE.
COME ON IN!
YEAH.
WHICH ONE?
HM... DUNNO.
DASH
BUZZ
There they are!
DON'T PUSH!
stand in line!!
押

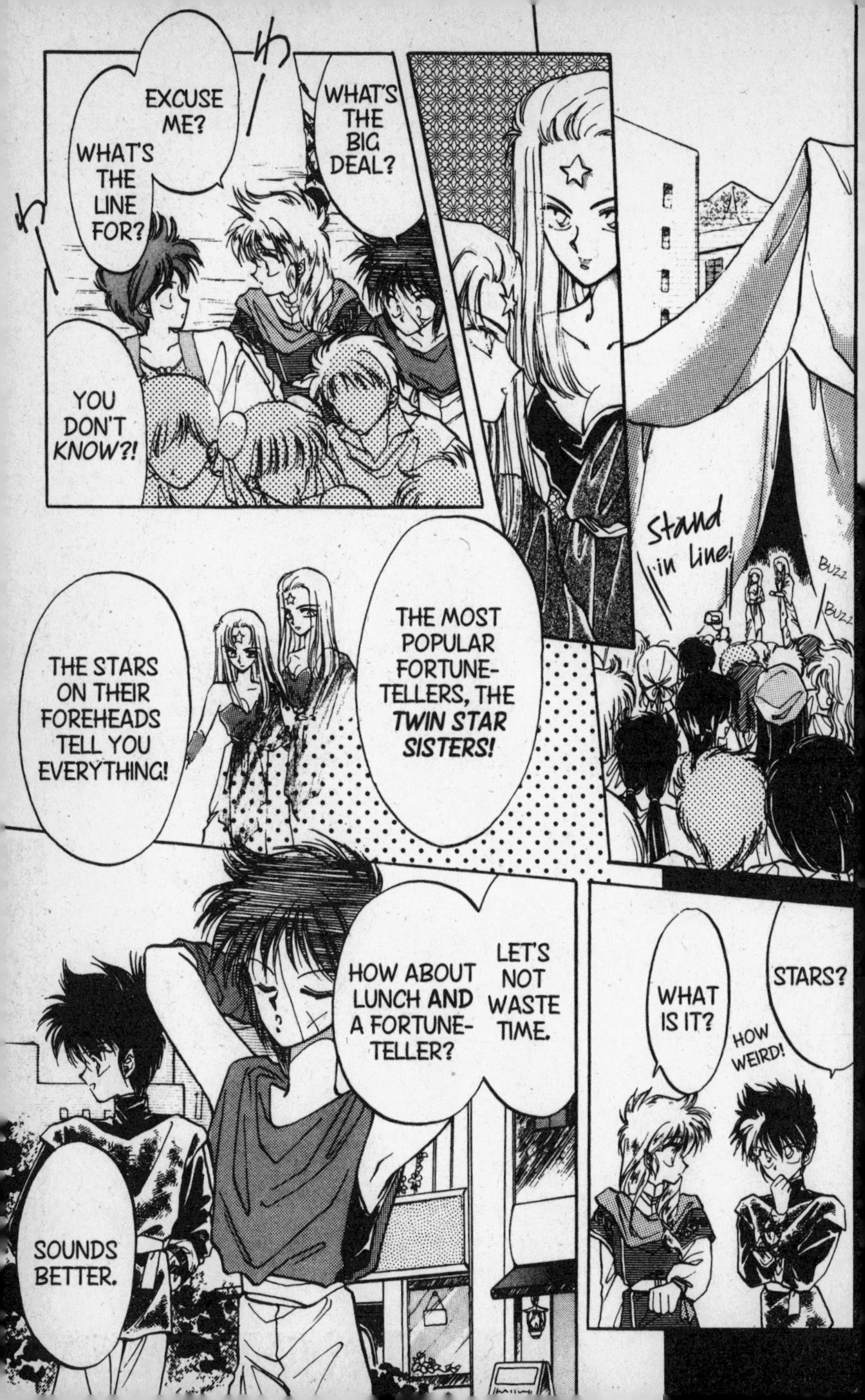
Stand in line!
BUZZ
BUZZ
わ
わ
WHAT'S THE BIG DEAL?
EXCUSE ME?
WHAT'S THE LINE FOR?
YOU DON'T KNOW?!
THE MOST POPULAR FORTUNE-TELLERS, THE TWIN STAR SISTERS!
THE STARS ON THEIR FOREHEADS TELL YOU EVERYTHING!
STARS?
HOW WEIRD!
WHAT IS IT?
LET'S NOT WASTE TIME.
HOW ABOUT LUNCH AND A FORTUNE-TELLER?
SOUNDS BETTER.

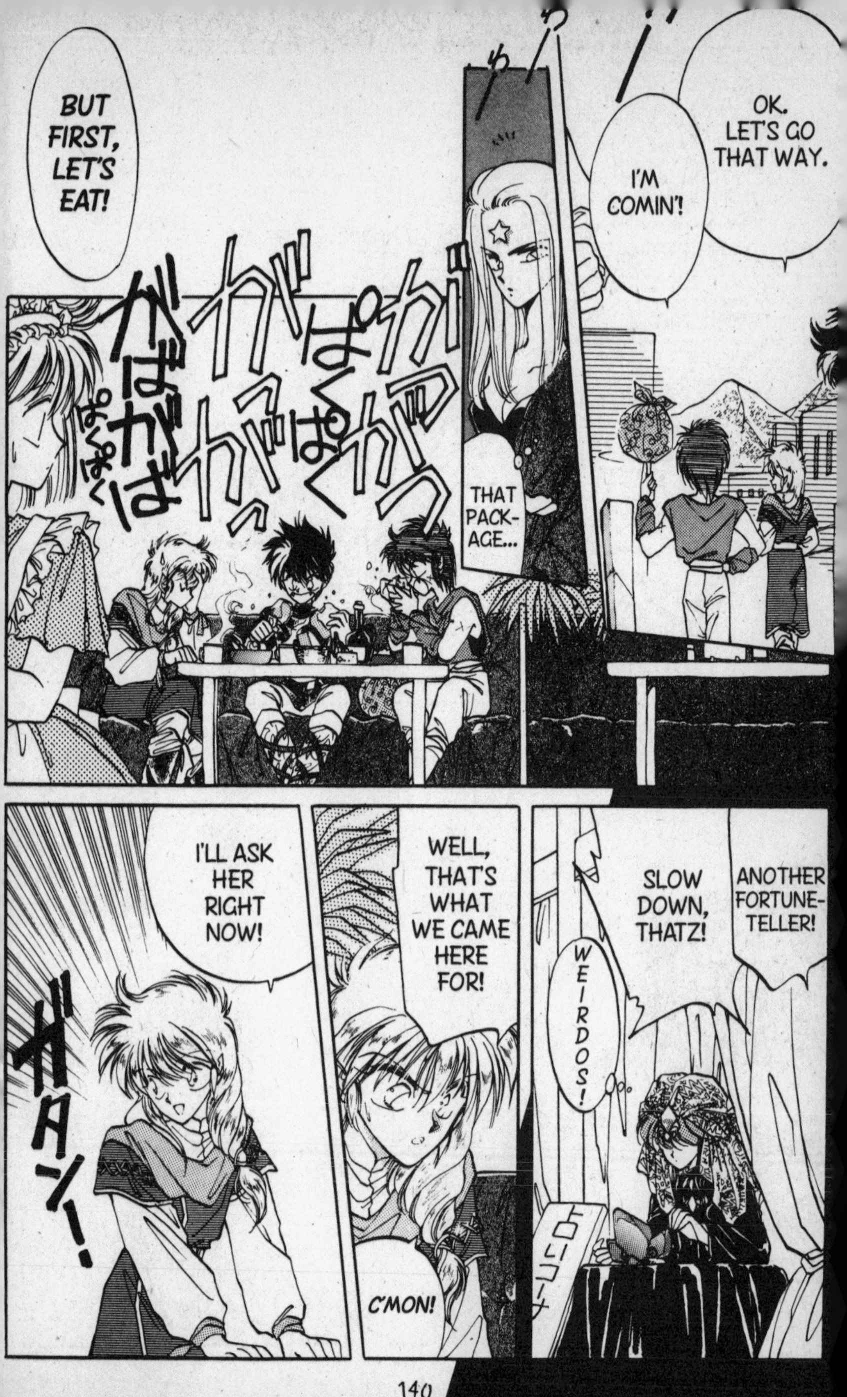
OK. LET'S GO THAT WAY.
I'M COMIN'!
THAT PACKAGE...
BUT FIRST, LET'S EAT!
ANOTHER FORTUNE-TELLER!
SLOW DOWN, THATZ!
WEIRDOS!
WELL, THAT'S WHAT WE CAME HERE FOR!
C'MON!
I'LL ASK HER RIGHT NOW!

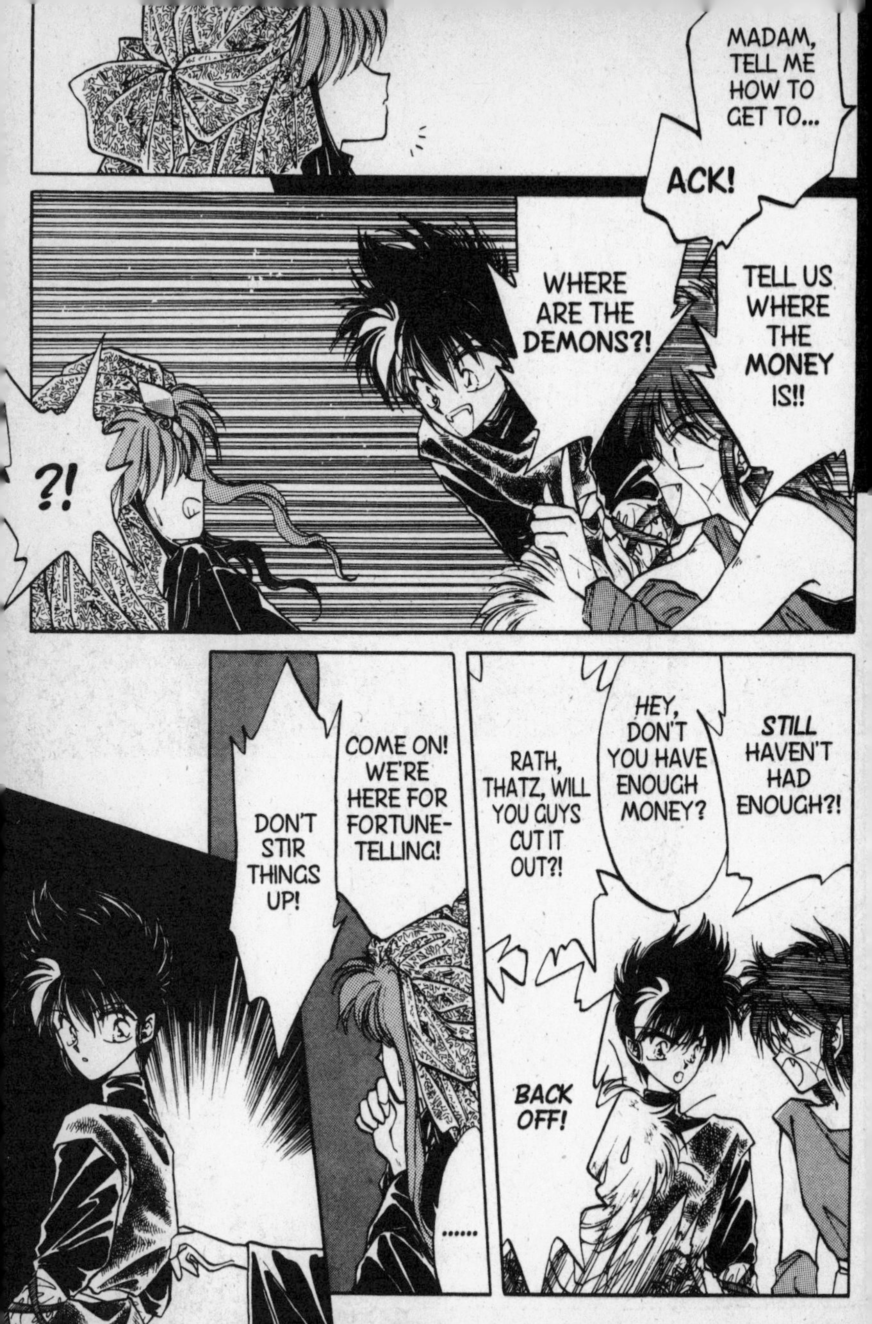
MADAM, TELL ME HOW TO GET TO...
ACK!
TELL US WHERE THE MONEY IS!!
WHERE ARE THE DEMONS?!
?!
STILL HAVEN'T HAD ENOUGH?!
HEY, DON'T YOU HAVE ENOUGH MONEY?
RATH, THATZ, WILL YOU GUYS CUT IT OUT?!
BACK OFF!
COME ON! WE'RE HERE FOR FORTUNE-TELLING!
DON'T STIR THINGS UP!
......

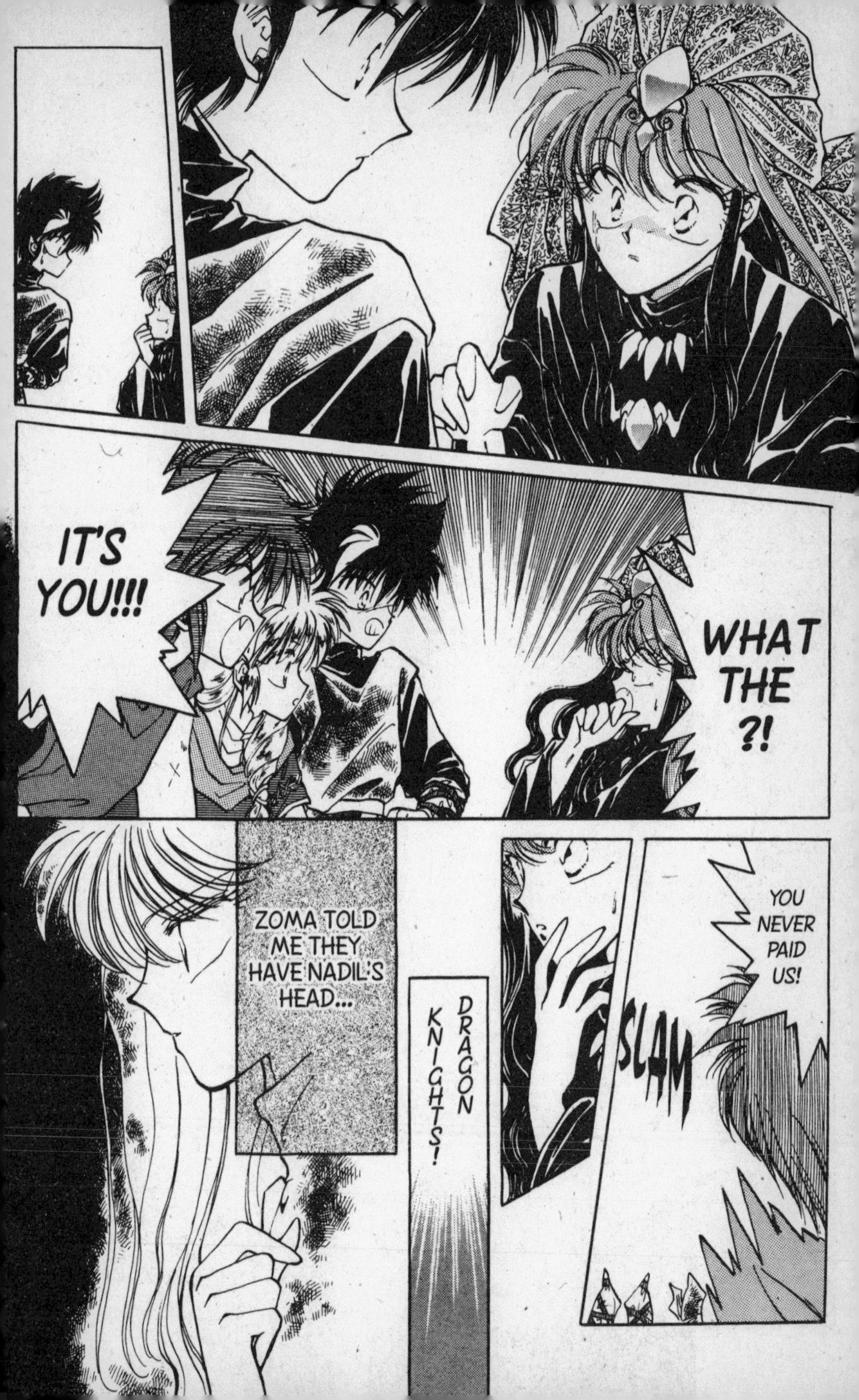
WHAT THE ?!
IT'S YOU!!!
YOU NEVER PAID US!
SLAM
DRAGON KNIGHTS!
ZOMA TOLD ME THEY HAVE NADIL'S HEAD...

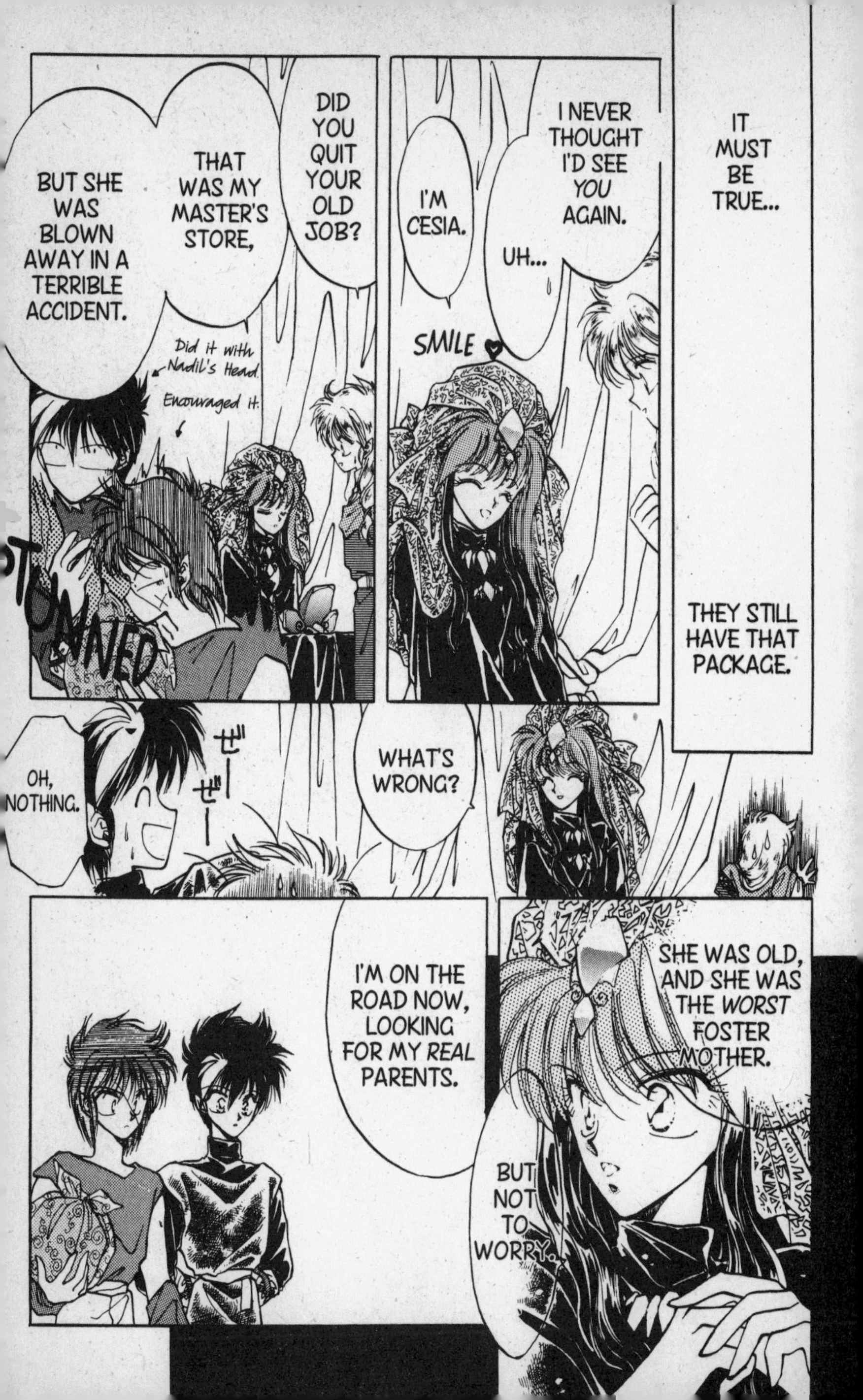
IT MUST BE TRUE...
THEY STILL HAVE THAT PACKAGE.
I NEVER THOUGHT I'D SEE *YOU* AGAIN.
UH...
I'M CESIA.
SMILE ♥
DID YOU QUIT YOUR OLD JOB?
THAT WAS MY MASTER'S STORE,
BUT SHE WAS BLOWN AWAY IN A TERRIBLE ACCIDENT.
Did it with Nadil's Head
Encouraged it.
STUNNED
WHAT'S WRONG?
ゼーゼー
OH, NOTHING.
SHE WAS OLD, AND SHE WAS THE *WORST* FOSTER MOTHER.
BUT NOT TO WORRY.
I'M ON THE ROAD NOW, LOOKING FOR MY *REAL* PARENTS.

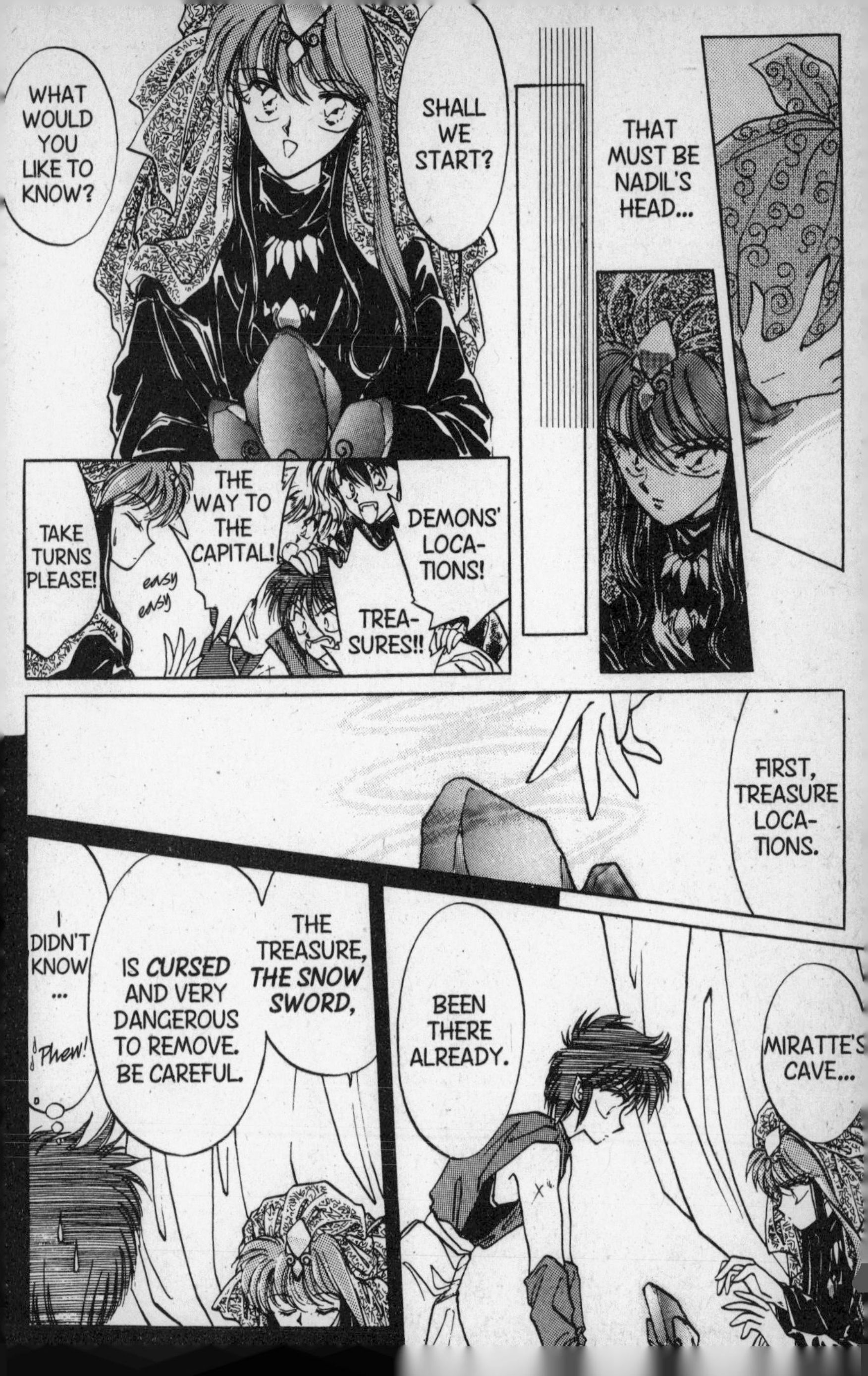
THAT MUST BE NADIL'S HEAD...
SHALL WE START?
WHAT WOULD YOU LIKE TO KNOW?
DEMONS' LOCATIONS!
THE WAY TO THE CAPITAL!
TREASURES!!
TAKE TURNS PLEASE!
easy easy
FIRST, TREASURE LOCATIONS.
MIRATTE'S CAVE...
BEEN THERE ALREADY.
THE TREASURE, *THE SNOW SWORD*,
IS *CURSED* AND VERY DANGEROUS TO REMOVE. BE CAREFUL.
I DIDN'T KNOW ...
Phew!

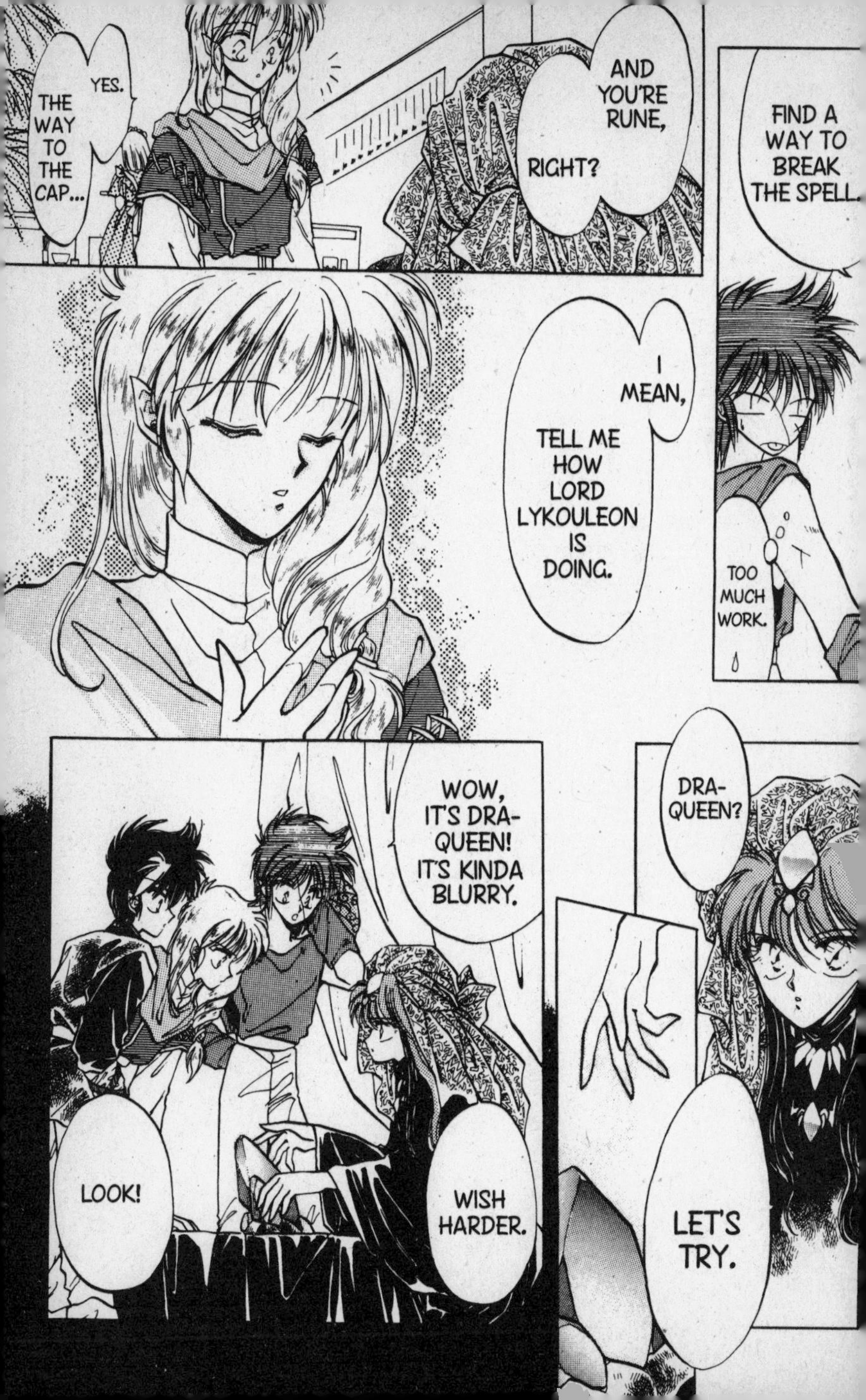

FIND A WAY TO BREAK THE SPELL.
TOO MUCH WORK.
AND YOU'RE RUNE,
RIGHT?
YES.
THE WAY TO THE CAP...
I MEAN,
TELL ME HOW LORD LYKOULEON IS DOING.
DRA-QUEEN?
LET'S TRY.
WOW, IT'S DRA-QUEEN! IT'S KINDA BLURRY.
WISH HARDER.
LOOK!

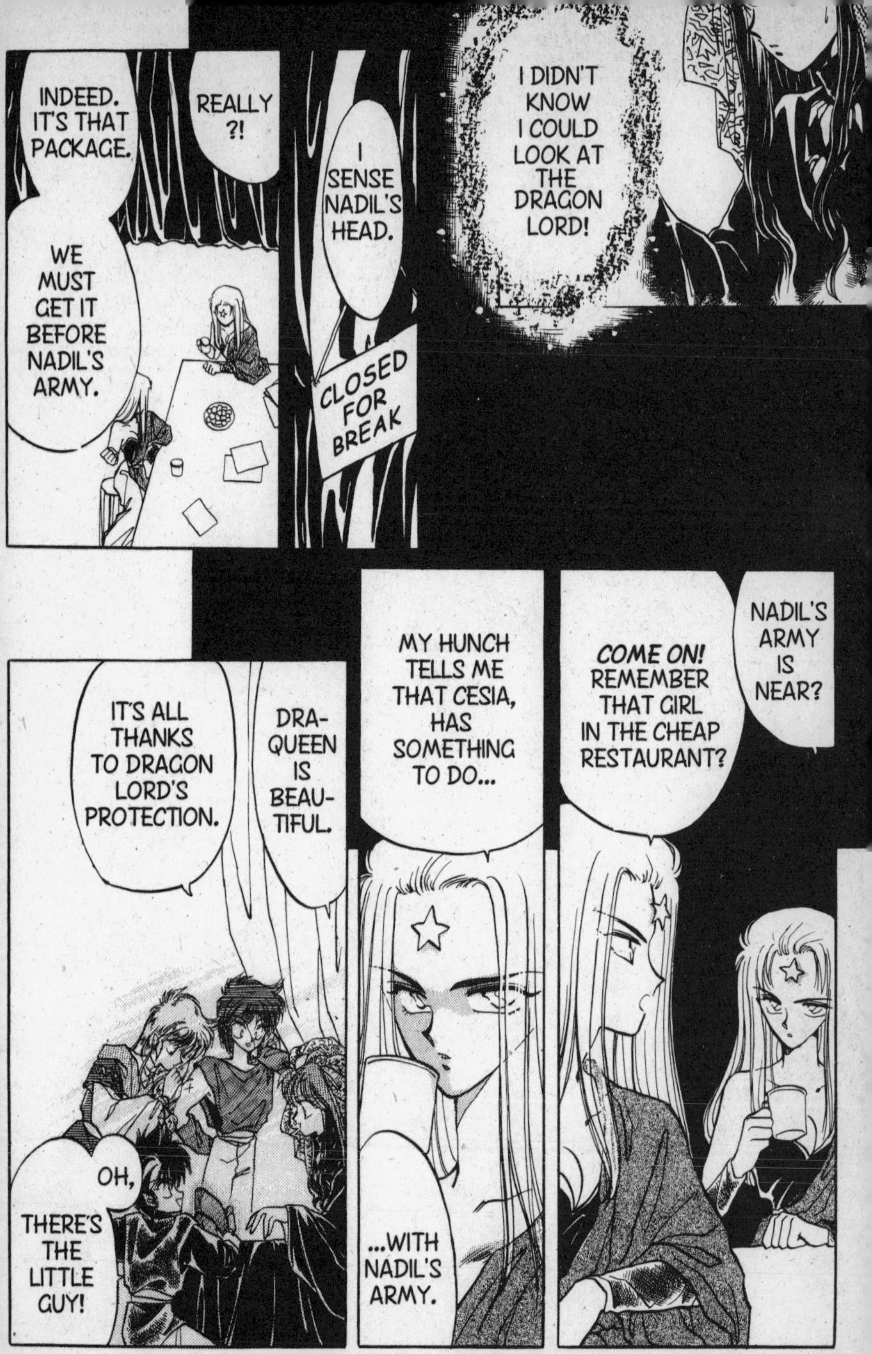
I DIDN'T KNOW I COULD LOOK AT THE DRAGON LORD!
I SENSE NADIL'S HEAD.
CLOSED FOR BREAK
REALLY ?!
INDEED. IT'S THAT PACKAGE.
WE MUST GET IT BEFORE NADIL'S ARMY.
NADIL'S ARMY IS NEAR?
COME ON! REMEMBER THAT GIRL IN THE CHEAP RESTAURANT?
MY HUNCH TELLS ME THAT CESIA, HAS SOMETHING TO DO...
...WITH NADIL'S ARMY.
DRA-QUEEN IS BEAU-TIFUL.
IT'S ALL THANKS TO DRAGON LORD'S PROTECTION.
OH, THERE'S THE LITTLE GUY!

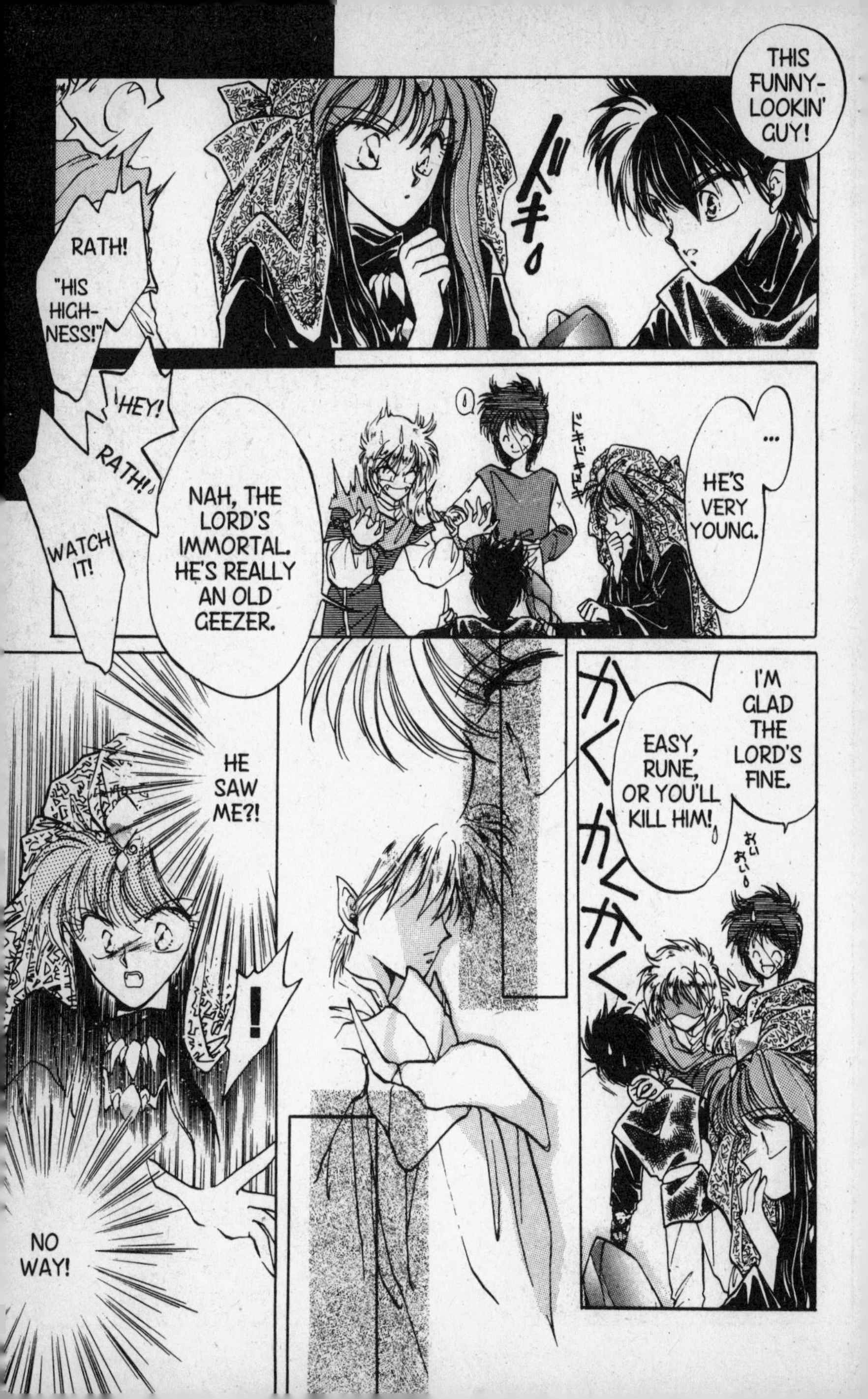
THIS FUNNY-LOOKIN' GUY!
ドキッ
RATH!
"HIS HIGHNESS!"
...
HE'S VERY YOUNG.
NAH, THE LORD'S IMMORTAL. HE'S REALLY AN OLD GEEZER.
HEY!
RATH!!
WATCH IT!
I'M GLAD THE LORD'S FINE.
EASY, RUNE, OR YOU'LL KILL HIM!
おいおい
かくかくかく
HE SAW ME?!
!
NO WAY!

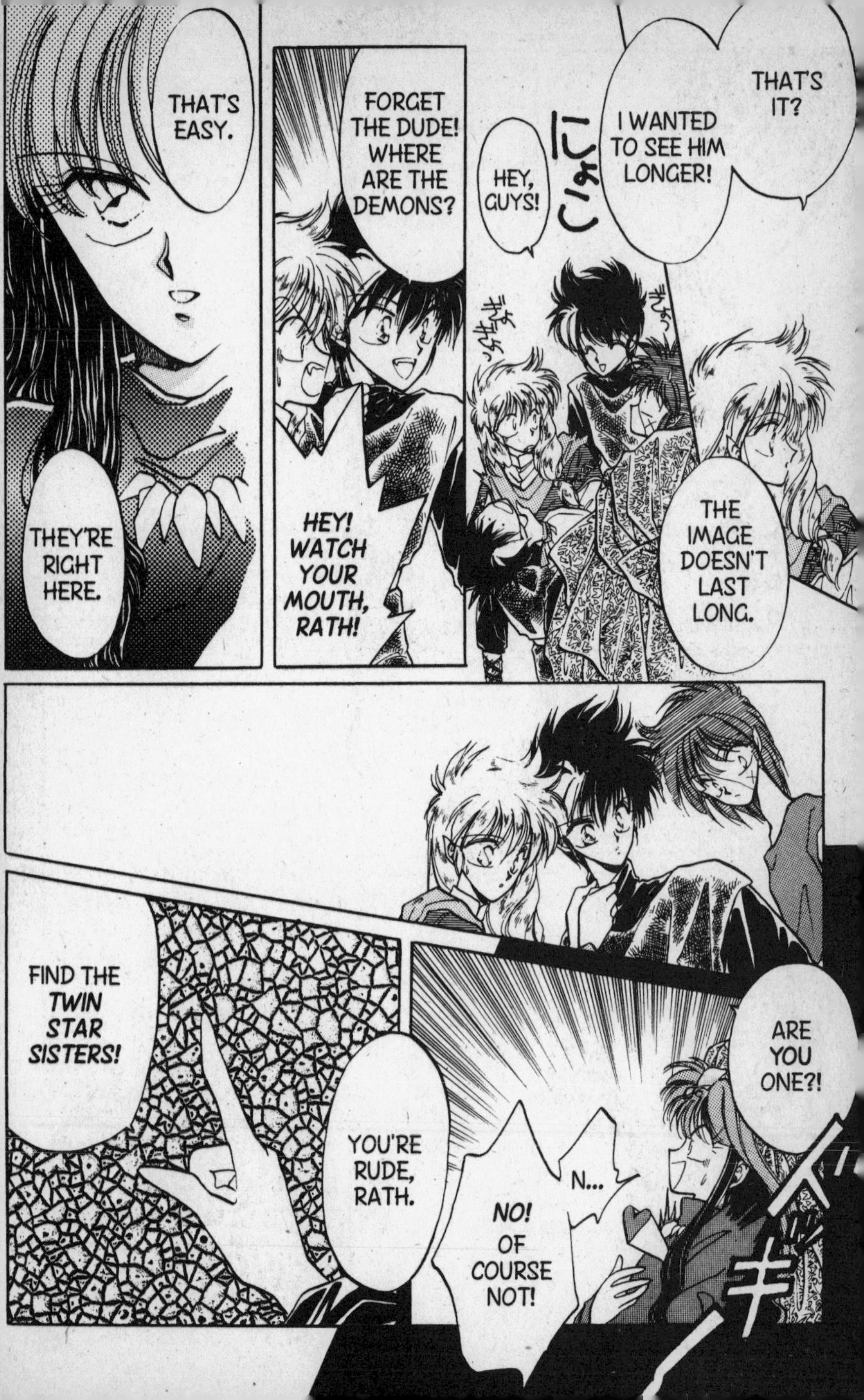
THAT'S IT?
I WANTED TO SEE HIM LONGER!
にょこ
HEY, GUYS!
THE IMAGE DOESN'T LAST LONG.
FORGET THE DUDE! WHERE ARE THE DEMONS?
HEY! WATCH YOUR MOUTH, RATH!
THAT'S EASY.
THEY'RE RIGHT HERE.
ARE YOU ONE?!
N...
NO! OF COURSE NOT!
YOU'RE RUDE, RATH.
FIND THE TWIN STAR SISTERS!

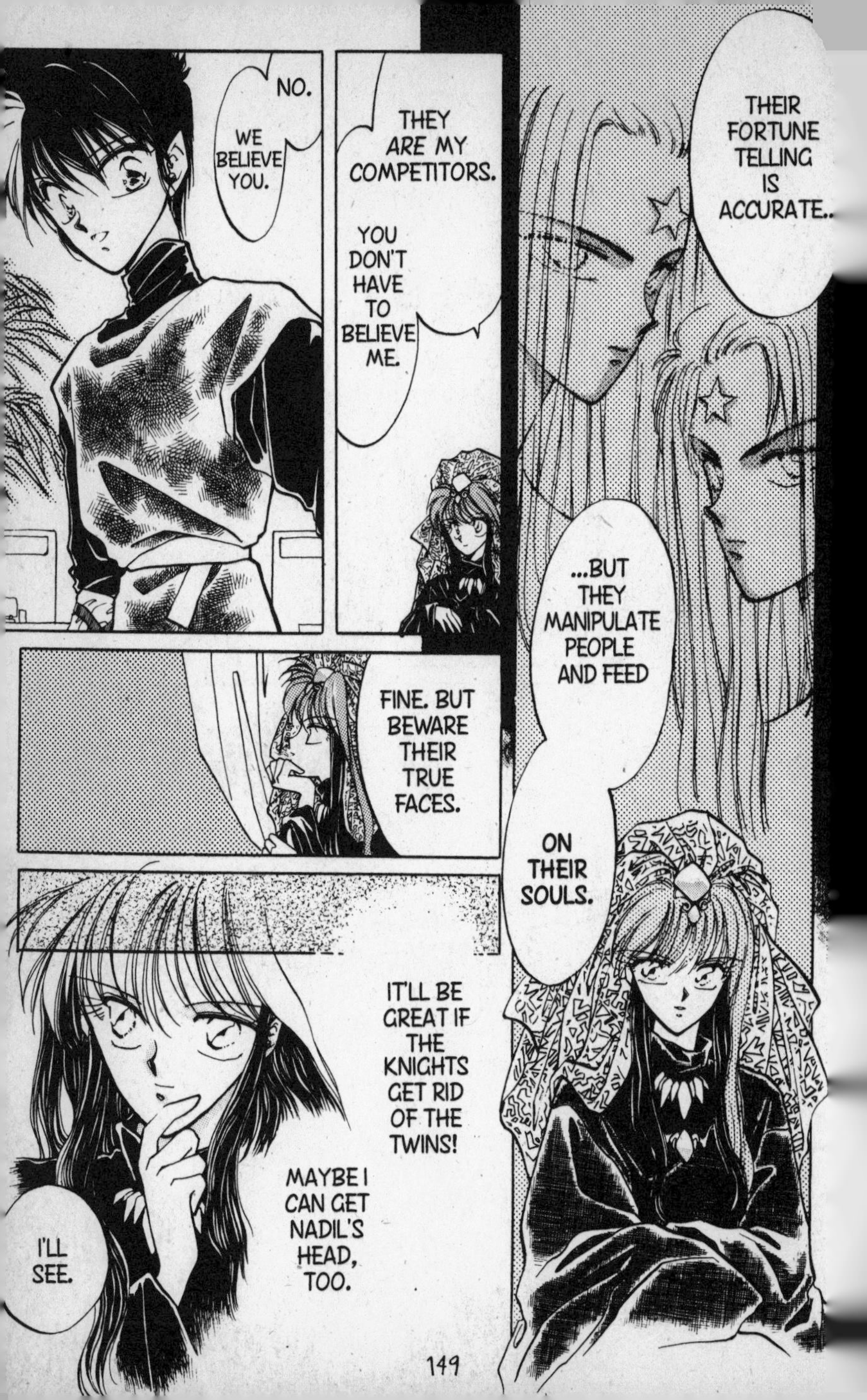
THEIR FORTUNE TELLING IS ACCURATE..
...BUT THEY MANIPULATE PEOPLE AND FEED
ON THEIR SOULS.
THEY ARE MY COMPETITORS.
YOU DON'T HAVE TO BELIEVE ME.
NO.
WE BELIEVE YOU.
FINE. BUT BEWARE THEIR TRUE FACES.
IT'LL BE GREAT IF THE KNIGHTS GET RID OF THE TWINS!
MAYBE I CAN GET NADIL'S HEAD, TOO.
I'LL SEE.

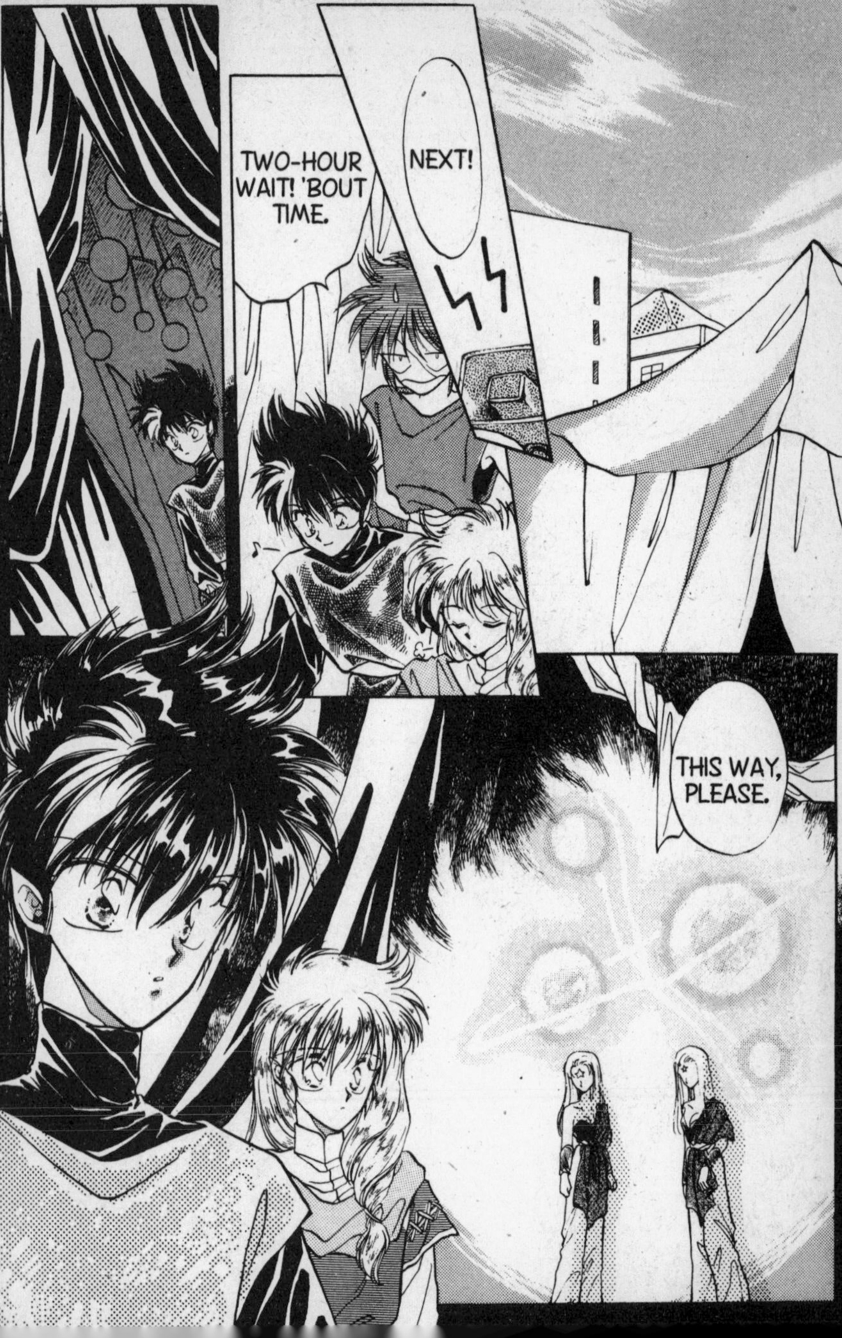
NEXT!
TWO-HOUR WAIT! 'BOUT TIME.
THIS WAY, PLEASE.

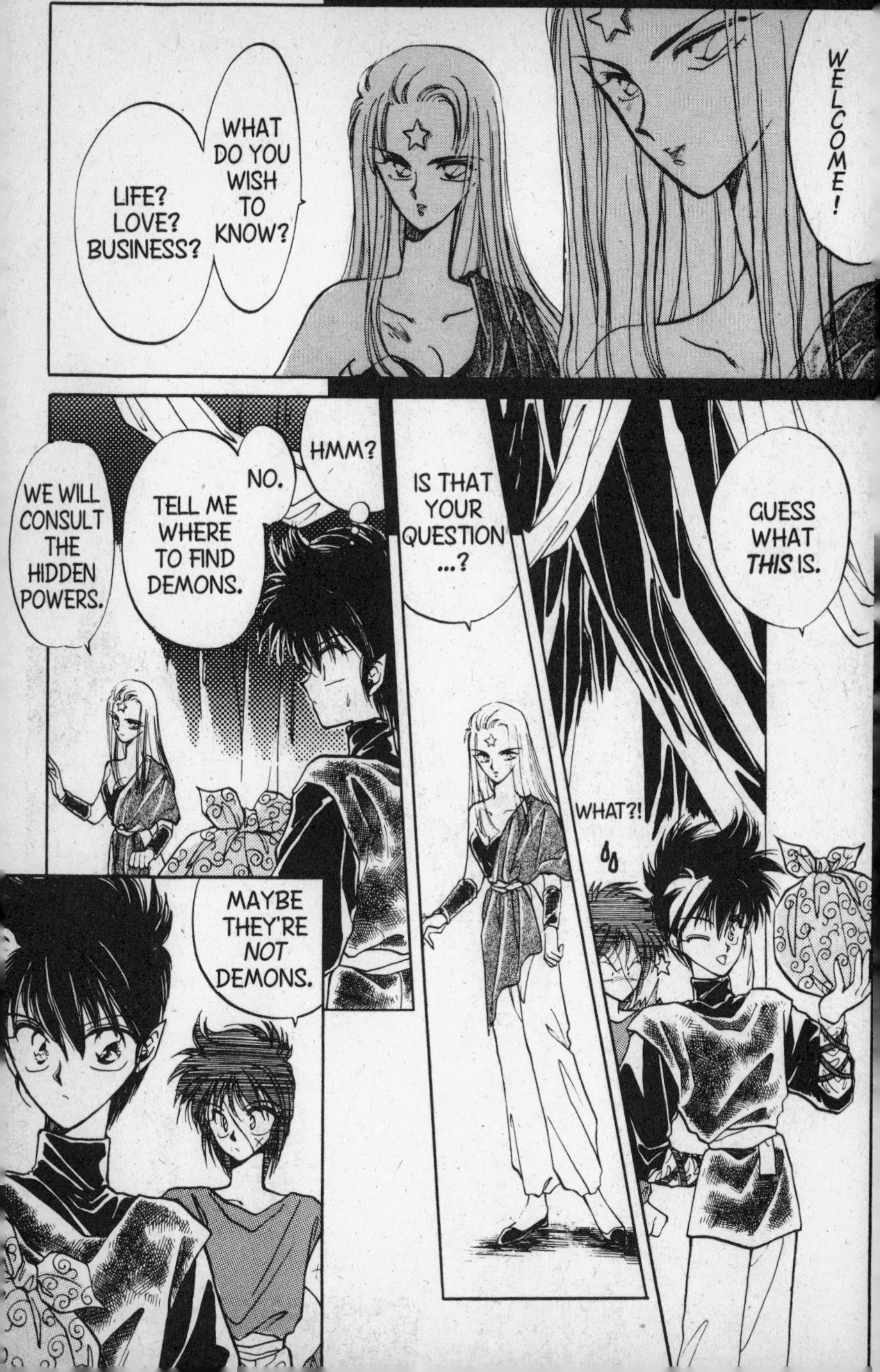
WELCOME!
WHAT DO YOU WISH TO KNOW?
LIFE? LOVE? BUSINESS?
GUESS WHAT *THIS* IS.
WHAT?!
IS THAT YOUR QUESTION ...?
HMM?
NO.
TELL ME WHERE TO FIND DEMONS.
WE WILL CONSULT THE HIDDEN POWERS.
MAYBE THEY'RE *NOT* DEMONS.

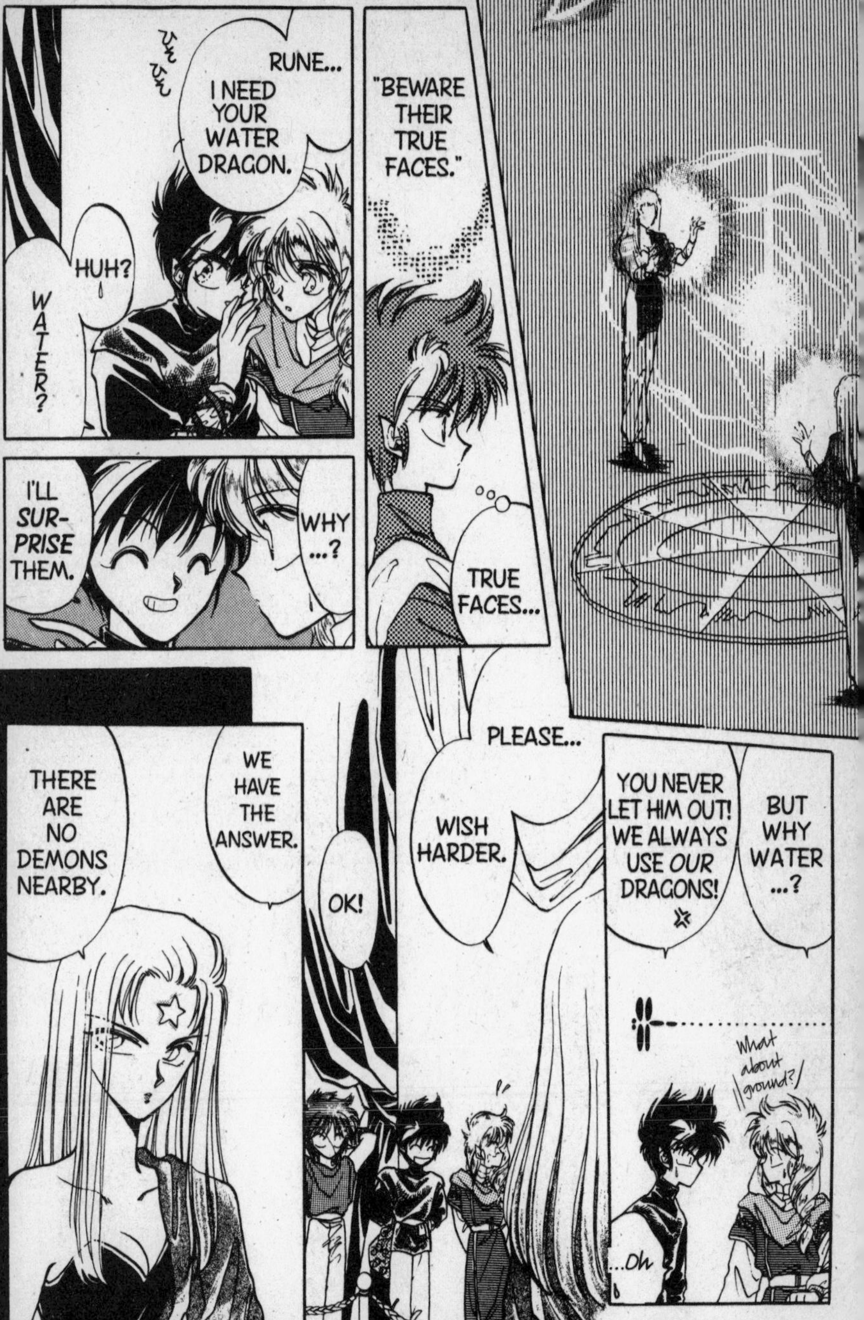
"BEWARE THEIR TRUE FACES."
TRUE FACES...
ひそひそ
RUNE... I NEED YOUR WATER DRAGON.
HUH?
WATER?
WHY ...?
I'LL *SUR-PRISE* THEM.
BUT WHY WATER ...?
YOU NEVER LET HIM OUT! WE ALWAYS USE *OUR* DRAGONS!
What about ground?
...Oh
PLEASE...
WISH HARDER.
OK!
WE HAVE THE ANSWER.
THERE ARE NO DEMONS NEARBY.

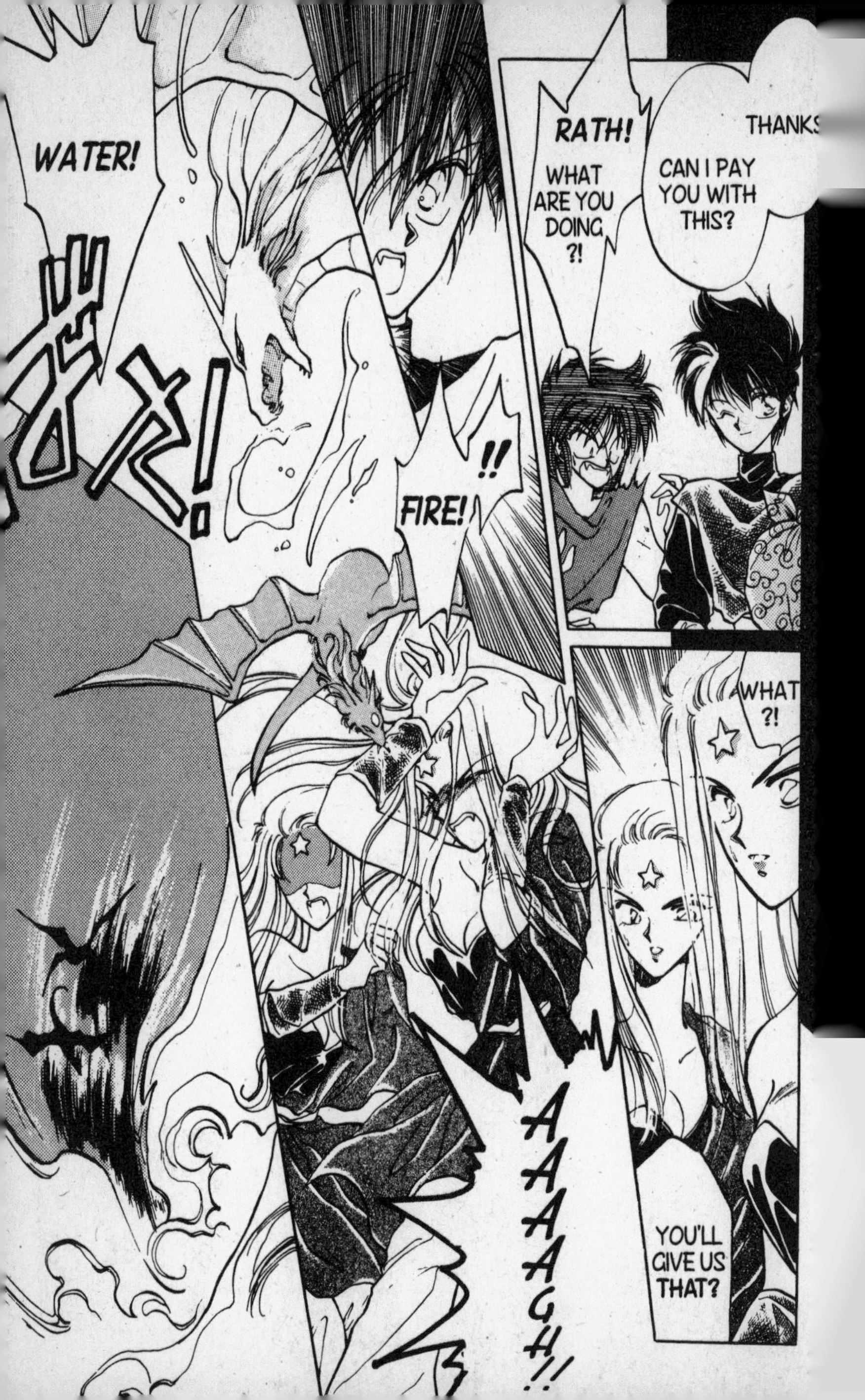
THANKS
CAN I PAY YOU WITH THIS?
RATH!
WHAT ARE YOU DOING ?!
WHAT ?!
YOU'LL GIVE US THAT?
FIRE!
!!
WATER!
AAAAAAGH!!

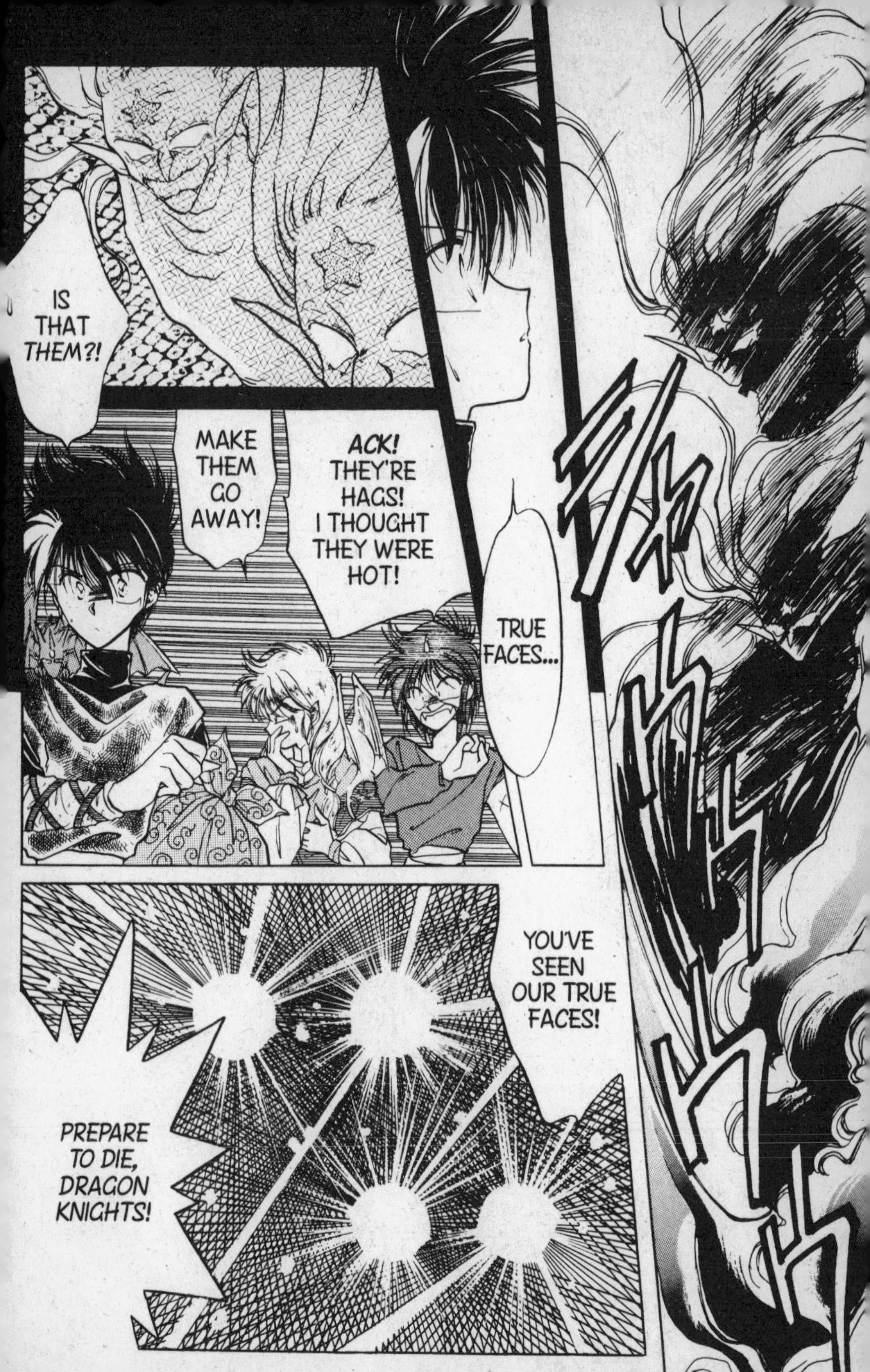
IS THAT THEM?!
ACK! THEY'RE HAGS! I THOUGHT THEY WERE HOT!
MAKE THEM GO AWAY!
TRUE FACES...
YOU'VE SEEN OUR TRUE FACES!
PREPARE TO DIE, DRAGON KNIGHTS!

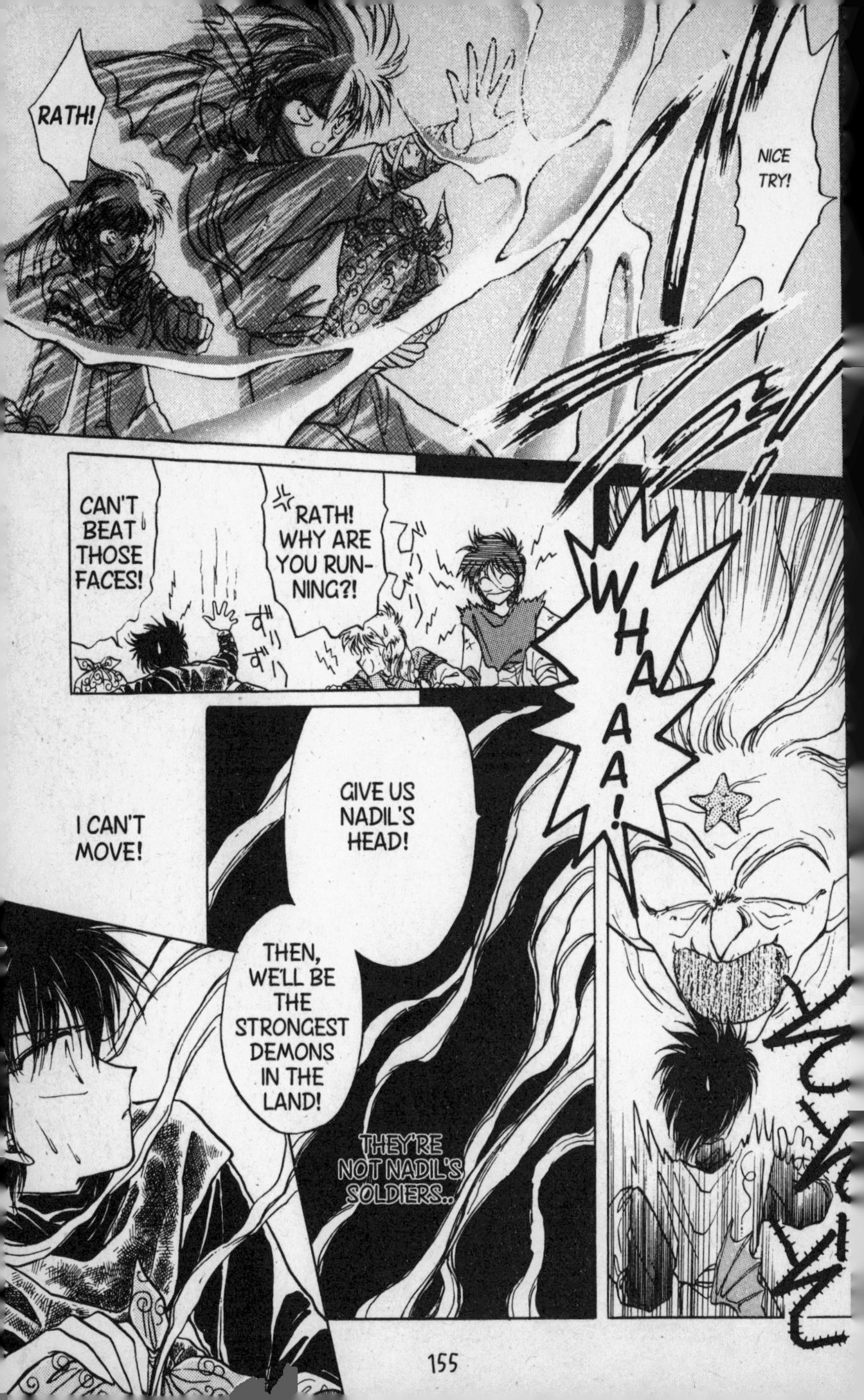
RATH!
NICE TRY!
WHAAAA!
RATH! WHY ARE YOU RUN-NING?!
CAN'T BEAT THOSE FACES!
GIVE US NADIL'S HEAD!
THEN, WE'LL BE THE STRONGEST DEMONS IN THE LAND!
THEY'RE NOT NADIL'S SOLDIERS...
I CAN'T MOVE!

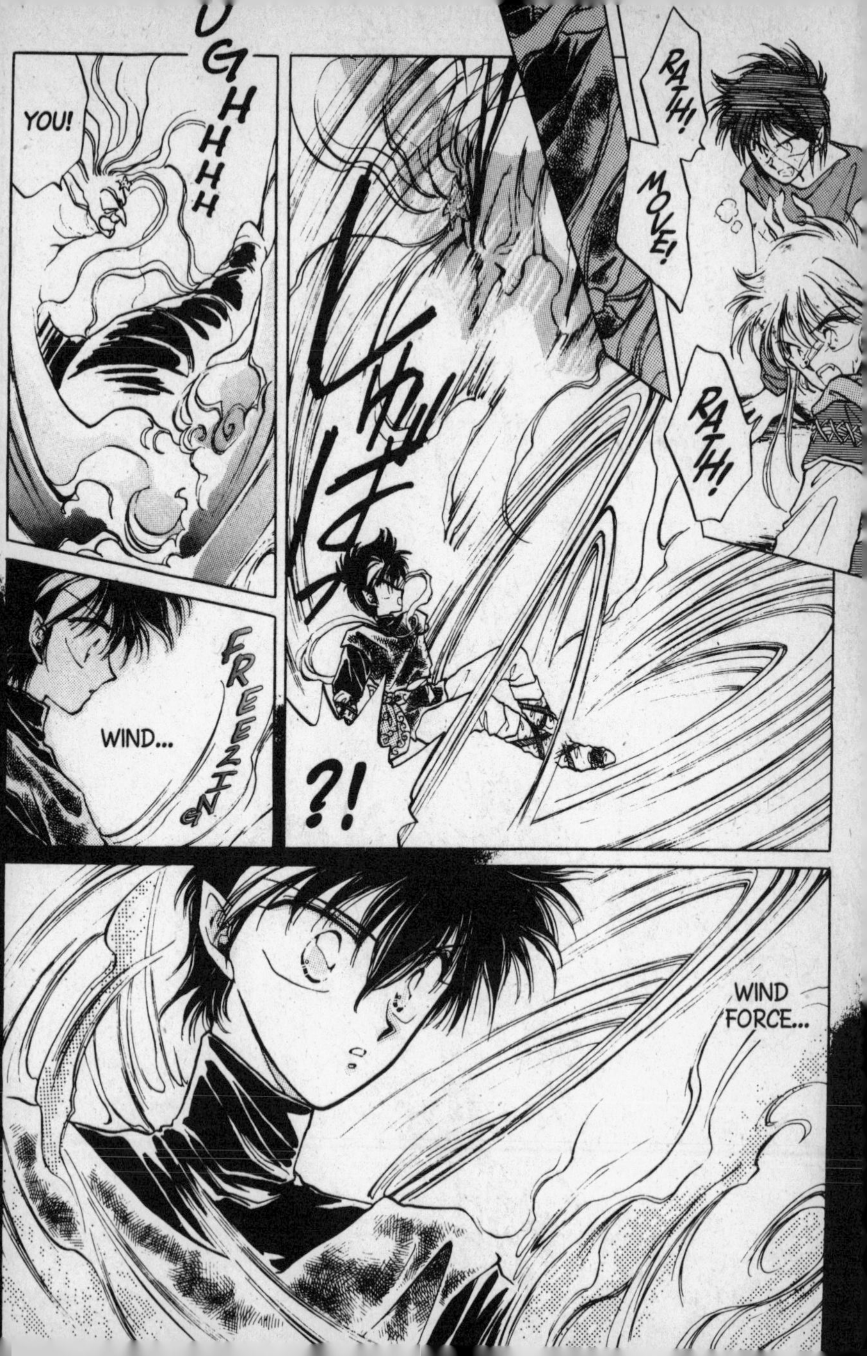
RATH! MOVE!
RATH!
?!
UGHHHHH
YOU!
FREEZING
WIND...
WIND FORCE...

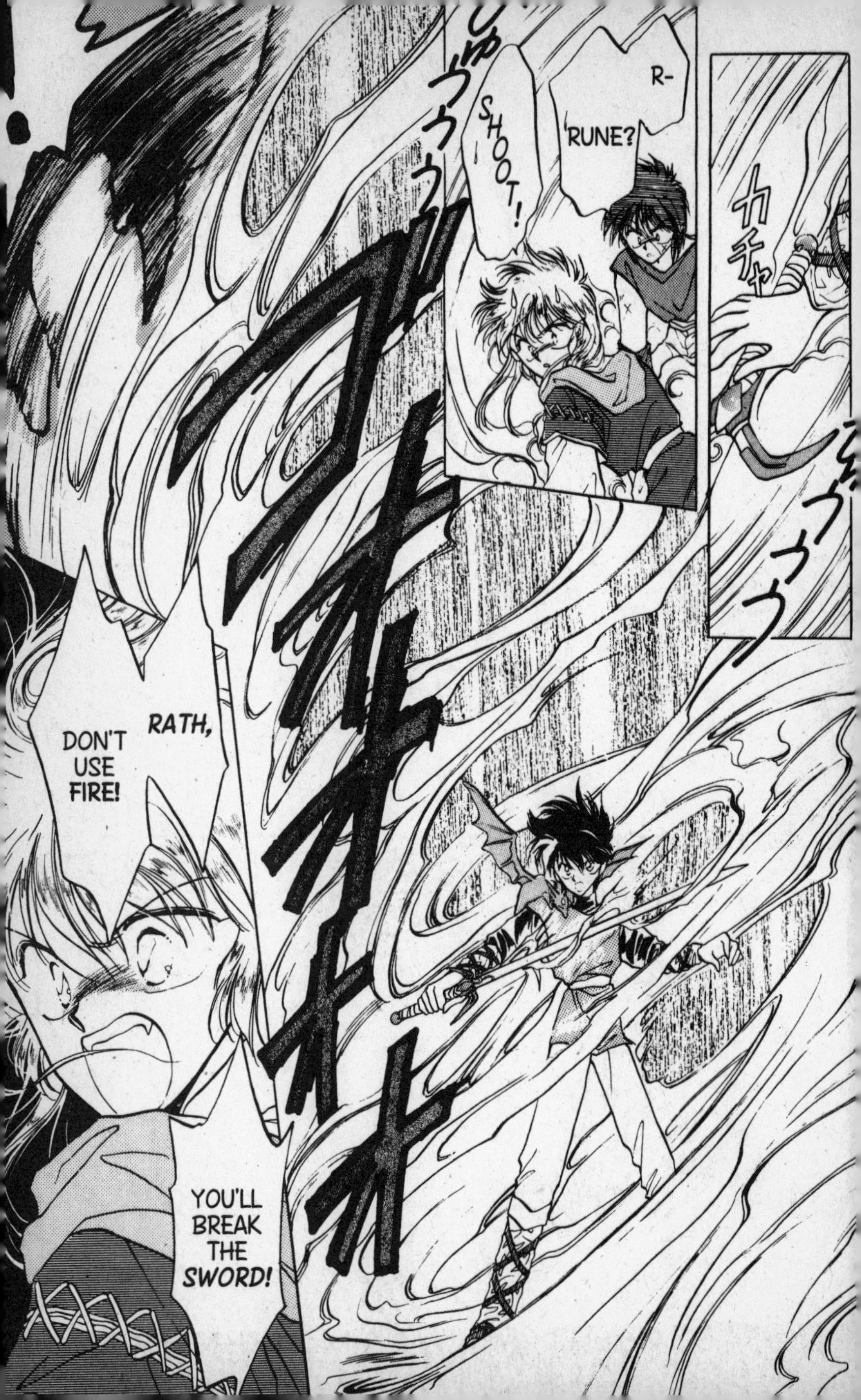
カチャ
R-
RUNE?
SHOOT!
しゅううう
ゴオオオオ
RATH,
DON'T USE FIRE!
YOU'LL BREAK THE SWORD!

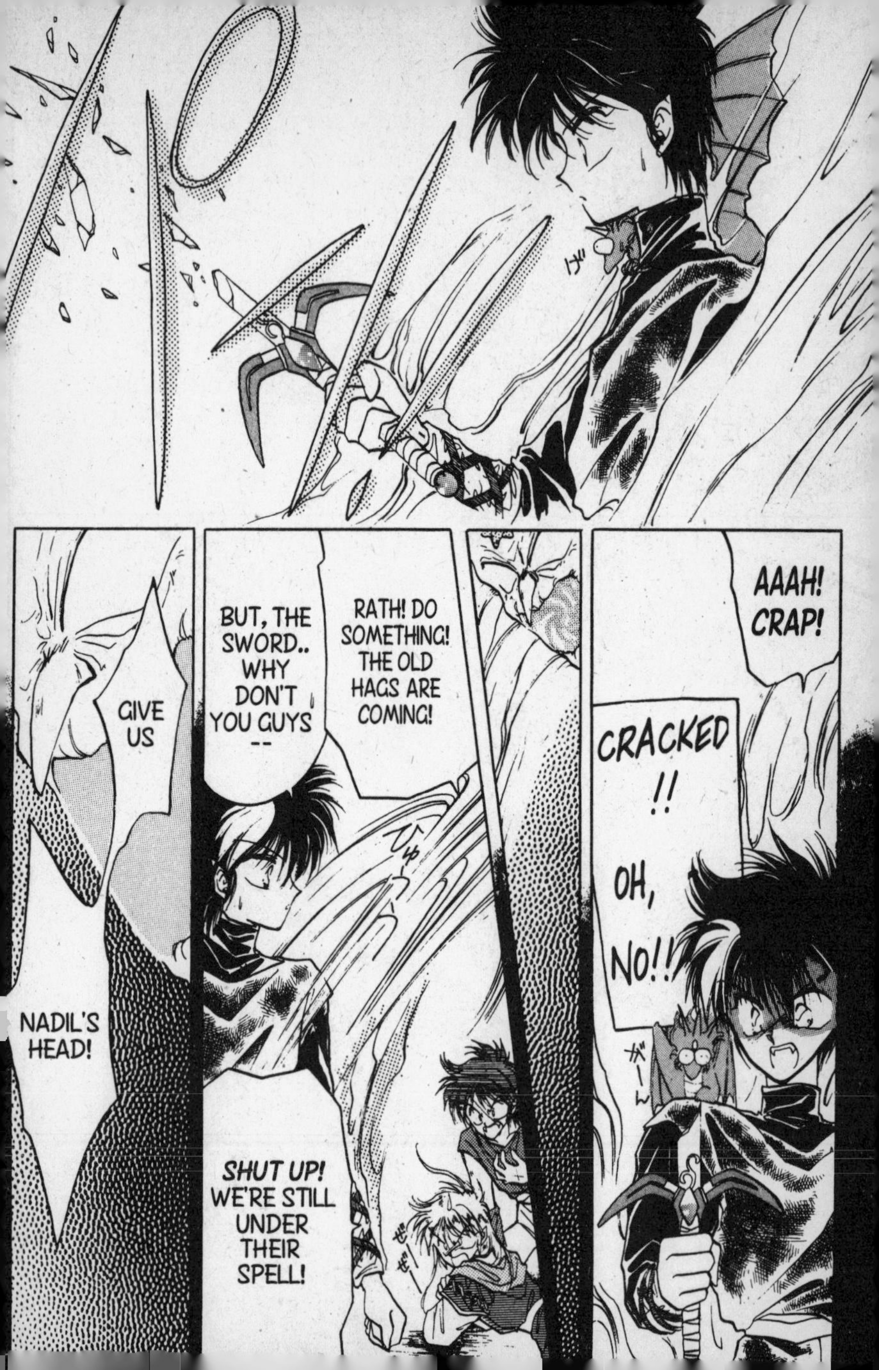
AAAH! CRAP!
CRACKED!!
OH, NO!!
RATH! DO SOMETHING! THE OLD HAGS ARE COMING!
BUT, THE SWORD.. WHY DON'T YOU GUYS --
SHUT UP! WE'RE STILL UNDER THEIR SPELL!
GIVE US
NADIL'S HEAD!

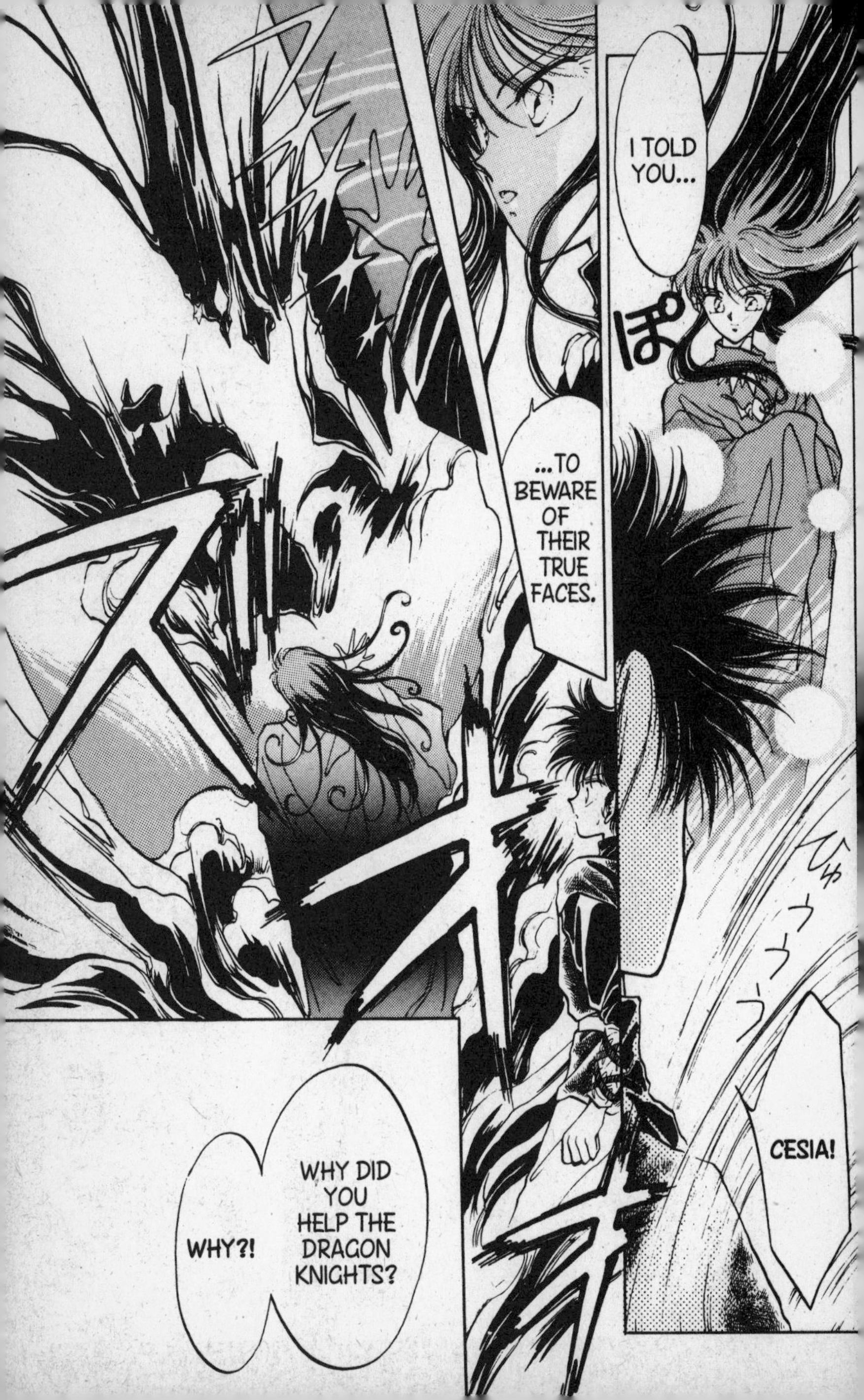
I TOLD YOU...
ぽ
...TO BEWARE OF THEIR TRUE FACES.
CESIA!
WHY DID YOU HELP THE DRAGON KNIGHTS?
WHY?!

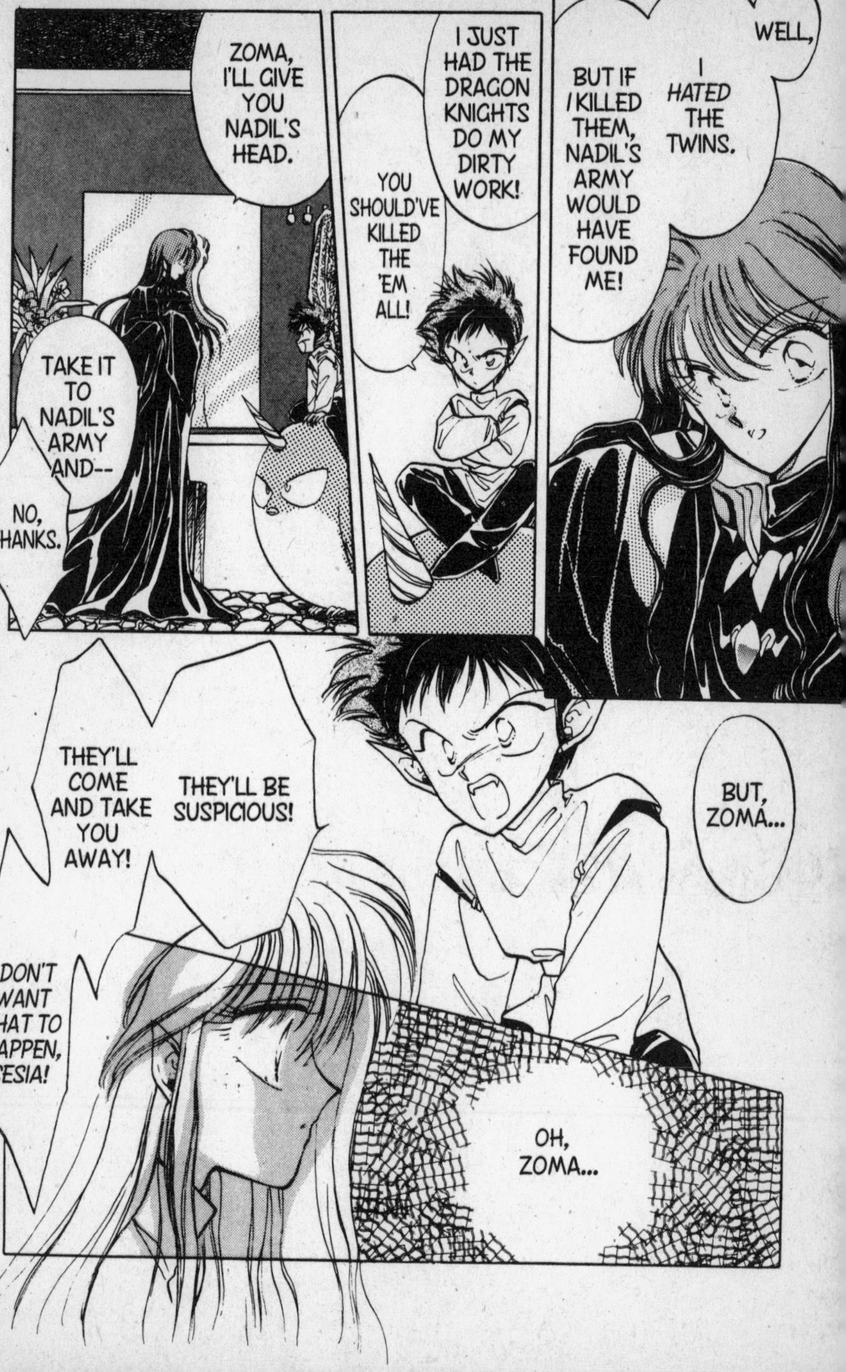
WELL,
I *HATED* THE TWINS.
BUT IF I KILLED THEM, NADIL'S ARMY WOULD HAVE FOUND ME!
I JUST HAD THE DRAGON KNIGHTS DO MY DIRTY WORK!
YOU SHOULD'VE KILLED THE 'EM ALL!
ZOMA, I'LL GIVE YOU NADIL'S HEAD.
TAKE IT TO NADIL'S ARMY AND--
NO, THANKS.
BUT, ZOMA...
THEY'LL BE SUSPICIOUS!
THEY'LL COME AND TAKE YOU AWAY!
I DON'T WANT THAT TO HAPPEN, CESIA!
OH, ZOMA...

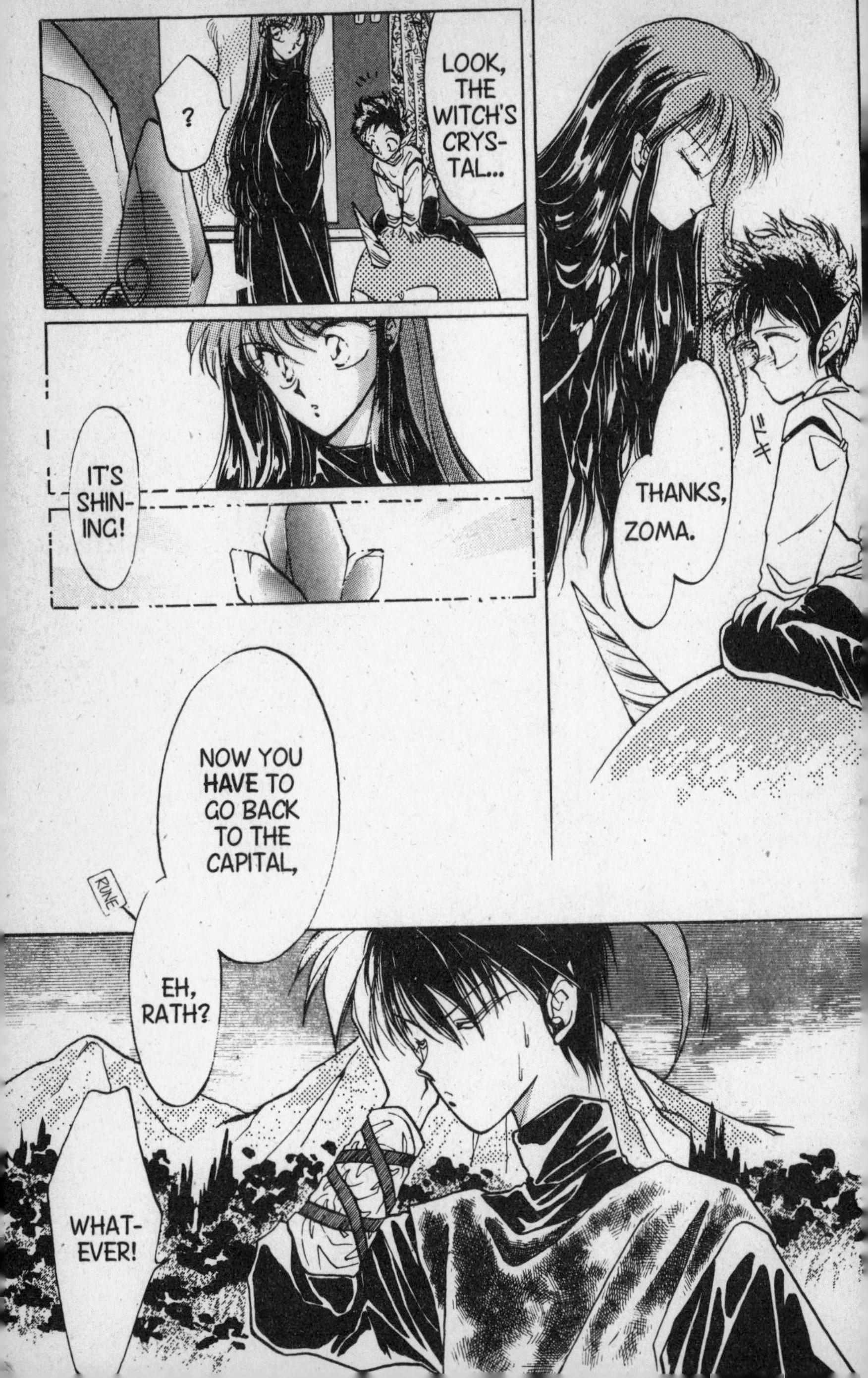
THANKS, ZOMA.
ドキ
LOOK, THE WITCH'S CRYS- TAL...
?
IT'S SHIN- ING!
NOW YOU HAVE TO GO BACK TO THE CAPITAL,
RUNE
EH, RATH?
WHAT- EVER!

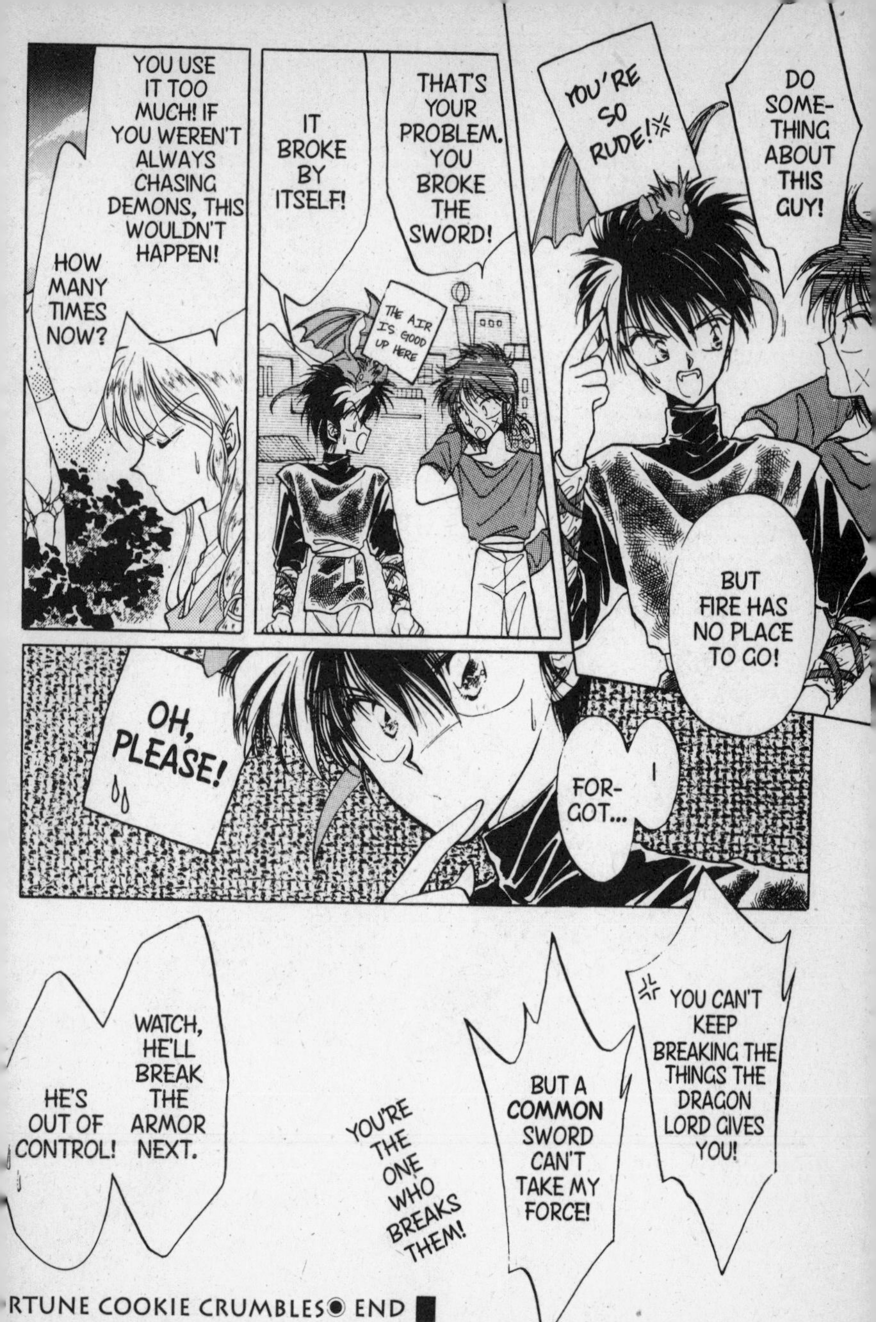
DO SOME-THING ABOUT THIS GUY!
YOU'RE SO RUDE!
BUT FIRE HAS NO PLACE TO GO!
THAT'S YOUR PROBLEM. YOU BROKE THE SWORD!
IT BROKE BY ITSELF!
THE AIR IS GOOD UP HERE
YOU USE IT TOO MUCH! IF YOU WEREN'T ALWAYS CHASING DEMONS, THIS WOULDN'T HAPPEN!
HOW MANY TIMES NOW?
I FOR-GOT...
OH, PLEASE!
YOU CAN'T KEEP BREAKING THE THINGS THE DRAGON LORD GIVES YOU!
BUT A COMMON SWORD CAN'T TAKE MY FORCE!
YOU'RE THE ONE WHO BREAKS THEM!
WATCH, HE'LL BREAK THE ARMOR NEXT.
HE'S OUT OF CONTROL!

RTUNE COOKIE CRUMBLES END

CESIA

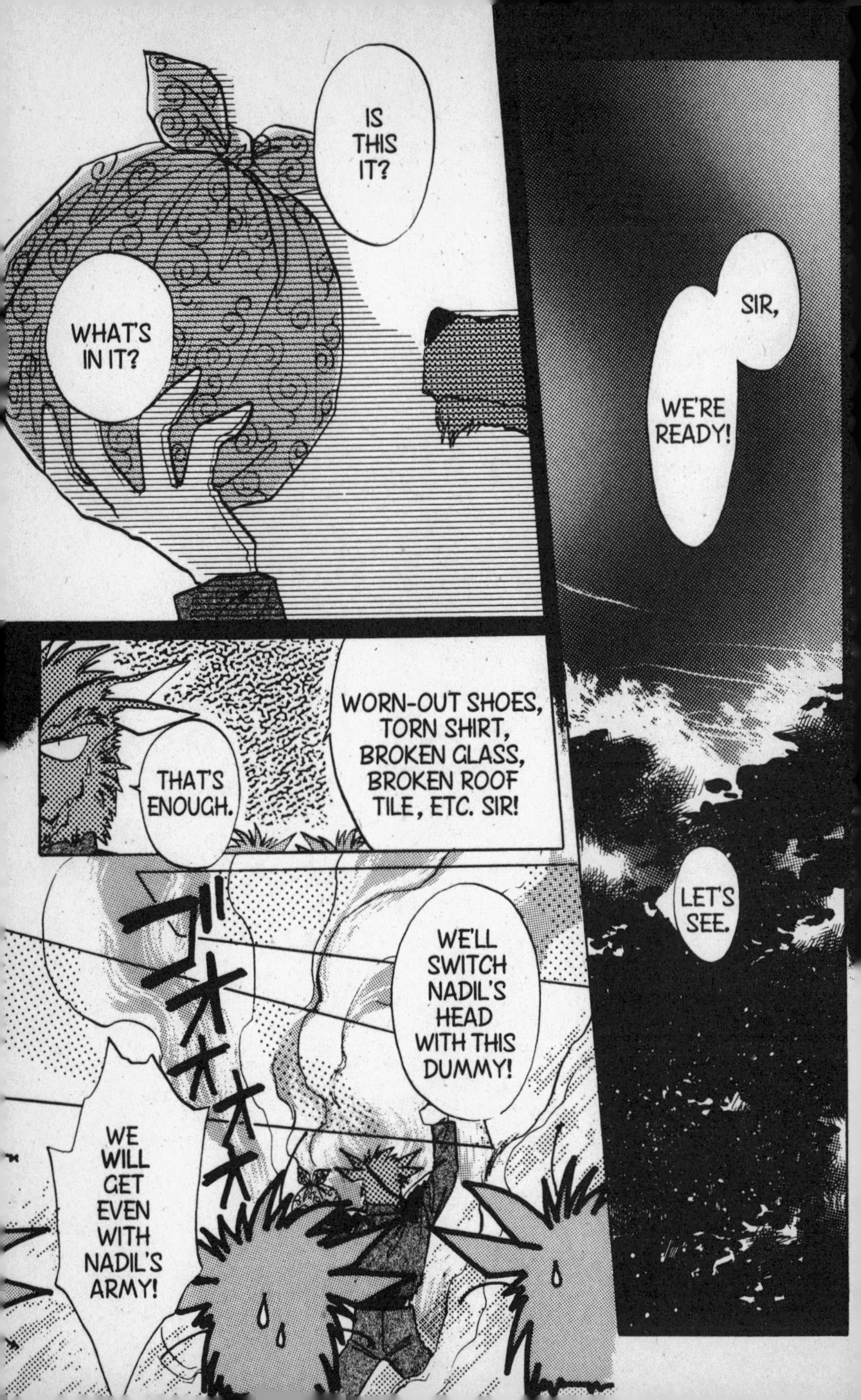
SIR,
WE'RE READY!
LET'S SEE.
IS THIS IT?
WHAT'S IN IT?
WORN-OUT SHOES, TORN SHIRT, BROKEN GLASS, BROKEN ROOF TILE, ETC. SIR!
THAT'S ENOUGH.
WE'LL SWITCH NADIL'S HEAD WITH THIS DUMMY!
WE WILL GET EVEN WITH NADIL'S ARMY!

DARK AND STORMY KNIGHTS

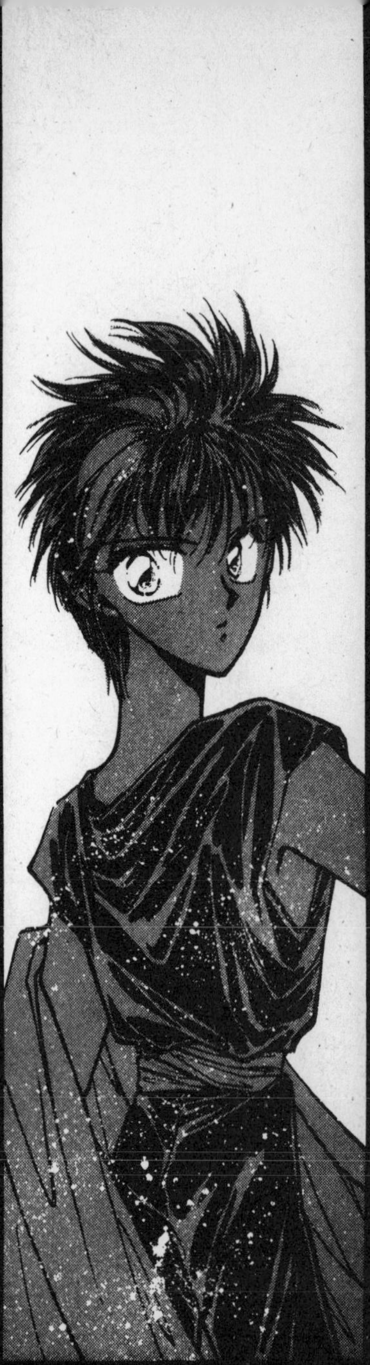

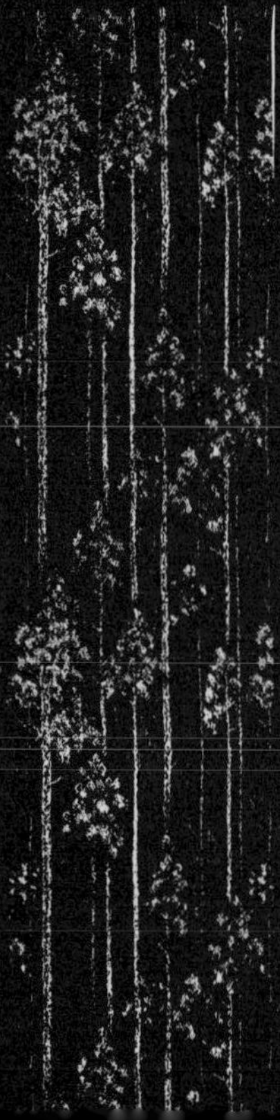

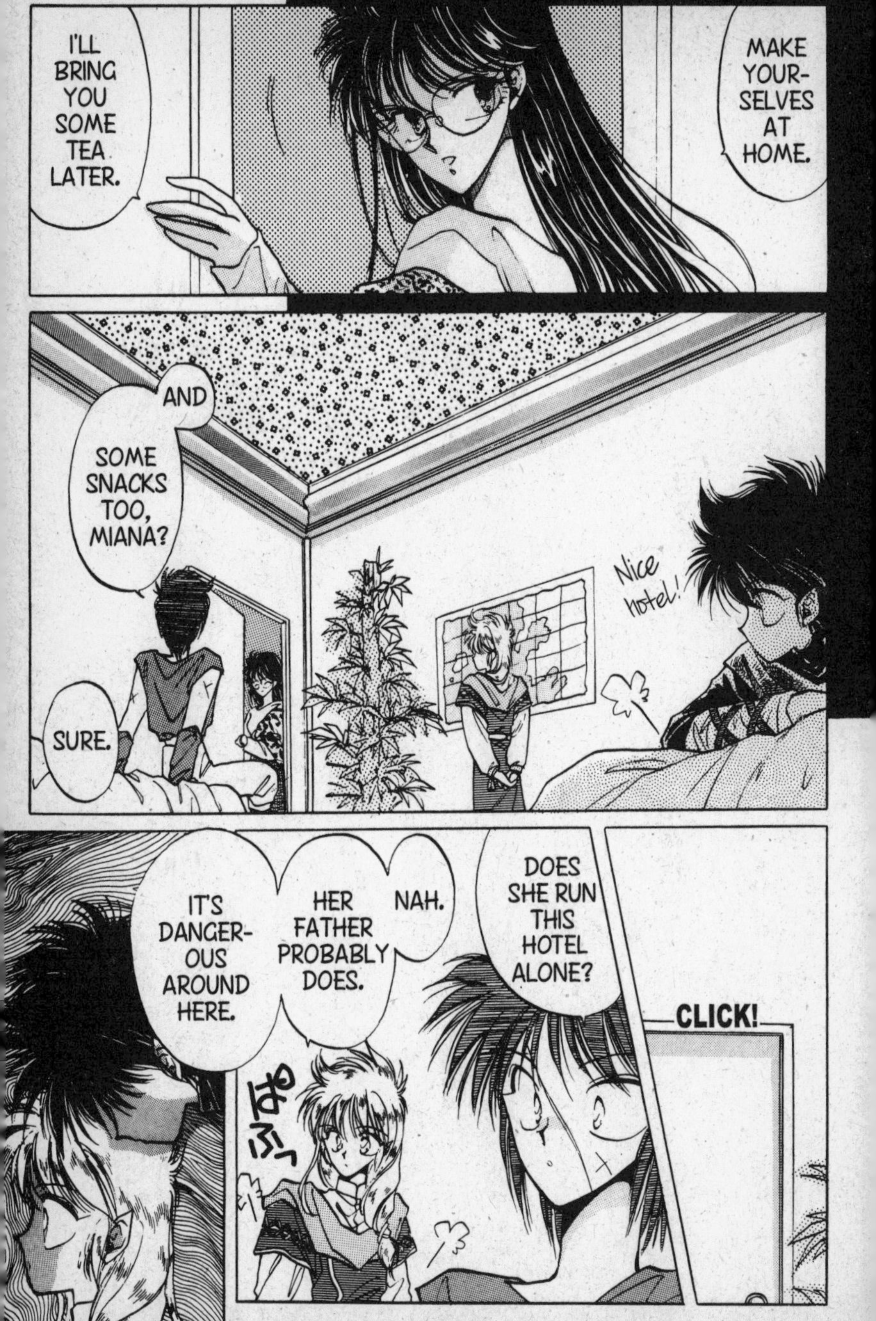
MAKE YOUR-SELVES AT HOME.
I'LL BRING YOU SOME TEA LATER.
Nice hotel!
AND SOME SNACKS TOO, MIANA?
SURE.
CLICK!
DOES SHE RUN THIS HOTEL ALONE?
NAH.
HER FATHER PROBABLY DOES.
IT'S DANGER-OUS AROUND HERE.
ぽふっ

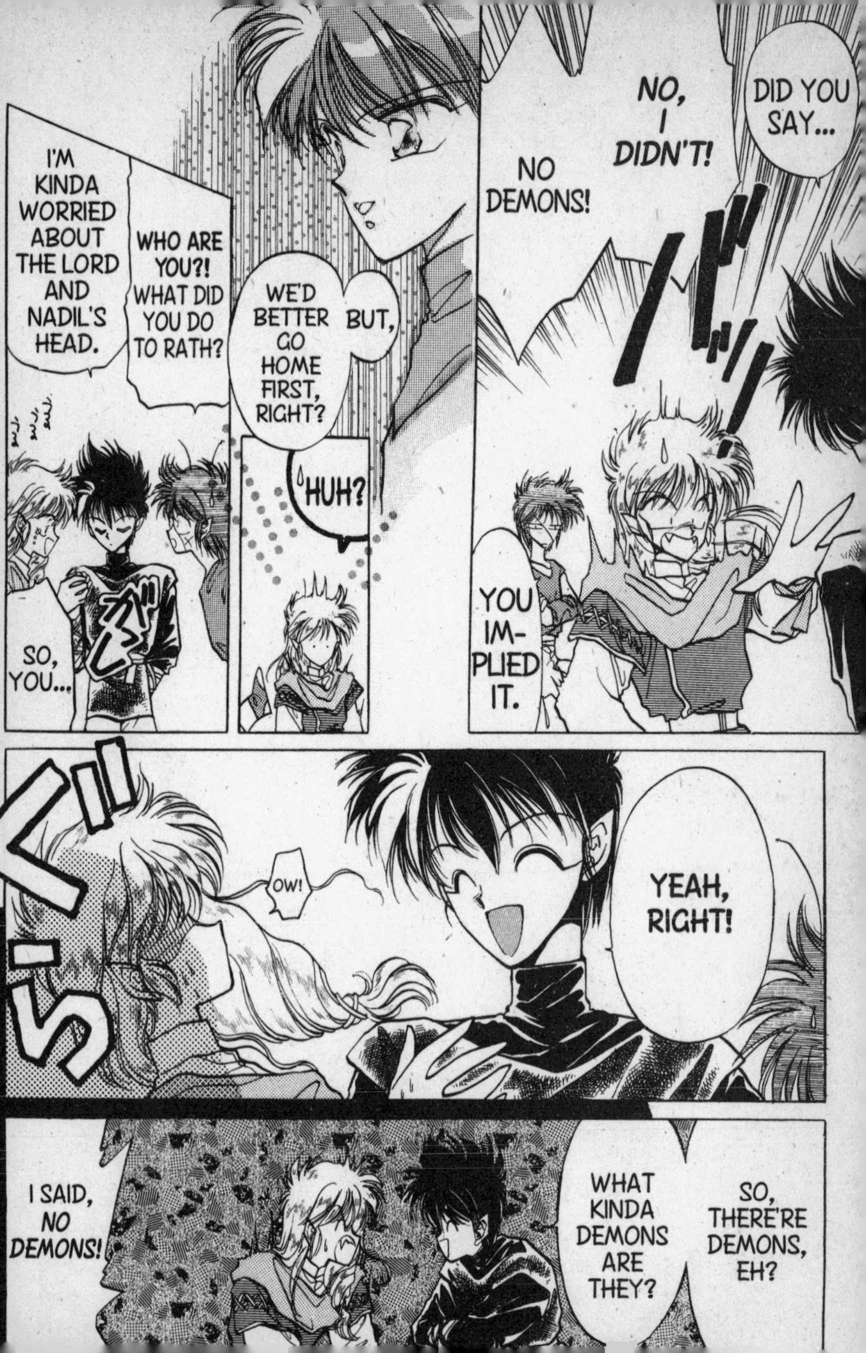
DID YOU SAY...
NO, I DIDN'T!
NO DEMONS!
YOU IM-PLIED IT.
BUT,
WE'D BETTER GO HOME FIRST, RIGHT?
HUH?
WHO ARE YOU?! WHAT DID YOU DO TO RATH?
I'M KINDA WORRIED ABOUT THE LORD AND NADIL'S HEAD.
SO, YOU...
YEAH, RIGHT!
OW!
SO, THERE'RE DEMONS, EH?
WHAT KINDA DEMONS ARE THEY?
I SAID, NO DEMONS!

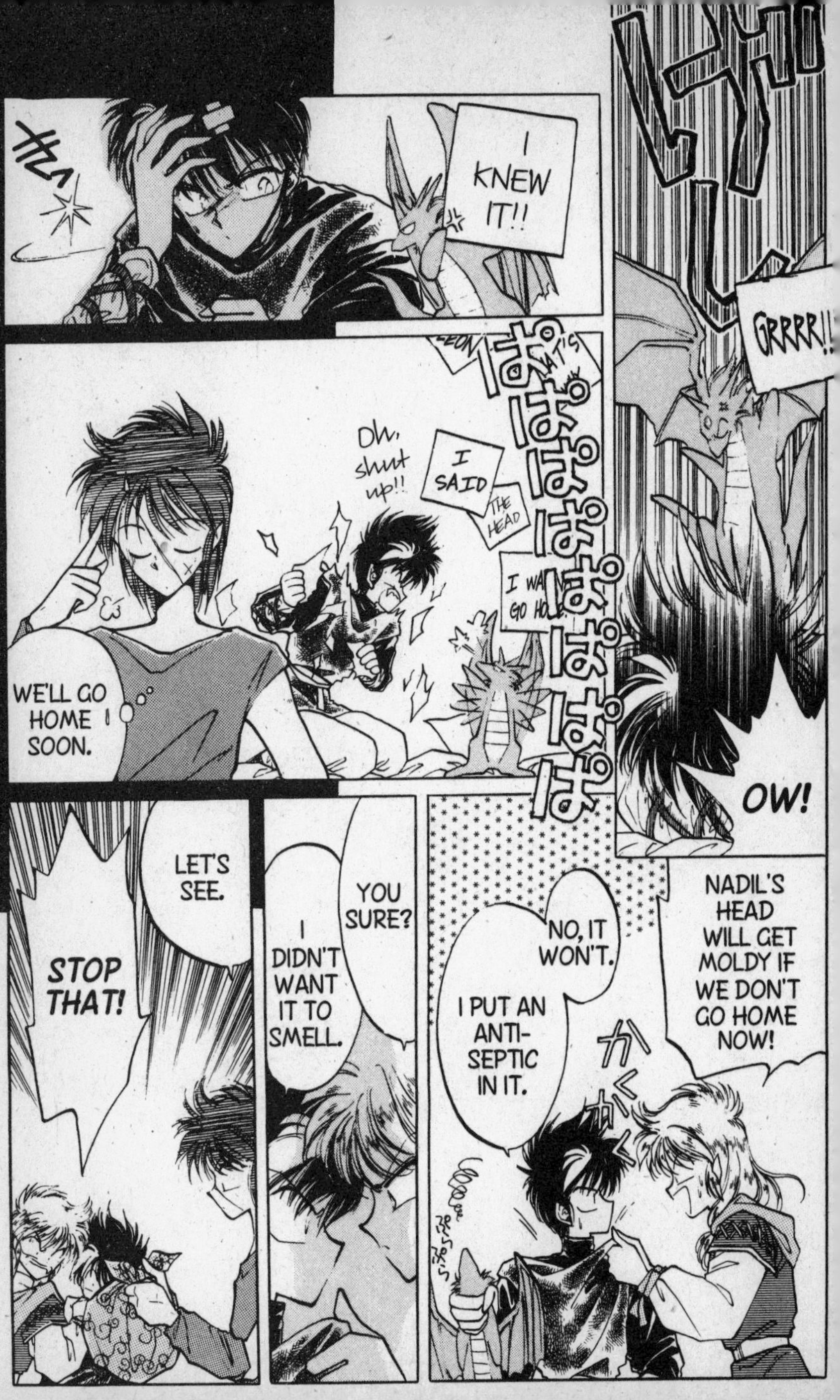
GRRRR!!
OW!
I KNEW IT!!
I SAID
THE HEAD
Oh, shut up!!
WE'LL GO HOME SOON.
NADIL'S HEAD WILL GET MOLDY IF WE DON'T GO HOME NOW!
NO, IT WON'T.
I PUT AN ANTI-SEPTIC IN IT.
YOU SURE?
I DIDN'T WANT IT TO SMELL.
LET'S SEE.
STOP THAT!

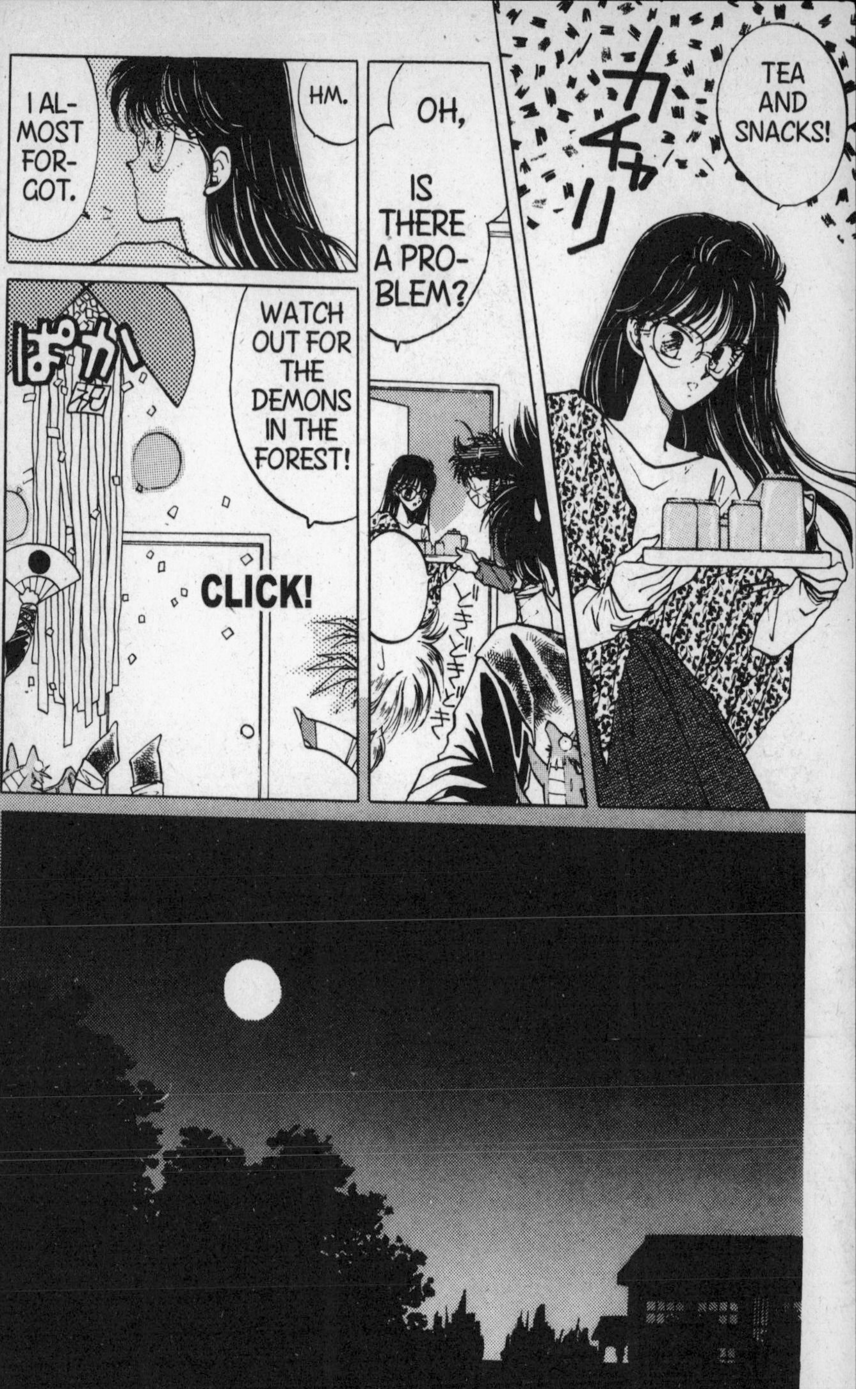

カチャリ
TEA AND SNACKS!
OH, IS THERE A PROBLEM?
HM.
I AL-MOST FOR-GOT.
WATCH OUT FOR THE DEMONS IN THE FOREST!
ぽか
CLICK!

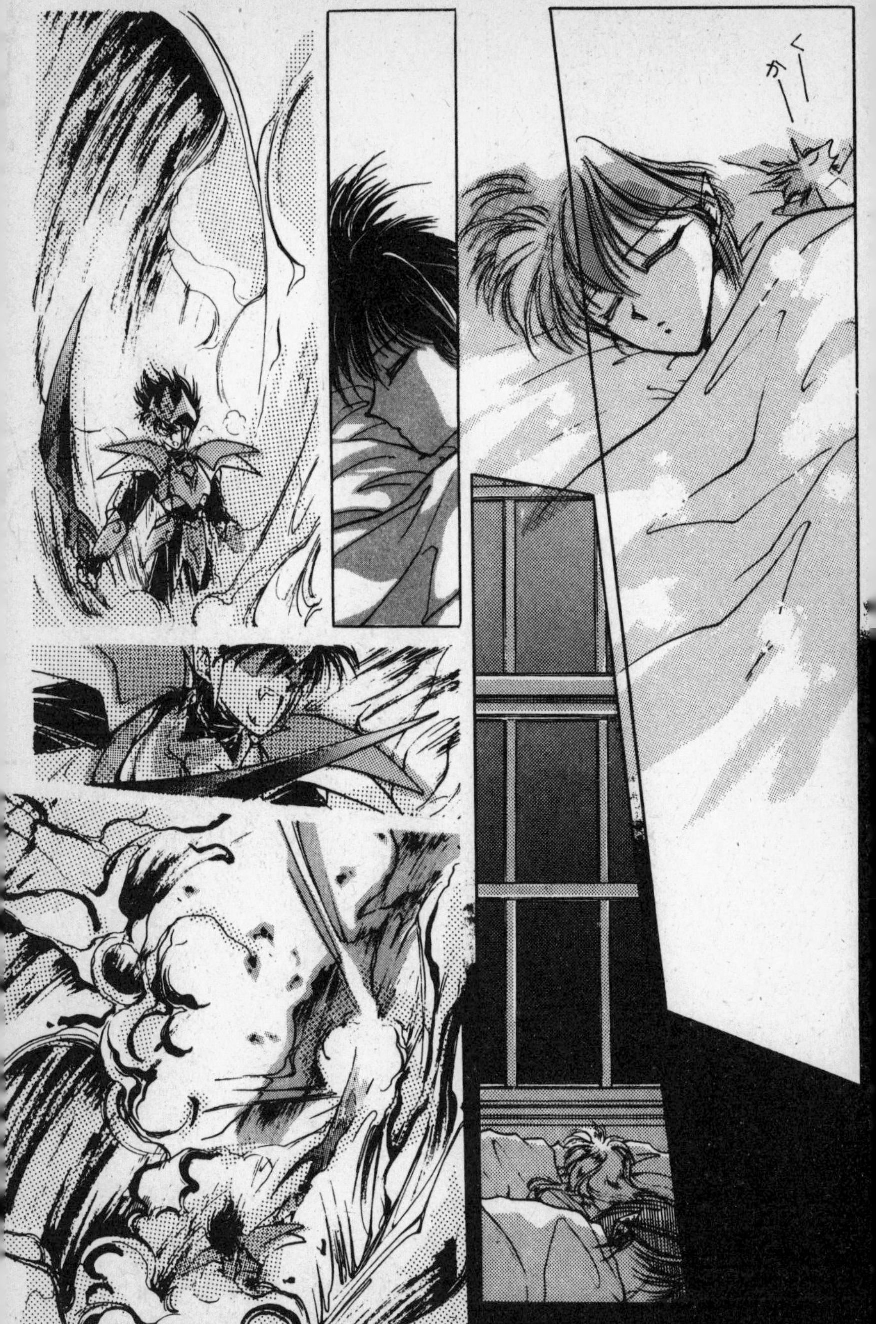
くー
かー

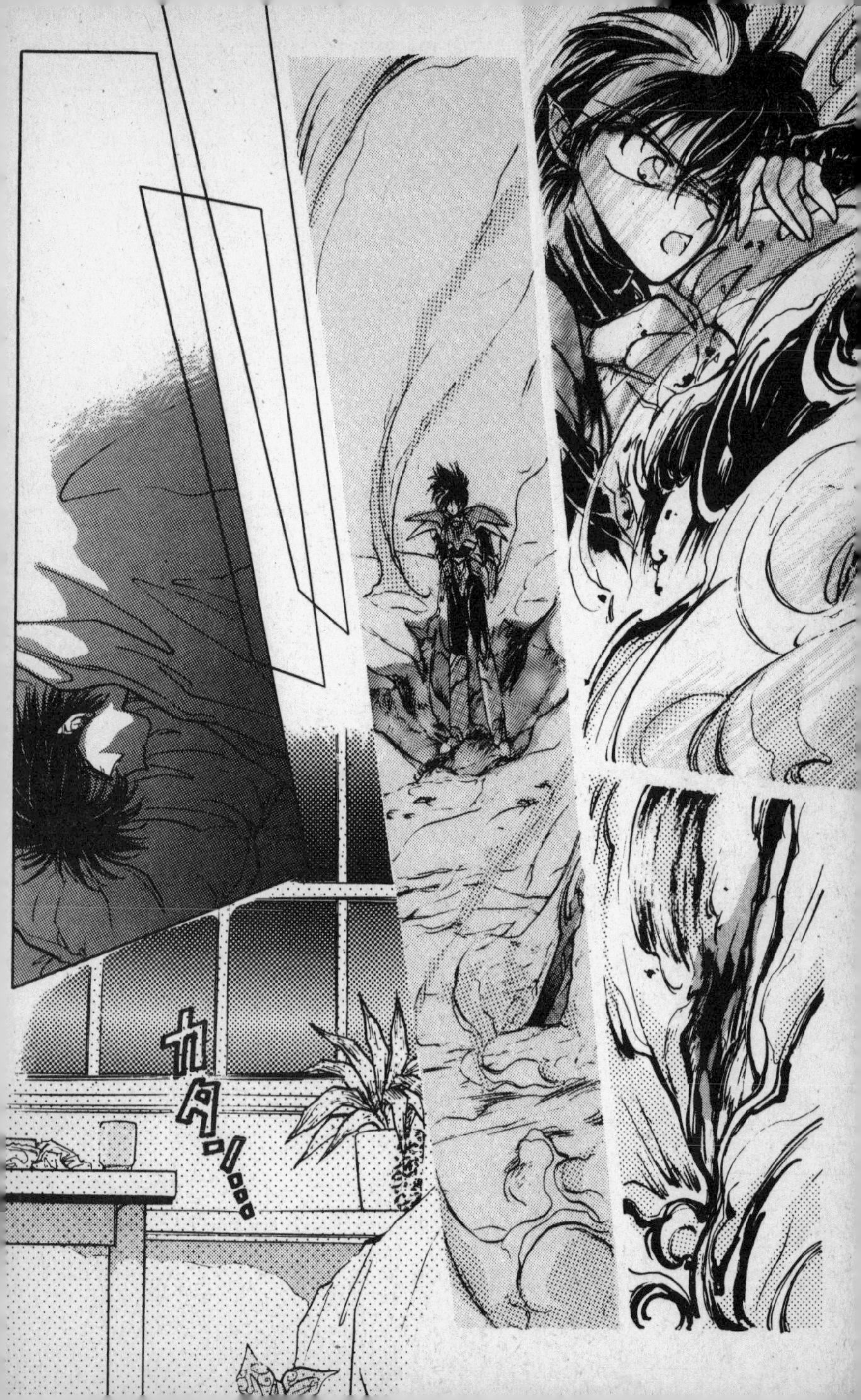
カタ

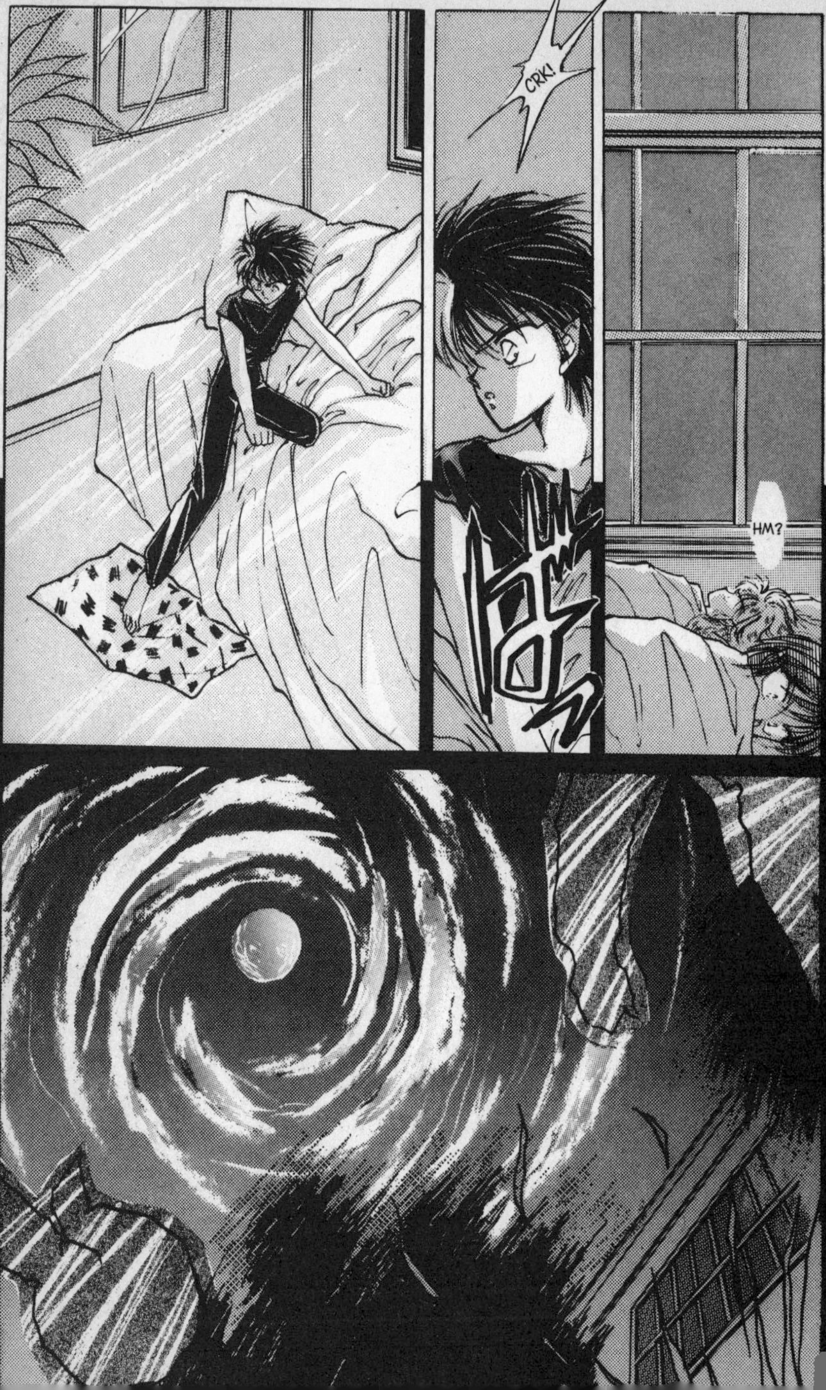
HM?
CRK!

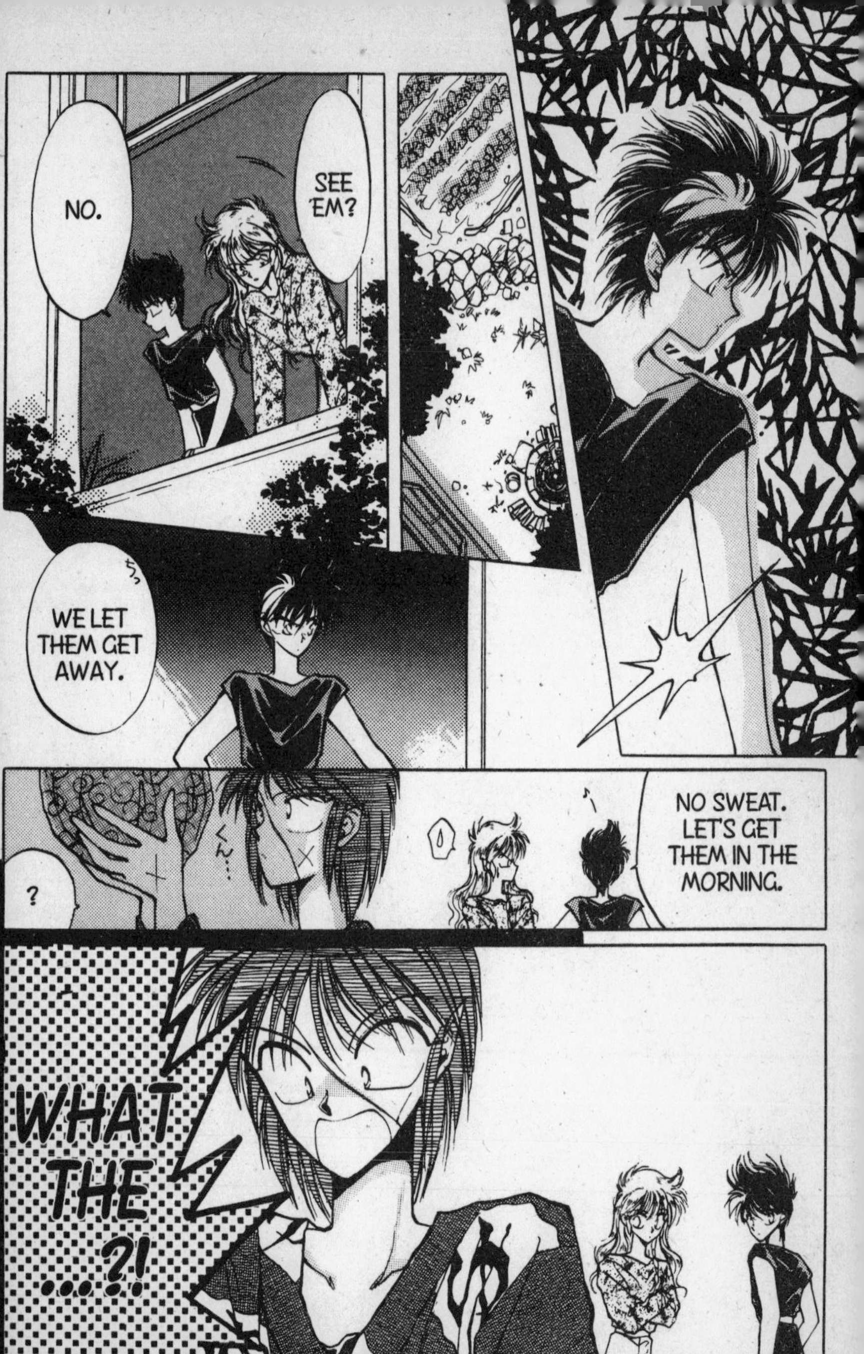
SEE 'EM?
NO.
WE LET THEM GET AWAY.
NO SWEAT. LET'S GET THEM IN THE MORNING.
?
WHAT THE ...?!

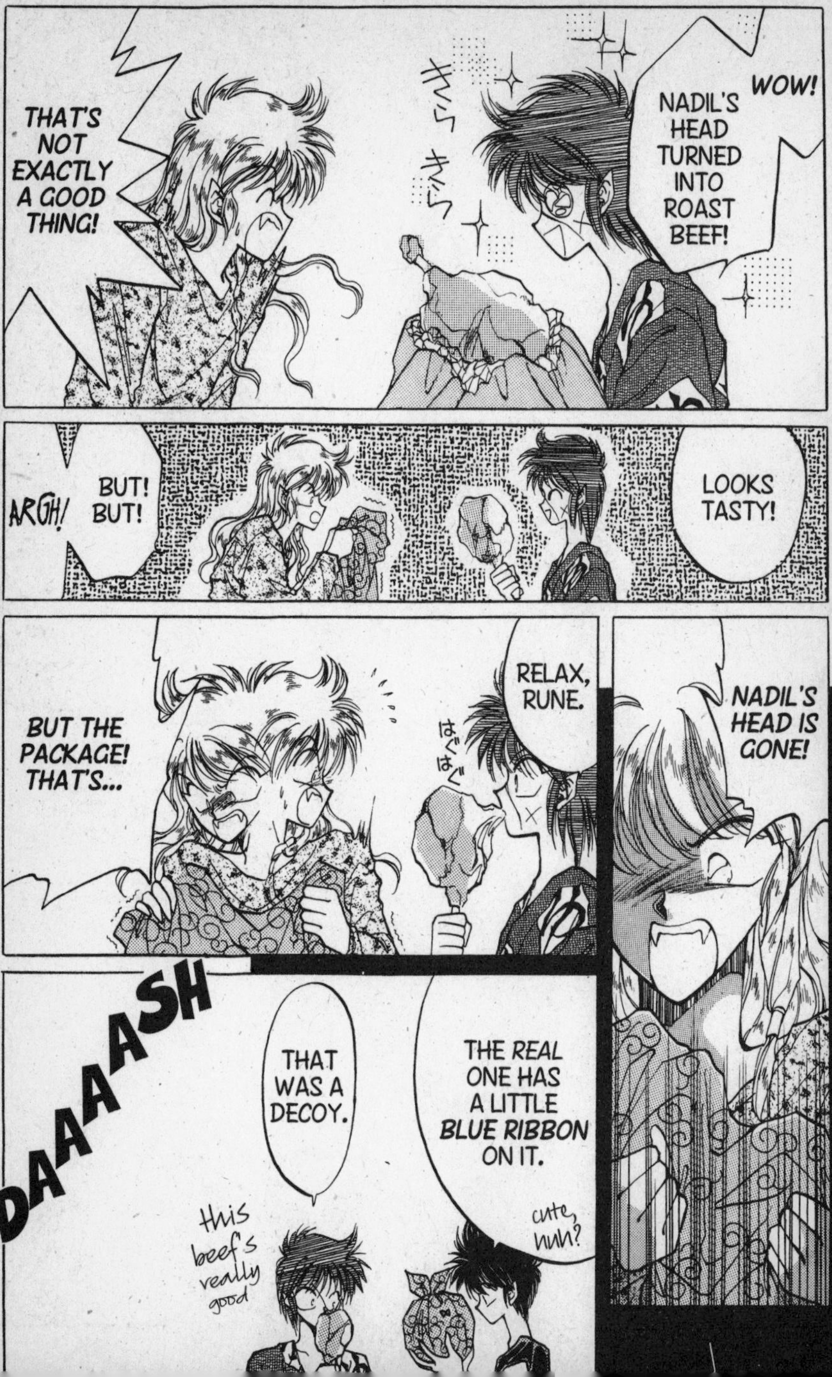
WOW!
NADIL'S HEAD TURNED INTO ROAST BEEF!
きらきら
THAT'S NOT EXACTLY A GOOD THING!
LOOKS TASTY!
BUT! BUT!
ARGH!
NADIL'S HEAD IS GONE!
RELAX, RUNE.
はぐはぐ
BUT THE PACKAGE! THAT'S...
THE *REAL* ONE HAS A LITTLE *BLUE RIBBON* ON IT.
cute, huh?
THAT WAS A DECOY.
this beef's really good
DAAAASH

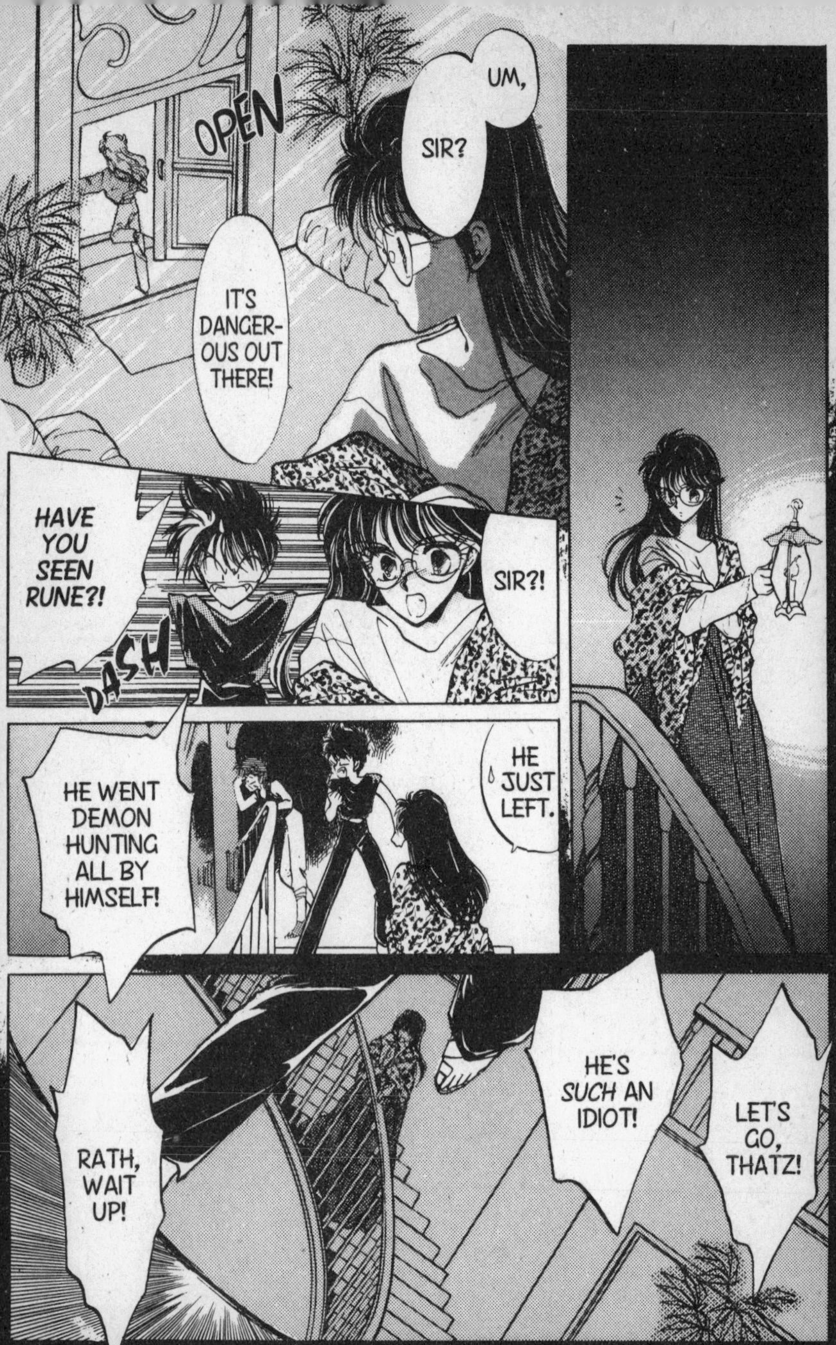
UM,
SIR?
OPEN
IT'S DANGER-OUS OUT THERE!
SIR?!
HAVE YOU SEEN RUNE?!
DASH
HE JUST LEFT.
HE WENT DEMON HUNTING ALL BY HIMSELF!
LET'S GO, THATZ!
HE'S *SUCH* AN IDIOT!
RATH, WAIT UP!

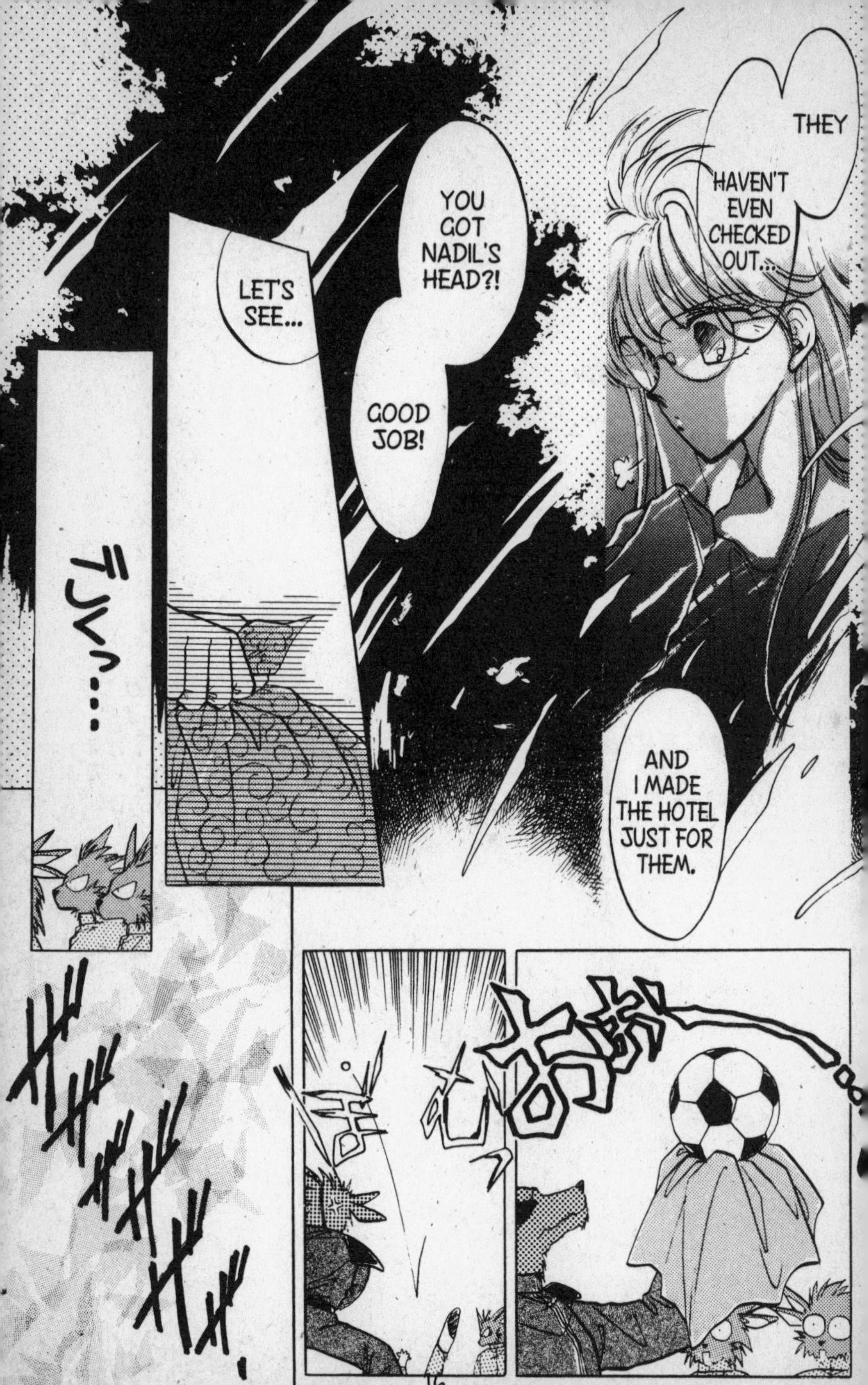
THEY HAVEN'T EVEN CHECKED OUT...
AND I MADE THE HOTEL JUST FOR THEM.
YOU GOT NADIL'S HEAD?!
GOOD JOB!
LET'S SEE...

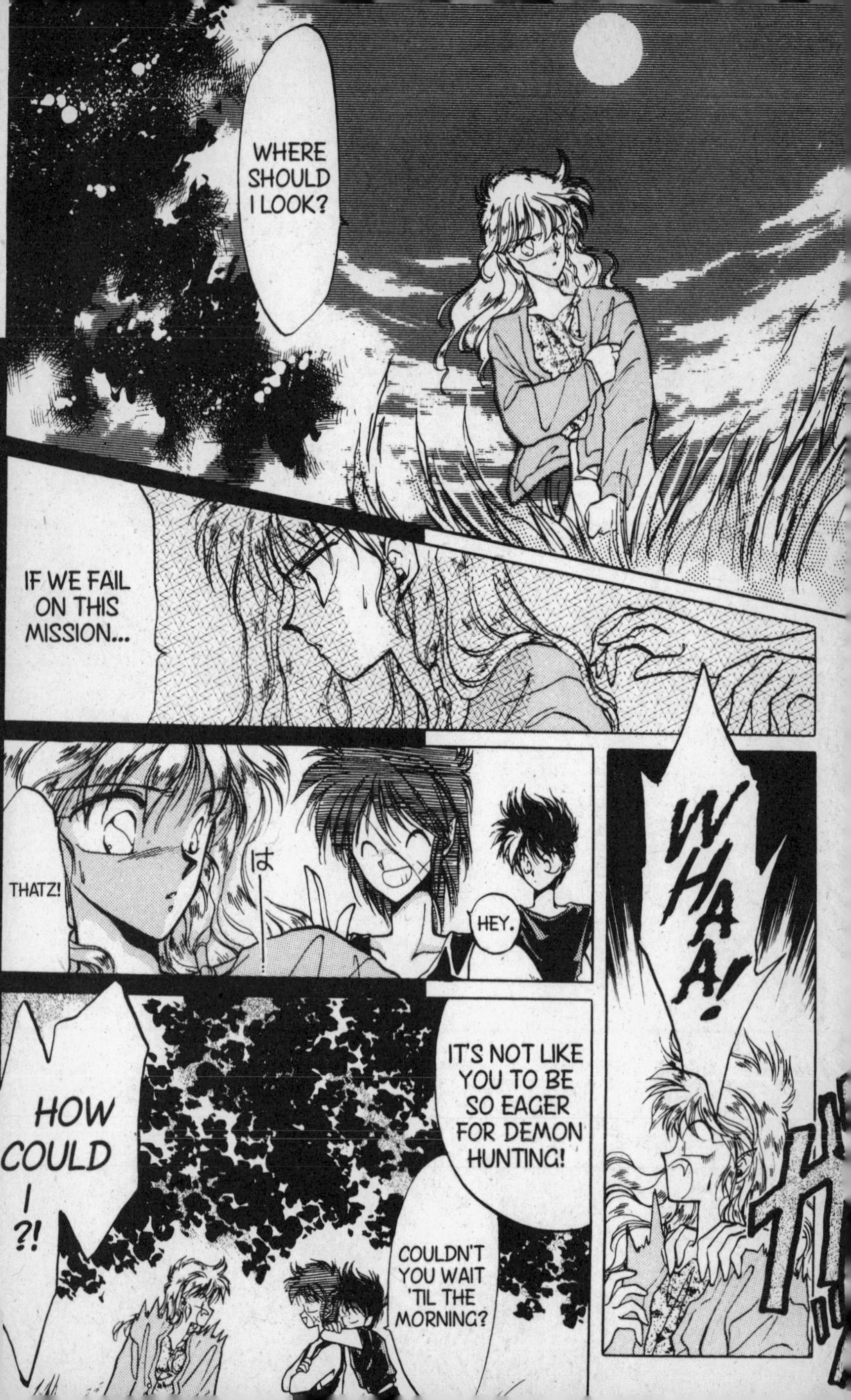
WHERE SHOULD I LOOK?
IF WE FAIL ON THIS MISSION...
WHAHA!
HEY.
は
THATZ!
IT'S NOT LIKE YOU TO BE SO EAGER FOR DEMON HUNTING!
COULDN'T YOU WAIT 'TIL THE MORNING?
HOW COULD I ?!

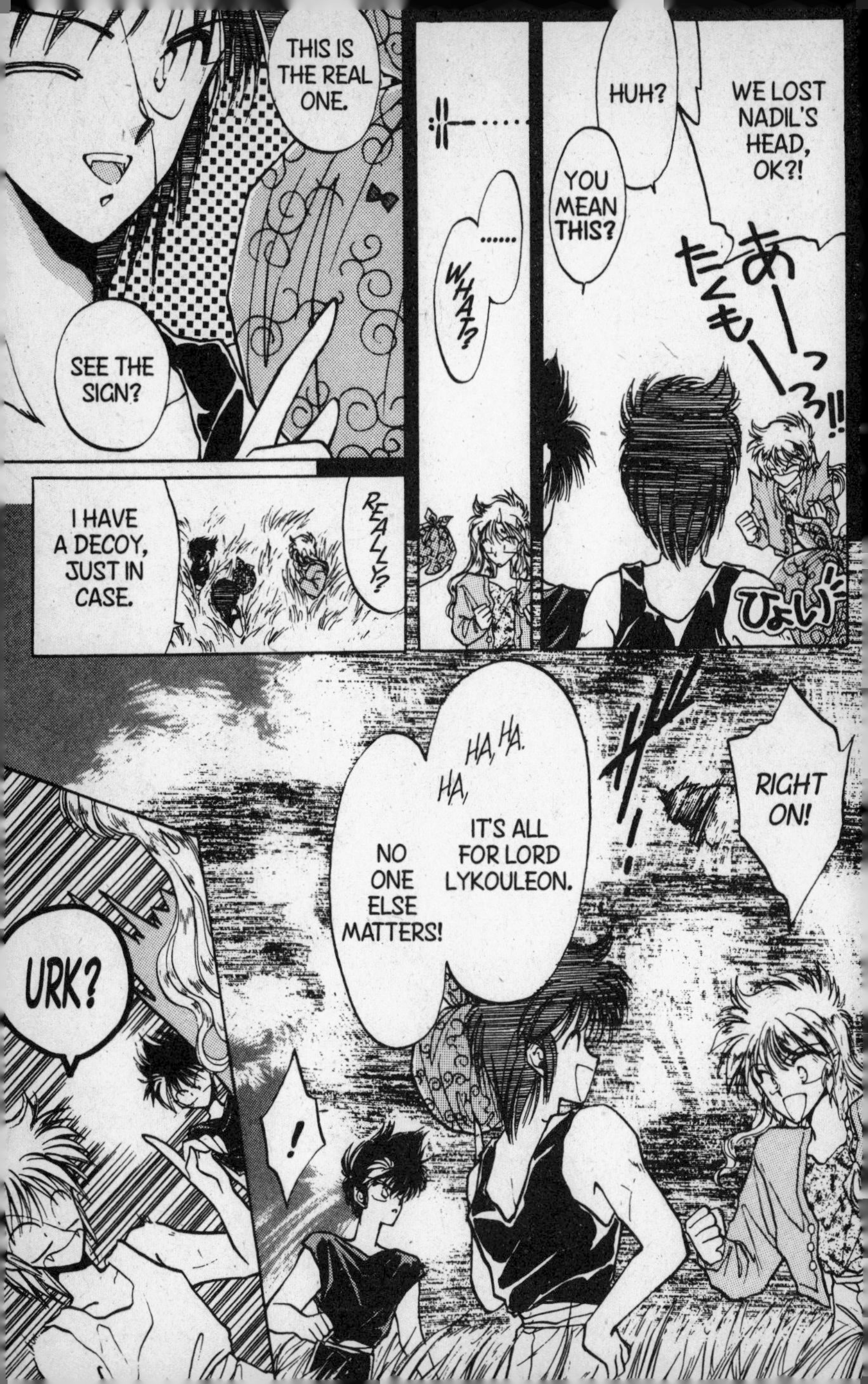
WE LOST NADIL'S HEAD, OK?!
あーっ
たくもーろ!!
HUH?
YOU MEAN THIS?
ひょい
......
WHAT?!
!!-.....
THIS IS THE REAL ONE.
SEE THE SIGN?
REALLY?
I HAVE A DECOY, JUST IN CASE.
RIGHT ON!
HA, HA, HA.
IT'S ALL FOR LORD LYKOULEON.
NO ONE ELSE MATTERS!
!
URK?

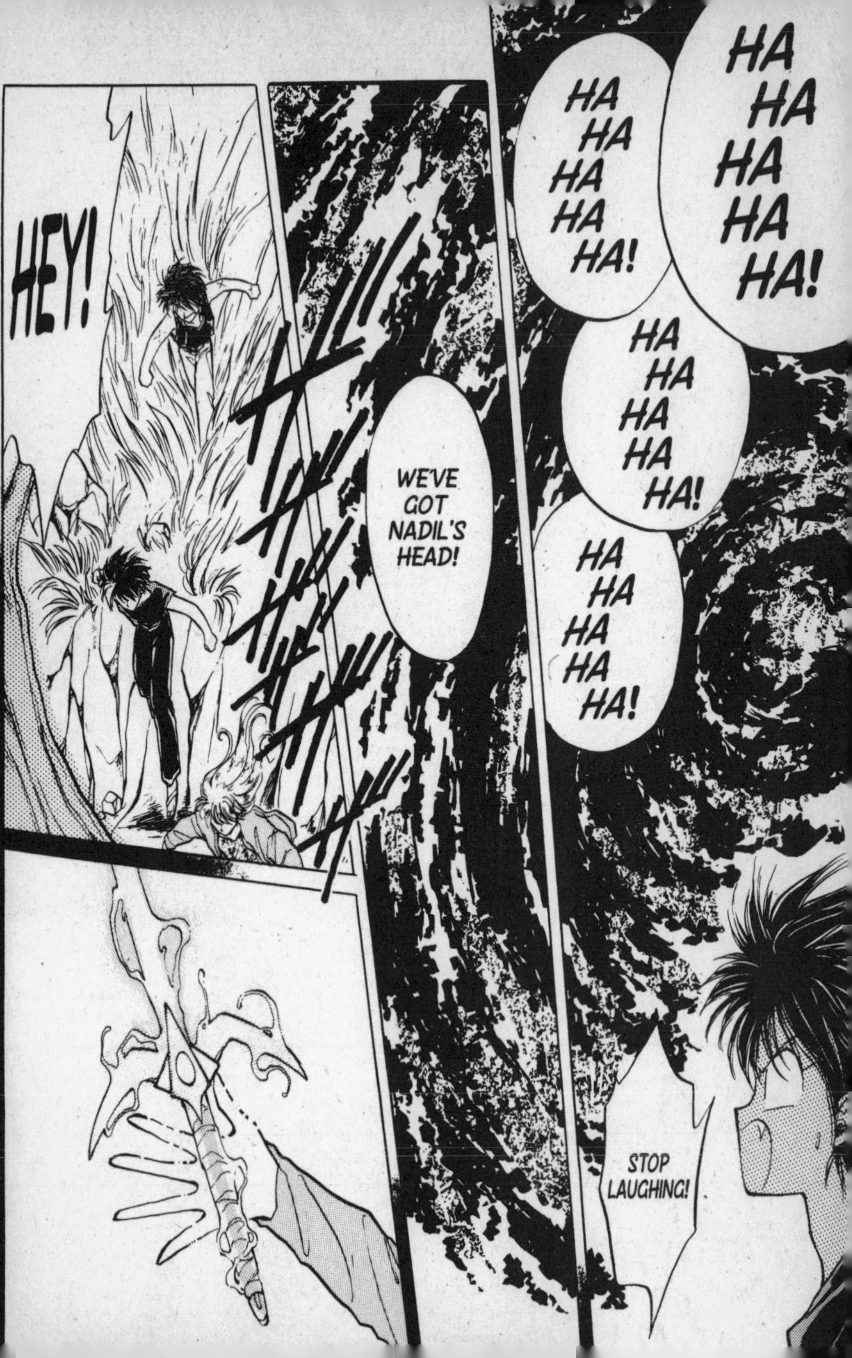
HA HA HA HA HA!
HA HA HA HA HA!
HA HA HA HA HA!
HA HA HA HA HA HA!
STOP LAUGHING!
WE'VE GOT NADIL'S HEAD!
HEY!

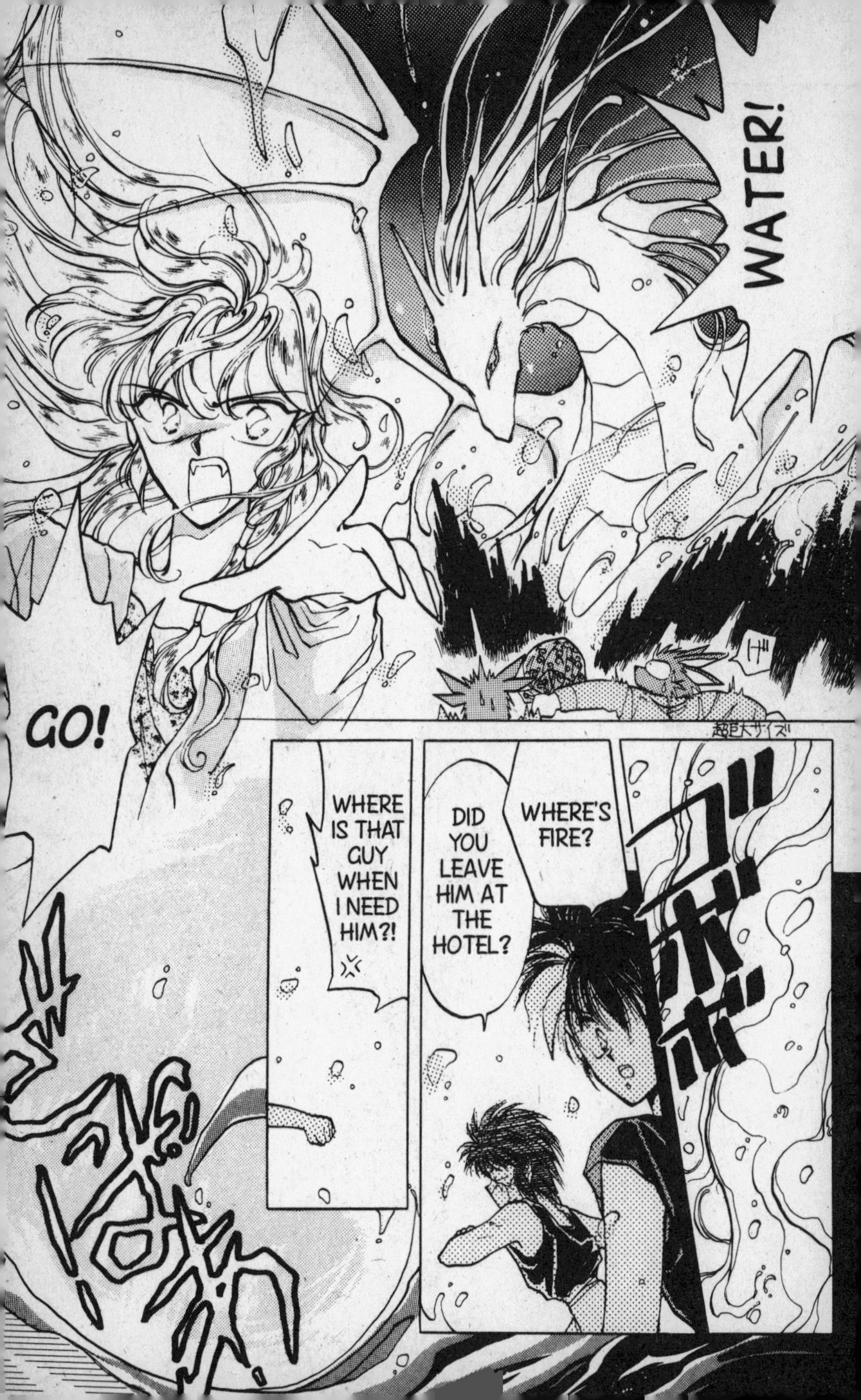
WATER!
GO!
WHERE'S FIRE?
DID YOU LEAVE HIM AT THE HOTEL?
WHERE IS THAT GUY WHEN I NEED HIM?!

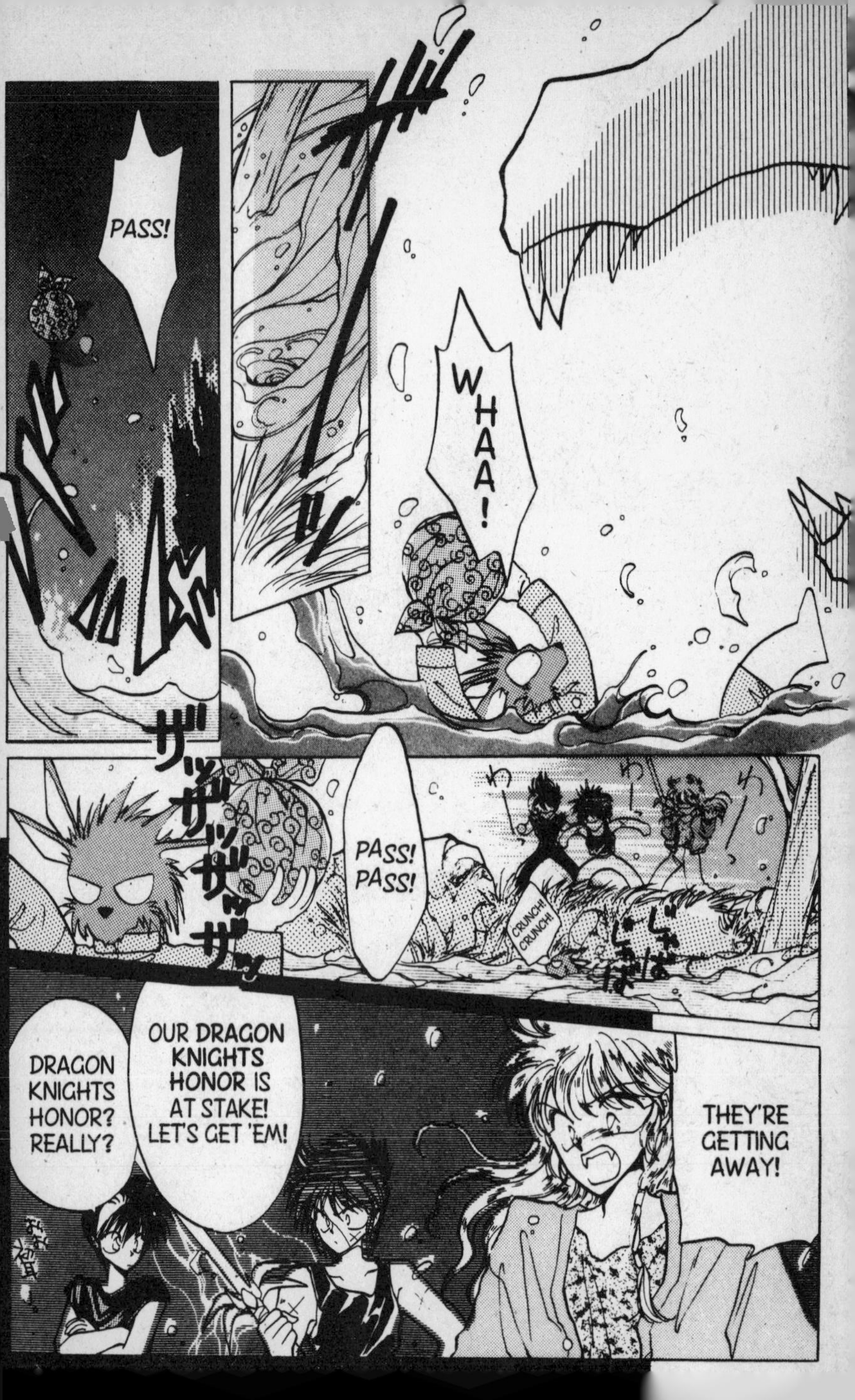
WHAA!
PASS!
PASS! PASS!
CRUNCH! CRUNCH!
THEY'RE GETTING AWAY!
OUR DRAGON KNIGHTS HONOR IS AT STAKE! LET'S GET 'EM!
DRAGON KNIGHTS HONOR? REALLY?

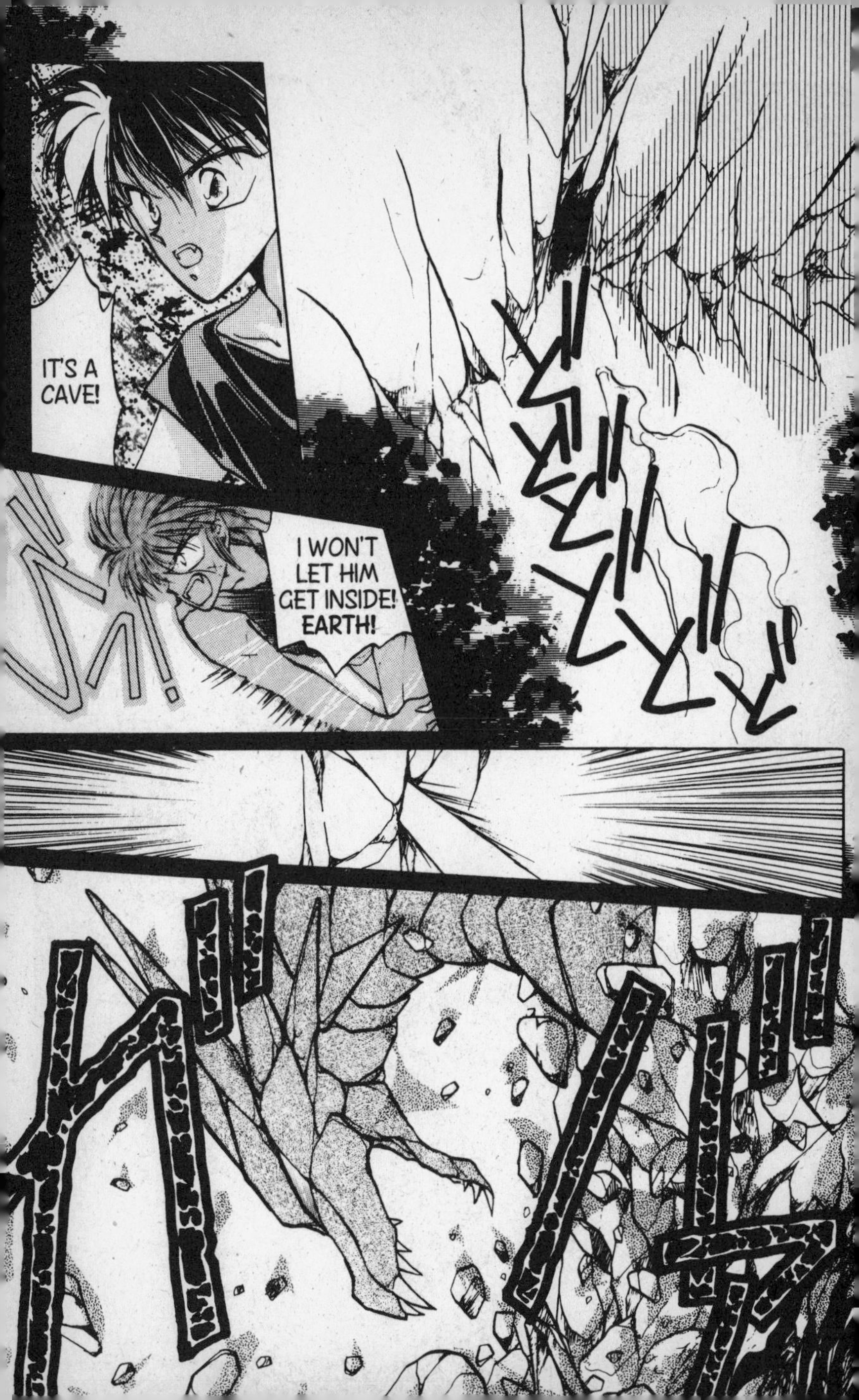
IT'S A CAVE!
I WON'T LET HIM GET INSIDE! EARTH!

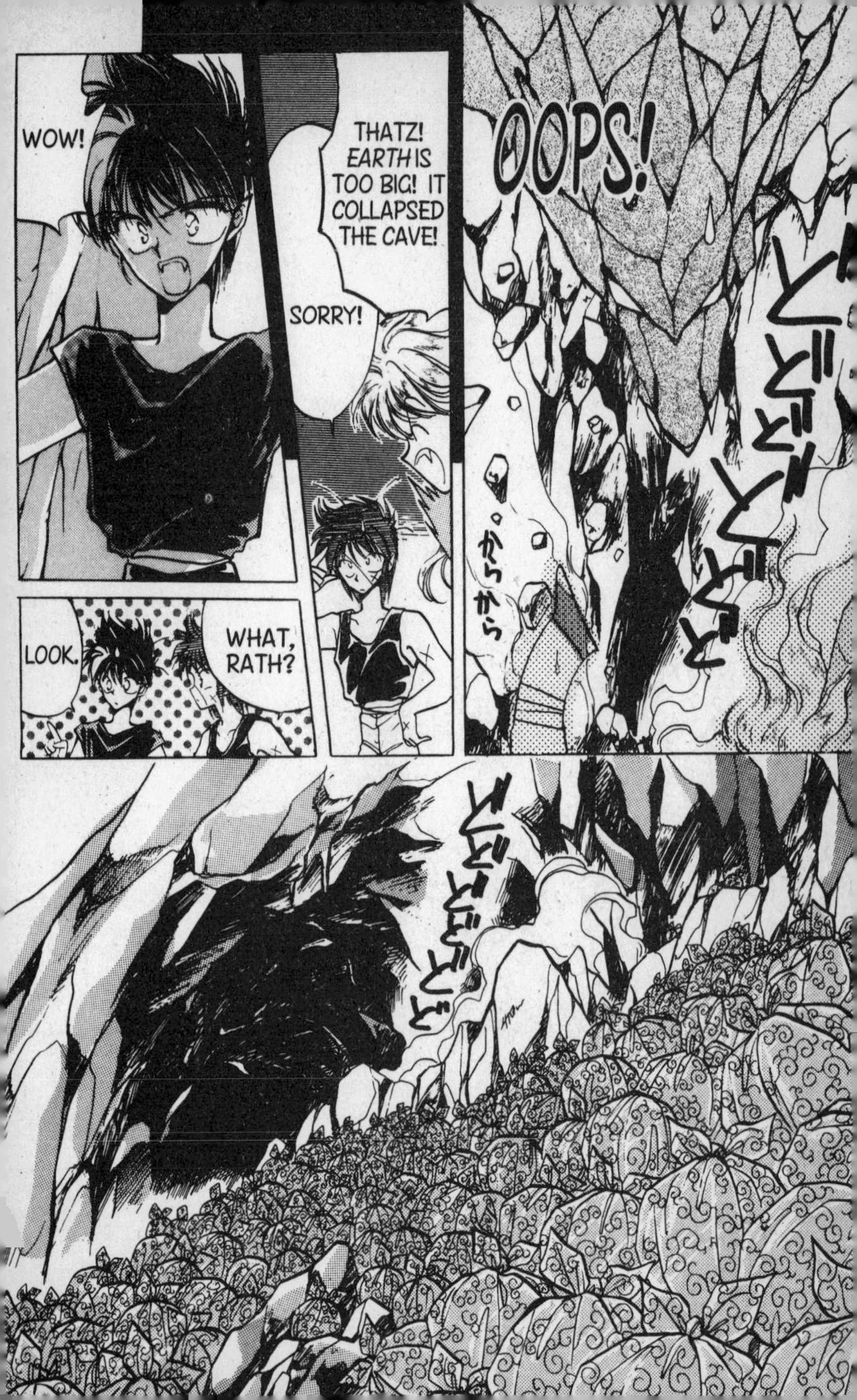
OOPS!
どどど
どどど
からから
THATZ! EARTH IS TOO BIG! IT COLLAPSED THE CAVE!
SORRY!
WOW!
WHAT, RATH?
LOOK.
どどどどど

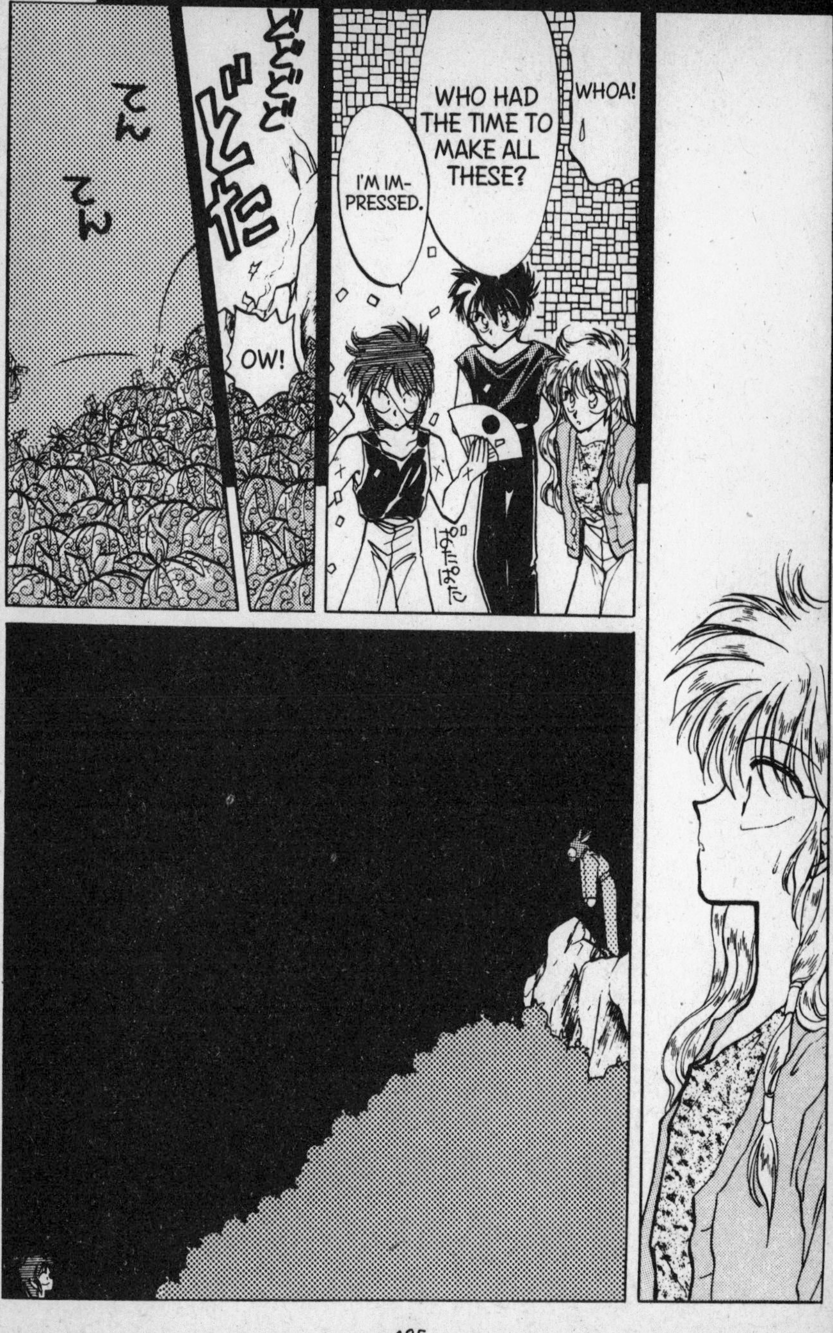
WHOA!
WHO HAD THE TIME TO MAKE ALL THESE?
I'M IM-PRESSED.
ぱたぱた
どどど
ぱたた
OW!
てん てん

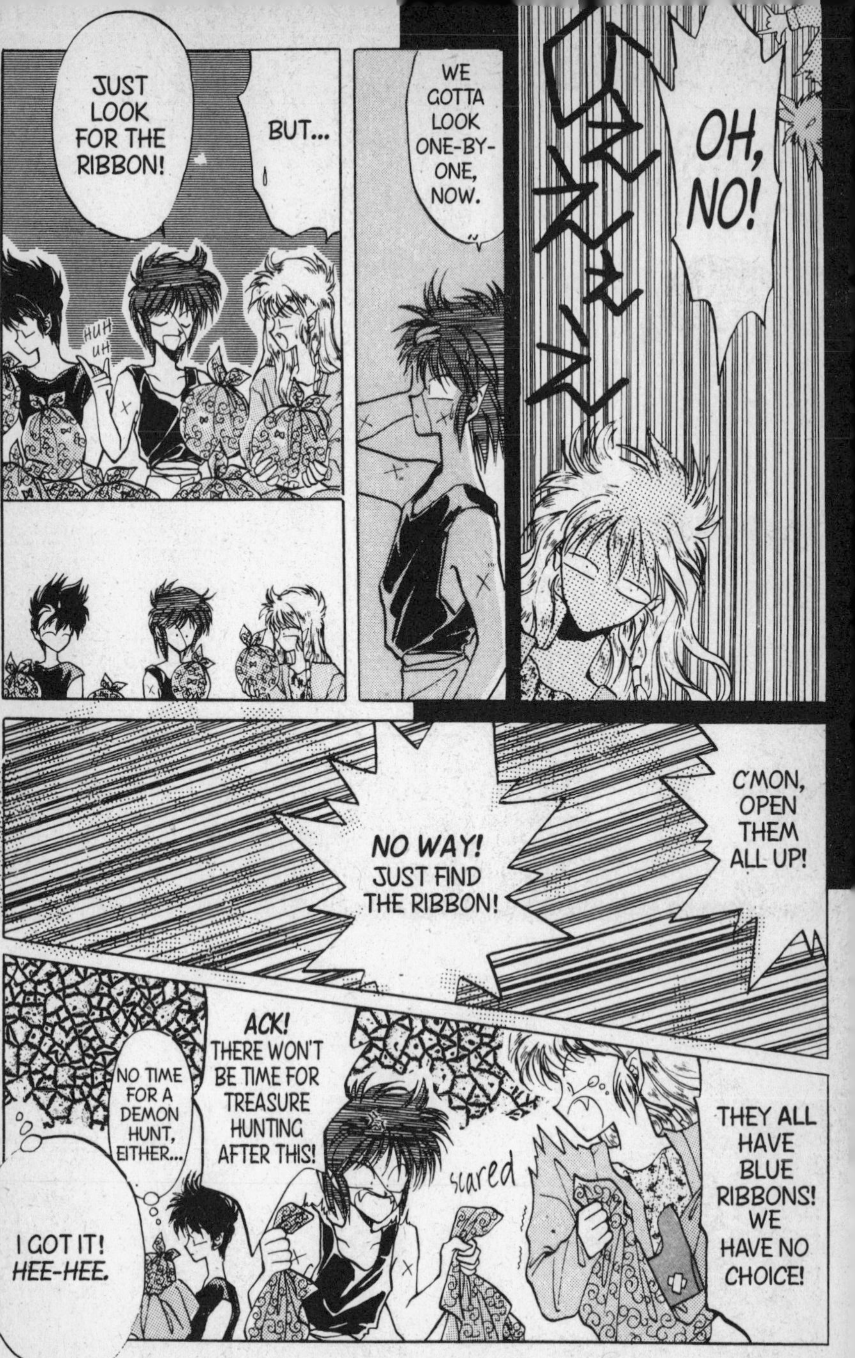
OH, NO!
WE GOTTA LOOK ONE-BY-ONE, NOW.
BUT...
JUST LOOK FOR THE RIBBON!
HUH UH
C'MON, OPEN THEM ALL UP!
NO WAY! JUST FIND THE RIBBON!
THEY ALL HAVE BLUE RIBBONS! WE HAVE NO CHOICE!
scared
ACK! THERE WON'T BE TIME FOR TREASURE HUNTING AFTER THIS!
NO TIME FOR A DEMON HUNT, EITHER...
I GOT IT! HEE-HEE.

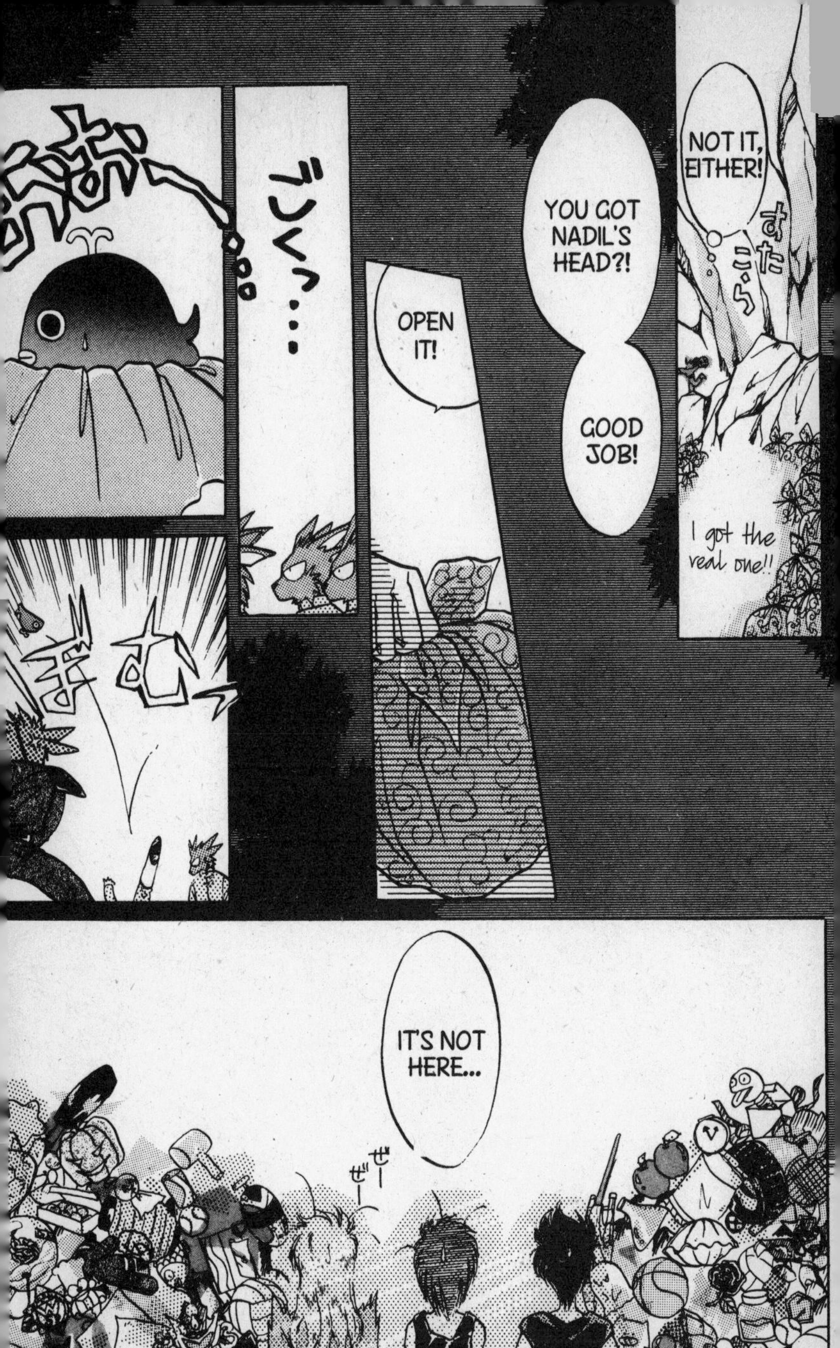
NOT IT, EITHER!
すたこら
I got the real one!!
YOU GOT NADIL'S HEAD?!
GOOD JOB!
OPEN IT!
ごくっ…
IT'S NOT HERE...
ぜー ぜー

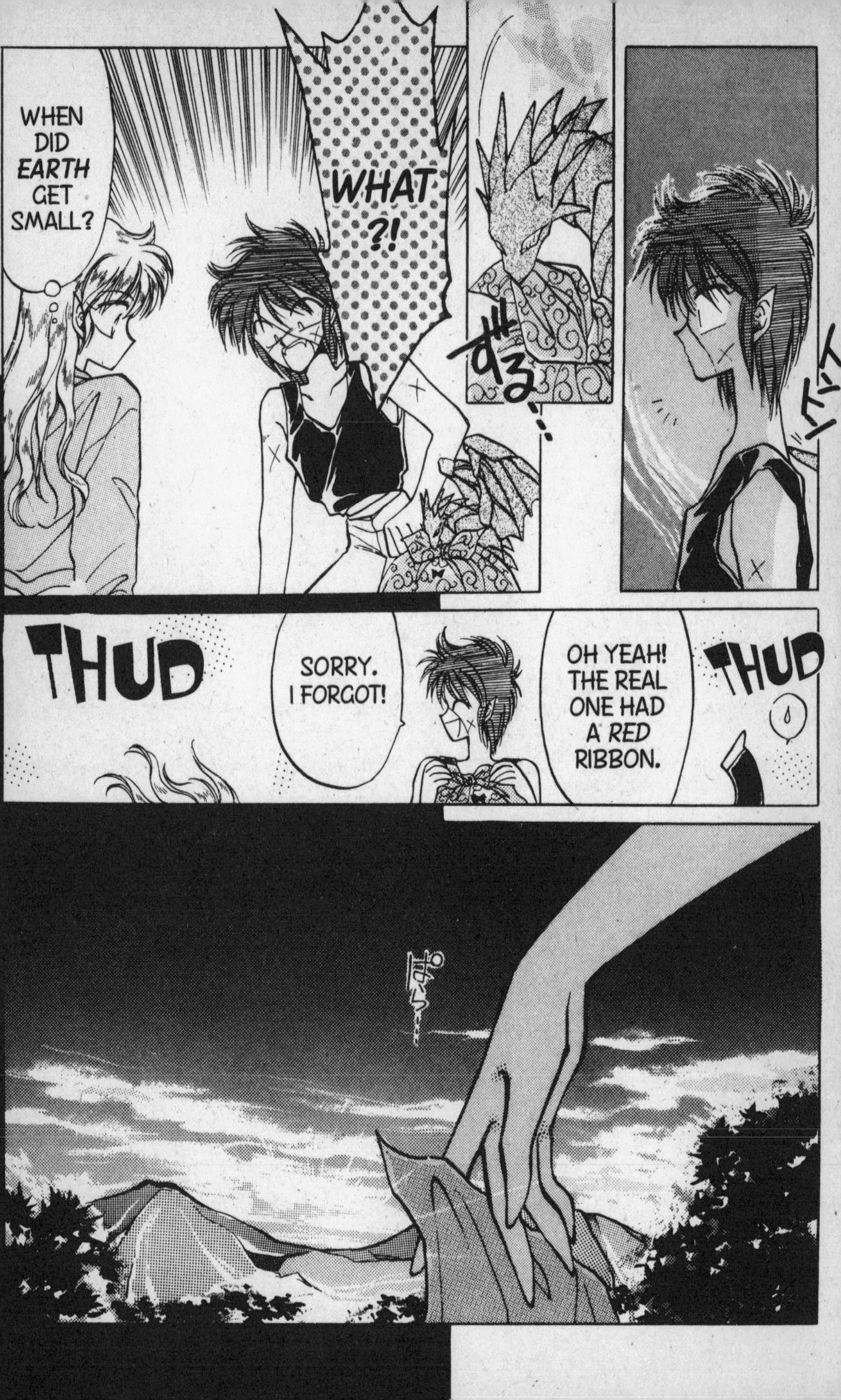

ずる…
WHAT ?!
WHEN DID EARTH GET SMALL?
THUD
OH YEAH! THE REAL ONE HAD A RED RIBBON.
SORRY. I FORGOT!
THUD

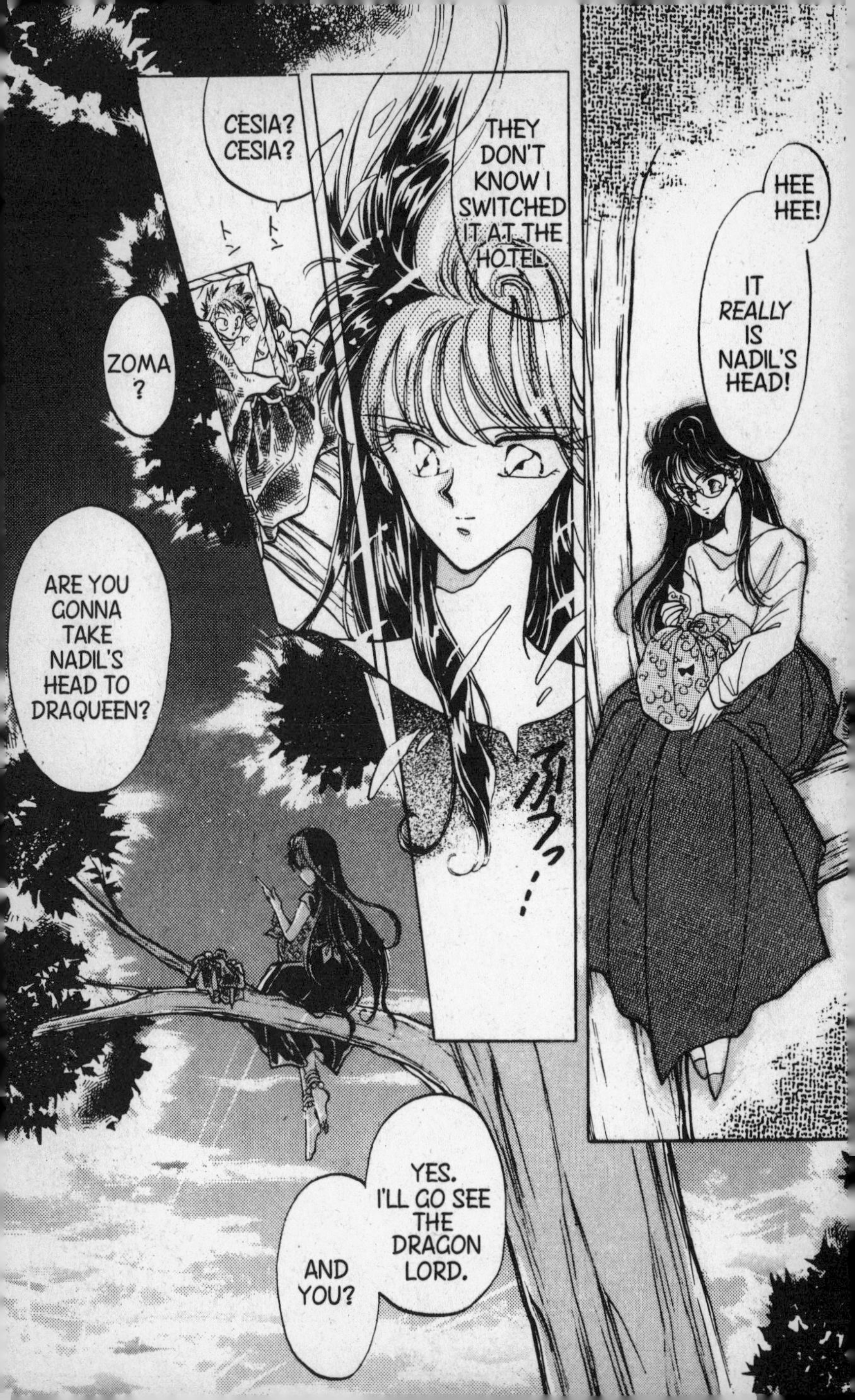
HEE HEE!
IT REALLY IS NADIL'S HEAD!
THEY DON'T KNOW I SWITCHED IT AT THE HOTEL.
CESIA? CESIA?
トン トン
ZOMA?
ARE YOU GONNA TAKE NADIL'S HEAD TO DRAQUEEN?
YES. I'LL GO SEE THE DRAGON LORD.
AND YOU?

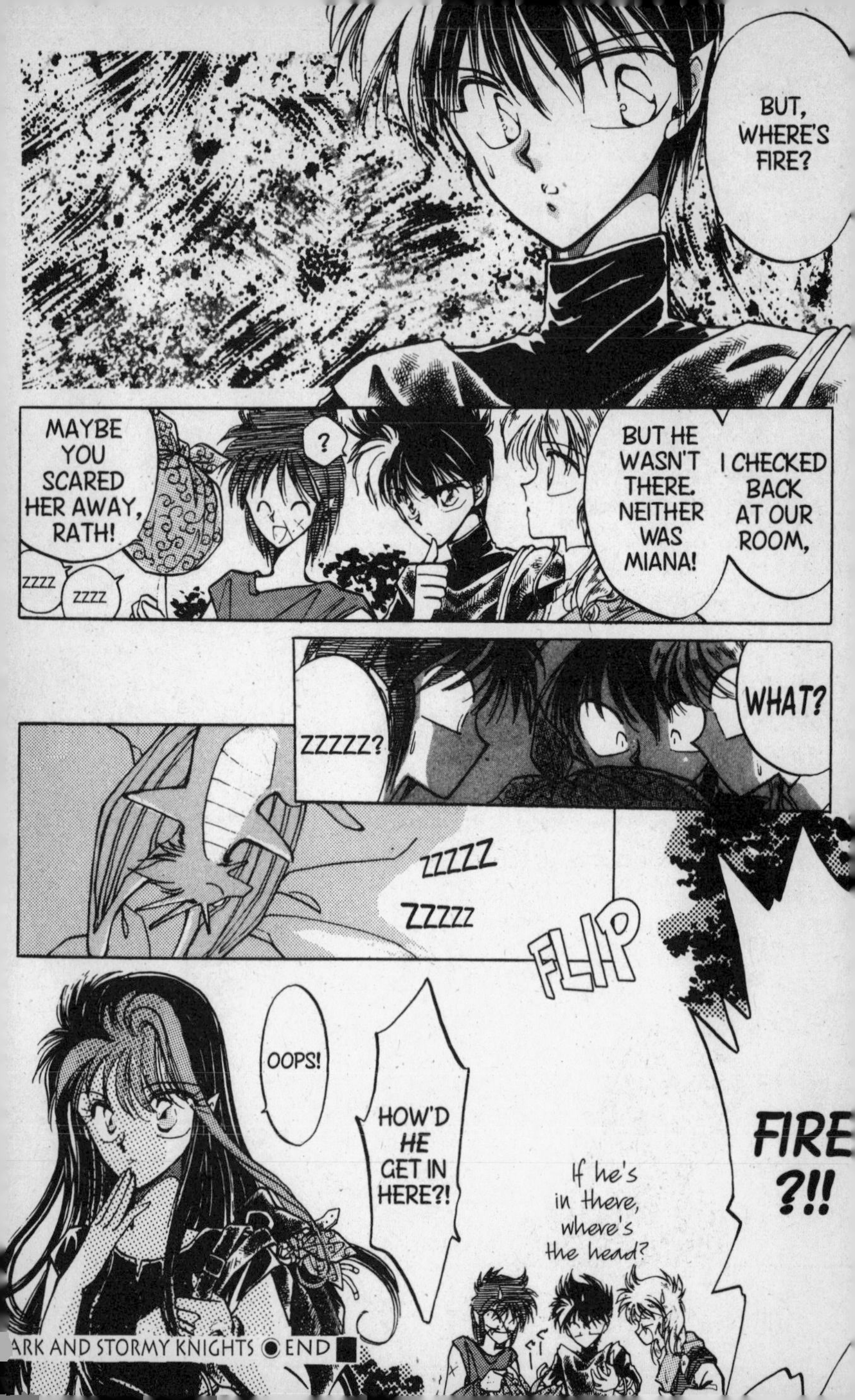
BUT, WHERE'S FIRE?
I CHECKED BACK AT OUR ROOM,
BUT HE WASN'T THERE. NEITHER WAS MIANA!
?
MAYBE YOU SCARED HER AWAY, RATH!
ZZZZ
ZZZZ
WHAT?
ZZZZZ?
ZZZZZ
ZZZZZ
FLIP
FIRE?!!
If he's in there, where's the head?
HOW'D HE GET IN HERE?!
OOPS!
ARK AND STORMY KNIGHTS ● END

Before they were Dragon Knights!

Local gangbanger makes good!

Everyone knows about "expert treasure hunter" Thatz's recent adventures in the Kingdom of Draqueen, defending justice in the name of Lord Lykouleon, but did you know that he used to be a common burglar? Juicy details, coming up!

How Nadil Lost his Head

You've seen the trouble that Nadil's head has caused for the Dragon Knights. In the next exciting volume you'll meet the man from the neck down and learn how he got his just desserts.

Lykouleon's knight a prince?

The Dragon Knights are a lofty bunch, but one of the three adventurers is genuine royalty. Find out which one in the next issue!

PAPERBACK

STOP!

This is the back of the book.
You wouldn't want to spoil a great ending!

This book is printed "manga-style," in the authentic Japanese right-to-left format. Since none of the artwork has been flipped or altered, readers get to experience the story just as the creator intended. You've been asking for it, so TOKYOPOP® delivered: authentic, hot-off-the-press, and far more fun!

DIRECTIONS

If this is your first time reading manga-style, here's a quick guide to help you understand how it works.

It's easy… just start in the top right panel and follow the numbers. Have fun, and look for more 100% authentic manga from TOKYOPOP®!

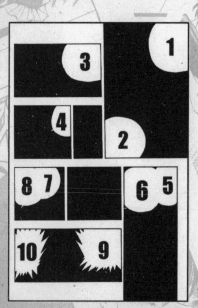